Dr Keshia N. A...
Binghamton U...
scholar and a J... ...ustice and Equity in Diversity and Inclusion) educator. *Black Victorians* is her first book.

Dr John Woolf is a nineteenth-century specialist who read History at Cambridge and Goldsmiths, University of London. He has researched and produced history documentaries for the BBC, co-authored a number of Audible Originals including *Stephen Fry's Victorian Secrets* and *Stephen Fry's Edwardian Secrets*, and is the author of *The Wonders*.

Further praise for *Black Victorians*

'An important survey based on painstaking research. *Black Victorians* provides an indispensable introduction to the subject told through the lives of some of the most eminent personalities of the era, as well as those hitherto little known. A significant contribution to the field'
Hakim Adi, Professor of the History of Africa and the African Diaspora, University of Chichester

'The book's telling details are liberating for, in spite of Black Victorians' subjection and degradation, they are presented not as victims, but rather as resourceful, inventive, assertive human beings in their quests for betterment. Their cumulative experiences are skilfully woven into an engaging, richly textured book – an insightful work of scholarship'   Ron Ramdin, author of
The Making of the Black Working Class in Britain

'An important contribution to the history of Africans in Britain. Woolf and Abraham's work complements that of many, many others... Given the subject matter, the book's accessibility is

remarkable and Abraham and Woolf are truly to be applauded'
Onyeka Nubia, author and Assistant
Professor of History, Nottingham University

'A triumph – both of collaborative writing and, more importantly, of Black agency, as delineated in an exhilarating range of historical fields and in the face of an equally sobering range of challenges. The clarity and deftness of Abraham and Woolf's work is exemplified by their beautifully succinct demonstration of how slavery led to racism, rather than the reverse. As the cast before us moves from the prison or asylum to the stage and the summit meeting, we begin to feel, not just anger and admiration, but something that might just be hope'
Oskar Jensen, author of *Vagabonds*

'Fascinating, thorough, well-researched and extremely readable, *Black Victorians* provides invaluable insight into a history of Victorian Britain that is not often told'
Hafsa Zayyan, author of *We Are All Birds of Uganda*

'Timely... This book will generate discussion and change mindsets. It is brilliant'
Dr Maggie Semple OBE

BLACK VICTORIANS
HIDDEN IN HISTORY

KESHIA N. ABRAHAM
JOHN WOOLF

First published in the United Kingdom by Duckworth in 2022

This paperback edition published in 2023

Duckworth, an imprint of Duckworth Books Ltd
1 Golden Court, Richmond, TW9 1EU, United Kingdom
www.duckworthbooks.co.uk

For bulk and special sales please contact
info@duckworthbooks.com

© Keshia N. Abraham, John Woolf, 2022

No part of this publication may be reproduced, stored in a retrieval system, or transmitted in any form by any means electronic, mechanical, photocopying, recording or otherwise, without the prior permission of the publisher.

The rights of Keshia N. Abraham and John Woolf to be identified as the Authors of this Work have been asserted by them in accordance with the Copyright, Designs and Patents Act 1988.

A CIP catalogue record for this book is available from the British Library.

1 3 5 7 9 10 8 6 4 2

Text design and typesetting by Danny Lyle.

Printed and bound in Great Britain by Clays.

Paperback ISBN: 978-0-7156-5488-0
eISBN: 978-0-7156-5446-0

Dedicated to our parents:
Henrietta Abraham, Gregory Abraham
Fay Hetherington Woolf, Michael Woolf

A portion of the royalties will be donated to
the Black Cultural Archives, London.

Winner of the John C. Laurence Award, Society of Authors,
'for work that helps improve understanding between the races'.

Content warning:
Among other topics, this book explores racism, slavery and
colonialism, recounting traumatic experiences, including
instances of abuse, rape, murder and mental health distress.
Some of the material may be emotionally challenging.

Nations reel and stagger on their way; they make hideous mistakes; they commit frightful wrongs; they do great and beautiful things. And shall we not best guide humanity by telling the truth about all this, so far as the truth is ascertainable?

W. E. B. Du Bois

Contents

Foreword by Keshia N. Abraham ... xi
Introduction by John Woolf ... xv

Part One: Context and Concealment
1. Hidden in History ... 1
2. Land of Hope and Glory ... 15

Part Two: Struggle and Survival
3. Broadmoor: William Brown ... 41
4. Bearing Witness: John Flinn ... 52
5. Hearing Joseph Peters ... 61
6. Rights: Edward Albert ... 70

Part Three: Church and State
7. Protest: William Cuffay ... 81
8. Black Aristocracy: Sarah Forbes Bonetta ... 97
9. The Bishop: Samuel Ajayi Crowther ... 118
10. Young Soldier: James Francies Durham ... 135

Part Four: The Arts
11. Sounds from the Diaspora: Samuel Coleridge-Taylor ... 149
12. 'African Roscius': Ira Aldridge ... 161
13. The Circus: Pablo Fanque ... 179
14. Art and Beauty: Fanny Eaton ... 189

Part Five: Fighting for Freedom
15. Defiance: Henry 'Box' Brown	209
16. Daring to be Heard: Sarah Parker Remond	227
17. Crossing Borders: Ellen Craft and William Craft	242
18. Anti-Racism: Ida B. Wells	257
19. Looking Forward: The Pan-African Movement	270
Conclusion: Not the First, Not the Last	281
Acknowledgements	*287*
Further Reading	*289*
Bibliography	*291*
List of Illustrations	*309*
Notes	*311*
Index	*343*

Foreword

by Keshia N. Abraham

The great force of history comes from the fact that we carry it within us, are unconsciously controlled by it in many ways, and history is literally present in all that we do. It could scarcely be otherwise, since it is to history that we owe our frames of reference, our identities, our aspirations.

James Baldwin

To see my ancestors in it, I had to learn to read history for clues, not for the facts. Many of us have learned to read in this way because the facts only tell part of the story. To be whole, we need to see what else we can know, what else might have been if we simply consider the facts together with more texture, more consideration for the variety of lived experiences that made that time (whatever time it may be) what we've known it to be. What would we carry within us collectively if we were more conscious of what's hidden in our shared histories? How does your sense of the world change when the people who made it become visible?

I come from an old city; old for the United States… Until I was twelve, I thought I was growing up in an ancient city. And then I went to Scandinavia and then to Europe, then to Africa, followed by the Caribbean, and eventually to Asia…

And in each of their most ancient and treasured places, I saw evidence of people who not only looked like me, but perhaps felt like me, who were a presence in the painted or storied versions that I could connect with and through which I could begin to see myself as tied to legacies greater than what I'd been taught in school. For years I'd been crafting my own what-ifs from the paucity of information on offer in canonical US history courses about Africa and the African diaspora in the UK. There were stories behind the eyes of the Black children in Byzantine paintings that I wanted to hear, there was a curiosity about the scale and influences in architecture and design that I wanted to feed. The electricity and 'rootsiness' that greeted me as I emerged from Brixton Station was thick with too many layers of history not to question what I thought I knew of the Empire.

After reading Sam Selvon's *The Lonely Londoners*, which came to me years after shuttling between Harare, Hackney and other global cities, my curiosity about Black life in Britain continued to grow in tandem with burgeoning socio-political support for better Black education and cultural awareness. I dove deep into contemporary Black British literature and found those novels that grappled with untold Black lives in different eras of British history – such as Bernardine Evaristo's 2001 novel in verse, *The Emperor's Babe* – of particular fascination, probably because, until I reached Spelman College, the notion of Black people existing and building what we know as Britain was never a part of my formal education or any academic conversation I encountered. In fact, just the opposite – in the histories I was taught it was as if all of the Blackness had been plucked out and systematically erased. Literature, good creative literature, is yoked to truths, and therefore provides opportunities to see history in new ways just as good historical writing can be the antidote to histories we've been taught as factual, when they are really fictions masquerading as facts.

Foreword

In every place I have visited in the world I've asked questions, connected with elders to hear oral narratives about its people and culture, tried to fill in the outlines with colour, with flesh, with wholeness. It has been an expression of my need to see more, to know more about the people to whom we pay homage as icons but whose experiences often seem to lie outside of the conventional interests of historians or of our imaginations. History is like a kaleidoscope where all of the pieces are inside, but what you see is dependent on how you turn it, how the pieces fall into place.

For me, collaborating on this book, *Black Victorians: Hidden in History*, was like colouring in the pages of history with more texture and substance and possibilities, turning and turning the kaleidoscope. And it couldn't have come at a more meaningful and synchronous time for John and me because both international education and global history as discipline and practice were being turned inside out in 2020 by both COVID-19 and a more mainstream consciousness of global racism which, once exposed, revealed the space that has been at my core this whole time – the space where John and I seemed really to connect on a curious desire to see and understand the history of Africans in diaspora with justice, equity, dignity and intention.

What seems crucial about the present is how we understand our past and what we do with that understanding. When this book was being researched and written, we were all, around the world, connected to a web of conversations, actions and choices about the coronavirus pandemic and about actions against racism that impacted our lives in different ways, according to our race, class and gender. My professional approach to navigating these 'twin pandemics' was through the development of International JEDI (Justice and Equity in Diversity and Inclusion) frameworks for global educators and through building bridges between the forms of education (abroad) that we've known and that which many of us have dreamed of – one with justice and equity at its centre. For several decades, my work has included an approach to teaching that prioritises dignity and equity in 'diversity' as a matter of social justice and aims to create more lasting change in the way we see the world and especially Africans in diaspora as they exist in and move around it.

Black Victorians seeks to bring people who were among the ancestral icons of my childhood to brand-new light and situate them within the making of Britain at that time, alongside less well-known but significant figures whose names, presence and impact we would not otherwise have encountered or considered. From the legendary Ira Aldridge to Henry 'Box' Brown, from Saartjie Baartman to Sarah Parker Remond, we have sought to flesh out history in order to advance the cause of making Black lives not only matter but valued, considered, appreciated, elevated, honoured… centred.

To centre Blackness need not involve the decentring or othering of anyone else. In shining light on the Black presence in Victorian England, no shade is placed directly on others. It is, rather, an attempt to understand the climate and implications of Black Victorian life, which brings us all into the light, and might help us begin to consider what our shared aspirations really are now, 'since it is to history that we owe our frames of reference, our identities, our aspirations'.

As we shape a collective future, while reading this book about the past, I hope that you also find yourself intrigued by the possibilities it suggests for thinking about our shared his/herstories in a new light. I hope that you are as moved as I am by these narratives of individual lives and historical moments, and encouraged to consider the implications of their spheres of influence, which are so much broader and deeper than many of us had previously imagined. For our futures to be different, we might need to rethink what's hidden in history.

Introduction

by John Woolf

At No. 222 Piccadilly, London, in the year 1810, you could pay two shillings to see the 'Hottentot Venus'. She had wide hips and large buttocks. She could be poked and prodded by spectators. A lady with her parasol and a gentleman with his cane jabbed the flesh to check it was 'natural'. The 'Hottentot' naturally resented such treatment, and on these occasions, 'it took all the authority of the keeper to subdue her resentment,' noted one observer.[1]

The 'Hottentot Venus' was Saartjie Baartman, a Khoekhoe woman from South Africa, who was displayed across the UK as a racial, sexual object. She was forced to pose naked for images that appeared in a book on natural history, and when she died in 1815, her body was dissected. Baartman's sex organs were preserved in a jar and her skeleton was displayed in Paris' Natural History Museum. It wasn't until 2002 that her body was repatriated and buried with dignity in the small farming village of Hankey on the Eastern Cape.[2]

'Ethnic shows', 'human zoos' or 'ethnographic exhibitions' were to be the subject of my next book: the commercialised display of foreign people deemed different. I planned to explore 'human zoos' within the context of debates concerning 'race', racism and ethnic otherness, building on my earlier research into nineteenth-century so-called freak shows.[3] But the more I researched, the more I was taken into spaces beyond ethnographic exhibitions; the more I found human beings defined way beyond their apparent ethnic freakishness. The more I sifted through primary and secondary materials, the more the Victorian age was revealed anew. And then I met Dr Keshia Abraham – a Black feminist and African diaspora scholar – who worked with me – a white socialist and British cultural historian – on this book. Our collaboration ultimately reflected our thesis: Black history and British history are intimately connected.

Black Victorians: Hidden in History reinstates marginalised stories to throw a new light on the Victorian era, illuminating how people of African descent helped create Great Britain. In the pages that follow, we resurrect human stories which coax an engagement with the possibilities of liberation and reimagination. Saartjie Baartman, for example, may have been treated like an object when she was alive and dead, but in life she was also a woman with agency: a performer, celebrity, mother, wife and publisher, who wrested back control over her representation as the 'Hottentot Venus'. She helped fashion a form of ethnographic entertainment that developed in scale and ambition as the century progressed; she was so much more than the 'Hottentot Venus' on display.[4] This brief account of Baartman's story offers a glimpse of how *Black Victorians* not only seeks to challenge our vision of Britain as the land of the white Anglo-Saxon, but is above all concerned with documenting agency, more than simply the Black presence in Britain; it is concerned with resilience, not victimhood.

By highlighting the lives of Black Victorians, we recognise the individual amid the collective, and situate these biographies within their broader historical context, illuminating the multivalence of 'race' in Victorian society. As such, this book unfolds as a study of 'race', racism and the Victorian mindset as much as a study of individual experiences. Many of the figures in it hailed from numerous places across the globe and from various backgrounds; in resurrecting their stories, we make new discoveries, amplify silenced voices and seek to offer a revisionist account of the age.

We acknowledge, meanwhile, that there have been many books published about the African (Black) presence in Britain, originating from independent and mainstream presses in Britain, the Caribbean, Africa, Europe and the USA. Some of these have focused on colonialism, ethnography, or the legacies of slavery and empire, among other topics. Therefore, this book builds on the work of authors who have shown how Black history and European history are not exclusive categories. We are especially indebted to the work of Hakim Adi, Caroline Bressey, Ray Costello, David Dabydeen, Peter Fryer, Gretchen Holbrook Gerzina, Paul Gilroy, Jeffrey Green, Jan Marsh, Martyn Hoyles, David Olusoga, Mike Phillips, Ron Ramdin, Folarin Shyllon, Marika Sherwood and others, whose names will appear and reappear in the text, notes and bibliography. There has been a tendency in the scholarship to fail to recognise the contributions of these historians, who have helped make our own research possible. We encourage readers of *Black Victorians* to engage with the wider historiography and amplify their understanding. At the end of the book there is a suggested further reading list (not exhaustive or definitive) that aims to acknowledge the contributions of some of these historians. It includes: Dusé Mohamed Ali, John Archer, Runoko Rashidi, J. A. Rogers, Edward Scobie and Ivan Van Sertima. They have long suggested that the Black presence in Europe predated enslavement, as Onyeka Nubia has also emphasised in his work, *Blackamoores*.

* * *

As we were researching and writing, on 25 May 2020 George Floyd was murdered by police in Minneapolis. The protests that followed pushed the Black Lives Matter movement, first established by three Black women in 2013, into the global public consciousness.

In Britain, statues of slave traders and colonialists became the focus of protest and fierce debate – the statue of Edward Colston in Bristol Harbour was pulled down and thrown into the dock, while the cultural centre once named in his honour was renamed the Bristol Beacon. English football players were booed because they took the knee. Institutions like the National Trust started seriously to examine the past connections of the properties and estates under their stewardship.

British newspapers either raged that this was all 'wokeness' gone insane or mused on whether it was an important reckoning with our history – a critical reflection which threw light on the present day. History became a site of public discourse and, as such, explicitly politicised. Some of the engrained microaggressions, macroaggressions and racist violence, which are woven into the fabric of society and often emanate from the very institutions designed to keep people safe, were placed under a brighter collective spotlight on both sides of the Atlantic. Some commentators and some of my friends did not want to talk to white people about 'race'; others, including many of my colleagues, did.[5]

If you will humour me on this important issue of 'race' and politics as it relates to the book in your hands: whether we like it or not, history and politics are connected. Historians, like the subjects of their study, are products of their time and background. The questions we pose about the past, the subjects we choose to explore, are invariably influenced by the beliefs we hold, our personal ideologies and the circles we move in. To do solid history, the historian needs to ensure that present realities do not conceal or distort past realities, which are messy and rarely fit neatly with our preconceived ideas. But it would be misleading to claim that historians can adopt an ahistorical, objective perspective: we are subjective creatures.

We have long been presented with a version of white British history which itself is political, and this book, as a counter to that presentation, is self-consciously political insofar as it unashamedly embraces diversity and inclusivity. But the point is not to mount a political polemic. It is not about bashing Britain, nor about romanticising people of African descent. Rather, it is driven by a commitment to the historical record. It is concerned with better understanding the past, capturing valuable individual experiences and keeping the issue of 'race' in the foreground – which is especially important for historians concerned with the Victorian era, as we will see.

The historian Peter Fryer, in his seminal book *Staying Power: The History of Black People in Britain*, posed an important question relevant to my own authorship: 'Can such an account be written by a white author in a way that is acceptable to black readers?'[6]

Decades earlier, in response to the publication of the anthropologist Kenneth Little's *Negroes in Britain* (1948), the African American sociologist St Clair Drake had commented, '[We] distrust people who survey us and study us, who write about us and publicize us, and who try to reform and lead us.'[7] It was a valid point.

Fryer, in answer to his own question, explained that he tried to 'think black' which, he wrote, meant 'to grasp imaginatively as well as intellectually the essence of the black historical experience'.[8] Personally, I don't know if I can, or even should, 'think black' – if 'the white man is locked in his whiteness' and 'the black man in his blackness', as Frantz Fanon argued, can that assumed mental divide truly ever be bridged?[9]

Alternatively, can one homogenise Black thinking or experience across genders, classes, contexts and continents? There are other issues, too: in a context marred by the scars of slavery and colonialism, is it *right* that a white person should write any form of Black history? And why, with many talented Black historians and writers on hand, should a white person be paid to write Black history? These too are important questions. They were the same questions I earlier considered as an able-bodied historian writing on the history of disability.[10]

Black Victorians has confronted each of these questions. It is not the product of a white historian 'thinking Black'; rather, it is a collaborative history that contemplates questions of 'race' in the nineteenth century. It is born from the conviction that to properly understand British history we need to understand Black history. Moreover, as historians of the nineteenth century, there is an imperative to centralise 'race', for we are, by definition, historians of Atlantic slavery and imperialism. Indeed, we will see that the economic, cultural and intellectual climate of the Victorian era was, to a large extent, informed by the issue of 'race' and this reality can no longer be ignored in the writing of our history. Academics have recently and rightly called for the 'undisciplining' of Victorian studies – that is, centralising 'race' in the era – and this work concerns us all.[11]

But a white author must proceed with humility and caution, so I am humbled and grateful to collaborate specifically with Dr Keshia Abraham: a self-proclaimed international JEDI, an expert on the African diaspora and a committed Black feminist. Her expertise on Black history has met my work on nineteenth-century British cultural history, producing a book that is very much ours, though all mistakes and flaws are solely mine.

Separated by the Atlantic Ocean, and shaped by differing lived experiences, we connected on a weekly basis to pore over the research. At our first ever meeting I was undergoing a personal crisis at home and, despite my desire to appear professionally cool, calm and collected, I was an emotional wreck.

Keshia offered such love and understanding, and even shared her own experiences of heartbreak, and from that moment we had a framework for our future collaboration: open, tolerant and full of human understanding.

In the proceeding weeks and months, we discussed politics and history; 'race' and identity; the diaspora and the dignity of our subjects. Keshia challenged my own subjectivity as it bore on my reading of history. She dared me to view the agents and their age in new, interconnected ways. She instilled what I can best describe as a liberating lens: a way of seeing the past, and writing about the past, which is infused with hope; which seeks to recast light rather than shadows over the past; which approaches history not as a dead weight but a tangible, dynamic terrain that is interwoven with our contemporary lives. She peppered the multiple drafts with comments and suggestions, directed our reading beyond what I expected of a historian's reading list, and she remoulded scribbled notes into something more coherent.

And so, with Keshia, I have tried to think imaginatively and sensitively, positioning myself not as an expert but as a learner, deepening my own understanding of the Victorian era by exploring the archives, revisiting my assumptions and deferring to experts (there are many, as the extensive bibliography shows). My aspiration is to pass that learning on to you, the reader. Our primary focus has been to root this history in individual lives, keeping as close to the first-hand accounts as the archives allow. We are influenced by Baldwin's critique that the 'rejection of life, the human being, the denial of his beauty' can lead to a place which insists on 'categorization alone'; and we take note, too, of the importance of considering individuality, reflecting on a line from Ta-Nehisi Coates's letter to his son, 'I have raised you to respect every human being as singular, and you must extend that same respect into the past'.[12]

In *Black Victorians*, we meet an array of individuals from different walks of life. After setting out the context in Part One, in Part Two we begin our biographical focus on the social margins with the little-known stories of William Brown, John Flinn, Joseph Peters and Edward Albert, who struggled for survival inside notorious asylums and on the urban streets. In Part Three, we move from the social periphery to the centre, exploring the life of one Black Victorian, William Cuffay, who sought to bring down the state, and others, such as Sarah Forbes Bonetta and Samuel Ajayi Crowther, who moved within the orbit of the establishment. Part Four considers the cultural contributions of the Jamaican-born artists' model Fanny Eaton, the Shakespearian actor Ira Aldridge, the composer Samuel Coleridge-Taylor and the circus proprietor Pablo Fanque; each, in their own way, informed and moulded Victorian art and culture. In Part Five, we enter a more overtly political arena, encountering the Transatlantic abolitionist movement in the figures of Henry 'Box' Brown, Sarah Parker Remond and Ellen and William Craft, and the feminist activism of the journalist Ida B. Wells.

The choice of whom to include was partly informed by the available source material for, as we will see, many lives are hidden in the archives and impossible to reconstruct fully; but was also driven by a desire to capture a diversity of experiences which, in turn, illuminate different facets of the Victorian world. There are many, many figures who aren't included and some – like Mary Seacole or Arthur Warton – who have been extensively covered elsewhere so only briefly appear.[13] Likewise, there are other avenues of enquiry not developed here – the distinct discourses concerning individuals of dual heritage, for example, or the different and sometimes overlapping experiences of other racialised peoples – because a lack of time and space prohibited a detailed exploration of many potential areas and groups, such as the Lascars, Chinese, Polynesians, Jews, Irish and Asians, who have their own rich histories deserving of their own historical treatment.

In this book 'Black' refers to people of African descent. The term 'Black Victorians' is imperfect – it cannot possibly capture the multiplicity of experiences – yet it signals the possibility of holding numerous identities. 'Black Victorians' seeks to challenge those who say they never 'see colour'; it's a 'provocation' that asserts Blackness into the traditional construction of the Victorian world as a white space, a point made powerfully by Olivette Otele in her book *African Europeans*.[14] Keshia and I capitalise Black because, as W. E. B. Du Bois retorted when campaigning for the capitalisation of 'Negro', 'Eight million Americans are entitled to a capital letter', and so are Black Victorians in this book.[15] And we apply quotation marks to the word 'race' because it is a cultural and historical category with a limited basis in biology ('ethnicity' is also occasionally used to denote cultural differences such as nationality, religion and language because that term moves away from the danger that 'race' is perceived as a fixed, heritable, innate, biological condition).[16]

In this book, 'race' refers to physical differences that are deemed socially significant; it is not the biology but the signification which is important.[17] As the sociologist and cultural studies scholar Paul Gilroy argued, '"race" has to be socially and politically constructed'; it involves power, politics and history. '"Race" is nothing special,' Gilroy continued, '[It is merely] a virtual reality given meaning only by the fact that racism endures.'[18] To put this another way: without racism, 'race' would mean little, and while the nature of racism is subject to much debate, here racism is used to denote 'an ideology which constructs a social collectivity with reference to real or imagined biological and cultural characteristics, which are negatively evaluated'.[19]

To expand slightly: racism (a word first coined in 1902 by a racist) reifies 'race', dividing humanity into separate and exclusive biological categories of difference under the guise of scientific authority.[20] Racism is more than an attitude, therefore, rather it is an ideology that lays claim to scientific truth. In the racist realm, differences between groups are real or imagined. Certain groups are assigned values and those values are applied to all members of a given group; a link is established between physical and mental qualities which are seen to be unchanging and constant – and this perspective justifies aggressive behaviour or actions.[21]

Racism is therefore concerned with relationships of power, discrimination and oppression, serving political, social and economic functions.[22] Racism is dynamic, multifaceted, historically contingent, embedded in social relations and involves active discrimination, impacting on individuals in a way that turns 'race' into more than *just* a social construction, but a lived reality.[23]

In this book, Keshia and I have attempted to think 'race' which, as other scholars have contended, is to think 'power, violence, the flesh, the human' but also 'to think resistance, relation, and the possibilities of freedom'.[24] We attempt to engage with that hope of freedom – liberating Black Victorians from the margins of history and challenging the idea that Victorian Britain, and the West more generally, was a unitary, homogenous field of whiteness.

In the end, this book attempts to sit with – and ultimately embrace – the tensions of difference and interdependence: between politics and history, past and present, the individual and the community, self and other, the seen and the unseen; between Black history and British history; authorial whiteness and Black subject matter. 'Community must not mean a shedding of our differences, nor the pathetic pretence that these differences do not exist', as Audre Lorde put it.[25] And from this corresponding state of difference and interdependence some definite convictions emerge: 'race' and racism are not just Black 'issues', then or now.

In fact, racism is 'primarily a white problem', wrote the twentieth-century African American novelist Richard Wright, 'because whites governed the conditions through which the discourse of race emerged and endures'.[26] The past, therefore, is not really past: it is imbricated in the present.[27] British history is not purely white, then or now, and fundamentally we *all* need to discuss and explore issues of 'race', both in the past and the present – unsettling assumptions, challenging beliefs, correcting the historical record and addressing inherited injustices that continue today.

* * *

Before we begin, it's important to keep in mind that, while individual lives act as our guide, this is not a history of 'Black exceptionalism': a narrative which promotes the idea that a Black individual smashed the glass ceiling through sheer hard work and exceptional qualities; the idea that they, and they alone, had what it took to enter institutions based on their skill and determination; that they were the 'first' to 'prove' themselves.[28] The inference is that other Black people lacked the skill to achieve such 'success' or, indeed, that a solitary Black individual who 'did something special' was strange, rare, a 'freak' even. The archives tell a different story. *Black Victorians* tells a different story, rooting individual lives within broader networks, milieus and contexts.

Furthermore, in the myth of 'exceptionalism' we render invisible the many societal barriers that had to be overcome. We need to consider the broader context and we need to confront white dominance. And this, indeed, is the focus of Part One: the obfuscation or whitewashing of British history and the shifting Victorian attitudes to 'race' across the long nineteenth century.

Part One

Context and Concealment

1

Hidden in History

In 1805, Ludwig van Beethoven published his Violin Sonata No. 9, Op. 47 in A major, and dedicated it to the virtuoso Rodolphe Kreutzer. The sonata became known as the 'Kreutzer Sonata'. But Kreutzer never performed the composition. He didn't even like the composition. In fact, Kreutzer didn't really care for Beethoven's work at all, and he only met Beethoven once, briefly. But the naming of the sonata was important. It sets the tone for this book.

In the original manuscript, composed two years earlier, Beethoven wrote a very different dedication, '*sonata mulattica Composta per il Mulatto Brischdauer gran pazzo e compositore mulattico*', translated as 'Mulatto Sonata composed for the Mulatto Brischdauer [Bridgetower], the great mulatto composer and lunatic'. Leaving aside the derogatory term 'lunatic', which appeared to reference other-worldly musical skills, the pejorative term 'mulatto', derived from the Spanish word meaning mule, referred to someone of dual heritage – in this case, the renowned violinist and composer George Augustus Polgreen Bridgetower (*c.* 1778–1860).[1]

Bridgetower's father might have hailed from Barbados, his mother from Germany or Poland, and both served in the courts of European princes. Their son was a gifted musician and by the age of ten was touring the continent as a violin prodigy, sometimes billed as the 'African Prince'. The Prince of Wales, the future King George IV, was impressed and employed Bridgetower to play in his orchestra and paid for his musical tuition too.

And on 24 May 1803, Bridgetower and Beethoven performed together at a concert in Vienna. Side by side, they brought to life the Violin Sonata dedicated to Bridgetower. He played the violin, Beethoven played the piano, and during one of Bridgetower's particularly inspired moments, Beethoven was so enthralled that he leapt from his seat and shouted, *'Noch einmal, mein lieber Bursch!'* ('Once more, my dear fellow!'). Beethoven – whose work drew on the classical traditions of Mozart but also looked forward to the Romantic lodestars of emotion and impact – was mightily impressed: he was right to have collaborated with Bridgetower and correct in his praise of the man's talent.

But then something changed. The details are hazy, but the result was erasure. When Beethoven published the Violin Sonata in 1805, the original dedication to Bridgetower was missing, replaced by the name of Rodolphe Kreutzer.

Bridgetower continued to have an impressive career – and was elected to the Royal Society of Musicians in 1807 – but that slight by Beethoven was emblematic of misguided and deliberate marginalisation. Whitewashing, in other words.

* * *

In 1817, six years after Bridgetower graduated from the University of Cambridge, John Edmonstone (sometimes spelled Edmonston), arrived in Scotland from Guyana, South America, where he had been enslaved on a plantation at Mibiri Creek. Edmonstone was previously acquainted with the renowned taxidermist Charles Waterton, having helped him trawl through the Guyanese jungle looking for natural specimens, and while on these expeditions he'd learned new techniques of preserving bird skins. So, by the time Edmonstone arrived in Scotland, he was well versed in natural history, held some cachet thanks to his association with Waterton and was now a freeman under Scottish law, which had outlawed slavery in the late 1770s.[2]

Edmonstone first resided in Glasgow, where many a table was sweetened by the sugar produced by the enslaved (which had helped to build the wealth of the town), before moving to Edinburgh, where the atmosphere was probably more congenial, 'well dressed young white men and women walking arm in arm with negroes in the street', noted one perturbed American visitor, adding with some consternation that 'it did not appear to be regarded with the same repugnance by the communities in Europe'.[3]

Edmonstone secured employment as a servant for Professor Andrew Duncan (the elder), a physician and professor at the University of Edinburgh. On the side, he conducted private taxidermy lessons in a space provided by the University Museum, building an association with a prestigious institution in the heart of the city of the Scottish Enlightenment.

Indeed, Edinburgh was home to former luminaries such as David Hume and Adam Smith. It was renowned for medical excellence: Old Surgeon's Hall stood proudly in Surgeon's Square, housing the illustrious Royal College of Surgeons. Revolutionary discoveries were just around the corner, too: chloroform amnesia in 1847, advanced antiseptic techniques in the 1870s. This was a city on the brink of an exciting future.

Edinburgh was also host to a rebellious science known as phrenology, which hierarchised humanity by reading the skull to reveal – allegedly – inner character. The titan of this spurious science, George Combe, lectured around the capital, arguing that 'faculties are innate' and each person 'has received a determinate Constitution from nature'. From this premise, Anglo-Saxons had apparently flourished thanks to their brains, while 'millions of Hindoos, Africans, and American Indies' had not because, well, they could not, said Combe.[4]

Edmonstone was living refutation of Combe's theory, quietly working away at the University Museum and offering private tuition to young students. In January 1826, he was engaged by a starry-eyed sixteen-year-old medical student eager to learn the art of stuffing birds. This teenage undergraduate was not really enjoying his studies and he found the cold Edinburgh winters hard to bear, but Edmonstone animated him as he imparted the skills of taxidermy. Every day for two months, for a fee of one guinea an hour and totalling over forty hours, Edmonstone taught the eager undergraduate the art of preservation.

Edmonstone almost certainly discussed his collecting expeditions in South America; we can imagine the teenager lapping up Edmonstone's adventures in the South American rainforest. He most probably shared his experiences of enslavement too, encouraging an abolitionist mindset in the white pupil, who found his Black teacher 'a very pleasant and intelligent man', as he later wrote, adding that their relationship was 'intimate'.[5]

It was also a fruitful one, for Edmonstone's student, who went by the name of Charles Darwin, directly applied Edmonstone's teachings on the voyage of HMS *Beagle* (1831–36), where the young Darwin preserved a mockingbird collection from the Galapagos. This became the raw material that informed Darwin's theory of evolution – the theory that mankind was rooted in a common descent and evolved by means of natural selection.[6] It was a radical theory developed, in part, thanks to the teachings of the formerly enslaved Edmonstone.

Years later, Darwin referenced Edmonstone in a sentence that expressed his commitment to monogenism (the belief that all humans are one species) while also articulating a sense that there was a separation between the 'races':

> The American aborigines, Negroes and Europeans are as different from each other in mind as any three races that can be named; yet I was incessantly struck, whilst living with the Fuegians on board the 'Beagle', with the many little traits of character, shewing how similar their minds were to ours; and so it was with a full-blooded negro with whom I happened once to be intimate.[7]

The relationship between Edmonstone and Darwin, much like the relationship between Bridgetower and Beethoven, is symbolically significant: demonstrative of a collective historical amnesia. Edmonstone has been forgotten.

Perhaps amnesia stems from obscurity: we know so little about Edmonstone. Darwin never mentioned him by name. He worked with many other people and there is the phenomenon known as the 'invisible technician', which describes those in the background who helped develop our understanding of science and medicine but rarely received recognition (unless something went wrong).[8] But in the case of John Edmonstone there is also the fact that he was Black.

* * *

Over forty years after Edmonstone taught Darwin in Edinburgh, the African American George Rice began his study of medicine at the University of Edinburgh in 1871. The city now had a different feel to the time when Edmonstone was around. As in several of Britain's principal cities, the introduction of railways in the 1840s and the tramway in the 1870s had led to greater mobility and a faster pace of daily life. New monuments peppered the urban landscape, slum clearances remade parts of the capital and there was a greater cultural offering too (the National Gallery of Scotland opened in 1859, for example).

Victorian modernisation was well underway as Rice dived into the study of medicine, surgery and obstetrics. He graduated in 1874 and subsequently worked at the Edinburgh Royal Infirmary under Sir Joseph Lister, the pioneer of antiseptic treatment.[9] The *Darmouth Alumni Magazine* (1935) wrote that Rice, as a house officer under Lister, was seen as a 'trusted and prized assistant'.[10] He received a glowing testimonial for his 'exceedingly efficient manner' and 'indefatigable zeal', and Rice was obviously equally appreciative of his time with the world-renowned surgeon, for he later named his son George Lister Rice.[11]

After working under Lister, Dr Rice moved to Manchester, where he was employed as the house physician at the Royal Infirmary. He then held posts at the Chorlton Union Hospital and the Woolwich Infirmary, where he met his wife-to-be, Florence Mary Cook (1849–1933), the daughter of a wealthy landowner. They married in 1881 and started a family.

A few years later, Rice secured a job as the Resident Medical Director at the South Metropolitan District School in Sutton, established in 1853 to rescue children from the workhouse. Rice and his family lived on the grounds in a purpose-built house and he received a healthy salary of £450 a year. His personal papers, housed at Sutton Archive, London, contain letters of commendation, correspondence and ephemera, including a bill for groceries whose quantities of sugar candies reveal a sweet tooth and a generous disposition.[12] There are also postcards and photographs, some of which show Dr Rice alongside hospital staff.

One photograph especially stands out. Dr Rice sits at the front of the assembled crowd surrounded by a sea of white female faces. And if you study each face gazing pensively into the camera, one in particular demands attention. On the back row, in the middle of the frame, there stands a Black nurse: who she is, we don't know, but standing two rows behind Dr George Rice, she offers silent testimony to the visible Black presence in Victorian Britain.[13]

Dr Rice with Hospital Staff, *c.* 1910–20

* * *

This presence did not exist in a vacuum. Go back far enough, say, some 10,000 years ago to the Mesolithic era, and hunter gatherers like the so-called 'Cheddar Man', whose remains were discovered in the Mendip Hills, Somerset, had skin pigmentation similar to that of Sub-Saharan Africans: dark skin, dark brown hair and blue eyes. Indeed, the ancestral skin colour in most of Europe was dark, with the genes for light skin emerging over the next few thousand years. This revelation upended deep-rooted assumptions about what our ancestors looked like.[14]

Fast-forward to the first century CE and Britain's population included people from North Africa, Syria, the Balkans and Scandinavia. After the Romans invaded in 43 CE, their multicultural and mobile empire expanded across Europe, North Africa and further afield, bringing more people of African descent to Britain. There were Black soldiers, Black people enslaved and free Black men and women, too – from the so-called Beachy Head Lady, raised in the south of England (around 200–250 CE), to the Ivory Bangle Lady, who was probably born and raised in Britain and buried in the fourth century.[15]

Leaping forward again to the Tudor period (1485–1603), long after the Roman Empire fell and following a period of disconnection from Africa, we discover people of African descent in the courts and societies of Henry VII, Henry VIII and Elizabeth I. They were living, working, trading, marrying and dying in Britain.[16]

And then, as the English colonised distant lands and enslaved fellow human beings, more people of African descent – whether enslaved, free or perceived to be enslaved – came to the British Isles, or became the 'property' of Britons. In 1555, John Lok brought five enslaved people from Guinea to England; the trader William Towerson enslaved people during his voyages from Plymouth to Africa; and from the 1560s, the naval commander John Hawkins embarked on slavery expeditions, 'pioneering' what became known as the (immensely profitable) Triangular Trade between England, Africa and the New World.

And so, as we enter the era of the Stuarts (1603–1714), we enter an age when Britain's involvement in slavery became entrenched. England followed the Spanish in colonising lands in the Americas and the Caribbean and embedding Transatlantic slavery. In 1663, King Charles II granted a royal charter to the Company of Royal Adventurers, later known as the Royal African Company (RAC), which gave the company a monopoly on the West Coast of Africa for 'the whole, entire and only trade for buying and selling bartering and exchanging of for or with any Negroes, slaves, goods, wares, merchandise whatsoever'.[17] This was royal sanction for the slave trade which, from the year the charter was issued until the end of the seventeenth century (by no means the end of the trade), enabled Britain to enslave some 332,000 Africans – and get rich as a result.[18]

Britain was responsible for transporting millions of enslaved Africans to the colonies, while many enslaved people were brought to Britain's shores to serve aristocratic and mercantile households. But in the famous Somerset Case of 1772, the British judge, Lord Mansfield, (who had a Black great-niece, Dido Elizabeth Belle, living at his home in Kenwood House) declared, 'It was impossible [that James Somerset, a formerly enslaved fugitive] could be a slave in England.'[19] This ruling inspired another enslaved individual, Joseph Knight, to go to the Scottish courts in 1774, which subsequently declared, after two appeals, that slavery was not compatible with the laws of the land. Legally, then, there was no slavery in Britain, but people could still be perceived as enslaved.[20]

By the eighteenth century, there were thousands of people of African descent living and working in Britain (as well as Asians and Native Americans). It has been estimated that, by the late eighteenth century, there were 10,000–20,000 Black people living in England, many more of them men than women.[21]

Large numbers worked as domestic servants – and having a male Black servant became a fashion – while others laboured as sailors and dock workers. There were a few craftsmen, labourers and washerwomen, and some successful businesspeople such as Cesar Picton, who became a wealthy coal merchant and, therefore, a member of the 'black labour aristocracy', claims one historian.[22] There were many notable Black individuals: the educated poet and classicist Frances Williams; the Arabic translator Job Ben Solomon; the composer Ignatius Sancho; and the 'Black Dandy', the man about town, Julius Soubise.[23] Then there were Black people within that broad category known as 'the poor': beggars, crossing sweepers, inmates of the workhouse and labourers in menial jobs with low pay.

There were also active Black abolitionists fighting to end Britain's involvement in the slave trade, forming the Black abolitionist organisation, Sons of Africa, which wrote letters, lobbied Parliament and appealed to the public in speaking campaigns. And there was a growing tradition of Black British writing, which flowed from the pens of Ottobah Cugoano, Olaudah Equiano, Ukawsaw Gronniosaw and Mary Prince, among others.

The thousands of Black people who lived in eighteenth-century Britain, naturally, married and had children, who married and had children, and so on. Over the years 'they became English people', the historian Gretchen Holbrook Gerzina writes, 'even though the records of their lives are obscured and scattered'.[24] It was curiously paradoxical, as historian Caroline Bressey notes, that in Victorian Britain there was 'a black presence that may have been observed but was simultaneously not present'.[25]

In her study of Black female migration (in the period 1700–1850), Montaz Marche uncovered records of over 100 Black women, including property owners, traders and servants, across the south-east of England, which show, she argues, that Black women assimilated into British society and, as such, they only appeared in the archives when scandal was afoot – they are largely hidden because 'they desired it to be so'.[26]

Photographs buried in the archives offer a visual record of the nineteenth-century Black presence, but on the whole, it is hard to find evidence of colour in the archives. The first national census in 1801, which amounted to little more than a headcount, was mute on questions of ethnicity. So, too, the national registration of births, marriages and deaths from 1837. This work was carried out by the General Register Office, which assumed responsibility for taking the census every ten years. But, despite the Victorian passion for record-keeping, cataloguing and taxonomising, there seemed to exist an institutional colour-blindness.[27] Indeed, the 1841 census listed the names of every individual in a household, including their age, sex, occupation and place of birth, yet none of the censuses mentioned ethnicity – until 1991.

These administrative decisions conceal Black Victorians in the archives. And even when information on an individual's place of birth is given, it is often a poor guide to establishing ethnicity because many white Britons were born and raised overseas. There are other issues that hamper genealogical research: names rarely reveal ethnicity; women habitually changed their surname upon marriage; and enslaved people were given the names of their captors.

Contemporaneous terminology was also concealing: the designation 'black' could refer to people of African descent, Asian descent or even native Britons with dark skin.[28] Some institutional files recorded the 'complexion' of an individual, in terms such as 'dark', 'fair', 'fresh', 'ruddy', 'sallow', 'pale', 'florid' and 'swarthy', yet 'dark' could be applied to both white and Black people (as I discovered when trawling the records in search of a particular Black police officer).[29]

Yet, despite our archival limitations, Black Victorians are not invisible, then or now. Local collections are a useful resource offering a window onto Black British life: in Haringey, London, one can find photographs of the Black footballer Walter Tull, and the nurses Sister Freda and Asarto Ward; at Waltham Forest, the stories of Madagascan Christian refugees; at the Museum of Croydon, materials on the Black composer Samuel Coleridge-Taylor; at the Lambeth Palace Library, the letters of the Black bishop Samuel Crowther. The Black Cultural Archives in London are also a treasure trove.[30] However, though local studies have shown that Black people were relatively common in densely populated areas such as London, Liverpool, Cardiff, Edinburgh and Kent, determining Black demographics in the Victorian era is more of a challenge. We can say that Black Victorians were present – not in large numbers, but present nonetheless.[31]

Indeed, among a general population which doubled to roughly 30 million between 1851 and 1901, Black Victorians were visible in areas ranging from politics to art, sports to entertainment, theology to law and the menial and skilled trades.

Black seafarers were a notably large contingent: people of African descent comprised a quarter of the British Navy at the end of the eighteenth century.[32] By 1880, there were thousands of Black seamen living in British ports. By 1890, one in five of Britain's seamen were born outside of the isles.[33] Many Black seafarers lived in growing 'sailor town' districts in Britain's major ports. Liverpool, for example, was home to Kru seamen from Liberia and East African seamen from Somalia, and there was a distinct Black community in the poverty-stricken district of Toxteth Park – where the writer Charles Dickens happened upon a public house run by a 'jovial black landlord' whose Black clientele 'generally kept together' due to racial abuse and poverty.[34]

A large number of Black seamen assimilated into the working class, which comprised the largest demographic group for Black Victorians (and the population in general). Many laboured as servants, nurses, travelling singers and circus performers.

When they were unable to work, for a multitude of possible reasons, poor Black Victorians (like poor white Victorians) could be found on the social margins, residing in workhouses, prisons, mental asylums and homeless shelters, also known as 'night asylums'. In his landmark four-volume tome *London Labour and the London Poor* (1851–65), social investigator Henry Mayhew calculates the average number of people inside one London night asylum in the early to mid-nineteenth century. He records 93 people per year hailing from Lincolnshire, 127.2 from Suffolk, 15.7 from Sussex, 75.1 from Bedfordshire, 31.8 from the West Indies and 9.4 people from Africa.[35] The ethnic diversity was such that Mayhew wrote, 'the poverty-stricken from every quarter of the globe are found', including Americans, Europeans, Asians and Africans.

At the other end of the social scale, we find figures like Nathaniel Wells (1779–1852), a Black country gentleman, who inherited a fortune from his slave-owning father and lived a life of respectability in Wales, or the Jamaican millionaire George Stiebel (1821–96), whose father was probably Sigismund Stiebel, a white merchant in London.[36]

A host of West African elites trained, studied, stayed, traded and worked in Britain, while others, such as Sarah Forbes Bonetta, were connected to royalty. There were, naturally, Black Victorians among the burgeoning professional middle classes too – like Dr George Rice and Mary Seacole, or Thomas Birch Freeman (1809–90), who was born in Britain and moved to West Africa as a Methodist missionary.

Africans and Asians came to Britain from the ever-growing empire; interracial couples cohabited, married and had children; the British drank Indian tea, ate Nigerian chocolate, chomped on New Zealand lamb. The empire was huge – by 1914, a quarter of the world's population and a fifth of its land were under the Union Jack – and crisscrossed by the tracks of thousands of people – white, Black or brown – travelling, working and settling.[37] Migration was always part of Britain's story.

But why, when Black Britons were so indubitably present and visible in many walks of life in this period, have they not, until very recently, been given a prominent place in nineteenth-century British history? Some Black Victorians were erased or whitewashed or overlooked – the likes of Bridgetower and Edmonstone. Others became hidden in the archives because they assimilated into British society – they remain the unknowns. There were Black Victorians, but archival obfuscation has concealed them from view.

There is a body of literature which explores the Black British presence, including, as we have noted and wish to emphasise, seminal work by Black historians such as Hakim Adi, Caroline Bressey, Christienna Fryar, Gretchen Holbrook Gerzina, Onyeka

Nubia, David Olusoga, Ron Ramdin, Edward Scobie, Folarin Shyllon and Sadiah Qureshi, but as a collective, many historians have simply failed to look for Black lives in Britain's past. Is this due to innocent historical oversight? Laziness? White indifference? Outright racism? The assumption that Britain's past was mono-ethnically white? The conviction that the Black presence was marginal at best?

Perhaps all of the above; perhaps there is some other reason. But it is a strange state of affairs, nonetheless, because, looking at it now, it seems beyond question that Victorian Britain was a time and place that, like others before and since, was marked and shaped by Black agency, ambition and achievement. It was also an era that witnessed an active Black presence within a society that *had* to confront the issue of 'race' in the light of the expanding imperial project, the international abolitionist campaigns and the upswing in racist ideologies and representations. In other words: the Victorian consciousness was saturated by concerns about 'race'.

So, before we move on to look at individual lives in the nineteenth century, we should first turn to a more detailed exploration of this Victorian context, confronting the obstacles and the ideas that tried to limit and obscure Black agency, and shining a light on a nation which increasingly believed that Black lives did not matter while, simultaneously and triumphantly, it boasted of its superiority as the Land of Hope and Glory.

2

Land of Hope and Glory

On 20 June 1837, the young Victoria assumed the throne, becoming Queen of the United Kingdom of Great Britain and Ireland. Deprived of a father from a young age and raised by her German mother in a fractious environment, Victoria nonetheless had a clear sense of destiny. 'Since it has pleased Providence to place me in this station, I shall do my utmost to fulfil my duty towards my country', she scribbled in her journal which, during her life, ran into 700 volumes approximating 60 million words, and which, as we'll see, contained references to the 'negros' whom she met, befriended and dismissed during the course of her reign.[1]

The young queen's intimations of destiny were certainly in keeping with the spirit of her times. The Victorian era was marked by imperialism and growth; change and modernisation; revolutions in industry, commerce and communication. There was optimism, self-belief and confidence in Britain. There were the railways; the expansion of the franchise; public health reforms; medical innovations; a growing and increasingly assertive middle class; urbanisation; electrification; new technologies. People had more time and money to enjoy entertainment and increased literacy rates enabled more people to gorge upon news, literature, sensationalism and imperial glory.

Yet this was also a period of paradox and contradiction: liberalism amid colonialism, poverty amid prosperity, optimism undercut by fear for the future. An expanding empire used bibles, bullets, guns and germs to infect, reform, conquer and subjugate people from across the globe. And by 1901, many in Britain could confidently sing 'Rule, Britannia!'

This sense of superiority was not merely imperial or naval or economic, or indeed racial. It was moral. Britain, its people believed, was civilising the world. The Victorians prided themselves on their open borders: the right to asylum; refugees welcome; all free to experience liberty and social justice – those central tenets of an idealised Britain.[2] Liberty, it was believed, flowed through Great Britain's veins: the very character of the English was linked to the unwritten constitution which, since the Levellers and Glorious Revolution of 1688, had been wedded to the idea of the freeborn Englishman.[3]

And now abolitionism was assuming its place as another cornerstone of national moral pride. In 1807, the Parliament of the United Kingdom triumphantly abolished the slave trade in the British Empire. In 1833, they went even further, passing the Slavery Abolition Act which immediately abolished slavery throughout most of the British Empire. When it passed into law on 1 August 1834, some 800,000 enslaved people were suddenly free. History was quickly rewritten. Britain's role in slavery was minimised, the history of abolitionism centralised and a Whiggish moral march was saluted, which focused on a small band of (white) abolitionists who, it was claimed, were enlightening the nation with their humanitarian cry.

The reality, of course, was rather different. Abolitionism had been fought for by a cross-section of British society: in 1787, the year that the Society for Effecting the Abolition of the Slave Trade was formed, Ottobah Cugoano, a formerly enslaved member of the Sons of Africa, made a radical case for immediate abolition. He drew on his own experience 'beholding the most dreadful scenes of misery and cruelty' and refuted pro-slavery arguments while also chiding Britain, 'But whereas the people of Great-Britain having now acquired a greater share in that iniquitous commerce than all the rest together, they are the first that ought to set an example, lest they have to repent for their wickedness when it becomes too late.'[4]

Two years later, another member of the Sons of Africa, Olaudah Equiano, who had experienced the horrors of slavery before purchasing his freedom and settling in London, wrote an autobiography that became a sensation. Eight editions were printed during his lifetime and Equiano became a celebrity of means, travelling around the country and igniting 'a sense of compassion for the miseries which the Slave-Trade has entailed on my unfortunate countrymen'.[5] And it was not only men who were involved in Britain's abolitionist movement: women played a vital role in propagating the humanitarian cause. The formerly enslaved Mary Prince powerfully made the case for abolition in her book *The History of Mary Prince* (1831): 'This is slavery. I tell it, to let English people know the truth; and I hope they will never leave off to pray God, and call loud to the great King of England, till all the poor blacks be given free, and slavery done up for evermore.'[6]

Internationally, meanwhile, blood was being shed by the enslaved as they rose up against their masters, most successfully in the French colony of Saint-Domingue where half a million enslaved people seized their freedom, creating the modern republic of Haiti in 1804. These long-running wars against enslavement, the memories of which were passed down the generations, were a crucial factor in the move towards emancipation.[7] So, too, were the declining economic importance of slavery, realpolitik on the international stage, a religious revival and the abolitionist campaigns – but the overwhelming Victorian takeaway was self-aggrandisement rather than self-reflection.[8]

Britain had risen to the challenge! Economic self-interest had been transcended! And how glorious it looked from on high!

Abolition revealed the hands of Providence guiding Great Britain to glory. Despite her domineering role in the slave trade, Britain now assumed the moral plane while other European nations – not to mention the Americans and Brazilians – languished in the quagmire of slavery.

This perspective proved, unsurprisingly, a helpful justification for British imperialism: a benevolent nation shining a beacon of light around the world.[9] This ideology of imperialism encompassed a 'sense of righteousness, self-assurance, and higher purpose', writes the historian Michael Adas, and provided a moral bolster that legitimised the bombardment of distant lands in a supposedly glorious civilising crusade.[10] And so – as the West African Squadron patrolled the seas, intercepting slave ships and freeing the humans inside, as missionaries spread the Gospel to 'heathens' across the seas, as the British Empire conquered foreign lands – Britain saw itself as purveying civilisation under God's watchful eye. Great Britain had God on its side; the Statue of Liberty, in comparison, was a devilish joke.

* * *

Such language is not hyperbole. Many Victorians firmly believed that morality and liberty emanated from its shores. The continuation of American slavery bolstered this jingoistic sense of self, and the presence of African American abolitionists heightened the belief in Britain's innate superiority as their rhetoric was often co-opted for a self-serving national discourse.

From the 1830s onwards, many Black abolitionists travelled from America to Britain to denounce slavery and segregation in their country: '3,000,000 of the coloured race are lying there under the heels of 17,000,000 of their white fellow creatures,' admonished the leading Black abolitionist Frederick Douglass in 1847.[11] He travelled for nineteen months across Britain, addressing thousands of people on the topics of slavery, temperance and suffrage, and building and strengthening an African American tradition which sought to erect a 'moral cordon' by isolating America from the global community and inflaming popular opinion against slavery.[12]

In major cities and small towns, in large assembly halls and tiny chapels, Black abolitionists delivered lectures, exhibitions, songs and panoramas to packed British crowds. Speeches could last for two or three hours. The instruments of human bondage – neck collars and chains – were shown. Runaway 'slave advertisements' were read. Songs from the plantations were sung. Daring stories of escape were told. Despite the powerful messages, ultimately this was perceived as spectacle and mass entertainment: these speaking campaigns fed the popular appetite for showmanship, exoticism, sensational narratives and morality tales that darkened America and enlightened Great Britain.[13]

And yet, Black abolitionists used supportive networks to further their cause. They exploited print culture to proliferate their message. They inspired letters in the press; they informed editorials, pamphlets, children's literature, religious reflections, songs, poetry and visual culture. Their stories were read and devoured. So-called 'slave narratives' (a literary genre better described as 'emancipation narratives') documented individual journeys from enslavement to freedom, and many became bestsellers.

Between the 1830s and 1860s, Black abolitionists appealed to the working classes by drawing comparisons between the plight of the enslaved and the plight of the industrial class. They also appealed to the middle classes, who perceived them as representing the much-cherished self-made man, and they appealed to the long held and widespread belief that Britain was morally superior – committed to liberty and abolitionism and a confident leader of the free world. In this manner, Black abolitionists directly contributed to Victorian Britain's sense of self.

In 1847, the *New York Express* was lamenting that 'the mother country, of late years, has signalized itself particularly in the great delight it has taken to avail itself of every opportunity to foster, and feed, and flatter, runaway American negroes'. There was, they argued, a pervasive 'English negrophilism'.[14]

And in a way they were right. As early as 1773, the formerly enslaved poet Phillis Wheatley wrote that in London the 'benevolent conduct towards me, the unexpected and unmerited civility and complaisance with which I was treated fills me with astonishment'.[15] In 1829, the African American David Walker stressed that 'the English are the best friends the coloured people have upon earth'.[16] In 1845, the formerly enslaved Harriet Jacobs visited Britain and wrote, 'For the first time in my life I was in a place where I was treated according to my deportment, without reference to my complexion. I felt as if a great millstone had been lifted from my breast.'[17]

In 1881, Frederick Douglass argued that in England 'character, not color, is the passport to consideration', and he was emphatic: 'there is no prejudice against color in England, save as it is carried there by Americans'.[18] To many Black abolitionists, who spent parts of their life enslaved or all of their lives segregated, Britain seemingly felt like a racial utopia, and the British in turn congratulated themselves by jibing the Americans:

'To the West, to the West, to the land of the free –'
Which means those that happen white people to be –
'Where a man is a man –' if his skin isn't black –
If it is, he's a n****r, to sell or to whack…[19]

But there was more that united Britain and America than the writers of that 1854 burlesque cared to believe. For starters, following the Slavery Abolition Act (1833), the British replaced slavery with 'apprenticeships', a system which forced the formerly enslaved over the age of six to continue working for their masters, partly or wholly for free, for four or six years, with continued punishments such as flogging and the treadmill. The system was almost impossible to administer and was terminated on 1 August 1838 (although not on the islands of Ceylon and St Helena and not in the territories belonging to the East India Company).

Then colonial officials in the Caribbean raised the price of land and raised the property qualification for holding office too, thus denying the formerly enslaved their political power. When they agitated for higher wages, thousands of indentured workers from China, South Asia and West Africa were brought to the Caribbean.[20]

Meanwhile, among the provisions of the 1833 Act, Parliament agreed to pay £20 million towards 'compensating the Persons hitherto entitled to the Services of such Slaves'.[21] The Slave Compensation Act (1837) was signed into law six months after the eighteen-year-old Queen Victoria assumed the throne with the blood money reinvested across Britain and her empire, going into mines, banks, railroads, civic buildings and the arts.[22]

In 1840, at the first World Anti-Slavery Convention (held in England, naturally), one delegate declared, 'It is known to every intelligent abolitionist in the United States, that the demand for American cotton in the Liverpool market, is the main support of American slavery'.[23] One South Carolina planter acknowledged that if the enslaved no longer picked cotton, 'England would topple headlong and carry the whole civilized world with her'.[24]

The raw materials harvested by the enslaved in the American South still powered Britain's industrial growth in the nineteenth century. The systems were enmeshed: the enslaved in America picked the cotton, which was then processed in mills and factories across northern England.

By the 1850s, Britain imported some £800 million of cotton every year, 77 per cent of which was produced in America by enslaved people. In England, almost a fifth of the population relied on cotton for their livelihood. As such, when cotton exports were disrupted during the American Civil War (1861–65), Britain suffered what has been dubbed the Cotton Famine. Poverty and unemployment led to riots across British towns while many sided with the Confederates.[25] At the same time, British companies still made the chains for enslaved people while British capitalists piled money into the American South, bankrolling steamships and railroads and buying up the debt of slaveholding states. And in the nineteenth century, the slave empire was replaced with a colonial one, which grew in size and ferocity as the century progressed, while the reality of slavery continued to have a material and psychological impact as it seeped into the very consciousness of what it meant to be Black.

* * *

'One ever feels his twoness,' W. E. B. Du Bois famously wrote. 'An American, a Negro; two souls, two thoughts, two unreconciled strivings; two warring ideals in one dark body, whose strength alone keeps it from being torn asunder.'[26] This double consciousness was characteristic of a subjectivity scarred by slavery, encumbered with racism and emanating from dislocation. And it was not just applicable to African Americans but was evident in the subjectivities of Black Britons too, for being European and Black meant negotiating two identities presented as mutually exclusive.[27]

Black Victorians were encased in a 'racial straight jacket' that marked them as 'Other', to quote from historian Edward Scobie, while Black women continually faced the dual threats of being Black and female. 'Slavery is terrible for men; but it is far more terrible for women,' wrote Harriet Jacobs. 'Superadded to the burden common to all, *they* have wrongs, and sufferings, and mortifications peculiarly their own.'[28]

The words of Du Bois and Jacobs serve as a general guide for understanding individual subjectivities in this book. And while a double consciousness brought inner conflict and ignited struggles with the external world, this consciousness did not denote powerlessness, as the stories that follow will also attest. Indeed, a double consciousness born out of the diaspora, itself born out of the transatlantic slave trade, could bring a clarity of perspective, as Richard Wright expressed:

> My point of view is a western one, but a western one that conflicts at several vital points with the present, dominant outlook of the West. Am I ahead of or behind the West? My personal judgement is that I'm ahead.[29]

The same could not be said for white consciousness, which was traumatised, in a very different way, by the transatlantic slave trade. 'They had to dehumanize, not just the slaves but themselves,' wrote the African American novelist Toni Morrison, and 'it made them crazy'.[30] It made them racist. How else could John Newton, the composer of the hymn 'Amazing Grace', turn to evangelical Christianity and *continue* to enslave fellow humans? In 1753, he wrote to his wife about the 'cargo' on his ship:

> The three greatest blessings of which human nature is capable, are, undoubtedly, religion, liberty, and love. In each of these how highly has God distinguished me! But here are whole nations around me, whose languages are entirely different from each other, yet I believe they all agree in this, that they have no words among them expressive of these engaging ideas: from whence I infer, that the ideas themselves have no place in their minds. And as there is no medium between light and darkness, these poor creatures are not only strangers to the advantages which I enjoy but are plunged in all the contrary evils.[31]

Newton could bask in God's love. He could proclaim the power of liberty. He could cherish sentient beings. And, at the same time, he could hear the cries of chained Africans on his ship. But there was no conflict here, for the ideology of racism denied Black humanity.

* * *

Racism was not created by slavery, but the latter became the material basis for the former. Until the last quarter of the seventeenth century, plantation labour was largely conducted by indentured European servants, but the move towards a total reliance on enslaved Africans, who were brutally dislocated, controlled and denied basic rights, transformed slavery into a relation of white–Black domination.[32]

After the English colonised Barbados in 1627, the Barbados Slave Code (1661) established the rules and justification which infected colonial thinking: an enslaved 'negro' was damned to slavery for life, as were their offspring, with violent retribution for resistance – and this was justified because Black Africans were deemed fundamentally inferior to white Europeans. This belief emerged at roughly the same time that the English started to self-describe as 'white'.[33] Simultaneously, the popular perception of what a slave might look like shifted from a European in the Ottoman Empire to an African in the Americas; slavery, in other words, became coloured.[34]

By the middle of the eighteenth century, justifications were hitting the printing press with regularity. David Hume was 'apt to suspect the negroes [...] to be naturally inferior to whites'.[35] In 1774, the Jamaican planter and slaveowner Edward Long published his widely read *History of Jamaica*, in which he declared, 'I think there are extremely potent reasons for believing, that the White and Negroe are two distinct species.' Heaping all manner of ignominy onto Africans, he finishes off, 'must we not conclude, that they are a different species of the same *genus*?'[36]

Others were starting to provide the groundwork that might support such a conclusion. In *Systema Naturae* (1735), the Swedish botanist Carl Linnaeus divided the human species into four 'varieties' (he did not use the term 'races'), which corresponded to the four then-known continents (Europe, America, Asia and Africa). Linnaeus reflected the prevalent belief that differences in skin colour were primarily due to climates and geographical variations, but by 1758 he rooted human differences in the temperaments or humours of the body. In this scheme, different physiologies corresponded with different moral and personal characteristics: white Europeans were deemed wise, muscular and inventive; Black Africans were sly and neglectful.[37]

By the late eighteenth century, the comparative anatomist George Cuvier was proposing three different 'races': Caucasians, Mongolians and Negros. Writing in 1790–91, he scoffed at the idea that Black people were inherently inferior, not least because his own Black servant was 'intelligent'. A decade later, he was proclaiming that the 'races of the human species' were anatomically different, and these innate differences likely reflected 'moral and intellectual faculties'.[38] An important conceptual shift was underway – 'Climate to Crania', as historian Bronwen Douglas has summarised it – which moved from explaining human variety in terms of environmental causes towards a belief in permanent, hereditary and innate differences among the 'races'.[39]

In the early nineteenth century, the dominant view remained nurture over nature: it was generally maintained that environmental factors caused human difference, not innate biology, which was a necessary position because Christian orthodoxy stipulated that all human beings were one species born from a single act of Divine Creation. This dominant view was known as monogenesis and it was given institutional authority with the establishment of the Ethnological Society of London in 1843 – its president, James Cowles Prichard, declared that 'all the tribes of men are of one family'.[40] The Ethnological Society of London grew out of the Aborigines' Protection Society, which was active throughout the Victorian age and sought to promote equal rights for people subject to colonial rule. Their motto was *Ab Uno Sanguine* ('Of One Blood').[41]

But there was an antagonistic theory, which became increasingly popular from the late seventeenth century and gathered steam in the nineteenth. Polygenism maintained that humanity was divided into distinct groups with separate origins – human variations were fixed, innate and biological. This theory found an institutional home in the Anthropological Society of London, first established in 1863, with its president James Hunt declaring that there was 'good reason for classifying the Negro as a distinct species from Europeans'.[42]

Members of this organisation, albeit on the margins of scientific debate, openly championed the slave-owning American Confederates and used the term 'abolitionist' as an insult. They were a rowdy, racist bunch who, after attending meetings denouncing 'Negros' and women (whose political participation threatened a 'hermaphrodite form of government', declared one member), might head to the Cannibal Club to read accounts of enslaved women being whipped.[43]

Monogenism and polygenism were not diametrically opposed, however. Between 1813–47, the president of the Ethnological Society of London oscillated between both theories while monogenists still established racial hierarchies with Europeans at the top.[44] Darwin's *On the Origins of Species* (1859) – which argued that man had a common descent (a triumph for monogenism) – nonetheless created a space for a shared racism as monogenists continued to establish racial hierarchies.

Polygenists, on the other hand, generally conceded that, OK, perhaps there was a common ancestry, but 'races' had been separated for so long that inherited differences had evolved.[45] By the 1850s, then, it was generally agreed that some 'races' were superior to others; that there were some innate differences between people; that these differences were not necessarily environmentally determined and that the white 'race' trumped all.[46] Little wonder, then, that the Ethnological and Anthropological Societies of London merged in 1871.

* * *

While science was bolstering racism (and, it should be noted, many people ignored these elite musings), the burgeoning entertainment industry was taking racism to the masses. Blackface minstrelsy, which peddled depictions of African Americans as lazy, comical and stupid, developed from backstreet entertainment in the 1830s into large-scale commercial shows appealing to the middle classes from the 1840s. A decade later, Frederick Douglass bemoaned the 'pestiferous nuisance' of blackface minstrelsy, observing how these racist representations were infecting British culture.[47] 'Ethnographic exhibitions' and freak shows were developing in size and ambition too, parading people from across the globe as 'Other', inferior, inherently strange and backwards.

In 1853, a group of Zulus from South Africa were displayed in London. The show was introduced by a white man who declared:

> Behind his agreeable outward bearing, [the Zulu] conceals the most vindictive feelings, and a capacity for perpetrating the most atrocious cruelty. Impulsive, emotional, and excitable even to frenzy, he makes no effort to control his impulses, nor at any time reasons upon the abstract justice of his deeds.[48]

Charles Dickens visited the display and was compelled to write an article which ridiculed the Enlightenment idea of the 'Noble Savage': 'His virtues are a fable; his happiness is a delusion; his nobility nonsense'.[49] Dickens was both condemning the white system that perpetuated the idea of the Noble Savage while also critiquing the actual people on display: they were deemed mentally and morally inferior.

The public flocked to these racially demeaning 'ethnographic exhibitions' – while in their leisure time at home they might simultaneously devour Harriet Beecher Stowe's *Uncle Tom's Cabin*, a forty-week serial in America which was first published in London in 1852. Drenched in sentimentality and the values of Christianity and abolitionism, the novel was an instant bestseller.

Readers were gripped when the fugitive slave Eliza Harris carried her child to freedom across the Ohio River. They cheered as her husband George battled slave catchers. They wept as the brutal slaveowner Simon Legree whipped Tom to death. They rejoiced when the enslaved Topsy embraced Christianity.

In England, where an estimated 165,000 copies were sold in the first year of circulation, the novel created a full-blown 'Tom-Mania', with spin-off dramas, songbooks, mementos, paintings, panoramas, card games and ornaments produced. The satirical magazine *Punch* declared that *Uncle Tom's Cabin* 'roused such a penchant for n*****s, that dark skins must now take precedence over white'.[50]

Though in 1837 the African American minister Hosea Easton wrote that 'n****r, is an approbrious [*sic*] term […] the practical definition is quite different in England to what it is here, for [in America], it flows from the fountain of purpose to injure', by the 1850s, in Britain too, the term was understood to be damning and injurious.[51]

In 1849, the Scottish writer Thomas Carlyle published an essay in *Fraser's Magazine* entitled 'Occasional Discourse on the Negro Question' – he did so under a pseudonym. But four years later, the same material was republished as a pamphlet under Carlyle's own name, *Occasional Discourse on the N****r Question*, a sharp shift in register that both reflected and contributed to growing racial hostility.[52]

By the 1860s, one Christian newspaper could sneer that some abolitionists and liberal humanitarians would invariably encourage the English 'to extend our sympathies to the blessed n*****s – we beg pardon – men and brothers of colour in the West Indies'; and this the editors would rather not do.[53]

This sarcastic, racist scoff reflected a recurring resentment within elements of British society, one based on the belief that more heed was paid to Black people abroad than to white people in Britain. Between 1814 and 1833, the journalist and MP William Cobbett actively demonised and scapegoated both free and enslaved Black people in order to ostensibly advance the cause of the British working class.[54]

As the century progressed, the working classes increasingly saw themselves as part of a national identity constructed in opposition to racialised outsiders.[55] And by the end of the 1850s, white Victorians more generally became aware of their own racial identity in an evolving 'racial Anglo-Saxonism' that assumed moral, intellectual and racial superiority.[56] So much so that in 1859, the writer Anthony Trollope declared that God 'created men of inferior and superior race' and the 'negro's phase of humanity differs from that which is common to ours'.[57]

* * *

This increasingly hostile, racialised environment made its effects known in the everyday lives of many Black Victorians. Mayhew wrote, 'It is only common fairness to say that negroes seldom, if ever, shirk work. Their only trouble is to obtain it.'[58] He went further, writing, 'Those who have seen the many negroes employed in Liverpool, will know that they are hard-working, patient, and, too often, underpaid.'[59]

Mayhew recorded the testimony of one 'Negro Beggar', who travelled from America to Britain having heard that in Britain 'n****rs were as good as whites; and that the whites did not look down on them and illtreat them, as they do in New York'.[60] Yet, the 'Negro Beggar' struggled to find work (his brother was luckier) and when he tried to get employment on English ships, 'They won't have me,' he told Mayhew.[61]

Black seamen had worked in a variety of roles on British ships, but from the mid-nineteenth century they were increasingly restricted to the engine rooms or the lower quarters.[62] An analysis of the 1901 census, for example, shows that a third of West Indian seafarers were deckhands (596), nearly another third were stewards and cooks (463, which included four women) and the remainder were confined to the engine room as firemen and trimmers (271).[63]

Denied even a lowly job on the ships, the 'Negro Beggar' was also denied access to public establishments – 'at some places they don't care to take a man of colour in' – and on the streets he was subject to racist taunts – 'the butchers call me Othello, and ask me why I killed my wife'.[64] Other stereotypes reared their heads: the idea that 'some blacks are peculiar in their dress', for example, or that most Black Victorians worked as crossing sweepers who cleaned the urban streets.[65]

Mayhew recounted a meeting of 'the lowest class of male juvenile thieves and vagabonds' and noted that when a Black boy entered the room, 'one of the young vagabonds would shout out "swe-ee-op." This would be received with peals of laughter, and followed by a general repetition of the same cry.'[66]

Racial attitudes were also informed by events abroad. The Indian Rebellion of 1857–59, a widespread revolt against the East India Company, was brutally repressed by the British Army, and subsequently perceived as a barbarous assault on Christianity, which was triumphantly controlled by 'the Great White Hand' (to borrow from the title of a novel documenting the 'adventure' overseas).[67]

According to *The Times*, however, 'the first great conflict of the races' occurred in 1863. 'It is time to consider whether the English or the Maories [sic] are to be masters,' the paper editorialised in response to continued fighting in New Zealand, a conflict which dated back to the 1840s and intensified in the 1860s.[68]

The American Civil War (1861–65) provoked more racial debate, dividing public opinion between support for the slave-owning Confederate states versus the Unionists. The 1865 Morant Bay Uprising, which the British turned into a massacre, similarly split opinion – and hardened racial attitudes – as the 'merits' of Britain's violent response were debated in Britain. By 1866, one commentator could write, 'English soldiers are in the field in four distinct wars of race in as many great divisions of the globe.'[69] The Victorians were fully aware that across the globe they were engaged in 'race' wars.

Racial conflict was a reality of colonial relationships, and it challenged the doctrine of assimilation. This had rested on the premise, however vulnerable, that some collaboration with colonised peoples was desirable. But colonial resistance shattered that illusion – and the result was often authoritarian, direct imperial rule. After the Indian Rebellion, Britain assumed direct rule over India; after the Morant Bay Uprising, Jamaica became a crown colony.

But the British also oversaw an 'empire of settlement' promulgated by the 'White Deluge' of European migrants to the Americas, Australasia and southern Africa between 1840 and 1890, as well as 'an empire of rule' practised in India and other colonial dependencies.[70] The former arrangement allowed self-governance in predominantly white colonies such as New Zealand, Australia and Canada, but the latter relied on authoritarian rule over people of colour. The mapping of empire was undeniably racial.

The brutal suppression of the Indian Rebellion and the Morant Bay Uprising shattered another comfortable illusion: the benevolent civilising British Empire was not so benevolent after all. But in 1864, the philosopher Herbert Spencer gave theoretical credence to imperial conquest overseas. He took Darwin's ideas about the natural world and applied them to the human world, using the theory of evolution and natural selection to explain human societies: 'This survival of the fittest, which I have here sought to express in mechanical terms, is that which Mr. Darwin has called "natural selection", or the preservation of favored races in the struggle for life.'[71] Although he was anti-imperialist, Spencer reasoned that human societies, like biological species, were governed by natural selection: humans existed in perpetual competition, which defined 'Nature's battlefield', so imperial domination was deemed natural and racial conflict inevitable.[72]

In the 1860s, Darwin's cousin, Francis Galton, similarly applied natural selection to human society, arguing that mental and physical ability – even morality – were inherited, and concluding that natural selection should be replaced with 'rational selection' of the 'well born'. These ideas underpinned what Galton termed the new science of 'eugenics' – the 'best' should reproduce; the worst should not – and this, of course, cut along 'race' lines.

Indeed, Galton was in no doubt that 'Negroes' were vastly inferior and that the 'Arab is little more than an eater up of other men's produce; he is a destroyer'.[73] He vehemently argued against racial equality and, instead, advocated childbearing among the 'fitter stock' (i.e., the Anglo-Saxon upper classes) and the cessation of breeding among the 'unfit' (i.e., the working classes and people of colour).[74]

By the 1870s, certain ideas were beginning to settle: there were fixed, heritable differences between groups; Black people were linked to notions of slavery and servitude; white people, and especially the British and more so the English, were the imperial leaders and superiors of the world.[75]

From the late 1870s, as the so-called 'Scramble for Africa' got underway, Britain's formal empire expanded exponentially, and within twenty-five years she and her imperial neighbours in Europe had partitioned 10 million square miles in Africa and were governing 110 million new subjects. Treasures were looted (and kept to this day), including from the Maqdala in Ethiopia, the Ashanti Kingdom in Ghana and the Benin Empire in present-day Nigeria. Uprisings were viciously suppressed and natural resources exploited, while people starved. By 1895, the *Spectator* could declare, 'The white race is taking charge of the black race everywhere [...] twenty years hence no black will be able to live happily except by consent of some white people.'[76]

By 1914, ninety per cent of Africa would come under European colonial rule. Empire emboldened and embedded racism in Europe, albeit with a cognitive dissonance that ignored, sanitised and/or justified imperial injustices overseas. In Britain, conflicts such as the Anglo-Zulu War and the Anglo-Afghan War prompted bursts of jingoistic excitement, and imperialist and racist ideas permeated a booming popular culture, in literature for adults and for children, in art, exhibitions, music halls and theatres.[77]

Despite this rising tide of racist thinking, there is evidence of countervailing forces including, around the end of the century, the rise of the Pan-African movement, which we explore towards the end of this book. From the world of entertainment, the Fisk University Jubilee Singers visited Britain from the United States in the early 1870s and, in opposition to racially degrading minstrelsy, they presented themselves as serious and refined, performing spirituals and honouring the memory of the enslaved while injecting Black music into British culture.[78] From the world of politics, in the 1890s the Black campaigner Ida B. Wells travelled to Britain to denounce racism and lynching in America, speaking to packed crowds and joining forces with the white Quaker Catherine Impey, who edited the anti-racist journal *Anti-Caste* and condemned lynching as a form of 'white supremacy' (her term).[79]

Elsewhere, Dadabhai Naoroji, the first Asian British MP (1892–95), directly challenged British rule in India; the African Association was founded in 1897 and three years later, they organised the First Pan-African Conference in London, which demanded self-governance for colonies in Africa and the Caribbean and political rights for African Americans, while anti-racist journals such as *Anti-Caste* did what its complete title suggested – *Advocates the Brotherhood of Mankind Irrespective of Colour or Descent*.

Despite this strengthening 'politics of resistance', by the end of the century racialism had intensified.[80] Science accepted that humanity could be divided into separate groups. Even Darwin's *The Descent of Man* (1871), which once again asserted the monogenist principle of racial unity, relied on a racial hierarchy or 'grade of civilization', which placed white men at the apex and Black 'savages' at the nadir.[81]

As the British Empire reached its apogee, mass culture peddled proliferating racist representations in large-scale freak shows, minstrel shows and ethnographic exhibitions. In 1899, for example, the Greater Britain Exhibition included 'A Vivid Representation of Life in the Wilds of the Dark Continent', with African animals and 174 natives from South Africa separated into four native villages that could be visited by spectators.[82]

Racism had become entrenched. By the 1890s, *The Times* would openly admit that 'the race prejudice which is prevalent with all white races, […] has kept the Anglo-Saxon race pure'.[83] Racism was necessary, they reasoned, especially in the American South, where 'no white woman is safe, from hour to hour, in those black country districts'.[84] In 1903 the *Westminster Gazette* ran with the headline 'A Colour Line in London? Publicans and "N****r" Customers'. The paper was reporting on a Black man and his friends who were refused service in a London pub. 'The incident, while not isolated, must not be taken to indicate that the colour problem which is so acute in America is to become established here,' they optimistically reported.[85] Six years later, however, *Britons Through Negro Spectacles* (1909) was published, written by the West African A. B. C. Merriman-Labor:

> [...] pray even now you never meet a troupe of school children just from school. They will call you all kinds of names, sing you all sorts of songs. Pray also that you never encounter a band of factory girls just from their workshop. Some of these girls will make fun of you by throwing kisses at you when not making hisses at you while others shout 'Go wash your face, guv'nor, or sometimes call out 'n****r, n****r, n****r'.[86]

Victorian racism was not black and white, however: the Italians and French, the Jewish community and the working class were all racialised, with the Irish, in particular, prone to endure racial scorn.[87]

There were seeming inconsistencies as well. Abolitionists could be racist; racists could be anti-imperialists. The ethnologist Robert Knox, who argued that the Black man 'is no more a white man than an ass is a horse or a zebra', was an ardent anti-imperialist and abolitionist.[88] The white abolitionist Richard Webb worried that the Black campaigner Frederick Douglass, 'after associating so much with white women' in the 1840s, would 'feel a craving void when he returns to his own family' (subtext: the fawning of white women will inflame a Black man's lust, which could destroy the nuclear family).[89]

These attitudes were, if not downright inconsistent, certainly complex. We should, for example, be careful in how we use the term 'racism', for the very notion of 'race' (and its reification, i.e., 'racism') was complex and invented and reinvented from classical antiquity to the Middle Ages to the Victoria era and beyond.[90]

The term 'race' was complex too. In the nineteenth century, the term was still vague. The anthropologist James Hunt once said, 'Hardly two persons use such an important word as race in the same sense.'[91] Imputing modern-day labels onto the past runs its own historiographical gauntlet and, as historian Matthew Sweet has argued, the Victorian era has been stereotyped and mythologised in such a manner that it not only does Victorians an injustice but also blinds us to our own contemporary fallibilities.[92]

And yet, as James Hunt recognised, 'race' was an 'important word' for the Victorians – it was reified by them too – but Black Victorians were not generally perceived as a threat (their numbers in Britain were relatively small). They did not, as a rule, worryingly challenge positions of power or compete for economic resources. Arguably, therefore, certain Black professionals could progress because they were deemed unthreatening: they weren't effective scapegoats, unlike the Irish or Jewish community. Indeed, the first anti-immigration act came about in 1905 – and that was in response to large-scale Jewish migration. It was the Jews, that 'Hebrew colony' in a Christian land, lamented the anti-Semite William Eden Evans-Gordon, who were condemned as 'a race apart'.[93]

But racial hostility directed towards Black Victorians, which was evident throughout the era and reflected a hardening of racial attitudes as the century progressed, would erupt on a larger scale with the harassment of Black communities during the First World War. In 1919, there were 'race riots' across South Shields, Salford, Hull, London, Liverpool, Cardiff and Barry, with whites attacking Black and Asian seamen.

As the twentieth century dawned, Du Bois would remark prophetically, 'The problem of the Twentieth Century is the problem of the color-line' – a barrier, division or obstacle created by whites, concerning, as Du Bois continued in *The Souls of Black Folk* (1903), 'the relation of the darker to the lighter races of men' – a white-made problem developed and manifest in nineteenth-century Britain too.[94]

Indeed, Du Bois first uttered this famous line in a speech in London during the first Pan-African Conference of 1900. He went on to say:

> ... the question as to how far differences of race – which show themselves chiefly in the color of the skin and the texture of the hair – will hereafter be made the basis of denying to over half the world the right of sharing to utmost ability the opportunities and privileges of modern civilization.[95]

The 'color-line', and the denial of human and civil rights and privileges that it represents, remains evident in many history books today. Black Victorians have been disaffirmed from British history and thus removed from the story of the making of modern Britain too – arguably reflecting a Victorian assumption that the 'negro' had no history worthy of note. In the 1884 edition of the *Encyclopaedia Britannica*, it was stated, with a staggering air of self-satisfaction, that:

> No full-blooded Negro has ever been distinguished as a man of science, a poet, or an artist, and the fundamental equality claimed for him by ignorant philanthropists is belied by the whole history of the race throughout the historic period.[96]

This book will show how obviously blind and ignorant that comment is but, before we meet the scientists and artists, we will begin with those individuals who lived, strived and survived on the social margins of nineteenth-century Britain.

Part Two

Struggle and Survival

3

Broadmoor: William Brown
(1832–85)

Sheerness, Kent, 18 January 1883 – in the early hours of the morning, the residents of Ebenezer Road were awoken by the sound of infantile cries. At the top of the street, at number seven, four terrified children were standing at an open bedroom window screaming, 'Murder! Fire! Murder! Fire!' One of the distressed youngsters, a girl of about nine, jumped from the window to escape the inferno. She alerted a watchman, who rushed to the scene and helped the other children down from the bedroom window to the street below.

The traumatised youngsters quickly relayed that their father had killed their mother and set fire to the house. A police constable burst open the front door. Out staggered a young man, around twenty years old, who collapsed in the street: blood oozed from open wounds in his thigh, chest and head. The police and local firefighters then entered the home of William Brown and quickly located his wife, Elizabeth, who was lying dead in a burning room. Her throat had been cut and her head bashed in.

The fire was quickly contained before the men searched for Mr Brown. At the top of the house, in an attic filled with smoke, they found him: his throat was slashed, and an open razor lay by his side. Miraculously, he was still alive. 'The tragic occurrence has caused immense excitement in Sheerness, where Brown was a familiar figure,' reported London's *Weekly Dispatch*, 'Formerly he was a seaman in the Royal Navy, and was discharged with a certificate for good conduct and a pension.'[1] But on that Tuesday night, he and his wife had an almighty row with terrible consequences:

> A black man named William Brown, about fifty years of age, after murdering his wife by cutting her throat with a razor, violently attacked his stepson, aged twenty, with the same weapon. He then set fire to the house, afterwards cutting his own throat.[2]

The harrowing scenes on Ebenezer Road were part of a story, not of evildoing, but of illness – of an individual undergoing a complete mental collapse. In exploring the story of William Brown, and a few others in similar tragic predicaments, we will encounter scenes of inner and outer despair and plumb the depths of the Victorian world of mental asylums, confronting poverty, destitution, tragedy and loss. But in the darkness of human experience, we will also see triumph, resistance, endurance, love and hope. We will meet the indomitable human spirit.

And it is important to state that our intention is not to give the overall impression that Black Victorians were only found in the lowliest stations of life – later, we will meet royals, aristocrats, politicians, clergy, activists and cultural figures. Rather, our hope is that this book, taken as a whole, will show the wide spectrum across which Black people contributed to, and were intimately part of, British life. Through the individual biographies that follow in this part, we want to examine a fundamental feature of existence: a question particularly acute in the depths of destitution and one beautifully summarised by Saidiya Hartman:

> Each new deprivation raises doubts about when freedom is going to come; if the question pounding inside her head – *Can I live?* – is one to which she could ever give a certain answer, or only repeat in anticipation of something better than this, bear the pain of it and the hope of it, the beauty and the promise.[3]

Can I survive? How do I survive? These questions haunt the subjects of Part Two, but they are not intended here as tragic or ruined figures, rather as ordinary Black people in a state of emergency, who ultimately survived in the archives.[4]

* * *

W. J. Harris, Coroner for the Sittingbourne District of Kent, immediately opened an inquest into the events at Ebenezer Road. Daniel Burrows, a local rigger employed at the dockyard, confirmed that the deceased Elizabeth Brown was his sister, aged forty-six, and the wife of William Brown, a local labourer. Brown had stabbed his stepson, Alfred Rump, who recalled waking up after hearing an argument and noticing smoke in his bedroom. Alfred went downstairs and found the backroom on fire with his mother lying in a pool of blood. He confronted his stepfather, who subsequently tried to throw him into the fire and, failing that, drew a knife and stabbed Alfred three times, penetrating his left lung.

Then came the moment when the police broke down the door, and Brown ran upstairs to the attic room, where he slit his throat with a razor. After his arrest, he was taken to the Union Hospital. According to the *London Dispatch*:

> His children had preceded him there, and the scene upon their arrival was of a most harrowing description. They cried most frantically, and would not be comforted, although they were treated by officials with great kindness.[5]

During the inquest, the Mayor of Queensborough gave William Brown a sterling character reference. 'He knew him to be a most industrious, persevering man, and he had frequently held him up as an example to his own workmen,' reported the press.[6] But who was William Brown before he arrived at this dock?

He was born in British Guiana during the era of slavery on 10 August 1832.[7] Following emancipation in 1838, many of the formerly enslaved moved from the sugar plantations to the towns and villages; others established cooperative ventures on the arable land. But with minimal capital to invest, these ventures struggled, while the white planter class replaced the formerly enslaved with indentured labour, bringing thousands of Portuguese, Chinese and Indian workers into British Guiana.[8] Rather than working the land, William Brown, when he reached his mid-twenties, instead chose to join the navy where he rose to the rank of petty officer. During the course of his twenty-one-year career, he also received a medal for good conduct which, at a time when Black mariners were facing increased hostility and limited promotional opportunities, was an impressive accolade.

As William Brown traversed the globe on British ships, it was in England where he met his wife-to-be, Elizabeth, in 1869. She was born in Sheerness, on the north-west corner of the Isle of Sheppey, in 1835 and, at the age of seventeen, married one William Burrows, who died five years later.

Records suggest that their union was an unhappy one for, during their marriage, Elizabeth gave birth to a son, Daniel Rump, who was possibly the child of another man, David Rump. Indeed, in the year that Elizabeth became a widow, she married David Rump and together they had four more children: two daughters, both given the first name Elizabeth, and two sons, David Rump and Alfred Rump. What became of Elizabeth's second husband remains unclear, but according to the family history, he had died by the time Elizabeth married William Brown in 1871.[9]

Elizabeth and William Brown had two daughters together, Anna Cecelia Brown and Mandy J. Brown, and one son named Donald Adolphus Brown.[10] William Brown retired from the navy in 1881 and, with his naval pension, settled down at Ebenezer Road with his wife, children and stepchildren. He was earning a second income as a labourer when his mental health began to take a turn for the worse. He was increasingly distant and depressive. He reportedly suffered from epilepsy and he started to argue with Elizabeth about the children. She too was reportedly depressed and turned to gin as a coping mechanism.[11]

The press speculated that 'Mr Brown, though usually a quiet man, was prone to a terrible temper when aroused or when frenzied by drink'.[12] But during his trial at the Lewes Assizes in April 1883, no motive or clear explanation for the murder was found. Brown was in a state of shock and unable to account for his actions – quite literally because, in his suicide attempt, he had severed his larynx and could no longer speak.

It was noted that when Brown was taken into custody, 'the prisoner was quite calm, and seemed not to know what had happened'. He and his wife had not been on good terms but there was 'nothing in her conduct to incite him to violence', wrote the press, 'and the only conclusion to be arrived at, his counsel urged, was that the man was insane'.[13] The jury took just forty-five minutes to concur with Brown's counsel. He was deemed not guilty by reason of insanity. He was thus declared criminally insane and, as such, was destined for an institution that has since become synonymous with madness and criminality.

* * *

Built high on a ridge above Bracknell Forest, Broadmoor Criminal Lunatic Asylum opened in 1863–64 with accommodations for ninety-eight female patients and 221 male patients. There were the Queen's pleasure patients like William Brown, found to be insane before or during their trials, and then there were the insane convicts who had lost their minds while serving time behind prison bars. Most of Broadmoor's patients were working class and there was no segregation on the grounds of ethnicity or 'race' (unlike in some colonial asylums).[14] The sexes were separated, and the most dangerous and disorderly patients were confined to Block One.[15]

When the Criminal Lunatics Act of 1800 was passed, those deemed criminally insane could be indefinitely detained until 'His Majesty's pleasure be known', yet there was no dedicated, secure accommodation for these patients.[16] They were initially housed in separate wings within London's notorious madhouse, Bethlem Royal Hospital, but it wasn't until the Criminal Lunatics Act of 1860 that the State was given the authority to build its own dedicated hospital for the criminally insane. Broadmoor was the result of that piece of legislation, opening its doors at a time when the Victorians were positive about the potential to reform the mentally ill.

The majority of Victorian psychiatrists were committed to 'moral therapy', a paternalistic approach pioneered at the end of the eighteenth century, which directed therapy towards the minds and emotions ('moral' characteristics) rather than seeing madness as inherently engrained in the brain. This moral approach dispensed with shackles and chains in favour of finding ways to develop a patient's self-esteem. Moral therapy entailed so-called 'moral management', which required the close supervision of patients, and 'moral architecture', which determined that the asylum should be a therapeutic environment.[17]

When William Brown was admitted into Broadmoor in 1883, a contemporary patient wrote to his sister:

Broadmoor: William Brown

[Broadmoor] is a splendid block of buildings [...] has an extensive view and is very healthy [...] the patients spend most of their time [...] exercising in the gardens, reading the daily papers, monthly periodicals etc., there is also a well selected library [...] a cricket club, billiards, cards and other amusements. In the wintertime we have entertainments given by the patients, such as plays, singing, etc. [We] have a good brass band which gives selections of music every Monday evening during the summer months on the terrace opposite the chapel [...] [We] are treat[ed] with kindness by the officials placed over us, [and] have free conversation among the other patients.[18]

Sketch of Broadmoor, 1880s

On a typical day, patients would rise from comfortable beds at 6 a.m. They would head to the chapel for morning prayers, followed by breakfast then work or rest. Employment, which was not compulsory and not paid, included labouring in the laundry room, kitchen, farm or gardens (the latter two were just for the men; women could undertake needlework and factory work). After a morning of labour, lunch was served, followed by more work or rest. In the evening, patients gathered for tea: the cutlery would be counted – wandering knives could have deadly consequences – then a meal was eaten, followed by another cutlery count.

Patients were visited by relatives and remained in communication with family and friends through letters. The staff were instructed to be compassionate and patient – restraints and the seclusion of inmates were frowned upon – and the institution remained committed to therapeutic, curative treatment. William Brown could have spent his time with other patients playing cards, dominoes and billiards, or he could have spent time reading novels and journals or playing croquet and cricket on the lawn. But we know this didn't happen.

In Brown's case files, staff reported how he would cry whenever he was spoken to. He was low in spirits. He was suicidal. He was diagnosed with melancholia and epilepsy. Thankfully he was eating and sleeping, but he was quiet and reserved.

At the beginning of February 1885, he deteriorated yet further. The Medical Officer reported that Brown was greatly depressed and emotional, writing, 'He only wanted to be allowed to "go in peace" – "on his long journey" – that no-one but God and himself knew what his feelings had been; then he commenced to sob and asked to be left to die quietly.'[19]

By late March 1885 the Medical Officer wrote in Brown's case notes:

Is very weak – lies on his back in a depressed lifeless fashion – has not energy enough to take food, but is fed at frequent intervals and takes a fair amount of nourishment. Is much emaciated. Will respond to questions, but has not strength to talk much.[20]

The following month was much the same. As was May. And June. In July, the master of the Sheppey Union Workhouse wrote to Superintendent Dr William Orange at Broadmoor:

Dear Sir,

A report has reached here that William Brown a man of colour, who was confined in your Asylum, is dead. I would be obliged if you would inform me if there is any foundation for the report.[21]

A reply was sent the following day:

William Brown died on the 9th instant of inflammation of the lungs. His funeral will take place tomorrow, Tuesday, afternoon, at 3 o'clock.[22]

Brown only lived in Broadmoor for a short period of time; through the archives we can only glean a partial insight into his life. We cannot know for sure what caused his mental collapse – if he was treated differently as a minority patient inside Broadmoor – or what sort of thoughts, pressures and torments he experienced, either before or after the tragic events on Ebenezer Road. But we do know that he was not abandoned by his family.

Following his incarceration in 1883, Mandy, aged around twelve, Anna Cecilia Brown, aged ten, and Donald Adolphus Brown, aged nine, were taken into the Sheppey Union Workhouse, which had a school, cemetery, infirmary and a ward for orphaned children. From the workhouse, Anna Cecilia Brown wrote to her father in moving letters replete with numerous kisses, opening with 'My Dear Father' and closing with 'your Ever Loving Daughter'.[23] In her letters, we learn that she was suffering from a degenerative eye condition ('Dear Father I have got very bad eyes and I am up in the hospital'); her brother Donald had been sent to the Greenwich Royal Hospital School to learn a trade; and her sister Amanda had just become a servant ('Dear Father Amanda is going to service this week').

Anna finished her letter dated 25 March 1885 with the words, 'Dear Father I think I have no more to say so Good bye and God bless your Ever Loving Daughter'.[24]

Asylum records are largely cold and matter of fact, so to confront such a young voice in the archives is a surprise. Here was a twelve-year-old girl whose father had murdered her mother and stabbed her stepbrother, who nearly died, along with her siblings, in a housefire also started by her father, nonetheless writing with such childhood innocence to her dad, whom she clearly loved. How William Brown responded to these letters, we can only imagine.

After the death of their father, Amanda married a man named Richard Forman in 1891, but little is known about the remainder of her life. The same is true for Anna Cecelia.

More is known about Donald Adolphus Brown who, like his father, became a sailor. In 1921, he averted a near-fatal explosion and was awarded two medals for bravery.[25] He married the political radical Eliza Adelaide Knight and together they started a family. Their daughter, Winifred Langton, compiled the family history, which was published by her great-nieces in 2007, tracing her parents' involvement in the Suffragette, socialist, trade union and adult education movements.[26] The family history continued, and indeed continues, long after William Brown had died.

* * *

The same cannot be said for another Black patient inside Broadmoor. John Flinn had no known family. There was no form of communication with the outside world; no love letters from children, parents or friends. Unlike William Brown, John Flinn spent most of his life within institutional walls. The archives only provide cold fragments of his life, the bare facts. Yet John Flinn, like William Brown, did exist, and continues to exist in the archives. He was an agent of 'the Black Atlantic' – the transatlantic network of the African diaspora that connected Britain and Africa – and he lived a life infused with an indomitable human spirit that survived a total of forty-seven continuous years behind four Victorian institutional walls.[27]

4

Bearing Witness: John Flinn
(1829–1902)

John Flinn was in his mid-thirties when he was admitted into Broadmoor in March 1864. On the admissions register it was written year of birth 'unknown', religious persuasion 'unknown', cause of insanity 'unknown' and degree of education 'imperfect'. In the column asking for the length of insanity, the superintendent simply wrote, 'about thirty years'.[1] But for all the vagueness of this official account, there are enough traces of John Flinn to enable a partial reconstruction of his life.

He was born in the West Indies in 1829 and, before his incarceration at Broadmoor, he worked for a number of years as a mariner. He had been in England only a few months when, in 1855, he was arrested for burglary and sent to Kirkdale County Gaol and House of Correction. In the prison records, he was recorded as a seaman, aged twenty-seven, degree of education 'N' (meaning: can neither read nor write), with a charge that read:

> Having at Knowsley on 13 March 1855 feloniously broken and entered the dwelling house of Thos. Travis, and having stolen therein, one watch, one knife, two ounces of tea, the property of the said Thomas Travis.[2]

Kirkdale Gaol, which opened on Merseyside in 1821, had its own courthouse and the country's largest treadmill. Each day, over 100 inmates stepped onto the treadmill to grind corn: step after step, typically for over six hours a day, the wheel would rotate as prisoners serving hard labour were made to atone for their sins. But Flinn was only at Kirkdale for a very short period of time. He began manifesting signs of insanity, and on 26 April 1855, he was transferred to Rainhill Asylum.

Private asylums were a long-standing feature of British life, but the 1845 County Asylums Act for England and Wales required all counties and boroughs to build asylums at the public's expense. This meant that by 1860 public asylums had sprouted the length and breadth of Britain (Scotland, despite having a different legislative framework, was equally passionate about locking up those deemed insane).

Rainhill was one of three lunatic asylums in Lancashire, built four years before John Flinn was admitted. In the register, the admissions clerk wrote, 'Social State: Single. Occupation: Mariner. Form of Mental Disorder: Dementia. Bodily Condition: Tolerably good. Complexion: Dark – Black hair and eyes. Expression of Countenance: Subdued.'[3]

At Rainhill, Flinn spent the greater part of his days sitting quietly in the men's dormitory and smiling to himself. He wet himself frequently and needed assistance going to the toilet. He began swallowing stones and buttons and pieces of lead; he needed near-constant supervision: 'He talks a great deal to himself and sometimes sings. He stands in a corner of the ward and looks at the ceiling his hands crossed before him.'[4]

What was he singing? What was he recalling? Was he creating the sign of the cross? Flinn was given 'tartar emetic', an antimonial medicine that induced vomiting, but to no restorative avail. He continued to swallow stones and buttons and began getting violent with other patients 'to whom it appears he entertains an antipathy', noted the doctor.[5] He went through periods of manic excitement (and may have been given morphine), but these were interspersed with periods of calm. He began pushing a two-wheeled handcart around the asylum farm and, by August 1858, there had been no purging for the last six months and working outdoors seemed to have been beneficial to his health.

But, according to his files, Flinn continued getting into fights with other patients, 'and as a rule has got the worst of it', and during one deadly fight in 1860 he 'effected such damage' on another inmate that 'the patient died about five hours later'.[6] What provoked the fight or how it was allowed to happen are not recorded. But, according to the coroner's jury, John Flinn had committed wilful murder. Due to his mental condition, he was incapable of giving evidence in court, so it was determined that, until he was in a fit state, he would be sent to one of the two criminal lunatic wings of London's Bethlem Royal Hospital.

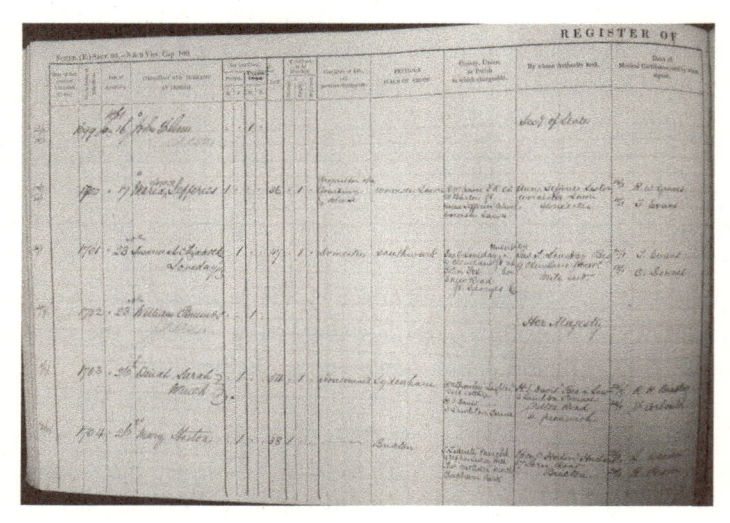

Joseph Flinn's entry into Bethlem archives, 1861

Broadmoor had not yet been built, so Bethlem, which also went by the notorious name Bedlam, was the principal repository for those, like John Flinn, deemed criminally insane.

* * *

Bethlem Royal Hospital was an archetypal Victorian institution whose image haunts the recesses of our collective imagination. Founded in the thirteenth century as a religious order, Bedlam, by the late seventeenth century, was an infamous London landmark, the oldest and only charitable madhouse in England. These were the days of dark cells, iron rings rivetted around inmates' necks and public visitations that allowed people to stare at and taunt the mad.

But following revelations of deprivation, mistreatment and squalor in the early nineteenth century, the asylum underwent a transformation in the 1850s. William Charles Hood became the resident Physician-Superintendent in 1852 and instigated sweeping changes. Moral therapy was established as the principal means of treatment; restraints were abolished; bedsteads replaced straw on the floor; pictures adorned the walls; carpets were laid out; and a library was opened.[7] The Chaplain, Edward Geoffrey O'Donoghue, wrote that the institution went from 'the grub to the chrysalis stage'.[8]

In the register of patients, Flinn's mental disorder was recorded as 'maniacal' (there was no detailed diagnosis), and it was noted that his physical health was generally good, though his case file contained the words 'homicidal propensity'.[9] On 18 February 1860, it was written, 'He is now at times maniacal and then very dangerous to others'. At other times, he was very quiet and subdued. He did not mix with other patients and 'when the gas is lit in the evening, he talks to it and treats it with reverence, indeed he worships it'.[10]

There was little change in his mental state for the next four years and, in March 1864, Flinn was transferred to the newly constructed Broadmoor, which succeeded Bethlem, inter alia, as the state's primary criminal lunatic accommodation. Unlike William Brown, who was admitted as a Queen's pleasure patient (that is, one found to be insane before or during his criminal trial), John Flinn was admitted as an 'insane convict' – a criminal who went insane *after* their crimes. They were treated very differently at Broadmoor. They were seen as an incurable criminal class – physically and mentally degenerate – who were capable of contaminating other patients with their murderous madness. Reformation was thought to be a waste of effort for this class of inmates; instead, they were to be punished.

This attitude reflected new thinking, which began to develop in the last third of the nineteenth century, as pessimism started to infect psychiatric thinking. This was largely because the number of asylum inmates were ever increasing, while discharge figures remained low, so the earlier Victorian optimism began to turn to despair as it became increasingly clear that those labelled insane were not being cured in high enough numbers. Psychiatrists started to wonder if, indeed, they could be cured, and they began to question the efficacy of moral therapy, probing the earlier belief that through compassion, dignity and a therapeutic environment patients could be cured.

Instead, a number of psychiatrists became increasingly convinced that madness was ingrained in some patients, that it was constitutional and hereditary, passed down from one generation to the next. This type of 'degenerationist' psychiatry maintained that some people were inherently 'degenerate' and 'defective' and the best thing was to lock them away and stop them from breeding.[11] This new psychiatric thinking did not just concern the insane but also the criminal man, who was increasingly seen as a fixed 'type' in legal and scientific circles, and perceived to be innately degenerate, indolent and manipulative.[12]

Criminal Man, published in 1876 by physician and psychiatrist Cesare Lombroso, designated four types of criminals: the born criminals, who could be identified by inherited physical stigmata (large jaw, shifty eyes, etc.); the insane criminals, including alcoholics, imbeciles and idiots; the 'criminaloids', whose crimes were opportunistic and occasional; and the criminals of passion, who committed acts out of anger, love or a wounded sense of honour.

According to Lombroso, the born criminal had prognathism, also 'found in negroes and animals', while the nose of the born criminal 'is frequently twisted, up-turned or of a flattened, negroid character'. And 'the lips of violators of women and murderers are', Lombroso stated, 'fleshy, swollen and protruding, as in negroes'. Even the feet of born criminals were 'often flat, as in negroes'.[13]

Such racialisation posited a direct biological relationship between people of African descent and the criminal class, both deemed physiologically and morally inferior. Lombroso was taking criminology to new depths, appropriating phrenology and evolutionary theory, and developing a biologically rooted understanding of crime that bled into racist eugenic ideas.

In the Anglo-American world, there was a nexus between ideas of 'civilisation', 'race' and insanity which permeated psychiatric thinking from the mid-nineteenth century until at least the 1950s.[14] (And the diagnosis and treatment of patients reflected – and still reflects – racialised power.)[15] The Victorian psychiatrist Daniel Tuke, who used ethnological observations to inform his theory of insanity, argued that madness was a disease of civilisation, so 'primitive people' could not actually suffer from it.

In America, pro-slavery advocates contended that slavery diminished instances of insanity because the enslaved were not burdened by the same worries as free white people. By the late nineteenth century, (white) European and American 'experts' were using evolutionary theory to explain a putative increase in insanity among 'dark-skinned races', which they attributed to an inability to cope with the trappings of civilisation.[16]

Mark Twain's *Adventures of Huckleberry Finn* (1884) incorporated and propagated the myth of the mad Black man of antebellum America, while learned circles around this time upheld the belief that insanity was physiologically innate in Black people like John Flinn.[17] Thus, the specific link that Lombroso was attempting to establish between Blackness and madness became entrenched.

We cannot tell to what extent these broader discourses impacted the life of John Flinn. Perhaps they didn't. There is no evidence to suggest that Flinn was treated differently because of the colour of his skin within either Broadmoor, Bethlem, Rainhill or Kirkdale Gaol. But, then again, the records don't reveal much.

We could speculate that Flinn's fighting at Rainhill Asylum, which ultimately led to his incarceration in Bethlem and then Broadmoor, could have been motivated by racism from the other patients. As we will see, there is evidence of racist attacks by the medical authorities on inmates in colonial asylums, although those institutions existed in a very different context.

We could speculate that, perhaps in Flinn's case, the medical authorities were careful to maintain the veneer of impartiality by deliberately omitting racist comments from their notes. We could certainly point to broader discourses and historical forces that would support the claim that Flinn's life was impacted by racism. We could also denounce such speculation as futile, misguided and anachronistic. The Victorians did not operate with 'the same models and patterns of race relations as recent scholars,' writes historian Christine Bolt, 'despite the Victorian passion for elaborate racial and linguistic hierarchies'.[18] But we also have to make sense of the past as best we can and it is perhaps enough to say that just because there was no direct reference to racism in the sparse archival traces of Flinn's life, it does not mean that there was an absence either.

* * *

Inside Broadmoor, John Flinn was frequently unwell and, due to his behaviour – which included walking around naked, attacking patients, throwing faeces and ripping his clothes – he was often placed in isolation. Eventually, he was moved to Block One with the other disorderly patients.[19] Staff claimed they could not understand him: adjectives like 'restless', 'unintelligible', 'muttering', 'demented', 'incoherent' and 'violent' frequently appeared in his files.

Would Flinn have been dismissed, ignored and deemed 'incoherent' quite so easily had he been white? The answer is probably yes. Patient William Ross Tuchet, for example, was also described as 'demented', 'muttering incoherently to himself', and was put in a straitjacket – and he was the son of the 20th Baron Audley.[20] In Tuchet's files, medical officers noted that he 'seldom speaks'; in Flinn's files, they scribbled that 'he is unable to give any account of himself'.[21]

Yet this wasn't true – at least not always. We know elements of his story because he told us. When Flinn was admitted to Rainhill Asylum, the medical officer wrote that he 'does not seem to have the power of recollecting things about which he should have no doubt', and yet, 'according to his own statements', Flinn did relay aspects of his life. He was able, at the very least, to state that he was 'a native of the West Indies'.[22]

This West Indian man – who had worked on vessels across the globe and was perceived as a criminal born bad, who was suffering from mental distress and seemingly alone in the world – managed to survive for thirty-eight years inside Broadmoor. He spent a total of forty-seven years inside four Victorian institutions, living the vast majority of his life incarcerated, dying on 5 January 1902 and outlasting Queen Victoria's reign. He had endured 'the great confinement' of the Victorian age, when asylums proliferated and took on huge institutional significance.[23] He answered, 'Yes' to that existential question: 'Can I live'? He was disoriented, distressed, often unable to express himself in a way that could be appreciated by those into whose supposed care he had been placed, but he knew enough to tell the authorities where he was from: he laid claim to a crucial piece of his identity. And he wasn't the only Black inmate to do so.

5

Hearing Joseph Peters
(*c.* 1843–83)

Shortly after his admission into Broadmoor in 1877, Joseph Peters dictated his life story in a letter to the Medical Superintendent, Dr William Orange. This letter was kept in the asylum records and, like Anna Cecilia's letter to her father William Brown, it makes for fascinating reading, allowing us to largely retell Peters' life through his own words.[1]

'I should like you to release me that I may go to my own people,' he verbalised as Mr Thomas, a schoolmaster employed to teach patients at Broadmoor, transcribed Peters' words, 'I want to tell you my life that you may know all about me'.[2]

It was not uncommon for patients to write to the Superintendent, explaining why they were persecuted or innocent of their crimes, and these letters usually manifested the intense delusions suffered by the patients. But what is remarkable about Peters' letter is the personal backstory, which is presented purely as a biography rather than part of a structure of delusions. In discussing this letter with Broadmoor's archivist, Mark Stevens, he notes the genuine, believable voice of Peters, finding no reason to doubt the veracity of his words. Neither do we. From this letter, it is clear that Peters was determined that his story should be told to the authorities, understood by the authorities, and his story functioned as a plea for freedom and an assertion of identity: this was his story, and he wanted to return home.

Peters was born on the West African coast in the early 1840s. His mother was formerly enslaved in America and, before Liberia became an independent state in 1847, she was transported to the region by the American Colonization Society (ACS), an organisation of white Americans worried that the increasing number of freed African Americans would jeopardise Southern slavery. Agents of the ACS coerced local African chiefs into selling them land, which was subsequently settled by thousands of the formerly enslaved, including Peters' mother.[3]

Peters recalled, 'As soon as I was able to talk and walk my father took me from home up to his factory [corn and rice store] and as far as I can remember I was there about four rice harvests.' But after Peters' father died when he was young and his mother remarried, they moved to the neighbouring settlement of Sierra Leone and then to the island of Matakong, just off the coast of Guinea:

> [...] being sent for by a Mr Rider an Englishman to do farming work. We stayed there 2 years. From there my mother brought me back to Sierra Leone leaving my step-father behind, being very glad to as he had fallen in love with another woman and not loving my mother anymore he ill-treated her.[4]

As they adjusted to life in Sierra Leone, which like Liberia had been settled by the formerly enslaved, Peters and his mother had to confront further hardships, additional to the vicissitudes of a life already lived under domestic and social intimidation:

> I went to school in Sierra Leone for a little while, but afterwards I had to take bread and ginger-beer for sale, which my mother made to get a living for us. She set up a shop, but this

didn't answer [didn't work out] as the woman who kept my mother's books knowing that my mother did not understand books, robbed her.[5]

Peters and his mother lived on the breadline, perilously close to destitution, and when she fell ill he 'was forced to do for myself and went to sea'. We can only imagine how that parting might have felt.

Still in his teenage years, Peters joined a trading ship and, shortly after going to sea, 'I had a letter saying my mother was dead and I felt very sad'. Alone, he traversed the globe, working on ships. He turned to drink, and found himself incarcerated in Liverpool, London, Bristol, Calcutta and Rio de Janeiro. When he resisted arrest in Buenos Aires, he sustained a deep cut on his thumb which precipitated a mental collapse. He became convinced that everyone was talking about his thumb.

After a long voyage to Liverpool, he sought a cure from a doctor, but the thumb still failed to heal. The cut then developed into an abscess during another arduous voyage to Montreal: 'My finger became so bad so bad that I told them on board, but they wouldn't believe it until it burst.'[6] He had the thumb amputated and became even more convinced that people were talking about the amputation – mocking it and writing songs about it.

In October 1876, he was reported in the *Shipping and Mercantile Gazette* for refusing to perform his onboard duties. He was suffering a serious mental collapse, but this went unnoticed. The *Gazette* only recorded:

At 8 o'clock in the morning he [David Moore, the ship's captain] sent the Chief Officer to ask the prisoner [Peters] to work, but he still refused. At 4 o'clock in the afternoon he went to the forecastle [the sailors' living quarters], as they were short of hands, but the prisoner said he would not work. On the Chief Officer going to speak to him he struck him over the arm with a belaying pin [wood or metal device use to secure lines].[7]

Peters was apprehended after trying to stab the captain and second mate with a knife. He was placed in chains, taken into custody and sentenced to three months. Following his release from prison, Peters found work on a ship bound for Australia, but on the return voyage his distress was absolute:

> [...] on my return to London they commenced the remarks again, and did all kinds of things which I can't mention, and didn't know how they did them. The 2nd engineer on board used to annoy me all he possibly could, and when I come on in the morning trying to be agreeable and pleasant, he would begin to tease and vex me and when I was in a great rage he would say 'that's how I like to see you'. One day he wanted me to do another man's work as well as my own, and I would not. He made me very angry and I pushed him down on his forehead on the coals and hit him on the head with my fist. I really think I should have hurt him if a man from behind had not got hold of me. They then placed me in irons and kept me 8 days in a hot place in the ship where a man ought not to be kept 4 hours. I was tried and they said I was mad and was sent from Newgate [prison] here [to Broadmoor].
> The remarks are still about.
> Hoping you will give me my liberty
> I am etc Joseph Peters.[8]

Joseph Peters did not get his liberty: his paranoid thoughts continued to torment him, and during a surgical procedure to amputate his leg, which had become infected due to a large tumour, his femoral artery was severed and he died. He was buried in the asylum cemetery in 1883, the same year that William Brown came to Broadmoor, at the same time that John Flinn continued to survive inside the asylum walls.

* * *

By telling his story, Joseph Peters asserted his identity; he wrestled back some power and agency in a system designed to isolate and control deviance. Numerous scholars have explored the various ways in which mental institutions exerted control over human agency and, in the colonial domain, scholars have explored how Western medicine and psychiatry could be a tool for social and racial control as well.

Yet scholars have also warned against analysis which *merely* describes Western medicine as an agent of colonialism.[9] Power could flow in numerous directions, not least from African doctors working in colonial asylums, but also from patients themselves.[10] Patients like Joseph Peters or Ann Pratt, a Jamaican woman whose mediated pamphlet *Seven Months in the Kingston Lunatic Asylum, and What I saw There* (1860) generated a colonial dispute, as historian Christienna Fryar has deftly shown in her discovery and analysis of the case.[11, 12]

In Pratt's pamphlet, she revealed the horrific treatment she suffered in the asylum, which included being publicly stripped and racially abused – staff called her 'a damned negro man's wife' and an 'imprudent mulatto thing'[13] – and being forced to endure a form of punishment known as tanking, which involved submerging patients in water:

> Scarcely, however, had I drawn my breath when I was again subjected to the same horrible treatment, with the addition of having my head hurt against the sides of the tank, and my poor body beaten and contused with blows, till the fear of murder prompted them to desist.[14]

Ultimately, Pratt's testimony altered imperial policy. Her pamphlet led colonial asylums to assess their standard of care against the theory of moral therapy, the more compassionate form of care.[15]

Peters did not affect such change, but he spoke to the experiences of others who traversed the Black Atlantic. William Brown, John Flinn and Peters were all international sailors, and we might tentatively speculate that syphilis – known to cause insanity – could have been a factor in their mental ill health, though there is no record of it. But there were also social conditions that are likely to have caused or perpetuated mental illness: maritime work was hard, rootless. It meant separation from homeland and family. It could be dangerous, hostile, precarious and isolating.

The Black Atlantic also marked the graves of Africans trafficked into New World slavery: it was a site of 'racial terror', as Paul Gilroy argued.[16] The Black Atlantic represented dislocated nationality, confused identity and painful, often bloody memories. It symbolised 'forced labour, European hegemony, and racial capitalism', which, argue contemporary scholars, 'constituted a critical matrix through which most Black Atlantic as well as African cultures were produced'.[17] It is not unreasonable to assume, therefore, that the Black Atlantic induced mental torment. It was also the network in which many Black Victorians came to Britain, often finding themselves forced to reside in conditions of poverty and rootlessness and subsequently entering asylums, workhouses and other forms of Victorian incarceration.

In his voluminous study, Henry Mayhew documented the lives of many of the London poor, covering a number of Black Victorians, including a Black woman who used to feed stray cats, a nameless Black crossing sweeper, Black men residing in lowly lodgings, itinerant entertainers like 'Black Sambo' and 'a real black – an African', who performed in a minstrel troupe, and a 'black sailor with his large fur cap' at the London docks.[18] In Volume Four of *London Labour and the London Poor*, Mayhew dedicated a whole section to 'Negro beggars', recounting an interview with a 'coloured man, with the regular negro physiognomy', wrote Mayhew without ever naming the individual.[19]

The man was in his twenties when he spoke to Mayhew, and his story was a familiar one: born in New York, he worked as a cabin boy and then as a cook before sailing to Liverpool, where he got a job in the city loading hay. He was told that London offered better employment opportunities so, after selling some clothes to finance the journey (clothes being among the few portable assets the poor had), he began the walk to London. Despite being over 200 miles away, with railways connecting the two major cities, those on the breadline often had to make the journey on foot.

By the time the nameless Black Victorian arrived in London, he had no money and few clothes:

> I was often out all night, perishing. Sometimes I slept under the butchers' stalls in Whitechapel. I felt the cold very bitter, as I was used to a hot climate chiefly. Sometimes I couldn't feel my feet.[20]

A policeman told him to go to the Asylum for the Houseless Poor located in Islington where, for a few nights, he would be given a ration of bread. A surgeon was on hand for anyone suffering from cholera, fever, exhaustion or starvation and the residents would reside in 'lofty, barn-like rooms, divided into sections by wooden pillars' with a large stove in the centre. Lining the room were mattresses filled with hay, topped with blankets made of leather to keep the vermin away.[21] On policy, this 'coloured man' would have been turned out of the shelter after a few nights, a week at most. But he had an ambition: 'I want to get a ship. I have a good character as a cook; my dishes were always relished; my pea-soup was capital, and so was my dough and pudding.'[22]

Whether this gentleman managed to find employment, we do not know, but if he was unsuccessful, he might have entered the dreaded workhouse – the last port of call for the poor, to be avoided whenever possible. Before the seventeenth century, those struggling could apply for 'out relief' in the form of grants for money, clothes and food, but during the seventeenth century, the workhouse evolved, offering 'indoor relief' to the poor. The system was consolidated through the Poor Law Amendment Act of 1834, which was explicitly designed to turn workhouses into deterrents.

Inside the blackened walls, inmates were put to hard work, usually without pay, and conditions were dire. Dickens described it thus:

> Groves of babies in arms; groves of mothers and other sick women in bed; groves of lunatics; jungles of men in stone-paved down-stairs day-rooms; longer and longer groves of old people, in up-stairs Infirmary wards, wearing out life, God knows how – this was the scenery.[23]

Featuring in this picture of despair were Black Victorians, such as Louis James Grant, aged ten, who was indicted for stealing from a fellow inmate at the workhouse of St Martin's-in-the-Fields. In the Proceedings of the Old Bailey, Grant was described as a 'black boy' and his father, who also resided in the workhouse, was labelled a 'negro'.[24] What their fate was, we do not know: they are silent agents of the Black Atlantic who appear momentarily in the archives.

There are other records of Black Victorians caught – temporarily or more permanently – by circumstances of poverty or emergency in night asylums, workhouses or rescue homes: in Pentonville Prison; in Barnardo's Children's Home; in Colney Hatch Lunatic Asylum.[25] And on the streets – the stage of urban life.

* * *

Here, on London's streets to be precise, could be found another man who, like William Brown, was loved by his family, like John Flinn, managed to survive and, like Joseph Peters, told his story. Indeed, from the margins of social life, Edward Albert let people know that he existed.

The Black Atlantic was not simply a site of desolation leading to continued despair on the streets of Western cities. The Black Atlantic, and the Victorian streets, were also places of struggle – for freedom, autonomy and recognition.[26] Edward Albert stayed in England to tell his story, establish his roots and assert his rights.

6

Rights: Edward Albert
(Dates Unknown)

'I will never leave England or Scotland until I get my rights,' Edward Albert declared. 'The loss of my limbs is bad enough, but it's still worse when you can't get what is your rights.'[1]

Disabled and poor, abused and abandoned, Albert never gave up the fight. He lived with his family in London, a city marked by paradox: sophistication and brutality; wealth and poverty – 'Two nations; between whom there is no intercourse and no sympathy', as Benjamin Disraeli wrote in 1845.[2] 'The very turmoil of the streets has something repulsive, something against which human nature rebels,' Friedrich Engels opined around the same time, 'the dissolution of mankind into monads, of which each one has a separate principle, the world of atoms, is here carried out to its utmost extreme.'[3]

But Albert was more than a monad: he was based in the city by his pursuit of his rights, and he had an intimacy with both its 'upper' and 'lower' realms, occupying one and communicating with the other. And while his story was lumped into the category of 'Crossing-Sweeper' in Mayhew's *London Labour and the London Poor*, Albert defied such categorisation in more ways than one.

* * *

Rights: Edward Albert

Edward Albert was born in Kingston, Jamaica. 'I was a little boy when the slaves in Jamaica got their freedom,' he told Mayhew, 'the people were very glad to be free; they do better since'.[4] Aged nine, Albert joined the royal navy as a cabin boy, before working his way up to cook and eventually head cook. So, he trudged a path along with many others such as William Brown, Joseph Peters and John Flinn.

In 1851 Albert joined the *Madeira*, a Scottish ship which set sail from Glasgow en route to California and then on to China. As the ship sailed off the Cape Horn, temperatures plummeted, and Albert suffered frostbite to his legs:

> In the course of the next day after my limbs became affected, the master of the vessel, and mate, took me to the ship's oven, in order, as they said, to cure me; the oven was hot at the time, a fowl that was roasting therein having been removed in order to make room for my feet, which was put into the oven; in consequence of the treatment, my feet burst through the intense swelling, and mortification ensued.[5]

His terrifying treatment was all the more shocking because, by the early nineteenth century, it was known that placing frostbitten legs in an oven could lead to amputation or even death.[6] Either the shipmates were ignorant of this common knowledge and it was a terrible mistake, or Albert's ordeal was an unforgivable homicidal act:

> The vessel called, six weeks after, at Valpariso [*sic*], and I was there taken to an hospital, where I remained five months and a half. Both my legs were amputated three inches below my knees soon after I went to the hospital at Valpariso. I asked my master for my wages due to me, for my service on board the vessel, and demanded my register-ticket; when the captain

told me I should not recover, that the vessel could not wait for me, and that I was a dead man, and that he could not discharge a dead man; and that he also said, that as I had no friends there to get my money, he would only put a little money into the hands of the consul, which would be applied in burying me. On being discharged from the hospital I called on the consul, and was informed by him that master had not left any money.[7]

There was a long history of discrimination against Black mariners. Following the American War of Independence, Black servicemen hardly ever received compensation from the Loyalist Claims Commission. Black sailors rarely benefitted from the relief scheme administered by London's Greenwich Hospital, founded in 1696 'for the Encouragement and Increase of Seamen'.[8] Furthermore, in 1747 the Merchant Seamen's Fund was established for 'the Relief and Support of Mariners and Disabled Seamen', but because the scheme was discontinued in 1851, Edward Albert, who had previously paid into the fund, received nothing.[9] Neither did he receive a penny for his work on the ship that led to the loss of his legs.

Yet, after he was discharged from hospital, Albert was determined to secure what he called 'his rights' – the wages for his work on the ship. He travelled the length and breadth of the UK, soliciting the support of the English Consul and the Lord Mayor of London.

In pursuit of his rights, Albert led a transitory life between Glasgow and London. He did find some temporary financial success, opening a coffee house and selling homemade pastries in Glasgow, until he reported being robbed of his business by an unscrupulous trader. Moving down to London, he began to sweep the streets but only during the winter months when the cold weather numbed his amputated stumps, so he could move around with minimal pain.

Mayhew introduced Albert as 'The Negro Crossing-Sweeper, Who Had Lost Both His Legs', and placed him under the broader category of 'The Afflicted Crossing-Sweepers'. His story appears in Mayhew's study between the case of 'The Most Severely Afflicted of All the Crossing-Sweepers' and 'The Maimed Irish Crossing-Sweeper', establishing Albert on a racial and disability continuum that enhanced his 'otherness' as a working man on the social margins.[10]

Mid-century crossing sweepers like Edward Albert lived on the breadline, earning eightpence or a shilling a day – if they were lucky. In the summer, when his amputated legs caused him too much pain to work, Albert was forced to beg. He always appeared immaculately dressed. He sat perfectly still in his sailor's shirt and trousers and wore a black neckerchief tied in the nautical fashion. In front of him was a placard:

> KIND CHRISTIAN FRIENDS
> THE UNFORTUNATE
> EDWARD ALBERT
> […]
> AS I HAVE NO OTHER MEANS TO GET A
> LIVELYHOOD BUT BY APPEALING TO
> A GENEROUS PUBLIC
> YOUR KIND DONATIONS WILL BE MOST
> THANKFULLY RECEIVED.[11]

* * *

When Mayhew met Albert, he was living in a poverty-stricken part of London in a sparsely furnished parlour with his wife and child. Albert told Mayhew:

> I am married: my wife is the same colour as me, but an Englishwoman. I've been married two years. I married her

from where she belonged, in Leeds. I couldn't get on to do anything without her. Sometimes she goes out and sells things – fruit, and so on – but she don't make much.

Albert evokes both belonging and estrangement. He married a Black British woman of dual heritage 'where she belonged', in her country of England, but his sense of belonging is more fraught. While he states, 'I was born in Kingston, in Jamaica; it is an English place, sir, so I am counted as not a foreigner', he is equally clear that England is not his home. 'My country', as he says, 'is Jamaica'.[12] His Caribbean origin was important in other ways. 'I have one child – it is just three months and a week old. It is a boy, and we call it James Edward Albert. James is after my grandfather, who was a slave.'[13]

The naming of his son was an act of remembrance, an evocation of familial trauma and brutal dislocation reconfigured into new life that affirmed Albert's own identity. But in the hands of social investigators like Mayhew, such individualisation was overlooked.

Mayhew sought to supply a 'scientific' representation of the metropolis, capturing the 'authentic' voices of people working in the casual economy. He was interested in classification, in taxonomising the working people of London, and he was interested not in the singular individual but in the mass. Mayhew lumped Albert into the category of 'Negro Crossing-Sweeper', one example within that 'large class of the Metropolitan poor' who were subdivided into further 'classes' which seemingly existed within a hierarchy:

I shall begin with the *Able-bodied Males*; then proceed to the *Females* of the same class; and afterwards deal with the *Able-bodied Irish* (male and female), who take to the London causeways for a living. This done, I shall then, in due order, take up the *Afflicted* or *Crippled* class; and finally treat of the *Juveniles* belonging to the same calling.[14]

For Mayhew, crossing sweepers existed within a broader social division. He perceived humanity within, as he wrote, 'two distinct and broadly marked races, viz., the wanderers and the settlers – the vagabond and the citizen – the nomadic and the civilized tribes'.[15] Drawing on the work of the naturalist Andrew Smith and the physician James Cowles Prichard (who largely divided humanity into three groups – savages, nomads and the civilised), Mayhew attributed different physical and moral dimensions to the two 'races' of settlers and wanderers.

Mayhew was not alone: there was an army of social investigators who constructed the urban poor as a racialised homogenous mass, treating the urban slums as colonial adventurers treated imperial outposts. Indeed, colonialists and urban 'explorers' advanced similar racial rhetoric: the language of exotic rootlessness – 'wild tribes', 'wandering tribes', 'savage races' and 'nomad races' – was applied to the urban poor by social investigators from Mayhew to Phillips Watts to James Greenwood, with the result that the entire urban poor were lumped into one racialised inferior category, and variously labelled by Victorian commentators as 'City Arabs' or compared to Bedouins and Bosjesmans.[16]

By the late nineteenth century, the trope of the 'urban savage' was firmly established. Some of the poor were deemed more 'savage' than others (sex workers, casual labourers or sweatshop workers were perceived to be more 'untamed' than the educated working-class man), but nonetheless these social investigators developed a discourse which meant that racialisation was not confined to skin colour, but could be heaped onto an entire class.

* * *

He might have been labelled 'The Negro Crossing-Sweeper', yet Edward Albert defied the bald category. He was a father, husband, veteran, businessman, cook, pastry chef and an author who sold his own memoir, *Brief Sketch of the Life of Edward Albert or the Dead Man come to Life again* (n.d.), which was first printed in Hull. Only one copy survives, currently housed at the

Edward Albert, *Brief Sketch of the Life of Edward Albert* (n.d.)

University of Washington and recently discovered by literary scholar Natalie Prizel.

Those titular words 'to life again' were crucial. Albert's familial history was one of enslavement and his own, one of dislocation and loss – yet Albert had life. By publishing his life story, he was undertaking a literary resurrection, while continuing his protest against the injustice he had suffered at sea.

Like the author, his memoir defied simple categorisation. Across eight pages, it shifted between genres and connected with different literary traditions, making reference to everything from the Bible to *Uncle Tom's Cabin* to blackface minstrelsy to the theme of posthumous endurance found in other Victorian texts. Opening with a legal affidavit (an account 'in the presence of [...] one of Her Majesty's Justices of the peace') and proceeding in a prose narrative, the memoir concluded with a ballad which regaled his life story:

I cannot labour for my bread
Give what you can afford,
And God who doth the ravens feed
Will in heaven reward.[17]

It is not clear if Edward Albert ever secured his rights: the wages from the ship's voyage that cost him his legs. But like William Brown, John Flinn and Joseph Peters, Albert's story is testimony to survival and then endurance after life – his story endured in the archives.[18] In this sense, as historian Olivette Otele has written, 'complete erasure of the past is illusory, because residues lurking in the outskirts of memory and history always resurface'.[19]

And, as we have seen, this re-emergence is rarely passive. We need to search for these stories in the archives, and then we invariably find that the historical subjects had to put up a fight to be heard and remembered. Brown, Flinn, Peters and Albert put up their fight from the social margins; next, we will meet others who moved *within* establishment circles or agitated against its structures, as royal favourites, representatives, employees of the state or as political dissidents.

Part Three

Church and State

7

Protest: William Cuffay
(1788–1870)

In September 1848 at London's Central Criminal Court, in the imposing surroundings of the Old Bailey, William Cuffay, aged sixty, addressed a sea of white faces with the following words:

> I know my cause is good, and I have a self-approving conscience that will bear me up against anything, and that would bear me up even to the scaffold; therefore I think I can endure any punishment proudly. I feel no disgrace at being called a felon.[1]

The cause for which he stood was Chartism, a working-class movement seeking democratic reform, and the obstacles he faced were racism, capitalism and an authoritarian state. But the consciousness which drove Cuffay on was undimmable. It bred determination and endurance; it was rooted in hope. And while he was denounced as a 'felon', mocked as 'half a n****r', ultimately banished from Britain having been found guilty of intending 'to levy war against the Queen', his determination for political change ultimately bore fruit.[2]

By 1918, five of the six Chartist aims had been realised: a vote for every adult man over twenty-one; secret ballots; abolition of property qualifications for becoming an MP; salaries for MPs; and constituencies of equal size (the one Chartist aim that has not been realised was annual parliamentary elections). The actualisation of these goals required a fight. They required conviction, collectivism and working-class consciousness. They required people with the drive and resolve of William Cuffay.

* * *

Born in Kent in 1788, Cuffay (or Cuffey, Cuffy or Coffey) was honest, hardworking, humorous and high-spirited. He was diminutive in height, a person with some physical disabilities, and he burned with anger at the injustices of industrial capitalism.

His paternal grandfather hailed from Africa and his father from St Kitts; both had been enslaved. His father emigrated to southeast England in 1772 and, aged around seventeen, was baptised after the name of the town where he had landed, Chatham, which had a notable Black presence by the eighteenth century. He found work at Chatham Dockyard on the River Medway which, by the nineteenth century, had grown to cover 400 acres and employed thousands of workers who lived in the town.

Chatham Cuffay was probably employed as a cook on the prison hulks – floating jails 'like a wicked Noah's ark', as Dickens described them – before serving onboard HMS *Chatham*.[3] In 1786, he married Juliana Fox, 'both of this parish,' their wedding certificate stated, and a couple of years later their eldest son William was born.[4]

William grew up learning about slavery in Jamaica while witnessing the realities of industrial life in Chatham which, 'in night's aspect,' wrote Dickens, was 'a mere dream of chalk, and drawbridges, and mastless ships in a muddy river'.[5] Cuffay lived in a town of dingy two-roomed houses built back to back along narrow, winding alleyways. He used the communal toilets found in open courtyards. And he rubbed shoulders with the ever-growing population of sex workers and their drunken punters, who were served by around fifty public houses in the town.

Cuffay was capable, and aged around twelve he began an apprenticeship with a local tailor, learning how to measure, cut, sew, reinforce and finish items of clothing. It's possible he studied the first English-language manual for tailors, *The Taylor's Complete Guide* (1796), which detailed the art of tailoring with materials like silk, wool and cotton.

There was dignity and precision in this work and, for the seven years of his apprenticeship, Cuffay sewed for self-elevation, learning an art that would allow him to survive in the free market. Across the pond, his Black contemporaries sewed for freedom – Ellen Craft sewed the trousers that would be part of a disguise to enable her escape from slavery, the enslaved Elizabeth Keckley saved enough money from sewing that she eventually purchased her freedom and that of her son.

After qualifying, Cuffay headed to London, that 'Human awful wonder of God', as William Blake described it, where love and loss defined the next phase of his life. In 1815, his father died. In 1819, he married, but he was widowed five years later. In 1825, he married again, and in 1826, he became a father. Yet, his second wife died in childbirth and his daughter died soon afterwards. Cuffay married once again in May 1827, this time to a straw-hat maker named Mary Ann Manvell, and death did not touch their lives until 1837 when Cuffay's mother died – by which point Cuffay's fortunes were under threat from another source.

In the eighteenth century, tailors made or mended clothes by hand. The work was unmechanised, skilled and conducted in small businesses. But the advent of large factories with cheap workforces mass-producing lower-quality clothing had the effect of depressing wages and driving exploitation and unemployment. The whole profession was threatened, but the tailors fought back.

Since the Middle Ages, they had organised themselves into guilds for their mutual benefit, and in 1833 they established the

Grand Lodge of Operative Tailors of London to improve their working conditions. Only a year later, they were instrumental in the establishment of the Grand National Consolidated Trades Union, which promptly called a strike.[6]

Cuffay was initially reluctant to join, probably aware that the chances of success were limited, but in the face of declining wages he took the plunge and faced the wrath. Strike breakers were enlisted from France and Germany, tailors were coerced into denouncing the strike and Cuffay was fired from his job. Materially and emotionally depleted, he nonetheless tapped an inner resource – his working-class consciousness, which propelled him through the rest of his life.

* * *

According to historian E. P. Thompson, the working class as a distinct and conscious entity had been formed by 1832. The realisation of this identity, akin to a collective spiritual awakening, was acquired through turmoil and repression, economic depression and collective action. The Reform Act of 1832 barred the working classes from voting but passed electoral power to the middle classes. As we saw in the previous chapter, the Poor Law Amendment Act (1834) consolidated the hated workhouse system and mechanisation, industrialisation, urbanisation, poverty, overcrowding, disease and insufficient social reforms added to the plight of the working poor. But there was a tradition of resistance which went right back to the Peasants' Revolt of the fourteenth century and the Levellers of the English Civil War (1642-1651).

The French Revolution of 1789 asserted the 'Rights of Man' (set out by Thomas Paine in his 1791 treatise of that name). The Second French Revolution of 1830 advocated the principle of popular sovereignty, while the contemporaneous struggle for Polish independence was closely followed in the proliferating radical press (radical, in this context, simply meaning a belief in democratic reform).[7]

Working-class consciousness expressed itself in unionism, which was especially evident between 1830 and 1834, as well as in Chartism, which emerged and converged around one primary cause – working-class male suffrage (women were actively involved in the fight, with some prominent members involved in the abolitionist campaigns, but female suffrage was not on the Chartists' agenda).

The Chartists, who took their name from the People's Charter of 1838, which listed the six main aims of the movement, were never a homogenous group. They were defined by different localities, traditions and means – moral suasion and/or physical force – but through strikes, riots, petitions, mass demonstrations and seditious acts, they fought for reform which recognised the working man. The context was ripe for Cuffay's activism.

Awakened and invigorated after the 1834 strike, Cuffay became involved in a dizzying array of activities: he helped form the Metropolitan Tailors' Charter Association in October 1839; he was elected to the Metropolitan Delegate Council in 1841; he was unanimously elected to chair the Great Public Meeting of the Tailors in 1842; and he was appointed president of a small interim executive following the arrests of prominent Chartist leaders. The specifics of his politics were expressed in his commitments: he was a member of a committee which opposed legislation that would have dangerously empowered employers; in 1846 he attended the Birmingham Land Conference as one of three London delegates supporting the redistribution of land; he was elected joint auditor to the National Land Company (a Chartist cooperative founded in 1846); and he was a director of the National Anti-Militia Association, which opposed working-class men joining the militia when they had no vote in Parliament. He was also a member of the Democratic Committee for Poland's Regeneration, having supported the Polish uprising of 1846, and he attended rallies and demonstrations in favour of Irish nationalism. Through various other committees, conferences and commitments, William Cuffay fought for the franchise and the empowerment of the working class.[8]

He was not just an activist; he was a leader – 'the black man and his party' wrote *The Times* – and a militant leader at that.[9] He had witnessed Parliament's rejection of three Chartist petitions in 1839, 1842 and 1848, and he had seen the heavy hand of the State imprison and transport fellow Chartists. He never preserved a diary, autobiography or papers outlining his views, but in reported speeches we know that he railed at the 'tyrannical oligarchy' that sought to deny 'the rights of labour' and he appealed directly to his own class – those who obtained 'our livelihood by the work of our hands', who knew first-hand how 'capital has encroached upon the rights of labour'.[10] He was a man who spoke his mind and backed up his words with actions. Even if that meant embracing a rebellion.

In 1848, William Cuffay joined a plotting committee, which comprised London and Irish militants. The aim was to overthrow the Queen and spark a revolution in Britain. On 15 August 1848, the 'Ulterior Committee', as it was dubbed, met above a London beer shop where an intelligence report was delivered: comrades in Manchester and Birmingham were planning an uprising and London could – should – join their brothers in arms. One member of the committee asked the assembled group if they were ready for the fight: there could be no doubts, no flinching when the time came. William Cuffay, the secretary of the committee, suggested the question be put to the room. All bar two agreed that a potentially violent insurrection was the only course to take. The plans were formulated and at the close of the meeting one of the revolutionaries exclaimed, 'May God's bitterest curse hang upon the head of any man who would betray us.'[11]

God's wrath would be called upon within twenty-four hours. A government spy had infiltrated the group and by 6 p.m. the police had arrested eleven of the conspirators. William Cuffay was located on the third floor of eleven Hollins Street, Soho. He demanded to see a warrant, but the arresting officer refused, for Cuffay was charged 'with wilfully and unlawfully combining against her Majesty' and this required no warrant. Cuffay responded, 'Oh that is quite sufficient; I am a Chartist; I understand it.'[12] He knew that a court of law awaited him.

* * *

From 25 September 1848, at the Old Bailey, William Cuffay and two co-conspirators were tried on the charge that 'they, with others, feloniously did compass, imagine, devise, and intend, to levy war against the Queen'.[13] Before the sentence of the court was passed down, Cuffay addressed the chamber with 'great vehemence', wrote one newspaper, projecting the 'air of a deeply-injured patriot', wrote another.[14]

> My Lords, I say you ought not to sentence me, first, because although this has been a long and important trial, it has not been a fair trial, and my request was not complied with to have a jury of my equals. But the jury as it is I have no fault to find with; I daresay they have acted conscientiously.[15]

Cuffay had no grounds to criticise individual members of the jury, but they were not of his own social class. He was concerned with the working-class consciousness born of hardship and solidarity.

The next reason that I ought not to be sentenced is on account of the great prejudice that has been raised against me in particular, for months past. Everybody that hears me is convinced that almost the whole press of this country, and even other countries, has been raising a prejudice against me. I have been taunted by the press, and it has tried to smother me with ridicule, and it has done everything in its power to crush me.[16]

Punch, the satirical magazine run and read by the middle classes, was one of many publications which mocked the 'unhappy crack-brained spooney'.[17] *The Times*, on the other hand, painted Cuffay as a destabilising alien import. 'The English are not conspirators,' they stressed. 'The nation abhors it,' they proclaimed, but 'Cuffey, the very chief of the conspiracy, is half a n****r. Some of the others are Irishmen.'[18]

Cuffay used his appearance in court to decry the injustices of his trial, but without self-pity or opprobrium. 'I pity the Attorney-General and the Government that they could descend to such means as to raise up a conspiracy against me by infamous and base characters,' he chided, in reference to the government spies whom even the high court judge deemed 'odious'.[19] In fact, the judge warned the jury that the prosecution's evidence needed to be treated with caution and there were suggestions, too, that the spies had colluded.[20] The 'regular organized system of espionage', lamented Cuffay, was 'a disgrace to this great and boasted free country'.

It was as if Cuffay was channelling the spirit of William Davidson who, some twenty-eight years earlier, stood in the same courtroom charged with high treason. In his address to the court, Davidson chastised the spies, 'always instrumental to the death of innocent men', whose dubious evidence led to his conviction.

Born in Jamaica to an attorney general father and an unknown Black mother, Davidson was sent to England when he was fourteen. He studied, went to sea and eventually trained as a cabinet maker. He was radicalised by his experiences of poverty and witnessing the repressive actions of the British State – notably the Peterloo Massacre of August 1819 and the Tory Government's oppressive Six Acts, promulgated the same year with the aim of quashing further popular protest.

The so-called Cato Street Conspirators of 1820 planned to assassinate the British Cabinet and spark a revolution. But, like the Ulterior Committee nearly three decades later, they were infiltrated by a government spy and apprehended before the execution of their plans.

In court, Davidson maintained that he was 'a silent spectator from the nature of my colour', and he was only apprehended because he was mistaken for another 'man of colour'.[21] He declared to the judge, 'You may suppose that because I am a man of colour I am without any understanding or feeling and would act the brute; I am not one of that sort.'[22] Still, Davidson was hanged, decapitated and buried in quicklime as a punishment for his alleged crime.

That same year, another Black activist and author, Robert Wedderburn, was sentenced to two years in Dorchester Gaol for blasphemy and sedition. Wedderburn's political convictions were forged in the hellhole of the Jamaican plantations, where his father, the slaveowner James Wedderburn, tormented his enslaved mother. 'By him my mother was made the object of his brutal lust, then insulted, abused, and abandoned', Wedderburn wrote in *The Horrors of Slavery* (1824).[23]

In the late 1770s, Wedderburn arrived in England and lived among a community of outcasts known as the 'London blackbirds'. Like Cuffay, he became a journeyman tailor and briefly a Methodist preacher, drawn to Methodism for its associations with working-class activism and anti-slavery sentiment. Then, after meeting the English radical and revolutionary Thomas Spence, he entered the world of underground revolutionary politics.[24]

Wedderburn's numerous publications articulated what one historian has dubbed a 'Black Atlantic radical rhetoric'.[25] Wedderburn wrote for a working-class audience in England and even managed to get some of his pamphlets to enslaved Jamaicans too. In *The Axe Laid to Root* (1817), he implored the enslaved, 'Above all, mind and keep possession of the land you now possess as slaves; for without that, freedom is not worth possessing', evincing a proto-communist commitment to communal ownership of land.[26]

Retribution was the cornerstone of his revolutionary zeal. Writing in echoes of Shakespeare's Shylock, he demanded in *The Horrors of Slavery*, 'Hath not a slave feelings? If you starve them, will they not die? If you wrong them, will they not revenge?'[27] And, drawing a link between abolitionism and working-class radicalism, he argued that the British working class could learn from the enslaved, as reported by a government spy who witnessed one of Wedderburn's speeches:

> After noticing the Insurrections of the Slaves in some of the West Indian Islands he said they fought in some instances for twenty years for 'Liberty' – and he then appealed to Britons who boasted such superior feeling and principles, whether they were ready to fight now but for a short time for their Liberties.[28]

* * *

Twenty-eight years on, William Cuffay stood before the court charged with seeking to overthrow the Queen. He had no regrets:

> As I certainly have been an important character in the Chartist movement, I laid myself out for something of this sort from the first. I know that a great many men of good moral character are now suffering in prison only for advocating the cause of the Charter; but, however, I do not despair of its being carried out yet. There may be many victims. I am not anxious for martyrdom, but I feel that, after what I have gone through this week, I have the fortitude to endure any punishment your lordship can inflict upon me.[29]

The punishment handed down? Transportation to Australia – for life.[30]

But, demonstrating the promised fortitude, Cuffay kept fighting, even after he was banished. Just before he was transported alongside 'my brother martyrs', as he wrote, Cuffay appealed to his 'chartist friends to raise a few shillings' to help him on his journey.[31] This they did, in a sign of the high esteem in which he was held.

After sailing for 103 days, Cuffay arrived in Hobart, Tasmania, and was given a 'ticket of leave' which allowed him to ply his trade as a tailor. He remained political, 'a fluent and effective speaker', according to the local press, 'always popular with the working classes'.[32] His wife Mary Ann joined him in 1853 and, three years later, along with all political prisoners in Tasmania, Cuffay received a free pardon from the British State.

But he ended his days in poverty in Tasmania and was buried in a pauper's grave – and yet, as he had declared in the dock of the Old Bailey back in 1848, 'I crave no pity. I ask no mercy.'[33] Thanks to his dedication and energy, his cause lived and eventually came to fruition.

* * *

A number of historians have argued that, until the mid-nineteenth century, class rather than 'race' was at the forefront of people's minds. From trade union agitation to Chartism, to the Irish famine to the 1848 revolutions in Europe, these were primarily seen and discussed through the prism of class.[34] But 'race' and class were not so separable. At a discursive level, they were frequently collapsed and at an individual level, 'race' was the modality in which class was lived.[35]

In a speech William Cuffay delivered before his 1848 trial, he revealed how issues of 'race' impacted his class-based activities. One reporter summarised the content of his address:

> He was the immediate descendant of a West Indian slave, whose father was an African slave; but he was born amongst them a freeman – and he respected, he loved Englishmen, for their great exertions in breaking the chains of the bondmen, and abolishing slavery in their colonies. The people forced that measure, though it cost them twenty millions to do it; and he was grateful to them for it. He would now exert himself in their cause, and assist them to gain their freedom. (Cheers.) He considered them a noble and generous people, and in the name of his fathers and his relations – the slave class of the West Indies and of Africa – he thanked them kindly for what they had done for him, and ever, whilst he had life and reason, he would do his best to aid them in return.[36]

Did he really use terms such as 'their' and 'they' when discussing the English, which might suggest that he saw himself *in* rather than *of* England? The speech certainly implied that his African heritage and the traumas of slavery drove his involvement in working-class politics. The whole speech argued that the emancipation of the enslaved had been achieved and now it was his patriotic duty to help liberate the British working class.

The connection between abolitionism and Chartism was expressed in the working-man's paper, *Reynold's Political Instructor*, which carried a front-page, illustrated feature on William Cuffay in April 1850. The article inferred that he, 'a scion of Afric's [*sic*] oppressed race', was committed to the cause of democracy because of Britain's glorious abolitionist past:

> On arriving in England, himself and his parents became free, and during his services in the cause of Democracy, he, the stern man, has often shed genuine tears of gratitude for this boon, and declared that the sacrifices of his life and liberty if needed, was due to the complete emancipation of that nation which had inscribed his name upon the list of free men, and this burst of generous feeling has been, as events have proved, no idle boast, nor has it fallen without producing its effect upon the hearts of his fellow toilers.[37]

There were many inaccuracies in the article (Cuffay was born in England, for starters), but the attribution of political motive was revealing. Cuffay was purportedly motivated by gratitude for liberty (which was bestowed by Britain), rather than anger at the injustices of industrial capitalism (which would have implicated Britain). This was a useful narrative as it maintained Britain's moral standing as the glorious nation which emancipated the enslaved – a sentiment which suggests the article should be taken with a hefty pinch of salt.

But whatever its veracity, the article reflected a genuine solidarity between working-class radicalism and abolitionism.[38] There was an affinity between enslaved people and the British working class because, within radical discourse, they were both presented as the oppressed. This perceived affinity meant that Black working-class leaders like William Cuffay could be incorporated into radical political movements.[39]

REYNOLDS'S POLITICAL INSTRUCTOR.

EDITED BY GEORGE W. M. REYNOLDS,

AUTHOR OF THE FIRST AND SECOND SERIES OF "THE MYSTERIES OF LONDON," "THE MYSTERIES OF THE COURT OF LONDON," &c. &c.

No. 23.—Vol. I.]   SATURDAY, APRIL 13, 1850.   [PRICE ONE PENNY.

MR. WILLIAM CUFFAY.

WILLIAM CUFFAY, loved by his own order, who know him and appreciated his virtues, ridiculed and denounced by a press that knew him not, and had no sympathy with his class, and banished by a government that feared him, has achieved a celebrity that fully entitles him to a place in our Portrait Gallery. He was born in the year 1788, on board a merchant ship, homeward bound from the Island of St. Kitts, and is consequently sixty-two years old. Cradled on the vast Atlantic, he became by birth a citizen of the world, a character that, in after life, he well maintained. His father was a slave, born in the Island of St. Kitts; his grandfather was an African, dragged from his native valleys in the prime of his manhood. On arriving in England, himself and his parents became free, and during his services in the cause of Democracy, he, the stern man, has often shed genuine tears of gratitude for this boon, and declared that the sacrifice of his life and his liberty if needed, was due to the complete emancipation of that nation which had inscribed his name upon the list of free men, and this burst of generous feeling has been, as events have proved, no idle boast, nor has it fallen without producing its effect upon the hearts of his fellow toilers.

Soon after his arrival in England his father procured a berth as cook on board a man-of-war, and Cuffay spent the years of his childhood with his mother at Chatham: though of a very delicate constitution, he took great delight in all manly exercises. As he advanced toward manhood, he entered the ranks of the proletariat as a journeyman tailor, and was reckoned a superior lame: his only child, a boy, died in its youth. Scrupulously neat in his person, he carried a love of order and regularity even to excess in all his transactions, whether social or political, this characteristic procured him much esteem and adapted him to fill offices which men of greater talents sought for in vain: during his whole career, he occupied an active post in the ranks of his own trade and was never found wanting in any of the requisites essential to the maintenance of a character for sterling and unflinching integrity. In a letter written by one who has known him upwards of forty years, he says, "Cuffay was a good spirit in a little deformed case: I have known some thousands in the trade, and I never knew a man I would sooner confide in: and I believe this to be the feeling of thousands in the business to this day. It was always his great delight to take young men by the hand and instruct them, not only in the trade, but mentally." He disapproved of the Trades' Union movement in 1834, and was nearly the last of his society in joining the lodge; but ultimately he gave way, and struck with the general body, remaining out until the last, thereby losing a shop where he had worked for many years; since which time he has had but very partial employ. He early saw through the deception of the Reform Bill, and from 1839, when the struggle for the Charter commenced, until his banishment, dedicated his whole energies as a worker to the task of enfranchising the millions; in 1840 he was elected as a delegate from Westminster to the Metropolitan Delegate Council, an office which he ably discharged during the long and energetic existence of that body in 1842, when the Chartist Executive, with the exception by acclamation, together with Thomas Martin Wheeler, John George Drew, and James Knight, to supply that vacancy. In 1845 he was appointed one of the auditors of the National Land Company, which office he held until his arrest: he was a member of nearly every Convention which was called into existence during those exciting times, and fulfilled his duties with honour to himself and satisfaction to his constituents. Elected as one of the delegates for Westminster to the National Convention and Assembly of 1848, he allowed his enthusiasm to overcome his usual cool judgment, and was singled out by the press for ridicule and vituperation; he bore it unflinchingly, he even seemed to glory in it! As early as 1842 he had been especially singled out by the Times as a leader of the opposition in London to the Anti-Corn League, which facetiously denominated the Chartists as the "Black man and his Party." Entrapped by the infernal spy-system into an almost involuntary attendance at the so-called insurrectionary meetings in the autumn of 1848, he fell a victim, but he shrunk not: flight was open to him, but he refused to avail himself of it, and during his confinement, both prior and after his sentence, his spirits maintained their usual equilibrium.

Notwithstanding the Government punishment of transportation for twenty-one years, it has been intimated that on reaching his destination he will receive a ticket of leave giving him his freedom in the colony. We trust this is a fact; but whatever may be his after fate, whilst integrity in the midst of poverty, whilst honour in the midst of temptation are admired and venerated, so long will the name of William Cuffay, a scion of Afric's ...

William Cuffay, *Reynold's Political Instructor*, April 1850

But they were never fully accepted. Within the English radical tradition – heterogenous, shifting and complex as it was – there was always a sense of exclusionary nationhood and patriotism. The working class increasingly saw themselves as part of a national identity crafted in opposition to racialised outsiders (Jews, Irish, Asians and people of African descent) and many white radicals looked on aghast as, in their perception, bourgeois abolitionists focused on the suffering of Black enslaved people while overlooking the exploitation of the white working class in Britain.[40] The Chartist James Bronterre O'Brien wrote in 1833, 'We are no enemies to colonial emancipation; all we require is that when negroes are emancipated, it *shall not be* at the expense of those who are greater slaves than themselves.'[41]

The influential radical William Cobbett perceived middle-class abolitionists like William Wilberforce as far more corrupt and dangerous than slave planters in the Caribbean, and Cobbett espoused a vitriolic racism. In one lengthy tirade written in 1804, he turned his attention to 'the importation and propagation of negroes in this country', lamenting an assumed tolerance leading to intolerable miscegenation:

No black swain need, in this loving country, hang himself in despair. No inquiry is made whether he be a Pagan or a Christian; if he be not a downright cripple, he will, if he be so disposed, always find a woman, not merely to yield to his filthy embraces, that, amongst the notoriously polluted and abandoned part of the sex, would be less shocking, but to accompany him *to the altar*, to become his wife, to breed English mulattos, to stamp the mark of Cain upon her family and her country![42]

There was, in short, a pronounced working-class racism. There was never a single monolithic working-class racist discourse, but that such a discourse existed was undeniable – and it led to increased hostility towards abolitionism from the 1830s onwards.[43] Indeed, by the early 1840s, a number of white working-class radicals expressed their racism by disrupting anti-slavery meetings.[44]

So, William Cuffay had to negotiate this working-class racism while simultaneously advocating for the cause of the working classes. He never ignored them, he fought tirelessly for the whole of the working class, and he was admired *despite* the racism, not because of its absence, which might lead us to suspect that Cuffay might very well have seen himself as an outsider *in* rather than *of* England.

* * *

Like Brown, Flinn, Peters and Albert – though in different circumstances – Black radical leaders like William Cuffay, William Davidson and Robert Wedderburn all confronted that same question: 'Can I live?' They not only answered in the affirmative, but with an understanding of what was flawed in society, and how those flaws should be addressed. They were prepared to fight in the political realm for a vision of equality despite the risks.

Davidson was hanged, Wedderburn was imprisoned and Cuffay was transported. But they all engaged in emancipation struggles born out of the Black Atlantic; a site of racial terror but also a site of political dissent which generated energetic hopes of a brighter tomorrow. They challenged poverty, oppression and the State, pitting themselves against the white Establishment. But, as we will see in the following chapters, there were other Black Victorians who were seemingly not at odds with the Crown at all, who were, in fact, within the royal orbit. They did not experience Victorian poverty or destitution but, instead, saw the other side of that paradoxical society, one couched in riches and renown.

8

Black Aristocracy: Sarah Forbes Bonetta
(1843–80)

Though Queen Victoria had a strained relationship with her eldest son, writing that he 'is so idle and so weak' and 'a very dull companion' who 'fills me with indignation', on this special day such feelings were set aside.[1] It was a day of celebration after all.

Saturday, 9 November 1850, and Bertie, Prince of Wales, was turning nine years old. Victoria admitted that her boy had 'great truthfulness & great simplicity of character' and on his birthday he would be spoiled.[2]

Bertie came bounding down for breakfast and discovered a table laden with gifts: toys, books, even a bullfinch, which chirped merrily as the family – mama, pappa, grandmama and siblings – gobbled down the morning's culinary delights. Afterwards, the family enjoyed a royal parade at Windsor Castle, then Prince Albert dressed for hunting while Queen Victoria took the children for a pleasant country walk and a spot of fishing. Boisterous games between young Bertie and his brother Alfred preceded another lavish meal at the castle, eaten to the sounds of a harp. Here was the picture of domestic bliss that Victoria cherished and sought to project to the world.

This day was special and remarkable for another reason, too. Around lunchtime, Prince Albert and Queen Victoria met

Captain Frederick E. Forbes, a British naval captain in the West African Squadron, who had recently returned from Dahomey (present-day Benin). As a representative of the Crown, Forbes had been on a diplomatic mission to negotiate with King Ghezo (or Gezo), a key player in the West African slave trade, hoping to encourage Ghezo to abandon the commerce in humans.

Forbes' venture proved unsuccessful, but he did return with a number of gifts: cloth from Dahomey, a keg of rum, cowry shells, a footstool and a girl – an enslaved girl, in fact, whom Forbes had accepted in the name of Queen Victoria. In the grand corridor of Windsor Castle, Forbes presented the girl to Her Majesty, and in the evening, Victoria wrote in her journal about the 'poor little Negro', recently baptised Sarah Forbes Bonetta, 'She is 7 years old, sharp & intelligent, & speaks English. She was dressed as any other girl. When her bonnet was taken off, her little black woolly head & big earrings gave her the true negro type.'[3]

From this day forward, Sarah was imbued with a special purpose. She would be propelled into the highest echelons of British social life to demonstrate that under British guidance she had the potential to transcend the supposed limitations of her 'race'. She would forever be seen as a 'true negro type', a representative of her entire 'race', and through her natural abilities she could serve to prove a point: Africans could be 'improved'.

In this sense, then, Sarah's agency was co-opted, her life arranged to please others, and we only get glimpses of how she felt about this in the archives. We just don't have the intimate sources to provide a clear window onto her inner thoughts and feelings. But at certain moments in her life – when she was pressurised into marriage, for example – we get the impression that Sarah wanted independence, that she could be assertive and resistant to a life led at the behest of others. We know that she was smart, talented and concerned with her 'peace of mind', as she wrote in a rare letter that survives, and with those attributes and desires, she was nonetheless treated like a 'doll' in Britain, her life prettily arranged to suit others.[4]

* * *

Born in Dahomey of Yoruba descent, the girl who would be designated the name Sarah Forbes Bonetta was seized when she was around five years old during the Okeadon War of 1848, a 'dreadful tragedy', wrote Captain Forbes, in which Ghezo's army stormed the town of Okeadon following a conflict with the Egbado (now Yewa) clan of the Yoruba people.[5]

In his book *Dahomey and the Dahomans* (1851), Forbes wrote that of Bonetta's own history 'she has only a confused idea. Her parents were decapitated; her brothers and sisters, she knows not what their fate might have been.'[6]

After the murder of her family, she was sent to live at the Dahomian palace in the capital of Abomey where, in a central square, there stood a pavilion adorned with 148 human skulls, 'the victims of the dreadful tragedy of Okeadon', wrote Forbes.[7] With this haunting reminder of her childhood trauma, the young Bonetta lived in the palace for about two years before she was handed over to Captain Forbes as a 'gift'. He might have been the first white person Bonetta had seen – how she felt at that time we can only imagine.

Forbes accepted Ghezo's 'gift' because refusing 'so extraordinary a present' would have 'signed her death-warrant'. He feared that Bonetta might have been offered as a human sacrifice, which Ghezo was known to practise in his highly militarised kingdom.[8] Indeed, Ghezo had come to power in the 1820s and, following the disintegration of the Nigerian Oyo Empire in the 1830s, established Dahomey as an independent state. In his book, Forbes paints vivid scenes of the court:

[...] in the Dahomey palace, on a rich mat reclined the king; as usual attended by his host of female ministers, ladies of the blood, wives, amazons, and maidens. On the neutral ground were the skulls of kings, and strewed about large pieces of cooked meat, gorging on which were thousands of turkey-buzzards flying about with sickening familiarity.[9]

Since the eighteenth century, Dahomey had been a source of fascination to Europeans. There was a slew of books on Dahomey, all written by British subjects, including publications by Forbes (1851), Richard Burton (1864) and J. A. Skertchly (1874). Forbes and Burton, though each having their own differing perspectives and agendas, agreed that Dahomey's resistance to ending slavery stemmed from its militaristic society which, they argued, manifested in state-sponsored human sacrifices.[10] But Dahomey engaged in what the British described as 'legitimate commerce' (notably the trade in palm oil) and King Ghezo welcomed, or at least accepted, contact with Europeans.

However, Dahomey's reliance on and propagation of the slave trade put the kingdom at odds with Britain's foreign policy agenda. In West Africa, the British were driven by a desire to defeat slavery and promote 'legitimate commerce', which included trade in cotton and ivory, backed by a wish to gradually train suitable West Africans 'in the arts of Civilization and Government', stated the former Secretary of State for War and the Colonies.[11]

But colonisation remained a viable option. In 1861, after the King of Lagos rejected Britain's hand of 'friendship' in return for abandoning the slave trade, Britain invaded and took control. For now, though, the preferred tactic was diplomatic persuasion. King Ghezo had already been visited by William Winniett, Governor of the British Gold Coast colony, and now Forbes was following suit.[12]

Ultimately, he failed to persuade King Ghezo to abandon the slave trade (leading to a British naval blockade in 1852) but instead returned to Britain with the young girl in tow. Forbes maintained that Sarah, in not being sold to slave dealers but instead being handed over to him, must have hailed from a good family – a claim which became so exaggerated that in Britain she was variously described as a 'chieftain's daughter', a 'woman of noble blood' and a 'princess' (and she was not the only figure for whom claims of 'noble birth' served a racialised purpose of comforting white observers).[13]

As they prepared to set sail on HMS *Bonetta* in July 1850, Sarah Forbes Bonetta was baptised in Badagry, a former slave-trading port. The new Christian name bestowed on her was taken from that ship and its captain.

On the sea voyage, Captain Forbes remarked that Sarah, or Sally, as the crew called her, was 'a perfect genius' who could speak fluent English and 'has a great talent for music'. Forbes assumed she was around eight years old, and he praised 'her docile and amiable conduct'.[14] He continued:

> She is far in advance of any white child of her age, in aptness of learning, and strength of mind and affection; and with her, being an excellent specimen of the negro race, might be tested the capability of the intellect of the Black: it being generally and erroneously supposed that after a certain age the intellect becomes impaired, and the pursuit of knowledge impossible – that though the negro child may be clever, the adult will be dull and stupid.[15]

In this estimation, Bonetta served a function: she could determine the entire capability of her 'race'. So when the ship arrived in Britain, Forbes contacted Her Majesty via the Secretary of the Admiralty, and Queen Victoria 'was graciously pleased to arrange for the education and subsequent fate of the child', wrote Forbes.[16] According to the leading missionary Reverend Henry

Venn, 'Her Majesty wished the princess to be trained for missionary work', so it was quickly decided that Bonetta would be sent back to West Africa where she would be instructed into the ways of the mission.[17] Another function she could serve: spreading the Christian message to the heathens of the 'dark continent', and beginning this mission in Freetown, Sierra Leone.

* * *

Close to the mouth of the Sierra Leone River, Freetown was described in one contemporary Western account as 'well situated for commerce, and is increasing in wealth and population', and there was the feel and appearance of a European city in the Sierra Leonean capital. Clothes, architecture, educational establishments and language reflected the Western order of things.[18] The city was 'the base camp for the continental civilizing mission', as historian David Olusoga writes, with colonial administrators aiming to remodel liberated Africans with the same names, manners and attitudes as Western whites.[19]

While the Wesleyan Methodist Missionary Society had bases along the west coast of Africa, and the London Missionary Society had a foothold in southern Africa, the Anglican, British-based Church Missionary Society (CMS), which was first founded in the City of London in 1799, was particularly prominent in Sierra Leone.[20] The CMS was committed to the abolition of the slave trade, domestic social reform and world evangelisation. In seeming opposition to the idea that Africans were *inherently* inferior – a claim Forbes rebuked in his journal – the CMS believed that Africans could become agents of Christianity and civilisation and thus 'improve' themselves and their 'kind'.

The CMS largely believed in the potential for native missionaries to spread the Gospels, which was seen as a safer, sounder and cheaper option than sending white westerners to Africa. It was argued that Africans had a higher resistance to

African climates and diseases and would be more culturally adept at spreading Christianity on the continent.

Reverend Henry Venn, who served as clerical secretary of the CMS for thirty-two years, was one of the most influential missionaries in the nineteenth century and he was committed to a form of African leadership and evangelising by native agents.[21] In 1845, he founded the Native Agency Committee 'to encourage the social and religious improvement of Africa by means of her own sons'.[22] This included daughters such as Sarah Forbes Bonetta who, in May 1851, was sent to the CMS Female Institution in Freetown.

The relatively new school, established in 1849 and run by the missionary Julia Emily Sass, predominantly tutored students from Freetown and the neighbouring villages. Not only was it fee-paying, but a disavowal of roots and culture was also required. African girls had to don English dresses and bonnets and were taught English hymns. They had to learn housekeeping skills such as sewing and knitting and Bible studies, praying morning and evening, as well as studying arithmetic, geography and English grammar.[23] Bonetta also had piano and French tuition. Her school fees were covered by the Queen, and she had her own room adorned with a picture of Queen Victoria. Bonetta continued to receive letters and gifts from the Queen and, on 24 May 1852, was allowed to host a tea party in celebration of Victoria's birthday.[24]

But her time at the school came to an abrupt end for reasons which remain unclear. Academic Adeyemo Elebute contends that Queen Victoria wanted Bonetta to return to England following the death of the Bishop of Sierra Leone in 1855.[25] Other biographies claim that Bonetta wanted to return because she was unhappy in Sierra Leone.

Bonetta might have been struggling to find her identity too. She variously referred to herself as Sarah Forbes Bonetta, Sarah

Bonetta Forbes, Etta and Ina, so returning to England might have been a search for identity, a journey of self-discovery.[26] But we don't have Bonetta's words on the matter; like William Cuffay, there was no preserved diary or autobiography, we only have the bare facts.

After four years in Sierra Leone, she sailed back to England and, aged around twelve years old, arrived at Gravesend in July 1855. She was subsequently placed under the care of a missionary, Reverend James F. Schoen, who lived in nearby Gillingham and worked as chaplain at the Melville Hospital, which was treating a large number of wounded soldiers from the Crimean War. His daughter, Annie C. Higgens, later claimed she tutored Bonetta in English and French, while Reverend Schoen taught her German.

'She was very bright and clever,' recalled Higgens, 'fond of study, and had a great talent for music, and soon became as accomplished as any English girl of her age.' Higgens stated that Bonetta was 'extremely lively' and 'full of fun and mischief'.[27] She took her place in the loving, religious household alongside Schoen's seven children and two African servants (formerly enslaved children who helped Schoen develop his study of the Hausa language). Bonetta was 'very affectionate and warm-hearted', wrote Higgens, 'and seemed to quite feel herself to be one of our family, calling my parents "papa" and "mamma"'.[28]

She was also a constant visitor to Windsor Castle and Osborne House. Bonetta reportedly cherished her time with the Queen and almost always returned with gifts. One time it was a gold watch, another time a turquoise ring and yet another time, a gold bracelet engraved with 'From Queen Victoria to Sarah Forbes Bonetta'.[29] When Victoria received the Guards following their return from the Crimean War, Bonetta accompanied Her Majesty. When Victoria's eldest child was married, Bonetta was invited to the palace galleries to see the bridal procession.

In the late 1850s, having comfortably settled into the Schoen household, Bonetta was relocated to Brighton. Once again, the reasons why remain unclear, but most historians agree Bonetta did not want to move.[30] Yet, her life was directed by others, so Brighton it must be.

Bonetta lived with and studied under the elderly and experienced tutor Sophia Welsh and became a much-respected member of Brighton society. She was praised for her musical abilities, her sociable manner and her mastery of languages.[31] In August 1862, the *Brighton Gazette* wrote, 'her mind has received a moral and religious impression' and her 'knowledge and accomplishments make her an ornament for any society, and prove, most satisfactorily, that the African mind is capable of the highest intellectual attainments'.[32] Bonetta had passed the test, just as Forbes had hoped. All she needed now, according to Victorian values, was a husband.

A promising match presented itself in the form of James Pinson Labulo Davies, a Yoruba polymath born in Sierra Leone whose wife had recently died. He too had studied at the CMS Grammar School in Freetown before becoming a teacher at the school. Later, he had joined Britain's West African Squadron, starting as a cadet and rising through the ranks to become lieutenant, and then became a wealthy entrepreneur and philanthropist. When he declared an interest in marrying the teenage Bonetta, she was reluctant to wed an older widower and wrote to her 'mama' Elizabeth Schoen:

> Others would say 'He is a good man & though you don't care about him now, will soon learn to love him.' That, I believe, I never could do. I know that the generality of people would say he is rich & your marrying him would at once make you independent, and I say 'Am I to barter my peace of mind for money?' No – never![33]

Still, since the Queen approved of the match, Bonetta eventually acquiesced – this was not her life to live. On 14 August 1862, while the Queen was crippled by grief following the death of Prince Albert, Sarah Forbes Bonetta became Sarah Forbes Davies at St Nicholas' Church, Brighton, swapping one name for another one she didn't choose herself.

* * *

From 10 a.m., throngs of people assembled in the rain waiting for the doors to open at St Nicholas'. Tickets of admittance had been issued and guests arrived early to get the best seats. At 10.30 a.m., all eyes were diverted to the 'four bridesmaids – ladies of colour – apparelled in white dresses', wrote the press, who entered the church, followed by 'four fair bridesmaids' and then the bridegroom and 'five coloured groomsmen'.[34] Loud cheering and clapping signalled the arrival of the bride, who appeared in a pure white glacé silk dress with a wreath of orange blossoms and a veil of white lace trailing down to her shoulders.

Bonetta was visibly nervous, 'the incessant throbbing of her deeply-coloured breast being very perceptible through her thin garments', but it was nonetheless attested that 'of her personal qualities we may safely say she is one of the prettiest colour-ed ladies we ever beheld'. The report in the *Islington Gazette* continued:

> There is a distinct absence of that abruptness in the features so often seen in the females of the African race, which gives them an air of ferocity. She has an eye expressive of tenderness and beaming with intelligence, whilst her whole deportment is ladylike in the extreme.[35]

The bridal party were arranged at the altar. The service was conducted by the Bishop of Sierra Leone, assisted by Reverend

Henry Venn and William Nichol, 'a gentleman of colour'. The ceremony lasted forty-five minutes and, on signing the marriage certificate, Sarah née Bonetta gave her first name as Ina, perhaps a variant of her African name, and perhaps also a moment of reclamation.[36]

At the conclusion of the service, the church bells rang out as ten carriages took the bridal party to the wedding breakfast, where Reverend Venn proposed the health of the couple and the bridegroom expressed his indebtedness to 'Englishmen for their kindness since he had been amongst them'.[37] At 4.30 p.m., the celebrations concluded, and the couple left for their honeymoon in London.

* * *

The press were in a froth of excitement about the wedding: it was widely reported from Belfast to London and from Cork to Dundee.[38] Parroting many other accounts, the *South East Gazette* wrote:

> No marriage of greater interest ever took place at the altar of St Nicholas Church than that which was solemnised on Thursday morning, the parties who were united being of the pure African race, their previous history giving peculiar interest to the occasion.[39]

In analysing the press response, historian Caroline Bressey notes that while the racial mixing of the congregation was praised as a victory over prejudice, commentators were still drawn to the innate racial differences of the congregation and bridal party. Reports included phrases such as 'novel sight' and 'interesting marriage'.[40] Bonetta remained a representative of her 'race', and so successful was she in her bridal role that she was *'almost Caucasian'*, italicised the press.[41]

The *Brighton Gazette* put a slightly different spin on the same basic trope, declaring that the marriage was thought-provoking for those 'deeply interested in the African race, and who have watched the progress of civilization caused by the influence of Christianity on the negro':

> The ceremony will also tell our brethren on the other side of the Atlantic that British ladies and gentlemen consider it a pleasure and a privilege to do honour to those of the African race who have proved themselves capable of appreciating the advantages of a liberal education.[42]

British tolerance was implied in contrast to American intolerance. The bride and groom were praised because they had successfully digested white civilisation and the bride, in particular, was acclaimed because she 'showed herself capable of holding with dignity a position in any society', wrote the *Gazette*, 'and but for the difference in colour might be a scion of the best European aristocracy'.[43] Clearly, then, Bonetta could successfully *imitate* the best of European stock, but being Black was still a bar to becoming a 'true' (white) aristocrat.

Nonetheless, the newlyweds, who honeymooned at 60 Burton Crescent, Bloomsbury, had their photographs taken at the studio of Camille Silvy, a leading portrait photographer from an aristocratic French background, whose studio at Porchester Terrace was famed for its refined furnishings and status-defining backdrops and props. Silvy was in high demand, photographing all of the royal family bar Queen Victoria, most of the British aristocracy and, within that fashionable milieu, Sarah and James Davies in September 1862.

Their portraits display all the visual trappings of wealth and rank, and there is one image of Sarah Forbes Davies which we find particularly arresting. Adorned with the symbols of respectable Victorian femininity and prosperity – a ring on her finger, a bracelet on her wrist – she stares directly into the lens, her gaze unswerving, almost confrontational, certainly defiant. Her thoughts may be impenetrable, but she stares at us, not as a submissive doll or as a passive ornament, but as an unassailable agent whose image in this *carte-de-visite* photograph would have circulated throughout Victorian high society – an unforgettable

Sarah Forbes Davies by Camille Silvy, 1862

and unmissable visual reminder of the Black presence in Britain's uppermost echelons.

* * *

Indeed, at the apex of the Victorian social hierarchy, we find a number of Black Victorians who were assimilated rather than integrated into the upper echelons of the social hierarchy which, as Montaz Marche highlights, is an important distinction, for 'integration implies an acceptance of black cultural practices in the British community', while assimilation does not.[44] Nonetheless, there were Black Victorians who lived within the royal orbit, who went to prestigious private schools, trained at the top British universities, had their photographs taken by leading fashionable photographers and earned large salaries (in America, too, there were notable Black individuals who survived slavery to become millionaires).[45] In Britain, there was a long history of West African elites studying and staying in Britain and there were wealthy domicile Black Victorians as well.[46]

Nathaniel Wells (1779–1852) was educated in England and, following the death of his slave-owning father (who owned Nathaniel's mother), received a considerable inheritance which enabled him to purchase the magnificent Piercefield estate on the Welsh borders in 1802.[47] He became an established country gentleman who served as Justice of the Peace in 1806 and Sherriff of Monmouthshire in 1818.

In 1801, he married Harriet Este, and together they had ten children.[48] Following Harriet's death, Wells married Esther Owen, the daughter of an Essex rector, and together they had ten more children. The births, marriages and deaths of Wells' children were reported in the local press, testimony to the esteem in which he and his family were held.[49] Indeed, in the local press Wells was praised for his 'beautiful and elaborately finished' artistic drawings which attested to 'his devotion to the Art'.[50] A former employee cleverly advertised her association with Wells when opening her new school in 1850, taking care to include in her announcement the line, 'For many years Governess in the family of Nathaniel Wells, Esq., Piercefield House, near Chepstow'.[51]

Wells had standing. He appeared in the papers as an investor in the Bristol & Liverpool Junction Railway; he sat on a grand jury investigating the Chartist Newport riots in 1839; and he was a member of the General Committee overseeing the Monmouth County Election in 1847.[52] He became a warden of his local church and paid for improvements to the building. He was seemingly a good royalist too. Following an assassination attempt on Queen Victoria in 1840 (the would-be assassin, Edward Oxford, was ultimately transferred from Bedlam to Broadmoor with John Flinn), Wells publicly declared his support for the Queen and expressed 'deep abhorrence of the atrocious and traitorous attempt upon the life of her Majesty'.[53]

All this begs the question, though, if, as we have seen, racial attitudes were hardening across the nineteenth century, why were Black Victorians like Nathaniel Wells and Sarah Forbes Bonetta celebrated and seemingly accepted within society? From this distance, it's hard to be sure. Perhaps this seemingly contradictory attitude to 'race' was informed by missionary optimism, which could elevate and praise the attributes of Black Victorians like Bonetta. Perhaps there was a dose of British tolerance which, as we saw in Part One, was recognised by some African American abolitionists. Perhaps there was a novelty factor when it came to non-threatening African 'princesses', glamorous marriages between partners of African descent and Black country gentlemen (nonetheless matched by ruthless, racially informed expansion and discrimination overseas). Perhaps homegrown racism wasn't yet very developed when these events were taking place. Or perhaps factors such as class, connections and wealth elevated certain Black Victorians away from everyday racism.

Queen Victoria herself holds the key. 'It would be fair to say that, at a personal and intellectual level the Queen was generally opposed to the racism of the mid-nineteenth century', writes David Olusoga, but, like her subjects, she 'thought in terms of racial "types", and may well have believed, to some extent, that the races of mankind possessed innate, inner characteristics.'[54] Victoria could welcome, admire and praise Black Victorians, but this certainly did not mean she saw them as racial equals. She could commend Black Victorians while harbouring racist views – an attitude shared by many of her subjects too.

Historian Joan Anim-Addo notes Queen Victoria's personal tolerance, while recognising how her relationships with the likes of Sarah Forbes Bonetta helped domesticate what was, in reality, violent conquest abroad.[55] Scholar Adeyemo Elebute was even more generous, stating that the Queen's tolerance grew as she aged, which ran counter to the hardening racial attitudes among her British subjects at the time.[56] One could also contend that Victoria was lured by the perceived 'exotic' nature of her charges and that there was image-making going on – as much as a real person, Queen Victoria was a persona who projected a vision of domesticity and imperial benevolence outwards to her subjects. Embracing colonial subjects, and caring for African orphans went towards this presentation of imperial munificence. She embodied the image of the 'Great White Queen', or the 'White Mother', as one Kalanga (Nyai) man called out while watching a column of advancing troops during the First Matabele War of 1893 (which ultimately and bloodily led to the creation of Rhodesia).[57]

How Her Majesty's contradictory behaviour impacted Black Victorians in her circle is another matter. Sarah Forbes Bonetta was not the only young person of colour whom Victoria clasped to her. After the Emperor of Ethiopia, Tewodros II, committed suicide following his military defeat by the British in 1868, his son, the young Prince Alamayu (also known as Alamayou, Alemayehu and Alamaiou), was brought to Britain and met Queen Victoria in July of that year. Her Majesty kissed him in an embrace that the seven-year-old boy returned.[58]

He was the subject of a book, *Anecdotes of Alamayu* (1870), which claimed that, on coming to Britain, Alamayu developed 'a deep sense of all the kindness and sympathy extended to him' (a clever bit of national self-congratulation).[59] In October 1872, he was sent to Cheltenham College where, on the pupil nomination form, in the section requesting details of the father, it was written, 'Theodore King of Abyssinia: dead'.[60] After leaving Cheltenham in 1874, Alamayu went to Rugby School and then to the Royal Military Academy at Sandhurst.[61] His reports there were concerning – 'good but hopelessly unpunctual; failed at the probationary exam' – and he left Sandhurst after one year, dissatisfied with his life in England.[62] Shortly afterwards he fell ill and died at the tender age of eighteen. At Queen Victoria's request, he was buried in St George's Chapel, Windsor.[63]

There were a number of other colonial subjects who became enmeshed, with varying degrees of willingness, in ambivalent relationships with Queen Victoria. In the final years of her reign, Victoria was intimate with the *'Munshi'* ('clerk' or 'teacher') Abdul Karim, a young Indian Muslim originally from Uttar Pradesh, which was then under British control. Victoria appointed Karim to the position of Indian Secretary within the royal household and from him she received Urdu lessons, learning phrases such as *'Anda thik ubla nahi hai'*, translated as 'the egg is not boiled enough', and *'Ham ko mazbut Thamo'*, which means 'hold me tight' (make of that what you will…).[64]

Victoria was also the godmother to Princess Gouramma, daughter of the Rajah of Coorg in south-west India, who was deposed and exiled by the British in 1834, and Her Majesty was also godmother to Victor and Sophia, the children of the former

Maharaja of the Sikh Empire, Duleep Singh, who, once again, was deposed by the British and exiled to Britain in 1854.

These exiles in flight from acts of British imperial violence were largely embraced by the Queen, as were some of their children, yet there was resistance to her monarchical smothering. Gouramma was denied access to her father and ran away on several occasions; Duleep Singh eventually proclaimed his Sikh identity and in the 1880s made a doomed attempt to declare war on the British Empire, while his daughter Sophia became a leading revolutionary and suffragette in the Edwardian era.[65]

Abdul Karim and his family were dubbed 'the Black Brigade' and were expelled from their homes in Balmoral and Windsor after Queen Victoria died.[66] There was an undeniable colonial mindset that sought control over these lives and this could, quite naturally, breed resentment and resistance. Indeed, perhaps the defiant gaze captured in Silvy's studio, or the name Ina written on the marriage certificate, was Sarah Forbes Davies' stoicism, resistance and resolve in the face of white authority.

* * *

It is perhaps revealing, moreover, that Sarah Forbes Davies and her husband James left Britain shortly after their marriage. They returned to West Africa, where they re-entered the local elite. James continued to develop his financially successful business, pioneering cocoa farming and engaging in philanthropic work, while Sarah worked at the Female Institution at Sierra Leone, which had trained her as a child. It was very possible that she might have become principal of the school but for the fact that her first child, named Victoria, was born in 1863.[67]

Queen Victoria, the namesake and godmother of the infant, sent a golden christening set to mark the birth, and in 1867 the Davies returned to England, reuniting with Queen Victoria, who wrote in her diary that the young Victoria Davies was 'a lively intelligent child' and 'far blacker' than her mother.[68] Years later, at another meeting between Victoria Davies and Queen Victoria in 1873, the 'large melancholy eyes' which the Queen detected in 1867 had become 'fine eyes'.[69]

By this time, Sarah and James Davies had two more children, Arthur and Stella, but Sarah's health was failing. She was suffering from tuberculosis and stress over her husband's business endeavours, which were struggling in an economic downturn. She was eventually taken to Madeira in the hope that the climate would be restorative, but she died on the island in August 1880, aged only thirty-seven. The Queen saw Sarah Forbes Davies' eldest child Victoria on the day she learned of her mother's death:

> [...] saw poor Victoria Davies, my black godchild, now 17 who heard this morning of the death of her dear mother at Madeira. The poor child was dreadfully upset & distressed [...]. Her father has failed in business, which aggravated her poor mother's illness. A young brother & a little sister, only 5 were with their mother. Victoria seems a nice girl, very black & with very pronounced negro features. I shall give her an annuity. – Also saw Mrs Nicholson the missionary's wife, who brought her.[70]

Much like her mother, Victoria Davies was taken under the wing of Her Majesty and her missionaries. In 1881, at the young Victoria's own request, she was sent to be educated at the prestigious Cheltenham Ladies' College. Her fees were paid for by the palace. Years later, Victoria would write to the principal, fondly reflecting on her time at the school.[71]

In November 1890, she married John Randle, a Sierra Leonean graduate of Edinburgh University who worked as an Assistant Colonial Surgeon in Lagos (he went on to become a successful doctor and a philanthropist who fought for equal pay

Victoria Davies while at Cheltenham Ladies College, *c.* 1881

between Nigerian surgeons and their white colleagues).[72] Together, he and his wife had two children, John Romanes Adewale and Beatrice Helena Randle, who was the namesake and goddaughter of Princess Beatrice, Queen Victoria's youngest child.

The Randle family continued to visit the royal household into the 1900s while their family's achievements and connections to the British Establishment have proved long-lasting: their grandson Adekunle Randle served as a British Crown prosecutor until 2013, while his son Banyo was called to the Bar of England and Wales in 2012.[73]

Sarah and James Davies' son tragically died at sea, aged sixteen, while their other daughter Stella studied in England before resettling in West Africa. In 1905, she dedicated a school in Lagos to her mother, naming it Bonetta Memorial Ladies School, with the Latin motto *Cede Deo*: 'Yield to God'. One of the school's patrons – with whom Stella would go on to have a child – was the famous Nigerian nationalist, Herbert Macaulay. His grandfather was the renowned Samuel Ajayi Crowther, who exemplified that Latin motto *Cede Deo*.[74]

Crowther's origins were not dissimilar to those of Sarah Forbes Davies. Born in West Africa of Yoruba descent, Crowther rose within the missionary ranks and was intimate with Queen Victoria, Reverend James F. Schoen and Henry Venn of the Church Missionary Society. He moved in similar circles to Sarah Forbes Davies, but ultimately, he followed a different path, one which saw him enter the corridors of state and ecclesiastical power as an active agent of the Church of England – an Anglican bishop, no less.

9

The Bishop: Samuel Ajayi Crowther (*c.* 1807–91)

> And this gospel of the kingdom will be proclaimed throughout the whole world as a testimony to all nations, and then the end will come.
>
> Matthew 24:14

At 11.30 a.m. on St Peter's Day, 29 June 1864, three bishops-elect were consecrated inside Canterbury Cathedral. Every aisle was full for the occasion: upwards of 300 members of the clergy including deans, canons and bishops were present. The Epistle was read by the Bishop of Lincoln, the Gospel was delivered by the Bishop of Winchester and the choir sang the Nicene Creed. The sermon was delivered by the Reverend Professor Henry Mansel, who preached on the Epistle to St Peter. The choir then sang Mendelssohn's anthem, 'How Lovely are the Messengers', and the bishops-elect were formally presented to the congregation.

Francis Jeune took the bishopric of Peterborough, Charles H. Bromby took the bishopric of Tasmania and Samuel Ajayi Crowther (or Dr Crowther, thanks to an honorary PhD from the University of Oxford) took the newly established bishopric of Niger, West Africa.[1] The choir marked the consecration with Michael Wise's eighteenth-century anthem:

Ev'ry valley shall be exalted
and ev'ry mountain and hill shall be made low,
and the crooked shall be made straight
and the rough places shall be made plain.

As the words from Isaiah 40 echoed throughout the cathedral, the newly elected bishops retired to be fully robed. They returned, knelt at the altar and received the hands of the archbishop on their heads. In a clear and distinct voice, His Grace delivered the solemn declaration and exhortation prescribed by the prayer book.[2] At the conclusion of the service, a collection was made for the Society for the Propagation of the Gospel, a Church of England missionary organisation which supported hundreds of Anglican agents around the world, while the congregation and the press marvelled at the ordination of an African bishop into the holy Church of England.[3]

'A BLACK BISHOP!' wrote the *East Kent Times*.[4] 'The first Anglican bishop of his race and colour,' wrote the *Kentish Gazette*. 'No personal appearance in England prevents the appointment of a worthy man,' opined the press.[5] 'Dr. Crowther has long been known as one of the most able of the missionaries,' noted others, 'his presence in England has given a stamp of reality to the great work of the [Church Missionary] Society.'[6] Crowther's consecration was the realisation of the Great Commission: 'Go into all the world and proclaim the gospel to the whole creation', as Jesus exclaims in Mark 16:15–16, chiming with the missionary zeal within Victorian Britain.

Typically for the age, there were concerns about irreligious urban spaces, a decline in church attendance, creeping secularisation and malign outside influences. But this was met with a compensatory proliferation of Nonconformist chapels, church restorations and offerings of Sunday schools, church choirs, religious philanthropy and foreign missions.[7]

The latter chimed with the wider imperial project: there was a symbiotic relationship between imperialism and missionary proselytising, the latter providing a moral and ethical gloss on naked colonialism. Missionaries were 'civilised' expansionists (although missionary motivations were not always or simply imperialist by nature), and they were presented as heroes and social reformers, brave explorers who brought the Gospels to dangerous lands. Missionaries condemned the slave trade as they saved sorrowful souls. They went forth with authority over the unclean spirits of the world, to paraphrase from Mark 6:7.

In truth, however, the majority of missionaries were less global explorers and more everyday artisans, shopkeepers and wives, who were building Christian institutions in their local communities. Many Britons joined the missionary ranks for social advancement and most missionaries were women. But there were missionaries overseas and, by the 1840s, Protestant missionaries, in particular, were penetrating Africa at the same time that European economic and political hegemony was being established on the continent.[8]

Many missionaries vilified foreign cultures, especially in the early nineteenth century, and they emphasised foreign cannibalism, mistreatment of women, polyamory and other practices in order to justify their existence as saviours. By the nineteenth century, there was also a strand to humanise those seen as foreign unfortunates, denizens of heathen lands who tragically lacked the benefit of Christianity and civilisation, but who had souls that *needed* to be saved, souls that *could* be saved – souls 'like ours'.[9] And amid their numbers were the likes of Bishop Samuel Crowther.

Reverend Henry Venn of the Church Missionary Society (CMS), who had previously assisted Sarah Forbes Bonetta and was present at her marriage to James Davies, was mightily pleased with Crowther's consecration. He wanted to see Africans spreading Christianity and he longed for the establishment of non-Western churches which, in his slogan, were to be 'self-supporting, self-governing, and self-extending'. These 'three selves', also known as the 'three-self formula', were spearheaded by Venn in Britain and Rufus Anderson in America, and they formed part of a missiological strategy to establish African-led churches.[10] The plan needed native agents – African bishops, missionaries, ministers in the service of Christ – so it needed men like Samuel Crowther, the newly ordained 'Missionary Bishop, Niger Territory', as he soon signed in his letters.[11]

* * *

Ajayi, as he was called before his baptism, was born into a dangerous world around 1807. European slavers had occupied the ports on the coast of Yorubaland in West Africa, the old Yoruba Empire of Oyo was disintegrating and Islamic jihadis terrorised the region. When Ajayi was around thirteen years old, he was captured and enslaved by Fulani and Oyo Muslim raiders. 'It was the day on which I was violently turned out of my father's house and separated from my relatives,' he later wrote in a letter, 'and in which I was made to experience what is called to be in slavery.'[12] Although he never wrote an autobiography, we hear his voice through his copious letters and publications, learning that he was sold and resold as a child until he was liberated by a British anti-slavery vessel and taken to Freetown, Sierra Leone, in the early 1820s. On 11 December 1825, he was baptised Samuel Crowther by Reverend John Rahan of the CMS and subsequently educated at the CMS Grammar School.

Crowther was a bright, able and pious student, as proficient in carpentry as he was in contemplative learning, and in the mid-1820s he was taken to Britain where he studied at a parochial school in Islington, London, increasing his proficiency in English and deepening his knowledge of missionary work.

He returned to Sierra Leone in 1827 and attended Fourah Bay College in Freetown, an institution founded by the CMS with the aim of developing Sierra Leoneans for Christian service. Crowther, who was one of the college's first students, would later reflect in another letter, 'Our country is greatly improved and benefited by the labour of the servants of the Church Missionary Society'.[13]

Crowther rose to become an assistant teacher and then a schoolmaster. He assisted John Raban in his publications on the Yoruba language (Crowther's mother tongue) and he studied the Temne language while possibly helping linguist Hannah Kilham in her studies too. During this period, Crowther met his wife, the schoolmistress Asano, and together they started a family. In July 1841, Crowther expressed the pain of separation as he began his next mission:

> When I looked back on the colony in which I had spent nineteen years – the happiest part of my life, because there I was brought acquainted with the saving knowledge of Jesus Christ, leaving my wife, who was near her confinement, and four children behind – I could not but feel pain, and some anxiety, for a time, at the separation.[14]

Crowther had agreed to embark on the Niger Expedition of 1841, working as a representative of the CMS alongside the missionary James F. Schoen (who would later care for the young Sarah Forbes Bonetta). The mission aimed to bring Christianity, commerce and 'civilisation' to West Africa, and Crowther proved invaluable in helping it meet its aims. He negotiated with different tribes along the Niger and 'while the white people were prostrate with sickness', Crowther remained healthy and demonstrated 'beyond question the importance of working such a dangerous field with native agency', reflected a later biography.[15]

The Niger expedition convinced Crowther of the importance of native missionaries, and in letters preserved at the University of Birmingham, he made clear his belief 'that Africa can chiefly be benefitted by her own Children'.[16] In one message, written after the Niger Expedition, Crowther applied the arguments mounted by Thomas Fowell Buxton, a former MP and President of the Aborigines' Protection Society, to the field of missionary work:

> I have read in Mr Buxton's work on the Slave Trade and its Remedies, that some promising youths among the children of Africa should be sent to England for education, who would afterwards hold situations in their countries, and whose conduct would have a beneficial influence upon their country people. If such a plan could be in contemplation for other employments, could it not be adopted for the preparing missionaries too, from the coast of Africa, who might become useful among their countrymen?[17]

It was exactly this sentiment which determined Sarah Forbes Bonetta's fate some ten years later. Crowther had been moved to discover the story of Philip Quaque, a young man from the Cape Coast who was educated in England, studied theology at the University of Oxford and received holy orders in 1765. He was subsequently appointed chaplain to the British trading settlement at the Cape Coast.[18] He was not the 'first' Black chaplain – the 'first' African to be ordained into a protestant ministry seems to have been Jacobus Capitein in the 1740s – but for Crowther, it was Quaque who set a precedent that he wanted to follow.[19]

After the Niger Expedition, Schoen wrote to the CMS recommending Crowther's ordination, and in September 1842, Crowther was again brought to England to study at the Highbury Missionary College, London, a training college run by the CMS to prepare missionaries for work overseas. A year later, in a

Samuel Ajayi Crowther, James Johnson, Henry Johnson
and friends at the Wilberforce Oak, Kent, 1873

ceremony presided over by the Bishop of London, Crowther was admitted into the full orders of the Anglican Church.

The newly ordained Reverend Crowther returned to Yorubaland as an Anglican minister and opened a mission in Abeokuta. The *Church Missionary Record* boasted in April 1850 that Crowther's mission had 500 attendants, eighty communicants and nearly 200 candidates for baptism.[20] In 1851, he returned to London where he shared stories of his missionary work with government ministers, Queen Victoria and Prince Albert and, in the presence of British royalty, recited the Lord's Prayer in Yoruba.[21] Queen Victoria wrote in her diary, 'He is a negro extremely black, with woolly hair, 42 years of age, comes from Abekuta, speaks English extremely well & is very intelligent & pleasing with quiet unaffected manners.'[22]

By 1853 Crowther was being praised in a children's book, 'What a treat it was to see dear Mr. Crowther in England!'[23] He returned to West Africa and undertook further missions along the Niger in 1854 and again in 1857. He led whole teams of African missionaries who spread the Gospels from Sierra Leone into the heart of Africa.

According to a later biography, Crowther 'passed hither and thither along the banks of the Niger, establishing at different points fresh centres of Christian enlightenment'.[24] He erected missionary centres, promoted commerce and laid the groundwork for future missionary endeavours which included a dictionary of the Yoruba language and translations of the Bible into Yoruba. All this before his consecration at Canterbury Cathedral, which marked yet another step towards realising the missiological strategy of African-led churches under the 'three selves' formula.

* * *

During the service at Canterbury Cathedral, the registrar read aloud the licence to consecrate Crowther, 'Bishop of the United Church of England and Ireland in the said countries in Western Africa beyond the limits of our dominions'.[25] The *Kentish Chronicle* opined, 'What has Her Majesty, or if she pleases, the Head of the English Church, got to do with places external to her dominions?'[26] And there was one critical reflection in May 1864 which effectively conveyed prevalent views that were both contradictory and racist.

This anonymous article was originally published in the *Belle Weekly Messenger* before being reproduced in other papers. 'Hitherto we have sparingly employed negro agency in our attempts to civilise and to evangelise Africa,' it opened, before proceeding to outline two antithetical beliefs. Number one: Africans were inferior morally and physically and as such, they 'must not mount the pulpit'. Belief number two: there was an 'entire equality of the white and black races', but still 'the white man should himself undertake the missionary labour, and become the servant in Christ of his black brother'. The article almost immediately contradicts itself again by stating, 'If we are to get at the negro at all, we must reach him by means of his own race'.[27] Echoing Thomas Carlyle's loathing of 'rosepick Sentimentalism', the article continued in a racist rhetorical tradition:

> Few people take the trouble to ascertain what the negro is, and what he wants. He is a child in ignorance and selfishness, in vanity and recklessness, totally thoughtless as to consequences, lazy, sensual, careless of the truth, dirty and insolent. But then, on the other hand, he is docile and good-humoured, resigned to his lot, even when most unfortunate; gentle and affectionate; and capable, when well treated, of showing sincere and permanent attachment. High intellectual powers he has not, nor is he endowed with that energy which inspired great and long-continued exertion. His wisdom is but cunning at the best; and he imbibes, as he cultivates it, a love for chicanery, which corrupts his whole moral being. Exceptions to this rule there are doubtless – but only enough to prove its correctness.[28]

This damning and confused indictment contextualised Crowther's achievements as an exception that proved the racist rule. The article also echoed the narrative of the Black victim needing white saviours (a sentiment peddled by abolitionists and missionaries alike). And yet, perversely perhaps, the commentator perceived some 'hope' in the distant future:

> The experiment is a new one. Let Mr Crowther ordain a sufficient number of negro preachers; let him be satisfied with such as he can get. […] bear in mind that to make the negro race what it is capable of becoming is not the work of one generation. We must not be disappointed if years pass away, and we find little effect produced by our sable prelate; the seed will be sown far and wide, and must have time to come up.[29]

Certainly, from the perspective of Henry Venn and the CMS, the consecration of Crowther promised a new beginning. And despite dissenting views, it reflected changing attitudes in the church, noted by his 1890 biography: 'Many have treated the black man as having no mind, and more have virtually denied him a soul. That he has both, however, is the growing conviction of the Christian Church to-day.'[30]

The Bishop of London articulated this belief when he ordained Crowther back in 1843: 'Among a race who were despised as incapable of intellectual exertion and acquirement, He has raised up men well qualified.'[31] To many, Crowther was not simply on a mission from God, he was proof of God's handiwork. 'His life is a conspicuous proof of the power of the Gospel, and of the continued presence of the Spirit of God in Christ's Church' was how the CMS put it.[32]

Unfortunately, however, God's African Church enshrined the hierarchies in which white privilege could thrive and, as the century progressed, it would be the Book of Job, rather than the Gospel according to Mark, which reflected the spirit of Crowther's mission: 'For He crushes me with a tempest, And multiplies my wounds without cause' (Job 9:17).

* * *

Crowther's consecration at Canterbury Cathedral was a momentous occasion, but the reality of his mission on the ground was not without problems. The episcopate was essentially a mission by another name, with a number of restrictions placed on Crowther's jurisdiction, and his mission did not strictly deploy native agents either. African missionaries were spreading the Gospels but not necessarily to people from their own tribes or ethnic groups.[33]

Missionary work was arduous, dangerous and isolating. The Niger mission stretched 350 miles from the coast, deep into the interior, with missionary stations dispersed as much as 170 miles apart along the river. In an attempt to bring some structure, in 1877 Crowther wrote to the Archbishop of Canterbury requesting that the mission be divided into an Upper District and Lower District, with the Reverend Henry Johnson, of Yoruba heritage, becoming archdeacon of the upper region, and Crowther's son, the Reverend Dandeson C. Crowther, becoming archdeacon of the lower.[34] His request was granted, which greatly improved the Niger mission, but significant challenges remained.

In 1878, Crowther wrote again to the Archbishop of Canterbury pressing an urgent question: 'How far native converts in foreign countries not British subjects, may be bound by English Ecclesiastical law of marriage and divorce?'[35] The following year, he expressed his major concern at the Lambeth Palace Conference (a gathering of the Anglican Communion to collaborate on moral and spiritual matters): 'Christianity, I believe, your Grace and my Lords, is the only medicine that can heal the negro race of Africa from the leprosy of polygamy, which they have contracted.'[36]

Polygamy offended colonial and Christian mindsets. 'Polygamy is against the holy ordinance of God', Crowther wrote, and despite his best efforts, he lamented the continuation of the practice.[37] While all this smacks of cultural colonialism, Western Christian values were not simply and monolithically dumped onto West Africans – there was a protracted conversation between missionaries and natives – and Crowther even adopted some Muslim beliefs by way of compromise.[38]

Still, there were undeniable tensions even when things seemed promising. King Pepple, a committed Christian of the Kingdom of Bonny, agreed that Christ should replace Iguana, the deity of the kingdom, but the introduction of Christianity created resentments which ultimately led to his deposition.[39]

As the century progressed, the problems multiplied, and by the 1880s Crowther was old, frail, weary and heartbroken. His

Samuel Ajayi Crowther, 1888

beloved wife died in his arms on 19 October 1880. His mother died three years later. In 1889, Reverend Schoen left the world too, a painful parting for Crowther, who loved the man who first recommended his ordination. Henry Venn, secretary of the CMS, had been dead since 1873.

Crowther might have turned to his Bible and read from the Book of Job, 'Does it please you to oppress me, to spurn the work of your hands, while you smile on the plans of the wicked?' He might have wondered as Venn's support for native missions was increasingly attacked. European missionaries were now particularly keen to spread the Gospels on their own terms and Venn's ideals – notably self-governing churches led by a native episcopate – were being threatened, undermined and ultimately replaced.[40] What's more, the 'three-self formula' had become a poisoned chalice – 'self-supporting' translated into limited means and 'self-propagation' meant endless work with no home leave – and now European missionaries began to question the efficacy and morality of Crowther's native missionaries too.[41]

As new European missionaries came, Crowther was pushed aside, his staff dismissed or transferred, aspersions were made, and financial controls exacted over his mission.[42] Archdeacon Henry Johnson was dismissed for obscure reasons.[43] The Sierra Leonian James Johnson, who worked on CMS missions in Nigeria, Lagos and Abeokuta, was slandered. In one report, it was claimed that funds associated with Johnson's mission were being misappropriated, that polyamory was being practised, that the Sabbath was not being observed, that his church was rapidly emptying and all of Johnson's reports to his superiors were damned as 'highly coloured, even when partially true, and were very largely a tissue of lies'.[44]

As Black missionaries were cast aside, Europeans brought their guns. The Scramble for Africa, sometimes alternatively called the Rape of Africa, was underway as the Western colonial powers wrangled for control of resource-rich African territories. Between 1877 and 1891, Nigeria became three separate British protectorates – Lagos, Oil Rivers and Territories of the Royal Niger Company – while Bishop Crowther looked on, aghast.[45]

As Western nation-states clamoured for African land, European missionaries clamoured for African souls: white Anglican, Methodist, Baptist, Catholic and Protestant missions, Scottish Presbyterians, Scottish Presbyterians, French Calvinists and Norwegian Lutherans all competed in a chaotic mix that exacerbated tensions and confusions.[46]

By the 1880s, the nature of evangelical religion had changed too. It had become more individualised and otherworldly whereas, when Crowther was first baptised, there was a stress on salvation *and* schooling – a nod to the afterlife with a commitment to heaven on earth. That had material benefits for Africans, bringing education and practical support to the land, but the new hardnosed evangelicals were disinterested in that.

Crowther's world, as he had developed and known it, was coming to an end. He died on 31 December 1891 and was succeeded by a white European bishop.

* * *

Crowther was by no means the only significant Black clerical figure during this period. There was a long tradition of Protestant, English-speaking Black missionaries active across the Black Atlantic. From the 1780s, a small but steady stream of African American missionaries went to Jamaica and Trinidad. In the early nineteenth century, Black-led churches sent missionaries into Canada and the Caribbean. From the 1820s on, African American missionaries headed to Sierra Leone and Liberia, and throughout the nineteenth century, Africa continued to be a key location for their work. The argument for native missionaries, espoused by Henry Venn in Britain and Rufus Anderson in America, helped spur on these missionary endeavours, and it was Black agency that played a central role in evangelising the African continent.[47]

And Black missionaries were not only men. Amanda Smith from the African Methodist Episcopal Church (established in New York in 1821) spent one year in England, two years in India and eight years in Monrovia, Liberia. She later opened an orphanage in Illinois, the only institution open to Black orphans in the state.

Catherine Elisabeth Mulgrave was one of twenty-four missionaries who travelled from Jamaica and Antigua to evangelise in present-day Ghana, becoming the founder and director of a girl's school in Accra. Agnes Foster, born into slavery and later resident in England for four decades, was central to the development of the Salvation Army, expanding and entrenching its message in Jamaica. The first edition of the Jamaican *War Cry*, the Salvation Army's official magazine, noted that many Jamaicans had been converted by Mother Foster, as she was known:

> Mrs Foster, who has a daughter, an officer of the Army in England, and was herself engaged in the work there, came out here [Kingston] four years ago, and has since been carrying on a successful street mission work.[48]

Additional Black soldiers of the army included Cadet Joe Norton, Captain William Daniel Woods and Lieutenant Harry Nichols (sometimes spelt Nicholls).[49]

There were also other agents of God who were disconnected from official churches. From 1840, the freeborn African American Zilpha Elaw preached across the United Kingdom without any licence or financial backing. She had already travelled across America as an itinerant Christian preacher before bringing her spiritual mission to England. Elaw attended Nonconformist chapels and meetings, travelled to Ramsgate, Canterbury, Leeds, Hull, Liverpool and Newcastle, among other places ('My God hath made my ministry a blessing to hundreds of persons,' she wrote), and she ultimately settled, married and died in England.[50]

In 1846, she published her memoir, in which she emphasised her right to preach as a Black woman. 'I am here,' she simply and powerfully retorted to a group of patronising white men.[51] Her memoir worked to undermine the narrative of Black victimisation and functioned as an assertion of Black female agency in a space dominated by white clergymen.[52]

Elaw's was a spiritual autobiography similar to those written by Jarena Lee and Julia Foote in America around the same time. This literary genre informed and preceded 'emancipation narratives' by almost fifty years and sought to prove that Black people were chosen by God just as much as whites. 'I was sent to preach Christ, and Him crucified,' Elaw declared. 'I came in obedience to His sovereign will.'[53] In drawing close to God, she felt a connection to her authentic individualised self, which subsequently brought liberation from racial and societal constraints. With God, she was freed from the fetters of feminine subordination, freed from the bondage of racism and empowered as a servant of Christ.[54] As she wrote, after an ecstatic visionary experience in America, 'From that happy hour, my soul was set at glorious liberty.'[55]

* * *

Although the West African mission became complicated by conflicting forces towards the end of Crowther's life, he was a key agent in the evangelisation of the African continent and his many achievements had a lasting influence. Thanks to his lexicographical and translation work in the 1850s, Yoruba became a written language for the first time.

He wrote and promoted a slew of publications, creating a new 'age of literature' which moulded the next generation of Nigerian leaders.[56] Of his six children, two daughters married clergymen, two sons entered the world of business and his youngest son, Dandeson, remained Archdeacon of the Niger until 1926.

Crowther's other son, George Nicol, was educated at the CMS Grammar School in Freetown and the CMS College in Islington, London, and was ordained into the Church of England in 1849. Twenty years later, he received two vacant chaplaincies on the West Coast of Africa.[57] George Nicol's son, George Gurney Mather Nicol, also became a Sierra Leonean clergyman, having graduated from the University of Cambridge in 1879. Crowther's other grandson, Olayinka Herbert Macaulay, who had a child with Sarah Forbes Davies' daughter Stella, became an engineer, journalist, musician and famous nationalist who resisted the very forces that were being stirred up at the close of the nineteenth century and were, as we will see in the next chapter, sweeping up the likes of Jimmy Durham.

10

Young Soldier:
James Francies Durham
(c. 1885–1910)

The *Times* retrospective of January 1901 eulogised 'that solitary figure holding aloft the flag of England in the face of the dark hordes of Islam'. In January 1885, that figure, 'alone, in a dark continent, dauntless and unfaltering', had met his death and, claimed one contemporaneous newspaper, entered national mythology as Britain went into mourning.[1] A solemn service was held at St Paul's Cathedral. Statues were erected. Reverent articles appeared in newspapers, journals and books. The object of this outpouring was General George Gordon, a white senior officer who had lost his life in defence of British imperial ambitions in the Sudan, and the conflict in which he died, and in which the young boy who is the focus of this chapter was unwittingly caught up, exemplifies the tangled and deadly nature of the imperial enterprise – particularly as it meets questions of 'race', identity, belonging and ownership.

Who should and could control the Sudan had become an acute problem. For many years prior to the 1880s, Egypt asserted devastating control over neighbouring Sudan. And this vast region became a British concern after their invasion of Egypt in 1882 – an invasion which many historians believe fired the starting gun on the 'Scramble for Africa'. Britain assumed effective control over Egypt, which in theory remained an independent state, albeit subject to British financial, military and strategic objectives.[2] Britain was initially reluctant to get involved in – to them – the relatively unknown expanses of the Sudan, but the insurgent Mahdist army from the region, led by Muhammad Ahmad bin Abd Allah, a Nubian Sufi religious leader or self-proclaimed Mahdi ('guided one'), had been making significant military inroads. The Mahdi had urged jihad against the colonial occupiers and by November 1883 the situation had spiralled out of control: the Mahdist army took over the region surrounding Khartoum, the strategically important Sudanese capital near the head of the Nile, and then crushed an Egyptian force sent to restore control. The Egyptian government was panicked, which in turn panicked London, and that panic turned to dismay with the death of General George Gordon, who was killed trying to defend Khartoum after a ten-month siege.

In Britain, Gordon's death was treated as a martyrdom. On the ground, however, the combined British and Egyptian forces were falling back as the Mahdists continued making inroads right up to the Egyptian border. Raids were mounted against British-Egyptian forts and reinforcements were sent. At the Ginnis-Kosha fort in northern Sudan, two infantry brigades and one cavalry brigade were tasked with securing the frontier zone. On 30 December 1885, at 5 a.m., the Battle of Ginnis began.

The Anglo-Egyptian army advanced, seizing villages as they moved along the Nile towards the village of Ginnis, which was then under Mahdist control. The Mahdist riflemen and spearmen attacked, and the British 2nd Durham Light Infantry (DLI) ducked the bullets and the spears, eventually fighting the Mahdists at bayonet point. Lieutenant de Lisle, a man known for his relentless energy, commanded the DLI troops as they converged on Ginnis.[3]

According to reports, most of the Mahdists fled into the desert and Lieutenant de Lisle volunteered to capture the *nuggar*, an Arab sailing boat which was located three miles up the Nile and was reportedly carrying ammunition and supplies back towards the south. Around 100 troops, including volunteers from De Lisle's infantry, marched thirty-five miles before arriving at the village of Kohehmatto, where the local sheikh reluctantly revealed the boat's position about six miles upstream. At this point, twelve men under De Lisle volunteered to pursue and capture the vessel. They continued astride their horses, following the winding path of the river, hoping to reach the boat before nightfall.

About half an hour into the mission, the twelve men caught sight of the *nuggar*, which was being towed by donkeys and 'a swarm of Dervishes', according to the regiment's own magazine, the *Bugle* ('Dervishes' was Britain's name for the Sufi religious movement dedicated to the Mahdi).[4] De Lisle called a halt and, leaving behind three men to hold the horses, commanded the rest of his troops to advance. Concealed by the dark night, they silently crept up to the enemy forces and, when they were about 300 yards away, unleashed rounds of gunfire followed by a charge. The *Bugle* reported, 'The Dervishes no doubt bearing in mind the events of the previous day, did not remain to try conclusions; but vanished under cover of the darkness into the desert, leaving the nuggar as a prize.'[5]

The Mahdists left behind the boat, some ammunition, one wounded soldier and a small boy (the whereabouts of his mother were unclear), 'an infant of about two years of age standing beside a donkey', as reported in the DLI's Record of Service:

From the statements of the wounded Arab, it appeared that the child's father had been killed at the battle of Ginnis, and his widow, with two children, intended to make her way to Berber. The child who fell into our hands was to have been mounted on the donkey during the journey, but the attack on the nuggar changed the whole current of his life. He was taken charge of by the mounted infantry and has since accompanied the battalion through the vicissitudes of foreign service. He was christened James Francies Durham, his real name having been Mustapha.[6]

Just a little before the Battle of Ginnis unfolded, the Berlin Conference of 1884–85, convened by Otto von Bismarck, formalised the carving up of Africa as European powers vied for the continent's natural resources. At a time when notions of white superiority abounded, the peoples of Africa had no say in the partitioning of their homelands. By 1900, nearly ninety per cent of Africa was under the control of European states with the war in Sudan one stage in this global, imperial march. Mustapha was one of the casualties.

In the House of Commons, the Battle of Ginnis was praised. The Liberal Secretary for War, Sir Henry Campbell-Bannerman, stated in Parliament, 'Her Majesty's Government fully recognize the important results of the battle of Ginnis, and also the high qualities displayed both by officers and men who were engaged in it', yet Campbell-Bannerman determined that because only nine British deaths and twenty-six injuries occurred, a distinct medal was not necessary.[7] Instead, the men who fought at Ginnis were awarded the generic Egypt medal, which was given to all troops deployed on the Nile. Still, for the soldiers of the DLI, they had another trophy that was far more interesting – the young boy Mustapha, who would spend the remainder of his life within the DLI ranks.

* * *

The recorded details of Mustapha's 'discovery' evolved over time. In 1894, the *Bugle* stated that, as the mounted infantry of the

DLI ran up to the *nuggar*, 'the child perfectly undaunted held up its arms to De Lisle to take him up, which he did'.[8] In an 1896 article, however, the *Bugle* claimed that 'standing on the bank of the river, all alone, was a small child dressed in the full war paint of a Soudanese warrior'.[9] Much later, in 1934, John Fergusson of the DLI recalled that the boy's mother was riding a camel and dropped baby Mustapha as she retreated from the fighting.[10] Later still, in 1939, De Lisle wrote in his *Reminiscences of Sport and War*, 'On the bank was a small dervish child, under two years old, who, pointing his finger at me kept repeating "Bung-morto," imitating the sound of the rifle.'[11]

Despite these variations in the 'discovery' tale, most sources agree that the child was handed over to Sergeant Stuart of the Durham Division Mounted Infantry and was christened James Francies Durham, also known as Jimmy Durham. His namesakes derived from the name of the battalion and the two men who helped care for him, Sergeant Francies Fisher and Private James (Jim) Birley, who 'had as much affection for the boy as if he were his own child'.[12] According to the *Bugle*, 'Jimmy remained the pet of the Durham division of the mounted infantry.'[13] He was raised in their ranks. His expressiveness and bold wanderings around the camp were a regular source of amusement. He was a fearless toddler, who charged through the camp pointing a stick and shouting '*Bonsy Morto!*' (*morto* is the Arabic expression denoting 'death'). When he was hungry, he would shout '*Aus laben!*' (roughly translated as 'I want milk!') to anyone he could find.[14] It would appear that, aged two, he could speak English and Arabic and ride a horse bareback. He would dance and sing for the regiment too. 'To English mothers it must seem incredible,' boasted the *Bugle*.[15] He even acted as an interpreter, negotiating with local hawkers around the camp. He was an amusing mascot, or as the *Bugle* wrote, 'Our little Soudan Trophy'.[16]

JAMES FRANCIS DURHAM

James Durham with Sergeant Stuart, *c.* 1887–89

The earliest known photograph of Durham was taken in Cairo. He is pictured sitting between the legs of two sergeants wearing a khaki drill uniform fitted with a sergeant's stripes and red sash. On his chest are the Egypt Medal and Khedive's Star, awarded to soldiers who fought in Egypt between 1882 and 1891.[17] The *Bugle* noted that Durham had 'quite a martial air'.[18]

Reportedly, Durham was 'treated kindly by all' and was adored by Sergeant Stuart, who allowed him to join military marches astride his saddle.[19] When the battalion was called to India, a number of sergeants demanded that Durham come along, and they each promised to pay one rupee a month – amounting to about one day's pay – to keep Durham with them. De Lisle eventually agreed. 'Master Jimmy's banking account is now worth more than that of any Subaltern in the Regiment,' noted the *Bugle* in 1894.[20]

British geopolitical concerns about access to India directly impacted Durham and the DLI, just as they had in the prized Nile and Suez regions. Arriving in 1887, he was placed in a school designed for the children of regimental officers. The *Civil and Military Gazette*, which was published in Lahore, ran a short feature on 'Little Jimmy', claiming he was living at the Ghorpoorie Barracks in Pune, and mistakenly asserting that he was 'rescued at the siege of Khartoum among the dead and dying'. Unsure whether Durham was 'a curly-headed Egyptian, or Somali', the *Gazette* stressed that he was cared for by the DLI 'and is now a chubby child, able to say a few words of English, his pronunciation being of the true Moore and Burgess style'. He was living in comfortable quarters, had a white kitten as a constant companion, and was loved by the regiment 'whom he knows as "brudders"'.[21]

In 1898, when Durham was around thirteen years old (his exact age was never established), he travelled with the battalion to the province of Burma in British India which, following the

Anglo-Burmese Wars, had come under British rule. Durham resided at their station in Mandalay and a year later received his territorial number, reported in the *Bugle* as No. 6758.[22] Allegedly, his application went all the way to Queen Victoria. In the context of white rule, a Black teenager was bestowed with a number which tied him to the arm of the British State. What he felt about this was never recorded – pride? Belonging? Relief? Bemusement? Did he feel a deep connection with the regiment? Or a sense of profound dissonance?

He formally enlisted as a bandsman with the DLI, playing violin and clarinet in the regimental orchestra (it was also mentioned that he played the bugle), and he was often pictured with his instruments.[23] In 1902, the DLI was recalled from India to the north-east of England, and James Durham came with them, instruments in tow. In 1908, he wrote to Stella Robson, the daughter of Sergeant R. Robson, who was one of the men who had helped raise him:

> Dear Stella, I hope you will always reckon me as your brother. I have know you from when you was a dear little child [*sic*] and I always use to look to your father and dear mother as my mother as well. They have treated me like one of you all. [...][24]

The gratitude seems deeply felt, even if, from our perspective, misplaced, since it was the invading British forces who played a decisive role in the loss of his parents.

Years after Durham's death, John Fergusson of the DLI wrote that he was 'as British as any of us', and perhaps being raised by British soldiers from an early age enabled Durham to feel part of the regiment and, by extension, the imperial project.[25]

In the year in which he wrote to Stella, James Durham married Jane Green, the twenty-two-year-old sister of a quartermaster sergeant with the DLI. Her father, Thomas Green, was recorded on the wedding certificate as a foreman blacksmith, while Durham was penned as James Francis Durham, twenty-four years old, a 'Bandsman in 2nd Durham Light Infantry'. The column for his father's name was left blank.[26]

As a non-smoker and lifelong teetotaller (perhaps a mark of his Muslim background), Durham ran the Army Temperance Association for the 2nd Battalion and in 1908 won an award for his service to the temperance cause. According to *Reynold's Newspaper*, 'He had been introduced to many people in high social circles.'[27]

But a mere two years after his marriage to Jane, and just before the birth of their daughter Frances, Durham was struck down with pneumonia and died at the Military Hospital in Fermoy, Ireland, near to where he had been stationed. The Digest of Services of the 2nd Battalion of the DLI recorded:

Bandsman Durham was a Soudanese, and was picked up when a child a few months old, by the Battalion in a skirmish which took place in January 1885 shortly after the action of Ginniss [*sic*]. He was brought up in the Battalion and when 14 years old permission was obtained to enlist him in the Band. He always proved a universal favourate [*sic*] and his loss was much regretted by all ranks in the Battalion.[28]

* * *

Durham's story, while extraordinary, should be placed within a broader military context. Men of African descent had been fighting alongside Britain and helping Britain rule the waves since at least the eighteenth century.

While most Black servicemen worked in low-ranking positions, there were some exceptions. Sierra Leoneans, J. A. Horton and W. B. Davies were medical officers in the British Army in the late 1850s. Black Canadian William Edward Hall

Jimmy Durham and Sheep, 2nd Bn. Durham Light Infantry.

James Durham with sheep (1900–10)

received the Victoria Cross after his actions during the Indian Rebellion in 1857. Samuel Hodge, a West Indian soldier with the British Army, won the same medal in 1866 for his bravery on the west coast of Africa. He was part of the 4th West Indian Regiment, one of a number of West Indian Regiments (WIRs) formed at the end of the eighteenth century. Based in the Caribbean and West Africa, they were part of the British Army and they saw fighting during the nineteenth century (most notably against the Ashanti in 1873–74 and 1895).[29]

During the Crimean War (1853–56), the Zouaves, French soldiers originally from North Africa, fought alongside Britain and so inspired the British that in 1858 the Zouave uniforms were adopted for the WIRs. Henceforth, the WIRs were to wear white turbans, red waistcoats and dark blue pantaloons.

In 1888, the WIRs were unified into a single regimental unit, and at Queen Victoria's Diamond Jubilee, members of the West Indian Regiment took part in the military procession. This regiment would go on to fight in East Africa and the Middle East during the First World War.[30] Indeed, Black British soldiers, either born or domiciled in Britain, fought in both world wars – a collective reminder that Britain's military muscle, whether fighting for good or ill, relied on Black effort as well as white.[31]

But James Durham, the bandsman, did not fight with a gun and bayonet, and he was often charged with looking after the battalion's mascot – a sheep. In many ways, Durham was seen as the sheep's counterpart: the pet of the DLI and a jolly mascot. Around his twenty-first birthday, one newspaper praised the 'Soudanese Bandsman', while others celebrated 'A "pets" coming of age'.[32] In this sense, Durham existed within the tradition of Black musicians, singers and dancers performing for white people in authority, a tradition dating back to the twelfth century and reaching a notable apex in the sixteenth.[33]

In the nineteenth century, regimental bands were seen as crucial for uplifting flagging imperial spirits and, by the 1890s, a number of Egyptians and Sudanese were recruited into the British Army to play for colonial regiments. As academic Kevin Le Gendre argues, these 'native' musicians produced sounds that were part of the Empire; these Black musicians, like those who worked in other musical genres and contexts, were an indivisible part of Britain's cultural landscape.[34]

* * *

As we move into Part Four, we leave the corridors of monarchical, missionary and military power and enter that of Victorian entertainment, culture and the visual arts, beginning with Samuel Coleridge-Taylor. He was a musician whose intentions were very different to those of military bandsman James Durham, a composer who, through his work, reacted against the age of imperialism by merging classical music with the sounds of the African diaspora.

Part Four

The Arts

11

Sounds from the Diaspora: Samuel Coleridge-Taylor
(1875–1912)

Despite the lyrical ambition of his given name, Samuel Coleridge-Taylor (he didn't adopt the hyphenation until his teenage years) had a tough and in many ways unromantic start in life. Born to an unmarried mother in August 1875, he was raised in Croydon on the southern outskirts of London, a relatively poor area described by Dickens as 'the dingiest collection of shabby buildings ever squeezed together'.[1] At school, he was given the name 'coaley', and racism would be a constant threat throughout his life.[2] Yet there was something of the respectable working class about his early years raised in a nurturing, musical household. 'My first teacher in music was my maternal grandfather, Mr. Benjamin Holman, who gave me lessons on the violin when I was quite a child,' Coleridge-Taylor later explained to the *Musical Times*.[3]

At a young age he became a violin pupil of the music teacher Joseph Beckwith, who first saw the six-year-old Coleridge-Taylor playing with a bunch of marbles in one hand while holding a violin in the other. Beckwith recalled:

> I was so struck with his appearance – a well-dressed, curly-headed, little dark boy – that I invited him into the house and placed a copy of some simple violin duets before

him, some of which he read perfectly in time and tune. His grandfather had been giving him lessons. I was so taken with the boy that I have him lessons on the violin and in music generally.[4]

Reflecting on his early years, in 1908 Coleridge-Taylor wrote: 'It has been stated again and again that I was born in the West Indies. This is not the case. I was born in London [...] My father was an African medical man, my mother English, and my whole surroundings and education, I need hardly add, have been English also.'[5]

The father of this Black British composer, Dr Daniel Peter Hughes Taylor, had studied medicine in London but returned to Sierra Leone unaware that his lover, Alice Hare Martin, was pregnant with his son. And although Dr Taylor wasn't a physical presence in Coleridge-Taylor's life, he was not an unknown figure. 'My father interested himself in the instrument named colangee, known on the West coast of Africa', a paternal and musical link to the continent which Coleridge-Taylor would embrace.[6]

Aged ten, he sang in the choir at St George's Presbyterian Church, Croydon. Already known locally for his musical abilities, in 1890 he won a scholarship for the violin at the Royal College of Music (RCM), a relatively new institution that had been established in 1883 and was already boasting Amanda Aldridge, daughter of Ira Aldridge, as one of its alumni. A local paper reported, 'A plucky, persevering, and painstaking young Croydon musician [...] has just met the welcome reward of his labours'.[7]

At the RCM, Coleridge-Taylor met his wife-to-be Jessie, a fellow student and distant relative of the composer Thomas Attwood Walmisley, and 'although he found himself among a crowd of clever young musicians from all parts of the country', recalled his benefactor Colonel Herbert A. Walters, 'he soon attracted attention, and in 1893 succeeded in winning an open scholarship for composition'.[8] Under the tutelage of Sir Charles Villiers, Coleridge-Taylor won awards for composition in 1895 and again in 1896. Five of his anthems were published, in a sign of his rising stardom.

During his time at the RCM, he met the African American poet and novelist Paul Laurence Dunbar and they subsequently embarked upon several collaborations. The *Musical Times* reported on one concert, which included recitations by Dunbar and music by Coleridge-Taylor, waxing lyrical that the young composer 'of partly African descent [...] produced work after work showing remarkable originality in almost every bar'. The article went on, 'Mr. Taylor, while still a student, reflects neither his teacher's nor anybody else's music, such a case being, perhaps, without precedent in the history of our art.'[9]

The principal of the RCM, Sir Hubert Parry, reflected that, despite Coleridge-Taylor's 'strikingly unoccidental' appearance and a 'racial combination [which] could not leave people quite indifferent', he was also 'accepted on terms of full equality, and soon won the affection of every one with whom he came into contact' (a statement which undervalues the racism Coleridge-Taylor received, especially when he first entered the prestigious institution).[10]

The RCM, which holds a number of papers on Coleridge-Taylor, includes a report from his piano tutor, praising 'one of my cleverest pupils'.[11] In his last report, written in 1897, Sir Parry scribbled, 'We shall be very sorry to lose Mr Coleridge-Taylor. His career at the College has been honourable and distinguished in a high degree.'[12]

Coleridge-Taylor became a teacher at the Croydon Conservatoire of Music while continuing with his own compositions. His 'Ballade in A Minor', performed in Gloucester in September 1898, established him as a serious orchestral composer. *The Times* wrote, 'The chief honours of the evening fell to a new composer

– Mr. S. Coleridge-Taylor', praising his 'strong instinct for beauty of tone-colouring and for characteristic turns of melody'.[13] The composer Edward Elgar was impressed with Coleridge-Taylor too.

But it was on Friday, 11 November 1898, that the young composer rocked the classical world with his composition 'Hiawatha's Wedding Feast'. The music was set to Henry Wadsworth Longfellow's famous poem 'The Song of Hiawatha' (1855). 'The writing of the music of the cantata,' Coleridge-Taylor later recalled, 'came to me quite naturally, and I did not feel handicapped by the supposed monotony of the poem.' On the night in question, as music-lovers eagerly assembled to hear the first performance at the RCM's Concert Hall, Coleridge-Taylor later remembered:

> Sir Arthur Sullivan was present at the performance. He was then in a very poor state of health, and had previously said to me 'I am always an ill man, but if I have to be carried I shall come to the concert,' and he did. The students sang and played the work splendidly, and Sir Charles Stanford, to whom I owe so much, took great pains in securing a good performance.[14]

'Hiawatha's Wedding Feast' made the young composer world famous. Sir Parry wrote that it 'was one of the most remarkable events in modern English musical history'.[15] The music went global and was played as far away as Constantinople. A trilogy followed, with compositions 'The Death of Minnehaha' and 'The Departure of Minnehaha'. The entire work was performed by the Royal Choral Society at the Royal Albert Hall in March 1900.

The *Musical Times* began comparing Coleridge-Taylor to the greats: 'Like Sir Arthur Sullivan, Mr. Taylor's first published composition is an anthem, a melodious and very vocal setting.' Like Schubert, 'he transmits his thoughts to paper straight away with as much, and probably more ease than most people write an ordinary letter'. They concluded, 'His quick movements are full of tremendous vigour, strange rhythms, and a wild untrammelled gaiety suggestive of neither European nor Oriental influence.'[16]

'Hiawatha's Wedding Feast' premiered a week or so after the climax of territorial disputes between France and Britain in Eastern Africa. The fighting in the region that had begun in the early 1880s, costing the life of General Gordon at Khartoum and sweeping up the young Sudanese orphan James Francies Durham, had been running for eighteen years and had mutated into a bruising conflict between two imperial superpowers. France wanted to extend its dominions across Central Africa and the Sudan, Britain wanted to link Uganda and Egypt via a railway line from the Cape of Good Hope to Cairo. Sir Herbert Kitchener had, finally, defeated the Mahdists on 2 September 1898, and on 19 September, his troops confronted French forces at Fashoda in Sudan, forcing them to withdraw in an important British victory. Suddenly, Britain's imperial march appeared once again unstoppable.

Edward Elgar captured this renewed imperial mood. His 'The Dream of Gerontius, Op. 38' was composed while the British fought the Sudanese, and it dealt with the glories of military conquest. The work was based on a poem of the same name and Elgar owned a copy of that poem with extensive marginal notes scribbled by none other than General Gordon. In other words, Elgar's 'The Dream of Gerontius' served as a musical military eulogy.[17] Elsewhere, jingoistic tunes blared out from music halls – 'By Jingo', 'War Songs of the Day', 'Soldiers of the Queen', which roused and reflected a patriotic fervour – but Coleridge-Taylor's *Hiawatha* trilogy was a countervailing force.[18] He drew a connection between the traumatic, oppressive experiences of Native Americans and African Americans by setting the main theme of *Hiawatha*'s overture to the spiritual 'Nobody

Knows the Trouble I've Seen'.[19] And he elevated Longfellow's epic poem, which recounted the adventures of an Ojibwe warrior named Hiawatha and the tragedy of his love for Minnehaha, a Dakota woman.

Coleridge-Taylor saw himself in Longfellow's Hiawatha, who searched for the father who abandoned his mother, and perceived his own relationship with his white fiancée Jessie through the prism of Hiawatha's relationship with Minnehaha, who came from a different tribe. In the poem, they marry for love and to ensure peace between their peoples, and on the morning of Coleridge-Taylor's own wedding, he sent a telegram to Jessie which paraphrased Longfellow's poem, 'You shall enter in my wigwam for the heart's right hand I gave you'. He signed off as 'Hiawatha'.[20] Later that day, 30 December 1899, Coleridge-Taylor married Jessie. Soon they had their first child, aptly named Hiawatha.

In Jessie's memoirs, she recalled how her family were 'shocked at the idea of a mixed marriage' and were firmly opposed on the grounds of 'colour-prejudice' which, by the late nineteenth century, was reaching an apogee in Britain. Jessie remembered the measures her family undertook to separate the couple and the 'vile suggestions [that] were made to me, and horrid threats hurled right and left'.[21] She and Coleridge-Taylor had already faced an avalanche of racial abuse on the streets and, in a revealing comment, she wrote about 'the *shrinking fear* he used to suffer when obliged to mix with those who were not completely in sympathy with him [our italics]'.[22] To receive similar hostility from the family of his fiancée must have been devastating, if predictable.

Jessie's family were firmly middle class. Her stockbroker father, Walter Walmisley, was a conservative Church of England attendee who sent his children to private school and paid for Jessie's tuition at the RCM. Both he and his wife Emma, plus his son-in-law and three of Jessie's sisters, were against the marriage. When Coleridge-Taylor asked Walter for permission to marry his daughter, the composer was thrown out of the house. But Jessie's vicar approved and eventually her mother and father begrudgingly accepted. Walter even witnessed the marriage certificate and eventually grew fond of his son-in-law.[23]

Coleridge-Taylor continued to face racial abuse and ignorance, however. Jessie recalled one interaction in their family home:

> We were aghast at one of our visitors – a Canon of the Church of England – who joined us at tea unexpectedly and, it would seem, out of curiosity, for leaning forward across the table and gazing at Coleridge he remarked, 'It really is surprising; you eat like we do, dress like we do and talk as we do.'[24]

Coleridge-Taylor was too flabbergasted or pained to respond. But even his wife was not immune from racial anxiety. At the birth of their son, Hiawatha, she reflected:

> You will realize how I had been tormented about the results of mixed marriages when I tell you that the first question I asked Dr. Collard was, 'is it black, white, red, or yellow?' After recovering from the surprise I gave him he replied, 'Good gracious, he's none of these – a beautiful boy.'[25]

In an increasingly hostile environment, Coleridge-Taylor embraced his Black identity. In March 1897, he published a poem entitled 'Liberian Patriotic Hymn', which celebrated the half-century of independence of Liberia: 'Beloved Liberians! Now from Bondage free / May "God our Strength" your Motto and your hope for ever be!'[26]

His musical compositions demonstrated his commitment to African, Caribbean and American melodies. 'Symphonic

Variations on an African Air' (1906) was based on the theme of an African American spiritual, and 'The Bamboula' (1911) was based on an African dance melody. And in *Twenty-four Negro Melodies* (1905), Coleridge-Taylor sought to preserve 'the beautiful folk-music of my race', as he wrote in the foreword, 'What Brahms has done for the Hungarian folk-music, Dvořák for the Bohemian, and Grieg for the Norwegian, I have tried to do for the Negro Melodies.'[27] The melodies were arranged into geographical regions – South-east Africa, South Africa, West Africa, West Indies and America – and included spirituals such as 'Wade in the Water'. There was one West African song entitled 'Oloba', 'kindly supplied by Mrs Victoria Randall', the daughter of Sarah Forbes Davies née Bonetta.[28]

Coleridge-Taylor also referred to his friend Frederick Loudin, leader of the Fisk Jubilee Singers, from whom 'I first learned to appreciate the beautiful folk music of my race'. The preface for *Twenty-four Negro Melodies*, which was written by

Samuel Coleridge-Taylor, *c.* 1900

African American leader and educator Booker T. Washington, praised 'the most cultivated musician of his race, a man of the highest aesthetic ideals', who 'should seek to give permanence to the folk-songs of his people by giving them a new interpretation and an added dignity'.[29] This carried additional weight because, at the time, white minds associated Black music with ragtime and 'c**n' songs but, unlike Ira Aldridge or Henry 'Box' Brown, Coleridge-Taylor did not succumb to the popularity of minstrel sounds. Instead, and against the additional imperial background noise, Coleridge-Taylor offered the world an alternative in Black diaspora music.

Despite the success of *Hiawatha*, Coleridge-Taylor faced financial pressures. The copyright of his world-famous composition was sold for only £25 15s, and although the two sequels generated £250 – twice his annual income at the time of his death – without royalties (which was very common for composers at the time), and with a young family to support, he needed to generate a dizzying quantity and breadth of work to pay the bills.[30] He produced music for the theatre, choral compositions and pieces for strings and piano. He was Professor of Composition at Trinity College of Music and then at the Guildhall School of Music. He judged numerous competitions around the country. He conducted the Croydon Symphony Orchestra, the Handel Society, the Rochester Choral Society and other provincial orchestras, too.

In 1906, he founded the String-Players Club and was heavily involved with the Central Croydon Choral Society, acting as their vice president for a number of years.[31] In 1904, 1906 and 1910 he visited the United States at the invitation of the Coleridge-Taylor Choral Society of Washington, established by Black choral singers in 1901. Coleridge-Taylor later recalled, 'It is about five years since I paid my first visit to the States, when, it may be remembered, I conducted a series of concerts, and, if I may say so without immodesty, was very successful.'[32]

Indeed, on that first trip, he was received at the White House and performed his first concert in Washington to a crowd of 2,700. 'The fact that I was English, and not American, seemed to do away with the race prejudice that does undoubtedly exist, and I was welcomed everywhere and received by the President', he wrote.[33] On his 1910 tour, Coleridge-Taylor was conducting all-white orchestras. During his trips, he was widely praised and received numerous gifts, including a bag of a Native American design and a silver cup inscribed with the words, 'It is well for us, O brother, that you came so far to see us'.[34]

* * *

Tragically, just two years after that triumphant US tour, Coleridge-Taylor died prematurely on 1 September 1912, of complications from pneumonia – the same illness that had killed military bandsman James Francies Durham. Perhaps the strain of making ends meet and enduring racial prejudice over many years had taken a toll on his health.

His funeral in West Croydon was attended by the Mayoress of Croydon, the Consul for Liberia and Sierra Leone, the editor of *Sierra Leone Weekly*, the principal of the Guildhall School of Music and many others. West African mourners brought a wreath in the form of a map of the continent. The flowers were all white bar a red patch to mark Sierra Leone and an inscription which read, 'From the sons and daughters of West Africa resident in London'.[35]

A memorial concert raised £1,440 for the family, while his son Hiawatha and his daughter Gwendolen (later Avril) both received bursaries from the Guildhall School of Music, and his widow Jessie received a £100 pension from the Civil List and over fifty messages of condolence. The newspapers were filled with eulogies – 'Death of Famous Composer', 'A Brilliant Career', 'Croydon's World-Famous Composer' – and obituaries reflecting on the 'exotic raciality' he brought into English music, the 'African rhythms or folk-music pure and simple' and the 'racial characteristics' of his sounds.[36] 'I am a great believer in my race,' Coleridge-Taylor had once exclaimed, and his musical compositions testified to this fact.[37]

Among the hundreds of obituaries was a moving appreciation by the author Alfred Noyes, who knew Coleridge-Taylor well. Noyes wrote that great numbers of people would consider the death of the composer a personal loss. He recalled how Coleridge-Taylor was a great conversationalist, a great listener with a keen sense of humour, and a contented man who once said, 'Even without any moderate success I think I should have been one of those rare beings – a happy man'.[38]

He loved his home life, his music, the occasional cigarette and copious amounts of tea. He was modest, kind and gifted with an unassailable energy which he channelled into his work. He was devoted to his wife and children, who had successful musical careers themselves, and years later, his daughter Avril recalled the walks she would take with her father, hand in hand, 'through the fields and country lanes, and he would sing or hum some of the music he was writing. What fun we had!'[39]

He was loved by his family, celebrated in Britain and adored in America too. Noyes concluded his heartful obituary with these faithful words, 'I feel quite sure that as times goes on, it will be recognized more and more closely that the place of Coleridge-Taylor is among the musicians whose work will endure while music endures'.[40]

* * *

Coleridge-Taylor's work continued to be played and remained popular into the 1920s and 1930s. From 1924 to 1939, the Royal Albert Hall held an annual *Hiawatha* season. Members of the royal family, and other distinguished guests, dressed in Native

American attire to see a spectacle which included 200 dancers, a tepee, a snowstorm, a waterfall and a Mohawk medicine man. During that time, 'The Death of Hiawatha' remained one of the most performed choral pieces in Britain, on a par with Handel's 'Messiah' and Mendelssohn's 'Elijah'.[41]

At around the same time, at London's Savoy Theatre, another concert artist, Paul Robeson, was acting in 'a tragedy of racial conflict', as he described Shakespeare's *Othello*. 'Killing two birds with one stone', he added, 'I'm acting and I'm talking for the negroes in the way only Shakespeare can.'[42]

While Coleridge-Taylor merged classical music with the sounds of the African diaspora, Robeson used the canonical words of Shakespeare to express his real-world experiences of racism. Amid predictable racist sneers, the public nonetheless praised Robeson's performance as Othello, mistakenly proclaiming him to be the first Black man to play the part.[43]

But another African American actor had trod the London boards in the role of Othello some sixty-five years earlier. Like Robeson, and indeed like Coleridge-Taylor, Ira Aldridge was forced to confront vicious racism, but he managed, nonetheless, to showcase his talent and stake his claim both on the stage and on the Victorian cultural landscape.

12

'African Roscius': Ira Aldridge
(1807–67)

July 1858, the Lyceum Theatre, West End, London – the house was packed with the great and good, sporting the latest fashions. There were nobles and aristocrats; the author Sir Edward Bulwer Lytton and the formerly enslaved abolitionist lecturer William Wells Brown were there (and this wasn't even the opening night). The air crackled with electricity. An expectant audience awaited 'the celebrated and only AFRICAN TRAGEDIAN, IRA ALDRIDGE', the press proclaimed, 'who has received the immediate patronage of the Emperor, Empress, and Ex-Emperor of Austria, the King and Queen of Prussia, and the elite of the Sovereign Princes of Germany'.[1] As the excitement filled the auditorium, the heavy green curtain rose on a performance of *Othello*.

Act I, Scene I: an argument between Roderigo and Iago. The former mortified by Desdemona's marriage to Othello, Iago disgusted by the 'Beast with two backs'.

Act I Scene II: Othello enters. The audience cheer the actor playing the Moor, Ira Aldridge. Wells Brown recalled, 'Mr. Aldridge is of the middle size, and appeared to be about three quarters African; has a pleasant countenance, frame well knit, and seemed to me the best Othello that I had ever seen.'

When Iago began to whisper poison, 'the Moor's eyes flashed fire'. Later, Othello 'looked the very demon of despair'. When Othello seized Iago by the throat and declared, 'Villain!', 'the audience, with one impulse, rose to their feet amid the wildest enthusiasm'.

At the conclusion of Act III, with two more to go, 'Othello was called before the curtain, and received the applause of the delighted multitude'.[2]

The production was a triumph. Reporters from the *Morning Chronicle* were amazed to witness 'a man of fine commanding form, carrying himself with grace and dignity, every motion and action betraying, in the words of Shakespeare himself, the "well graced actor."'[3] Bulwer Lytton was similarly impressed. Even the *Athenaeum*, which had long reviled the actor, begrudgingly admitted Aldridge's skill and originality.

The next evening, Wells Brown went to see Aldridge performing as Hamlet, 'as perfect in that as he had been in Othello', and later wrote about the thespian in *The Black Man, His Antecedents, His Genius, and His Achievements* (1863).

* * *

In a career spanning more than forty years, Aldridge performed across Europe, Russia and the Austro-Hungarian Empire, winning awards, honours and medals. 'Nature has stamped this man as an actor of the first order,' an early British review declared, 'with a strong caste of face of the African mould; his action is most graceful and becoming; his pronunciation clear and distinct, with a deep and mellow tone of voice.'[4]

Yet not all the reviews were complimentary. Even that seemingly positive review carried the implicit assumption that Black people had erratic elocution – a stereotype peddled via blackface minstrelsy on the very stages Aldridge trod upon. Throughout his career Aldridge was hounded by elements of the

IRA ALDRIDGE AS "OTHELLO."

Ira Aldridge as Othello, 1887

British press and was continually forced to battle for equality – on and offstage – forever confronting the racist depictions of African Americans in the form of the minstrel.[5]

Many white commentators did not want to see a Black Shakespearean actor on the West End stage. It was a threat to white supremacy and high culture, which made Aldridge's reception at the Lyceum in July 1858 all the more impressive.

* * *

Ira Aldridge was born in New York on 24 July 1807. He attended New York's African Free School No. 2, which offered free formal education for young African Americans, before getting his first taste of acting at William Brown's African Theatre, commonly described as the first Black theatre in America. Black actors performed Shakespeare, pantomime and farce, jealous whites instigated riots and the young Aldridge soon set his sights on Britain as a less-fraught place to live and work.[6]

There had been a few Black actors in Britain before Aldridge. In the 1770s, a Black actress, whom we know very little about, appeared in *The Beggar's Opera* and *Romeo and Juliet* (as Juliet).[7] The formerly enslaved Julius Soubise may have acted as Othello in the late eighteenth century, and he was certainly known as an amateur violinist and singer who was taught oration by the actor and producer David Garrick. Garrick also hired Ignatius Sancho, who was born on a slave ship in 1729 and harboured acting ambitions and briefly worked for Garrick's theatrical company, although it is not clear if Sancho acted onstage.[8]

In the early nineteenth century, Billy Waters, a former soldier in the American War of Independence, appeared on theatre stages in London and Edinburgh, and in 1822 he was joined by the Black entertainer and dancer, African Sal. It is even possible that James Hewlett, from New York's African Grove Theatre, acted in England around 1824, the year Aldridge emigrated to England.[9]

In 1825, Aldridge performed as the lead character in *The Revolt of Surinam; or, A Slave's Revenge*, an adaptation of Thomas Southerne's play, itself based on Aphra Behn's earlier novel of the same name, *Oroonoko* (1695), in which the heroic African prince is tricked into slavery. The notice in *The Times* was vitriolic. In a racist rant, the reviewer made comparisons to London's Surrey Theatre, where 'a man plays a monkey in the most unnatural manner' and recalled the performance of 'a genuine n****r', who performed in a minstrel show. The review also focused on Aldridge's physical appearance, 'His figure is unlucky for the stage [...] owing to the shape of his lips, it is utterly impossible for him to pronounce English'. *The Times* suggested Aldridge should be replaced by a 'blackamoor', who 'sweeps the crossings at the end of the Fleet-market' – that is, the likes of Edward Albert, whom we met in Chapter 6.[10]

Alongside the racial bile, there was a strong cultural bias too. Aldridge was appearing in a working-class non-patented theatre – the Royal Coburg in Waterloo (now the Old Vic) – antithetical to the high-minded patented theatres that were licensed to perform 'legitimate' or 'spoken' drama. Non-patent theatres like the Coburg featured melodramas and burlesques. Their dramas had short scenes interspersed with musical accomplishments. They were immensely popular but not well regarded by the culturally snooty.

For a few months, Aldridge continued at the Coburg before heading for the provinces. He developed his craft as he performed across Brighton, Hull, Manchester, Newcastle, Liverpool and Edinburgh, appearing in abolitionist melodramas and musical farces and depicting around sixteen different roles in the course of a week and a half.[11]

From the mid-1820s, he probably travelled with his wife, Margaret Gill, whom he met shortly after his run at the Coburg. They married on 27 November 1825 and, as with the fictional union of Othello and Desdemona, Aldridge's marriage to Gill, a white woman, fanned the racist flames and led to periods of unemployment. Yet, the couple managed to survive, and in April 1833 Aldridge was back in London, this time playing Othello at the Covent Garden Theatre – a highly esteemed and, importantly, patented theatre. This was the West End debut for the 'African Roscius', a moniker that alluded to the eminent Roman actor born into slavery.[12]

Reporters from the *Standard* were keen 'to witness the performance of that singularly-gifted actor, the African Roscius', mistakenly describing him as 'the first performer of colour that ever appeared on the boards of any theatre in Britain'. Aldridge 'succeeded in deeply affecting the feelings of his audience', they observed, igniting 'an intense stillness, almost approaching awe'.[13]

But despite this positive review, many others among the London press demonstrated outright hostility towards a Black man performing Shakespeare in the refined setting of the Covent Garden Theatre. One review, published before Aldridge even opened, declared with vicious venom:

> [...] a further act of insolence is to be perpetuated, by the introduction to the boards of Covent Garden theatre, of that miserable n****r, whom we found in the provinces imposing on the public by the name of African Roscius. This wretched upstart is about to defile the stage, by a foul butchery of Shakespeare, and Othello is actually the part chosen for the sacrilege. [...] unless this notice causes the immediate withdrawal of his name from the bills, we must again inflict on him such chastisement as must drive him from the stage he has dishonoured, and force him to find in the capacity of footman or street-sweeper, that level for which his colour appears to have rendered him peculiarly qualified.[14]

It was claimed that admirers of the actress who played Desdemona 'were envious of the Moor's familiarity with her fair face, and ridiculed his privilege' and the white actors who performed alongside Aldridge did not like playing minor roles to his major role.[15] Furthermore, as Aldridge absorbed these resentments among the cast and attacks from the press, Parliament was debating the Slavery Abolition Act in the shadow of the Baptist War, an eleven-day revolt led by enslaved Jamaicans.

The London Society of West India Merchants and Planters ferociously peddled pro-slavery arguments and were in financial cahoots with a number of leading newspapers, which partly accounted for the campaign of hate against Aldridge. For the champions of slavery, a Black man playing such a sophisticated role completely undermined their claims of Black inferiority. One paper wrote that Aldridge 'practically contradicts the arguments of the advocates of slavery'.[16]

So, effectively hounded out of London, Aldridge gave only two performances at the Covent Garden Theatre (a flu epidemic forced the closure of many theatres), before returning to the provinces, and his next major London engagement was not for another fifteen years.

* * *

Returning to the provinces was not easy. Aldridge travelled incessantly for most of the year, performing an array of roles at venues large and small in villages, towns and cities. At any given theatre it was common for two plays to be performed each night, with the bill changing every day, so Aldridge needed a repertoire of ever-changing characters, which was difficult due to the conventionally limited number of Black roles. Aldridge, as such, got creative: he played serious tragic parts, offset with more comical characters such as the drunken servant Mungo from *The Padlock*, a comic two-part opera first performed in 1768. Aldridge played white characters such as Shylock, Richard III and Macbeth and, perhaps just as ingeniously, he developed his own character offstage, deliberately constructing a fictional biography as a defence mechanism against the racialised hatred he kept encountering.

In the anonymously published *Memoir and Theatrical Career of Ira Aldridge, the African Roscius* (1848 or 1849), the actor, who probably had an authorial role, claimed he was born into a royal family in Senegal. His 'forefathers were princes of the Foulah tribe', noted the memoir, which falsely claimed that a missionary had converted and 'civilised' his father, Daniel, who was taken to America for a 'Christian education'.

The story went that Daniel Aldridge trained as a Christian minister, married an African American and only returned to Senegal after the death of a rebellious chief who had previously killed his father. Soon after Daniel's return to Senegal, Ira Aldridge was born. But the country was then plunged into civil war, and it was another nine years before the Aldridge family fled back to America.[17]

This was a tall tale, a fiction, but one which elevated Ira Aldridge socially. As the son of an *African* prince, the story enhanced his exoticism, and as the son of a *Christian* African prince, it distinguished Aldridge from the 'heathens' of the continent. In short, Aldridge was able to present himself as exotic and 'Other', while also highborn, civilised and unthreatening. The memoir even claimed that his wife Margaret was the daughter of an MP, which was completely untrue, but the lie served to enhance the couple's social status and arguably erected a buffer to ward off racist attacks against their interracial marriage. The distinction between Aldridge's work onstage and his life offstage was eclipsed: both functioned as performance.

Aldridge continued to expand his repertoire by adapting plays as a vehicle for his acting. In 1847, he presented his own adaptation of *The Black Doctor*, a romantic melodrama in which the protagonist Fabian, the titular Black lead played by

Aldridge, gains his freedom from slavery by saving the lives of his white master's family, including the daughter Pauline Reynerie, with whom Fabian falls in love. Fabian declares, 'To it alone I breathe my fearful secret; that I, a mulatto, and late a slave, dare to love the daughter of a white man – the daughter of him who was my master! It is madness – madness!'[18]

It is significant that in the script Aldridge made Fabian a good-looking 'mulatto', which positioned the character within the convention of the 'swarthy' Romantic hero – a marginalised figure who displays integrity in the face of social opprobrium – and enabled Aldridge to sidestep the racial stereotypes of the 'mad Black man' or the 'unhinged mulatto'.[19] The Black doctor is presented as a noble man who assumes dignity in the context of his interracial marriage to Pauline. In his adaptation, Aldridge also created the Grimaud family, headed by Hannibal, a former soldier turned wine shop owner, who is able to countenance a Black man marrying into his family. Aldridge was perhaps making the suggestion that racial tolerance was more pronounced in the provinces and among the lower middle classes.[20]

In 1850, Aldridge adapted another play, Shakespeare's *Titus Andronicus*, with important variations from the original. The violence was consigned offstage, and Aaron the Moor was positively rewritten. In Shakespeare's original, Aaron's skin colour is linked to his villainy, which he himself celebrates, 'Let fools do good, and fair men call for grace, / Aaron will have his soul black like his face'. But in Aldridge's adaptation, Aaron becomes the hero, leaping into a river to save a child and demonstrating 'a noble and lofty character' which, the *Era* noted, 'Mr Aldridge delineated with judgement and great force of expression'.[21] Although there is no surviving manuscript, the following review from the *Sunday Times* gives a good insight into the heroism of Aldridge's Moor:

Aaron is made a model of valour and magnanimity [...] while Aaron is chained to a tree, from which he breaks by main strength, leaps into the river and saves his child. Saturninus, the tyrant of Rome, is the villain of the piece.[22]

* * *

In 1852, Aldridge undertook his first ever continental tour. He knew little of Europe or of its languages, but he travelled at various times thereafter, including to Stockholm and Constantinople, Hamburg and St Petersburg, and through France, Belgium, Holland, Germany, Switzerland and Hungary. He performed Shakespeare in English while his fellow actors recited their lines in their native languages.[23]

Despite the linguistic and racial barriers, Aldridge was able to connect with his audiences. He was awarded the Golden Order of Service by the Duke of Saxe-Meiningen, he became Chevalier Ira Aldridge, Knight of Saxony, and, in 1858, he was presented with a Russian tribute following his celebrated performances of Othello, Shylock and King Lear in St Petersburg.[24] The government of Haiti honoured him as 'the first man of colour in the theatre', and he was congratulated by the Jewish community in Zhitomir, Ukraine, for his sensitive and powerful portrayal of Shylock.[25]

By 1858, when he performed at the Lyceum Theatre, with its lofty proscenium, domed ceiling and grand Corinthian columns reaching to the gods, Aldridge had a continental reputation. On this, his return to the West End, he packed out the house. The *Morning Chronicle* wrote:

> We are free to confess that we went to see him rather out of curiosity than otherwise. We expected that he would act well for a black man, and that he would send us away simply pleased to think that negroes were capable of some little intelligence,

some faculty of mimicking what they see and hear with a certain degree of trust and propriety. Mr. Aldridge, however, showed that he was far more of an actor than a mere elocutionist, for he not only spoke the lines with perfect accuracy, but gave the true feeling of the sentiments which they expressed. A finer piece of elocution we never heard.[26]

The reference to Aldridge's elocution was a coded racist sentiment, yet the *Chronicle* concluded:

Mr Aldridge's acting rises almost to the sublime. The lingering looks of fondness, mingled with painful regrets, which he casts upon his sleeping wife, as he prepares to wipe out all trace of the shipwreck of their love, is the very apotheosis of murder. It becomes, with that calm motive, seeking only to efface an outrage upon virtue and pure love, a sacred deed, and it is more Othello that you pity than Desdemona.[27]

This was some feat indeed. Ever since the famous white actor Edmund Kean applied lighter make-up when performing the part, several decades earlier, audiences had become unaccustomed to the idea of an obviously Black Othello. In restating and reclaiming Othello's Blackness, Aldridge heightened the dramatic and racial tensions of the play at a time when racism was becoming pervasive. Indeed, the fact that some reviewers claimed to be surprised by Aldridge's perfect elocution suggests the insidious background influence of another phenomenon with which Aldridge had to contend, a form of entertainment that had infected the stage and further corrupted white perceptions: minstrelsy.

* * *

On 25 March 1824, the white comic Charles Mathews introduced his audience at the English Opera House to *A Trip to America*, a show supposedly based on observations made during his travels in the two years prior. The show featured a number of Black characters, including a minister who spoke in 'stump speech', a lazy and obese fugitive slave and a pretentious Black tragedian whom Mathews had apparently encountered at New York's African Grove Theatre (where Aldridge first performed). Mathews would burst onstage as Hamlet, muttering, 'To be, or not to be? That is the question; whether it is nobler in *de* mind to suffer, or tak' up arms against a sea of trouble, and by opossum end 'em'. He would then break out in a song, 'Opossum up a gum-tree'.[28] The public assumed that Mathews' Black Hamlet was a direct parody of Aldridge, and Mathews never corrected that impression – he even performed the role in the same theatres in which Aldridge appeared.[29] It was a nasty, racist pastiche that infected Aldridge's reception in the press.

More broadly, by directly mocking the association of Blackness with high culture, Mathews created an immensely popular character that would spawn other imitations. In 1829, for example, one character was doing the rounds described as 'A Negro. Loves acting and misquotes Shakespeare in the vein of Mathews.'[30] Only a year after Aldridge's short-lived 1833 Covent Garden run, there was a burlesque of Othello, who was described in the script as 'Moor of Venice, formerly an Independent N****r, from the Republic of Hayti [*sic*]', played by a white man who spoke in a bastardised African American dialect.[31]

Mathews had created what he called 'black fun', in what would prove to be a popular precursor to blackface acts, and he continued peddling these parts until his death in 1835.

Back in America, while enslaved people planned and executed revolts – in South Carolina (1822), Alabama (1827) and Virginia (1831), among other locations and dates – in which troops were called in and rebels executed, white producers created the minstrel show. Many of the creators were eccentric white performers from the northern states who had encountered the music and dance styles of African Americans and now turned their skewed impressions into popular entertainment.[32]

One of those manufacturers of 'mirth' was the American playwright and performer T. D. Rice, who seized on aspects of traditional Black music developed by enslaved people in the Southern states and added his own distorted language and exaggerated dance. He donned rags, blacked up his face and hands, and in so doing gave birth to a grotesque creation known as Jim Crow (the name, possibly already in existence as a Black folkloric character, also became a shorthand for America's racial caste system, which lasted from the promulgation of new segregation laws in 1877 to the mid-1960s).

A year after Mathews died, T. D. Rice introduced Jim Crow to Britain. Onstage, Jim Crow told jokes in a distorted imitation of African American vernacular English and performed so-called 'Negro ditties' to the accompaniment of the banjo, tambourine or fiddle. He danced in an eccentric style and acted the buffoon. His make-up was cartoonishly exaggerated: dark face, large red lips, wide eyes. He was joyous and stupid and lazy, and he proved to be a huge success.

T. D. Rice returned to Britain to perform his racist Jim Crow character between 1838 and 1840, and again between 1842 and 1843. He received rapturous applause and a proliferation of imitators, such as the onstage characters Jim Dandy and Zip Coon. The Virginia Minstrels – the first blackface American minstrel band to tour in Europe, in 1843 – signalled a growing trend for minstrelsy chorus acts in Britain. They were followed, in 1845, by the Ethiopian Serenaders – white musicians in blackface playing the violin, banjo, tambourine and bones – and in 1857 by the Christy Minstrels. Traditional ballads even began to take second place to minstrel songs in British popular culture.[33]

By as early as 1845, blackface minstrelsy was so ubiquitous that one commentator could complain that 'the Stage Negro has become a vulgar dancing brute, with a banjo in his hand [...] a wretch constantly jumping about'.[34] As the century progressed, minstrel shows evolved from small-scale entertainment into organised and lavish recreations lapped up by all the social classes.[35] A panoply of grotesque 'comical' Jim Crow-type characters was established, fixing a stereotype through which Blackness was increasingly seen and relegating genuine abolitionist sentiment in favour of the happy-go-lucky minstrel.[36] This was the context with which Aldridge had to contend.

* * *

Aldridge responded to minstrelsy in a variety of ways. Most surprisingly, perhaps, he incorporated minstrel acts into some of his own performances. He chose to act as the minstrel character, Massa Jeronymo Othello Thespis, a Black footman so enthralled by Shakespeare that he bursts forth in misquotations as he conducts his household duties. Aldridge went further, playing a character named Ginger Blue, who spoke in the so-called 'Negro dialect' and was described in playbills as 'an independent n****r, head waiter, always absent when wanted, yet mindful of his perquisites, remarkably familiar, bursting with fun and laughter'.[37]

Aldridge's other popular repertoires included ditties such as 'Jim Crow', 'Lucy Long', 'Coal Black Rose', 'Jim Along Josey' and 'Sich a Gittin Up Stairs':

On a Suskehanna raft I come down de bay,
And I danc'd and I frolick'd, and fiddled all de way,
Sich a getting up stairs I never did see,
Sich a getting up stairs I never did see![38]

'African Roscius': Ira Aldridge

Aldridge amused audiences with minstrel acts into the 1850s and beyond, winning fans as he appropriated popular racist culture for his own ends. But it's hard to do more than speculate as to why he performed minstrel acts rather than ignoring them altogether.

At one point, he declared to audiences that Charles Mathews' racist rendition of the Black Hamlet was 'ludicrous', and he fought against the onslaught of minstrelsy by developing dignified, heroic Black characters onstage.[39] When he did perform minstrel characters, they certainly had a level of humane subtlety that his rivals' caricatures did not, and he played a range of Black characters – Oroonoko, Gambia, Zanga, Hassan – who were infused with Enlightenment values and arguably reflected the idea that all human beings possessed the capacity for self-development. These characters demonstrated, to varying degrees, Black nobility, honour and Christian belief, which counterbalanced their fundamentally racialised nature.[40] As such, Aldridge both resisted the minstrel character and, paradoxically, contributed to the success and ubiquity of minstrelsy.

Perhaps, though, he was above all financially shrewd, knowing that these acts were wildly popular and lucrative. Perhaps, in the ultimate demonstration of versatility and resilience, he wanted to show himself as a gifted comedian as well as tragedian, who could outplay the white minstrel acts at their own game. Perhaps, then, he was engaging in a form of satirical reappropriation, playing off not only his white competitors and attackers, but also his audiences.[41]

There was a telling moment when, in 1851, Aldridge visited Shakespeare's birthplace on two occasions, a mere few days apart, and penned in the visitors' notebook at the Royal Shakespearean Theatre a quote from the dark-skinned Prince of Morocco: 'Mislike me not for my complexion, the shadowed livery of the burnished sun.'[42] In his choice of quotation from *The Merchant of Venice*, we can see an intimation of this surely painful cultural tussle that Aldridge was living through, as well as the expression of an ambition to be judged not on the colour of his skin but on the content of his performances. Above all, he simply wanted to act – and to be received as the actor that he was.

* * *

In 1865, following Margaret Gill's death, Aldridge married Swedish-born Amanda Pauline von Brandt. As with his first marriage, to guard against racist opprobrium he elevated her beginnings, claiming she was a baroness of noble birth, though in truth she came from a humble background.

Not long after their daughter, also named Amanda, was born, Aldridge planned to return to America, but before he could make that journey, he died from an apparent lung infection while touring in Poland. At a lavish funeral attended by the mayor of Łódź and the city councillors, Aldridge's body was 'interned in a *chapelle ardente*, covered with white and black cloth', wrote the *Era*, 'with tapers burning in the room', as thousands came to pay their respects:

> In conclusion, it may be observed that, although Shakespeare was not unknown even in the most remote parts visited by the lamented deceased, the latter certainly extended the reputation of that National Poet of English literature.[43]

This was a reputation that was continually attacked during Aldridge's career in Britain. In *Memoir and Theatrical Career of Ira Aldridge, the African Roscius*, the narrator notes:

> The disadvantage of colour, which excluded him from all chance of success in America, was not entirely overcome in England among a prejudiced, wanton, and unthinking few,

who could not let an opportunity pass for sneering at and ridiculing the 'presumptuous n****r'.[44]

That, in fact, was a conservative statement, yet Aldridge did manage to win over the majority of his audiences, and he certainly left an impressive legacy. He made theatrical history by performing his adaption of *Titus Andronicus*, which had not been staged in Britain for 128 years.[45] He predated African American artiste Paul Robeson's ecstatic reception in Russia by almost 100 years (and Aldridge's daughter Amanda gave elocution lessons to the young Robeson in 1930). Above all, he fought against racism to win renown as a talented actor. He challenged the prevalent belief in Black inferiority; he challenged the growing revulsion against Black people who, during his lifetime, were increasingly associated with slavery and ignominy; and he navigated the ubiquity of minstrelsy in the best way he could.[46]

Though he was by no means the first Black person to work in the British theatre, Aldridge was very much a trailblazer. A year after he died, a young African American actor by the name of George Gross was heralded as 'the only successor to the celebrated African Tragedian, Mr. Ira Aldridge'.[47]

Another celebrated successor was Samuel Morgan Smith, a former barber from Philadelphia, who went on to enjoy a sixteen-year acting career in Britain, appearing in over forty productions. Like Aldridge, Smith acted the parts of Othello, Shylock, Lear, Macbeth and Richard III, as well as continuing the tradition of performing in melodramas such as *Oroonoko*, *The Black Doctor*, *The Slave* and *The Revenge*. Smith, too, received a rough ride in the London press, but he was popular in the provinces and especially in Scotland and Ireland. He never achieved the same level of renown as his predecessor, but he did help open the door wider still for other Black Victorian actors, such as Gustavus Allenborough, George Dunbar and Paul Molyneaux.[48]

Black actors were not uncommon in Victorian Britain, therefore, and by the middle of the century a number of Black actors secured opportunities to perform, thanks to the enthusiasm for *Uncle Tom's Cabin*. Blackface minstrelsy provided another opportunity for Black performers, too.[49] And away from the theatre stage there were dancers, singers and musicians; Black performers in freak shows and ethnographic exhibitions; Black circus artists, Black lion tamers and, as we will see in the next chapter, one particularly impressive Black circus proprietor, Pablo Fanque, who was born into Victorian squalor and rose to become a respected member of the circus community, bringing the wonder of the circus to the people of Britain, and helping cement this artform as a central pillar of Victorian mass entertainment.

13

The Circus: Pablo Fanque
(1810–71)

His story began in the Dickensian world of St Andrew's Workhouse, Norwich: an institution described as 'dark and confined' and containing 700 inmates, among them an interracial couple named Mary and John Darby.[1] Their marriage, back in 1791, would have infuriated the author Philip Thicknesse, who lamented, 'In every country town, nay, in almost every village are to be seen a little race of mulattoes, mischievous as monkeys, and infinitely more dangerous'.[2] While John and Mary were incarcerated in St Andrew's workhouse, they had a daughter who was born and buried within its walls; then, on 30 March 1810, their son William Darby came healthily into the world.[3]

He was raised in the house of despair until, at some point between 1820 and 1831, he joined the circus. Some workhouse children were offered apprenticeships in 'respectable' trades, but the circus was not deemed one of them. Still, it was an escape for the teenage Darby, who was apprenticed to the 'strict disciplinarian' William Batty – a skilled equestrian and circus proprietor, who had 'indomitable energy and enterprise', noted the nineteenth-century chronicler, Thomas Frost.[4]

At the height of Batty's success in the late 1830s and early 1840s, he managed the ancestral and spiritual home of the circus, Astley's Amphitheatre in Lambeth, south London. This was named after the so-called father of the modern circus, Philip Astley, who united equestrian performances with acrobats, jugglers, clowns and rope dancers, giving rise to the modern circus.[5] As an apprentice to Batty, Darby's first task was to master acrobatics, which was painful, dangerous and laborious. As one acrobat shared with Henry Mayhew:

> When my father first trained me, it hurt my back awfully. He used to take my legs and stretch them, and work them around in their sockets, and put them up straight by my side. That is what they generally call being 'cricked'.[6]

Darby probably went through a similar routine, learning posturing, gymnastics and circus tricks before gearing up to equestrianism, the pinnacle of circus entertainment. There were three main equestrian acts: the *haute école* was a specialised form of dressage; 'trick riding' involved the equestrian performing acrobatic tricks on the back of a horse; and the trainer barking commands to a respondent horse was known as the 'liberty act'. William Darby mastered all three as he travelled with Batty's outfit around the country, following the rhythms of the English fairs.

Since before the Norman Conquest, the fairs roamed from village to village and town to town, bringing goods and entertainment to the public. The travelling folk were a diverse bunch, with jugglers and acrobats largely hailing from Italy and North Africa, rope dancers from the German states, and wild animal trainers from Eastern Europe. Without established roots, this assortment of social outcasts – which included a sizable Jewish and Romani contingent – were viewed with suspicion by townsfolk and the authorities, yet the crowds still flocked to see them.

In this lively, transitory environment, Darby began impressing audiences from the early 1830s. Billed as 'The American

Voltigeur and Flying Mercury', on a corde volante, a rope attached at two points from the ceiling, he mesmerised audiences with his dangerous stunts, which had left many other performers paralysed after a slip.[7] His youth, strength and natural ability won him acclaim and, to develop an exotic onstage persona, he began adopting the name Pablo Fanque:

> Pablo Fanque, the man of colour, the loftiest jumper in England, who will take a number of surprising leaps without the assistance of any elastic apparatus – first, over a garter 12ft high – second, through a hoop, 2ft 6in, in diameter – third, through cross hoops – fourth, through a balloon 2ft 9in diameter – fifth through two balloons – sixth, though a military drum 4ft 6in long – seventh, will take a surprising leap over 10 horses – eighth, will leap through a hoop of real steel daggers – and lastly an unparalleled leap over A POSTCHAISE [covered horsedrawn carriage], LENGTHWAYS![8]

In 1836, Pablo Fanque toured with Batty's circus in Nottingham, joining a company which included two zebras, an elephant, a wild ass, a stud of horses and two principal equestrians. There was also the head vaulter and the 'chief clown, with capacities for every branch of the profession, being an admirable vaulter and acrobat, and a good rider', noted Frost, who described Fanque as 'a negro rope-dancer'.[9]

The company went on to Birmingham, Newcastle, Edinburgh and Manchester, and in May 1839, Fanque made his first appearance at Astley's Amphitheatre. 'In the course of the evening Pablo Fanque, The Flying Indian, will execute his wonderful exercises on the Slack Rope', declared the press.[10]

Just two years later, the ethnically malleable Fanque – variously dubbed the 'negro', 'Flying Indian', 'man of colour' – was venturing into the circus world alone.

* * *

'It was my last night at the circus,' wrote the clown, William Frederick Wallett, 'and also that of Pablo, who left Batty to start an establishment of his own.'[11] The year was 1841. Fanque was thirty-one years old.

The chronicler Thomas Frost warned that 'young and struggling beginners had a hard battle to fight', and the stakes were high for Fanque.[12] He was a Black itinerant performer with a white partner, and they had a young son to support. But Fanque bristled with energy and optimism, and by 1842 he was presenting an exciting circus to the people of Preston. He had booked a magnificent amphitheatre 'fitted up with every attention to comfort', boasted his promotional poster.[13] For an entrance fee ranging from three pence to two shillings, his circus was open to all social classes who flocked to see his horsemanship, acrobatics, clowning and pantomime.

Fanque vied for the public's attention by presenting his circus as a respectable family affair. He also gave liberally to charity and held benefit performances for charitable causes. In these ways, he gave an air of respectability to his entertainment, not only distancing his circus from the licentious travelling fairs but helping to elevate the circus in the public's mind more generally.

His charitable work also reflected his character. He was known to be kind, optimistic, strong-willed and daring. What struck people was 'his cheerfulness and vivacity, his strong commonsense notions about business, and his buoyant anticipations of the future', the press declared.[14] One member of the public wrote, 'Ministers of religion, of all denominations, in other towns, have attended Mr Pablo Fanque's circus' and were satisfied because the proprietor was known for 'probity and respectability'.[15]

Stoking his burgeoning reputation, Fanque appealed to locals with an impressive band of musicians and innocent publicity stunts. In March 1846, for example, he triumphantly rode

Pablo Fanque, *c.* 1860

into Bolton with twelve horses in hand. He plastered towns with beautifully designed posters and engaged high-calibre performers such as the leading acrobat William Kite, the renowned equestrian John Henderson, and William Wallett, the 'Shakespearian Jester'.

The public loved Fanque's horse, Xanthus, and his son Lionel won applause too. But Fanque always stole the show. 'The extraordinary Jumping of Mons[ieur] Pablo Fanque, through hoops covered with paper and encircled with knives, over high garters, and over nine horses was deservedly applauded', the *Liverpool Mercury* proclaimed.[16]

Thomas Dawson Walker, known by the moniker Whimsical Walker, joined Fanque's circus when he was around eight years old. As an apprentice, Walker was in awe of his teacher, 'A thorough master of his profession, and I have to thank him for what I subsequently became – without vanity may I say it? – the greatest celebrity in my particular line in the circus business.'[17] Walker was not being immodest: by the time he published his autobiography in 1922, he was a celebrity clown in Britain and America who had performed before Queen Victoria.

Pablo Fanque first made Walker into a clown because, as Walker admitted, 'my face was not so beautiful', and Fanque taught him 'to ride, to tumble, to perform on the trapeze, to vault over horses, and indeed all the intricacies belonging to circus life'. He was 'certainly one of the best of masters'.[18]

Fanque worked his apprentices hard. At 6 a.m. they were instructed to get up, feed and groom the horses and then, at 8 a.m., eat breakfast for thirty minutes before practising acrobatics. 'Pablo Fanque did his duty towards us very conscientiously and sent us to church on Sunday mornings', recalled Whimsical Walker.[19]

By the middle of the century, Fanque's circus had burgeoned to thirty horses. He could easily fill a 3,000-seat amphitheatre and he had monopolised the northern market too. He was at the top of his game. But the 'showman's life, my friends, is not all glory', wrote the circus proprietor George Sanger, 'beneath the glitter and the tinsel is many a heartache. The open road is often strewn with thorns.'[20]

And on 19 March 1848, just before Fanque's son was about to perform to a packed audience in Leeds, the amphitheatre's pit collapsed. Timber frames went flying, people screamed, and the gas lights went out. Fanque rushed to the lobby and frantically sifted through the debris, managing to locate his partner Susannah Marlow, whose 'head hung down on her shoulder, and I never observed her breathe at all', he later recalled.[21] She was buried the following week.

'The show must go on', runs the old adage, and no sooner had Marlow been buried, than Fanque was on the move again, heading to Rotherham, Sheffield and the Knott Mill Fair in Manchester. Three months later, he remarried.

* * *

Fanque's family life is opaque. It is often claimed that in 1834 he married Susannah Marlow, the daughter of a button maker from Birmingham, and a year later their first son Lionel was born. But the marriage to Susannah might not have been legal, and there is little official evidence of it.

Lionel might not have been Fanque's first son either. Evidence suggests that he possibly fathered another child when he was eighteen years old. This boy, possibly William Darby Banham, was apprenticed to Pablo's circus, although he frequently fled for reasons unknown, which was also true for Lionel who, shortly after his mother's death, left Fanque's circus to make his own way in the world, at the age of only twelve.

By this time, Fanque had married Elizabeth Corker, an equestrian performer from Sheffield, and together they had two sons, George and Ted, and a daughter named Caroline. She died a year after her birth and was buried in the grave of Fanque's first wife, Susannah. After losing his daughter, Fanque appeared to leave his second wife Elizabeth, moving into the house of one Sarah Smith and fathering an illegitimate child, before reuniting with Elizabeth around 1861 or 1862.[22]

Despite the family tragedies and domestic complications, in the circus arena Fanque continued to shine. In the 1850s, he operated a circus in Liverpool while running a second company in Sheffield. In early 1851 he headed to Ireland with 'undoubtably the largest and most talented Company in Europe', claimed the press.[23] Born into the worst of poverty, he had emerged as a leading circus performer and proprietor; so much so that a contemporary could assert:

> In the great brotherhood of the equestrian world there is no colour line, for, although Pablo Fanque was of African extraction, he speedily made his way to the top of his profession. The camaraderie of the Ring has but one test, ability.[24]

In the world of the circus, skill was the key to success. Ethnic difference could even be an advantage, adding to the wonder and exoticism of the circus.[25] The very name Pablo Fanque was a deliberate move to create an exotic circus persona and he played on the public's interest in ethnic difference with some of his acts.

In the 1850s, for example, Fanque dressed up a white Irishman, shaved his head, dyed his skin yellow and gave him the name Ki-hi-chin-fan-foo, in a stunt which today we would deem highly questionable, if not downright racist. Another circus proprietor, George Sanger, hired some locals from the poor quarters of Liverpool, costumed them up, doused their skins in red pigment and placed them in a cage. The 'Red Indians' were a decided hit.[26]

* * *

A decade later, however, Fanque's fortunes were declining. He had been declared bankrupt in Leeds, although in the 1860s he continued to travel around the smaller industrial towns, and in a show of solidarity sent another struggling proprietor two shillings, 'which I looked upon as a very handsome present', recalled the grateful recipient.[27]

Now in his fifties, Fanque decided to partner with other proprietors, loan his name out and retain only a small company of performers to keep down the costs. Perhaps his final hurrah came when he hired the steel-fisted fighter Jem Mace. Full of animalistic energy and high-spirited, Mace brought a new lease of life into Fanque's circus. But Mace soon headed for America, leaving Pablo Fanque to soldier on. He passed away at the Britannia Inn, Stockport, on 5 May 1871, and was buried next to Susannah Marlow.

Despite his decline in later years, Fanque had proven his worth in the Victorian circus ring. By attracting the middle classes into his amphitheatres, he helped popularise the circus more generally, such that, by the end of the century, it had become a popular form of family entertainment, close to how we know it today.

Fanque was the most celebrated, but he was by no means the only Black performer in the world of the circus. In the first half of the nineteenth century, Joseph 'Mungo' Hillier developed his own act known as Cossack Riding, which saw him gallop, tumble and reel over and under a moving horse without ever touching the ground. Bar the occasional 'joke' – 'Hillier is looking as black as ever'; '[He] has ridden until he has become black in the face' – there was nothing to suggest that he was marginalised in the circus because of the colour of his skin.[28]

Meanwhile, in the travelling menageries, Arthur Williams, a Black sailor turned lion tamer, dressed 'as a wild man in skins and feathers' in order to wrestle with tigers and lions.[29] And the travelling fairs were also host to performers of Asian and African descent: Indian jugglers, Malay swordsmen, 'Savage African Cannibals', 'The Beautiful Spotted Negro Boy'.[30]

* * *

Fanque's two sons, Ted and George, went on to become successful circus clowns. Fanque's previous partners and protégés, William Wallett and Whimsical Walker, found international stardom, and almost 100 years after his death, Fanque found a kind of posthumous fame too. One day in January 1967, John Lennon took a break from filming a promotional video for 'Strawberry Fields Forever' and wandered into an antique shop in Sevenoaks, Kent. His eyes lighted on a gawdy Victorian poster with the headline, 'Grandest Night of the Season – 14 February 1843 – Pablo Fanque's Circus Royal, Town Meadows, Rochdale, and Positively the Last Night but Three!' Lennon bought the poster, hung it in his music room and was inspired. 'Being for the Benefit of Mr Kite!', released on *Sgt Pepper's Lonely Hearts Club Band* in May 1967, plucked lyrics directly from the poster and featured the name of the man, Pablo Fanque, who had risen from the workhouse to become a renowned circus impresario.

14

Art and Beauty: Fanny Eaton
(1835–1924)

In the spring of 1860, art enthusiasts flocked as usual to see the hundreds of paintings exhibited by living British artists at the Royal Academy of Arts (RA), then standing proud on Trafalgar Square, in the east wing of the building that now houses the National Gallery. Though, when it had been established in 1768, its founder members included two female artists, Angelica Kauffman and Mary Moser (a high point for representation not matched until the mid-twentieth century when the first Black artist, Ronald Moody, had work exhibited – it was not until 2005 that Frank Bowling was elected as the first Black academician), by the mid-nineteenth century, the RA had solidified as a bastion of white, male artists.

Entering the exhibition that spring, patrons first encountered Edwin Henry Landseer's *Flood in the Highlands*. 'A very fine work,' wrote one reviewer, '[featuring] such a variety of living creatures in one common peril [...] that it takes some time to unravel the general confusion, and examine the wonderful reality of the details.'[1]

Another painting lauded for its detailed realism was William Dyce's landscape, *Pegwell Bay*, 'a piece of the most true and literal rendering', as one press report praised it, and Londoners were particularly drawn to John Phillip's *The Marriage of Victoria, Princess Royal, 25 January 1858*, which vibrantly captured the union of Queen Victoria's daughter with Prince Frederick of Prussia.

In the West Room, John Stirling's *Lay Preaching* was celebrated for its impressive composition and fine coloration, 'and holds place most honourably among the fine works with which it is surrounded', which included one painting by the young, Jewish, homosexual artist Simeon Solomon, entitled *The Mother of Moses*.[2] The painting invites the viewer into an intimately

Fanny Eaton in Simeon Solomon's *The Mother of Moses*, 1860

domestic imagined scene: Jochebed, mother of the Prophet Moses, gazes into the face of her baby son, attended by her older daughter Miriam, who clasps the wicker basket which will carry the infant down the River Nile and away from the Pharoah's edict to drown Israelite boys (a pyramid is faintly visible through the open window behind the figures).

The scene pays careful attention to accurate historical details, from the decorated textiles to the ancient Egyptian harp, expressing a commitment to realism which was a hallmark of the Pre-Raphaelite Brotherhood: a group of painters, poets and art critics who were inspired by the art of the late medieval and early Renaissance periods – the era before Raphael (1483–1520) – and adopted naturalism, intricate detail and jewel-like colours in their work. The Pre-Raphaelites, who were also intensely focused on notions of female beauty and sexual yearning, found many of their models from among the working classes and Simeon Solomon was no different in this respect, modelling both Jochebed and Miriam on a dual heritage Jamaican working woman, Fanny Eaton (it's possible the baby in the scene was modelled on Eaton's own son, too).[3]

In the Victorian era, Black individuals were seen depicted in portraits, sculptures, photographs, caricatures, war illustrations, genre scenes, anti-slavery texts and documentary pictorial images. To support the abolitionist campaigns of the 1780s and 1820s, Black models were sought after for the depiction of enslaved people, and in the late Victorian era, an increased understanding of antiquity led to an increased desire for 'authentic' representations, which created another opportunity for Black models.[4]

This did not mean that Black subjects were centralised in artwork – often they were portrayed as figures in a crowd, harem attendants, servants or characters from the Bible or popular fiction – but it did mean that Black models were sought after.[5]

There were numerous Black performers from the world of entertainment who, with varying degrees of personal choice, were depicted in posters, pamphlets and newspaper illustrations, too.[6] Some, like Anna Olga Albertina Brown, known as Miss LaLa, 'Olga the Mulatto', 'Olga the Negress', 'La Vénus Noire' or the 'African Princess', were even sketched and painted. French artist Edgar Degas' preparatory drawings – which included one sketch of LaLa in a blue costume with darkly coloured skin – formed the study for his oil painting, *Miss LaLa at the Cirque Fernando* (1879), which vividly captured the agility and strength of the circus artiste. The painting was sent to the 1879 Impressionist Exhibition in Paris, where, especially from the 1860s, avant-garde artists sketched and painted the community of free Black Parisians.[7]

The Royal Collection Trust also holds a range of photographs and paintings of Black Victorians, including Cetshwayo, King of the Zulus, and Prince Alamayu.[8] There were numerous, anonymous models 'found' wandering the urban streets, who were subsequently photographed and sketched, as well as people like Louis Black, who was born into slavery and subsequently raised in Scotland, where he modelled for different artists. And although painters and sculptors could use reference guides, such as E. W. Lane's *An Account of the Manners and Customs of the Modern Egyptians* (1836), many artists preferred these living Black models.[9]

But, from our viewpoint today, there is something intriguing about this Jewish artist portraying a Jewish origin story, in *The Mother of Moses*, by means of Eaton. Throughout his artistic career, Solomon deliberately chose models with darker Semitic features, painting scenes of Jewish life and same-sex desire, and we can speculate that he may have felt some affinity with Eaton, whose outsider status as a Black woman in Britain perhaps echoed his own dissonance both as a Jewish man in a highly anti-Semitic society *and* as a gay man in a society that legally punished male same-sex desire. Solomon certainly believed that Eaton's features effectively reflected the look of Israelites in Egyptian captivity, and indeed the very subject of his painting, the oppression of Israelites, may have been influenced by his outsider status as a Jewish man in a world of gentile artists.

Perhaps unsurprisingly, therefore, some critics picked up on what they perceived to be the exaggeratedly Jewish features of the subjects in *The Mother of Moses*. One commentator sneered, with racial undertones, that 'two ludicrously ugly women, looking at a dingy baby, do not form a pleasing object'. Another, on the other hand, opined, 'I thought it finely drawn and composed. It nobly represented, to my mind, the dark children of the Egyptian bondage, and suggested the touching story.'[10]

We can feel sure that, as the RA's patrons contemplated the painting, they would have acknowledged its religious significance, the proficiency of the artist and his careful attention to detail. But it seems equally probable that they viewed Solomon's portrait of Jochebed and Miriam through the 'colonialist gaze', which perceived Black bodies from a white ethnic viewpoint, and their heads were likely filled with other, stereotypical images of Black bodies that were circulating in the broader visual realm. These included grotesque portrayals in popular caricatures, war illustrations and images of the slave trade – not to mention the tonally very different but no less manufactured images of African princes, warriors and missionary converts, such as Sarah Forbes Bonetta.

All these depictions of the 'exotic' served some sort of function – whether it was to elicit sympathy for the abolitionist cause or to confirm the efficacy of evangelism abroad. And at the same time, they increased the conceptual distance between self and other, white and Black, while paradoxically confirming the white observer's own sense of whiteness.[11]

While the choice of a Black model was not completely novel in the visual culture of the time, *The Mother of Moses* nevertheless has a unique status in white Victorian art: it is a *sensitive* portrayal of a Black model, centralised in the work of art, which seeks to communicate a story of religious significance and ethnic persecution. More remarkably, perhaps, in it we see the model Fanny Eaton, a Black migrant mother and domestic labourer, insert herself into a white, patriarchal cultural space. Indeed, following her work for Solomon, Eaton was embraced as a model by a litany of artists within the Pre-Raphaelite movement, and in this way her presence at the centre of a major strand of Victorian art was asserted.

* * *

Fanny Eaton, recorded on the parish register as Fanny Antwistle, was born in Jamaica on 23 June 1835 to a Black mother, Matilda Foster, who was probably formerly enslaved and likely worked on the Elim Estate in the parish of St Elizabeth. There was no mention of Fanny's father on the register, perhaps an indication that Fanny was born illegitimate, though it is possible that her father was a white British soldier named James Entwistle, who died in Jamaica eleven days after her birth.[12]

After emancipation, Matilda and her daughter followed the emigration pattern of a number of Jamaicans and travelled to England where, according to census records, they were living at 9 Steven's Place, St Pancras, in 1851. Matilda was recorded as Mrs M. Entwistle, a married laundress, and her sixteen-year-old daughter Fanny as a servant.

In the late 1850s, aged twenty-two, Fanny married or cohabited with nineteen-year-old James Eaton, a horse cab proprietor from the East End, and they went on to have a large family.[13] Their first daughter, Matilda, was born in 1858 and their son James was born roughly two years later (around the time that Solomon was likely painting *The Mother of Moses*). James was followed by Amelia in 1862, Mildred in 1863 and Julia in 1864. Then there was Miriam in 1868, Walter in 1871, Cicely in 1876 and the youngest child, Frank, in 1879. From the age of twenty-three to forty-four, therefore, Fanny Eaton was in a state of near-constant pregnancy. But, like many women in her situation, despite the physical demands of gestation, childbirth and childrearing, she continued to do paid work.

In the 1861 census she was recorded as a charwoman, living with her family in a part of London known as Tiger Bay: a moniker 'associated in the public mind with dangerous ruffianism and unscrupulous crime', noted one social commentator.[14] In his non-fictional book *The Wilds of London* (1874), the journalist James Greenwood described 'the sanguinary fights' in Tiger Bay, the 'white men and plug-lipped Malays and ear-ringed Africans', and 'the tigresses who swarm'.[15]

It is possible Simeon Solomon met Eaton somewhere around Tiger Bay, perhaps in the year 1859, and was drawn to her beautiful bone structure and distinctive look. She, in turn, must have sensed an opportunity. She allowed Solomon to execute a series of naturalistic drawings of her on 7, 8 and 11 November 1859.[16]

Unfortunately, beyond the dates on the drawings, there are no details of the meetings between Eaton and Solomon, who had entered the Royal Academy Schools in 1855, and was part of a sketching club which included the artists Albert Moore, Marcus Stone and Henry Holiday. They might have sketched Eaton around this time too.

Solomon's sketches of November 1859 demonstrate his superior draughtsmanship skills in a careful, lifelike rendering of Eaton. His drawing dated 7 November was a direct study for Jochebed, while the sketch executed on 8 November was a profile study for Miriam.

Thanks to the research of Fanny Eaton's great-grandson, we know that in 1860 she had forged links with the RA, where she was working as a paid model. Eaton used her seemingly passive role as a model for personal advancement – much like another Pre-Raphaelite muse, Elizabeth Siddal, who modelled for the Brotherhood to fund her own artistic career – and participated in the creative process. We should not forget that the models were integral to the creation of the art, assuming and performing a range of roles that brought a central animating force. Eaton had further RA sittings on 13 July and 20 July, receiving the large sum of fifteen shillings per day. The average pay for a

Portrait of Mrs Fanny Eaton by Simeon Solomon.
Graphite on paper, 7 November 1859

charwoman was around one shilling six pence per day, two shillings if one was lucky, so this was a significant fee that Eaton negotiated.[17]

It is perhaps no wonder then that, throughout the 1860s, Eaton allowed a whole host of Pre-Raphaelite artists to paint and sketch her, including Ford Madox Brown, Robert Hawker Dowling, Dante Gabriel Rossetti, Frederick Sandys, Walter Fryer Stocks, Albert Moore and Joanna Mary Boyce. Contemporary critics have debated the extent to which these artists 'othered' Fanny Eaton. Solomon's sister Rebecca, also an artist working in Pre-Raphaelite circles, depicted Eaton in her painting *A Young Teacher* (1861). The press assumed that the dark-skinned Eaton, pictured in a middle-class domestic interior with a young white girl in her arms, represented an Indian servant being taught by the twelve-year old child (which, indeed, may have been the artist's intention). Eaton's actual ethnicity was collapsed into the ethnic stereotypes of 'exotic' Indians, who were depicted with increased frequency in art following the Indian Rebellion of 1857.[18]

Eaton also sat for one of the founders of the Brotherhood, John Everett Millais, appearing as an anonymous 'Oriental' woman in his *Jephthah* (1867). She is positioned in the background, to the right of the frame, possibly depicting a servant in this scene of grief.

In Albert Moore's *The Mother of Sisera* (1861), another scene taken from the Old Testament, Eaton is presented as the apprehensive mother waiting for Sisera's return, unaware he had been killed in battle. Moore focuses on the mother's suffering. Anguish emanates from her gaze as she peers out through the lattice from the confines of the feminine domestic sphere. Yet there is an ambiguity in this depiction: in the Book of Judges, the unnamed mother of Sisera assumes that her son, the enemy of the Israelites, is enjoying the spoils of war, 'a womb or two

[...] a booty of many colors', and there is the implication that the mother approves, which thus links her, and her son, to sexual depravity and evil.[19]

Eaton appears in a very different painting, Dante Gabriel Rossetti's *The Beloved ('The Bride')* (1865–66), though she is not easy to spot right away in this crowded, intense composition. One attendant, ranged to the right, was a Romani model named Keomi Gray and in the foreground is a young Black boy whom Rossetti 'discovered' in London (apparently, he cried throughout the sitting). In the background behind Gray, her face barely visible, is Eaton.

Some critics have suggested that, in this painting, Rossetti celebrates diversity and beauty, while others have noted the ambivalent sexual energy in the painting – accentuated by the ubiquitous lilies – with the bride looking both virginal and nubile, while the attendants are made to appear suggestive. Still others have claimed that *The Beloved* imposes a white standard of beauty by literally centralising the white bride as the superior model. Eaton is here consigned to the margins and merely decorative, one could argue, but she was, to Rossetti at least, the Black equivalent of his favourite muse and lover, Jane Morris (who was also from humble working-class beginnings and took on an idolised status with the Brotherhood). Certainly, by Eaton's very presence in Rossetti's painting, she complicates the 'assumptions of what a black woman could represent', as one contemporary critic, Roberto C. Ferrari, aptly contended.[20] And for many Victorian men, at least, what the Black woman represented was unbridled sexuality matched with physical and moral ugliness.

* * *

A few years after Eaton made her debut at the RA, a thirty-five-year-old white civil servant named Arthur Munby – a

Art and Beauty: Fanny Eaton

Fanny Eaton in Dante Gabriel Rossetti's
The Beloved ('The Bride'), 1865–66

sinister Victorian figure – made the acquaintance of an Ethiopian husband and wife in London. They got chatting, went for a cold beer and Munby paid the pair one shilling to take their photograph. He wrote in his diary, 'Both of them were decently behaved and quiet; the girl, in spite of her black face, being fairly good looking also.'[21]

Munby was surprised by his own reaction. He fancied himself something of an urban ethnographer, indexing his voluminous private diaries 'Working Women, studies of', and he was generally repulsed by Black women.[22] In his notebooks and sketchbooks, now housed at Trinity College, Cambridge, 'race' permeates his observations. White working-class women were recast as racial others; their work was 'black work', he wrote.[23]

He recorded his observations of 'black-faced' dustwomen and sketched one coaldust-covered white collier woman as a 'grotesque caricature of the stigmata of racial denigration', writes academic Anne McClintock, 'her forehead is flattened and foreshortened; the whites of her eyes stare grotesquely from her black face; her lips are artificially full and pale'.[24] In Munby's voyeuristic and titillated gaze, working-class women (Black or otherwise) were racialised 'others' and, to him, they were gross.

It is perhaps not surprising to learn that Munby's revulsion was mixed with attraction. What was more, he was secretly engaged in a sadomasochistic affair with a white working-class servant named Hannah Cullwick, whom he first met in 1854. Munby would sit upon her knee. He loved to marvel at her large hands and he derived pleasure from seeing her toil in filth. She washed his feet, licked his boots and called him 'Massa'.[25]

Munby added a racialised aspect to this fetish for sexualised servitude in a poem he wrote about an enslaved Black woman named Cupassis, who was abused by her cruel white mistress, Queen Kara. Cupassis (derived from Latin terms approximating to 'degenerate desire') is kept naked, used as a 'mat' by other enslaved people and, either face down or on all fours, treated as a human footstool for her white queen. The racialised fetishism of his real-life relationship with Cullwick was taken to its ultimate expression – slavery being represented as the most extreme form of servitude – in his erotic poem.[26]

Elsewhere in his diaries, Munby recalled how, on another occasion while watching a blackface street performance, he was asked by one of the male performers if he wanted a private viewing. 'I can provide plenty of other women besides this one', the performer said, pointing to a blacked-up woman, titillating Munby with the promise of a private show where she would 'go through all the scenes of plantation life'.[27] Whether Munby accepted this offer of a slavery-inspired burlesque is not recorded.

These associations between servitude, slavery, sex and 'race' were not new or unique to Munby. The Black servant frequently appeared in European art and often signalled an atmosphere of illicit sexual activity – whether that be the Black servants in William Hogarth's *A Rake's Progress* (1733–34), the Black female attendant proffering the bouquet of blooms in Édouard Manet's *Olympia* (1865) or the deviant, sexualised servant rubbing the back of his white mistress in Franz von Bayro's *The Servant* (1890).[28] The very word 'slut' emerged in the seventeenth century as a shorthand for slattern or kitchen maid. In the nineteenth century, the 'servant names' John Thomas and Mary Ann doubled as sexual slang.[29]

The novella *Venus in Furs* (1870) by Leopold von Sacher-Masoch is another nineteenth-century depiction of sexualised slavery and 'race'. The male protagonist Severin (whose name, meaning 'severe, serious or strict', indicates his fetish for domination) asks to be enslaved to Wanda, the white woman of his desire, who sadistically degrades her masochist. Wanda enlists the help of three Black women to inflict pain and humiliation. Her 'black demons drove me out into the field,' Severin recalls, 'one of them held the plough, the other one led me by a line, the third applied the whip, and Venus in Furs stood to one side and looked on.'[30] The image barely needs commentary: Black women sexually dominating a white man marked the ultimate reversal. This was not an empowering depiction of Black sexual agency (we would have to cite other examples for that) but rather of 'race' objectified, of Black women in the service of white male pleasure.[31]

There was a long-running association between Black people and hypersexuality, which had roots in the Middle Ages (sexuality was often referred to as 'the African sin'), and in particular, an association between Black women and lasciviousness.[32] In varying ways, this obsessive association was played out in *Venus in Furs*, Munby's poem, or (if you can bear more troubling perversions) the sexual escapades of 'Walter', described in his anonymously published *My Secret Life* (1888).[33]

By the late nineteenth century, perceptions of Black women had merged with perceptions of the 'prostitute' – both viewed as primitive, sexualised outsiders – an association which inevitably manifested in nineteenth-century visual culture. Indeed, in a 1992 polemic, the artist Lorraine O'Grady, who was born to West Indian parents in Boston, described the Black maid in Édouard Manet's *Olympia* (1863), posed by the Black model, Laure, as 'Jezebel and Mammy, prostitute and female eunuch, the two-in-one', who stands outside the white construction of what it means to be a woman:

> She is the chaos that must be excised, and it is her excision that stabilizes the West's construct of the female body, for the 'femininity' of the white female body is ensured by assigning the not-white to a chaos safely removed from sight.[34]

In white Western thought and art, white skin was the prerequisite for the beautiful body; the Black body, its antithesis. Yet the Black female body, regarded as repulsive and placed outside the frame of Western notions of beauty, had the power to titillate and excite. 'Otherness' could be frightening and disruptive while also being sexually charged and alluring.[35]

However, in her seminal book *Posing Modernity* (2018), art historian Denise Murrell argues that, around this time, a new trend was emerging in modernist art which depicted the

Black body, 'not as an exoticized foreigner but in a modernist way, as part of the working class'.[36] Murrell points to Manet's *Olympia* (1863), in which the Black model Laure appears not simply as an anonymous exotic 'Other', but as a woman of significance, an active participant in the scene, whose presence reflects the reality of modern Parisian life.[37] Of Edgar Degas' *Miss LaLa at the Cirque Fernando* (1879), Murrell writes persuasively that LaLa's dual heritage symbolised this 'cultural blending', and it feels apt to draw similar conclusions for Fanny Eaton in Britain.[38]

So, the Black body was obviously not, either in reality or in its representations, a homogenous, unchanging form. Africa was certainly seen by white culture as the 'dark continent', populated by the 'Negroid' (while Europe was the region of the Caucasoid and Asia of the Mongoloid), but colonialists and painters nonetheless recognised ethnic and tribal variety in Africa – even if that recognition was often disparaging. The Scottish painter David Roberts, who travelled from Egypt to Palestine to draw the people and sites he encountered, admired Abyssinians, detested 'negresses' and wrote, 'Though Nubian women are dark in their complexions even to blackness, they have nothing else that should class them with Negroes; on the contrary, their features are finely formed, and even Greek in character' (by which he meant that they had elements of what Victorians conceived of as the Greco-Roman ideals of proportionality, symmetry and whiteness).[39]

Black and white were dichotomous but with shades in between. And, for white Victorians, the lighter the shade the better. Hence the Egyptians, racially and geographically closer to white Europeans, represented 'the white-negro body', argues scholar Charmaine Nelson, 'at once a marginal site of whiteness and a superior form of blackness'.[40] Arguably, Fanny Eaton fitted this mould.

Edgar Degas, *Miss LaLa at the Cirque Fernando*, pastel sketch, 1879

* * *

Eaton was enmeshed in this messy, hierarchical, racial and sexual visual domain, often depicted in sensual or exotic idioms and collapsed into an 'exotic' Other. She was variously intended to stand as Jewish, Arab and Libyan (rather than Jamaican). Madox Brown thought Eaton was a 'Hindoo', while Rossetti labelled her a 'mulatto'.[41] One critic described her as 'an Arab woman'.[42]

The colour of Eaton's skin, matched with the ignorance and indifference of her painters and observers, made her ethnically malleable. And yet, in the portraits and sketches of her, she is never overtly sexualised, nor does she represent the assumed ugliness of Blackness. Her portrayals stand in contrast to the overtly sexualised Black bodies or the downtrodden enslaved women or the asexual 'mammies' of other artworks of the period.

She was sensitively portrayed by Simeon Solomon as the mother of the Prophet Moses. She was dignified in Joanna Mary Boyce's portrait of 1861 – we can speculate that the female artist's gaze perhaps accounts for the especially atmospheric and exalted qualities of this profile portrait – while in Walter Fryer Stocks' sketches, Eaton is presented within the Pre-Raphaelite tradition of alluring and sensual feminine beauty, exemplified in her slightly parted lips and averted glance.[43]

In Eaton's indisputably beautiful look, she seems to occupy a liminal space between the tropes of Black and white, her depiction by the Pre-Raphaelites somewhat reminiscent of Botticelli's women. In her presence in Victorian art, she might appear to us to echo the words attributed to the Ethiopian Queen of Sheba, 'I am black and I am beautiful' – and I have power, she might have added.[44]

Fanny Eaton ceased modelling after 1867, although she or one of her daughters was recorded in the Royal Academy's account books in 1874 and 1879. By that time, Simeon Solomon had been publicly shamed, following his arrests and convictions for 'attempted sodomy' (that is, gay sex), while Fanny's mother Matilda had died in 1868. Fanny's partner James died in 1881.

Fanny continued to work as a needlewoman and housekeeper in different parts of London and, by 1901, was employed as a cook on the Isle of Wight. In 1911, she was living back in London with her daughter Julia. She died in 1924 and was buried in a common grave. But though she lived and died in humble circumstances, Fanny Eaton made an important and unmissable mark on Victorian visual culture, embodying the now internationally famous Pre-Raphaelite aesthetic. She was a working-class mother, a servant and a charwoman, who through her own tenacity carved herself a career as a model within the Victorian avant-garde, challenging representations of the Black body in art and culture and playing off lazy perceptions of her ethnic ambiguity in order to make a living.

* * *

In very different ways, the people we are about to meet in the next part of this book similarly asserted themselves in British popular culture and, like Fanny Eaton, challenged public perceptions. Back in 1788, during the early abolitionist campaigns in Britain, Reverend Peter Peckard penned the pamphlet *Am I Not a Man and a Brother?*, whose frontispiece was stamped with that emblematic image produced by Darwin's maternal grandfather: the kneeling enslaved African with pleading, manacled hands; an image that erased Black agency and offered a plain canvas for the projection of white guilt.[45] The image, which proliferated in the late eighteenth and nineteenth centuries, reflected and enhanced a stereotype of the passive Black victim requiring white saviours. Yet, as we will see in Part Five, there was a countervailing force in Britain; one spearheaded by African American abolitionists, feminists and Pan-Africanists, who set out, with courage and determination, to remould the political landscape.

Part Five

Fighting for Freedom

15

Defiance: Henry 'Box' Brown
(*c.* 1815–97)

Many will say 'This is the slaves' side of the question. The slave-holders would tell a different story.' You have heard the slave-holders' story 250 years ago. Now, I think it is time for the slaves to speak.[1]

Moses Roper, 1838

On 29 March 1849, a wooden box, around three feet long and two feet wide, marked 'THIS SIDE UP WITH CARE', was bound for Philadelphia from Virginia, entrusted to the Adams Express Company. At Potomac Creek, the box was placed on a steamer headed for Washington. The label 'THIS SIDE UP' was ignored. Two footsore men took a seat on top and started discussing the contents inside. They reasoned that the box must be 'THE MAIL'.

Arriving at Washington, the box was taken from the steamboat, placed on a wagon and driven to the depot. Once again, 'THIS SIDE UP' was ignored. The box journeyed on towards Philadelphia.

Over twenty-seven hours after leaving its original destination, and having travelled around 350 miles, the box finally arrived at the Philadelphia depot. It was stored alongside other luggage and remained there until 7 in the evening. The box was then collected, placed on a wagon and brought to a house in the city. A number of people circled around.

'Let us rap upon the box and see if he is alive,' said one.

'Is all right within?' queried another.

From inside the box, a weary voice responded, 'All right.' Henry 'Box' Brown, as he would come often to be known, recalled:

> When they heard that I was alive they soon managed to break open the box, and then came my resurrection from the grave of slavery. I rose a freeman, but I was too weak, by reason of long confinement in that box, to be able to stand, so I immediately swooned away. After my recovery from the swoon the first thing, which arrested my attention, was the presence of a number of friends, every one seeming more anxious than another, to have an opportunity of rendering me their assistance, and of bidding me a hearty welcome to the possession of my natural rights, I had risen as it were from the dead.[2]

Brown felt an immediate rush of gratitude and burst forth in a hymn of thanksgiving:

> I waited patiently, I waited patiently for the Lord, for the Lord;
> And he inclined unto me, and heard my calling:
> I waited patiently, I waited patiently for the Lord,
> And he inclined unto me, and heard my calling...[3]

Brown had been delivered to the Anti-Slavery Society's office in Philadelphia. The fugitive had arrived in a free state.

'I was born about forty-five miles from the city of Richmond, in Louisa County, in the year 1815', opens *The Narrative of*

Henry Box Brown, Written by Himself (1851). 'I entered the world a slave – in the midst of a country whose most honoured writings declare that all men have a right to liberty.'[4]

Indeed, the Preamble of the American Constitution declared that the purpose of the Federal Government was to 'secure the Blessings of Liberty', but five clauses in that cherished document of 1787 protected slavery, which had been present on America's shores since the sixteenth century.[5] And although all the northern states abolished slavery between 1774 and 1804, many Northern businessmen continued to grow fat on the trade, while the Southern economy was dependent on it.

Born in a state which first legislated for slavery in 1661 (later codified in the Virginia Slave Code of 1705), Henry Brown was fifteen years old when the person who legally owned him, John Barret, died and his animate and inanimate property was divided between four sons. Brown, the legal 'property', was subsequently separated from his parents and siblings, 'the most severe trial to my feelings which I had ever eudured [*sic*]', he wrote. 'This kind of torture is a thousand fold more cruel and barbarous than the use of the lash which lacerates the back.'[6]

Brown was taken to the city of Richmond, where his new master William Barret, son of John Barret, had a tobacco business. Brown was forced to work fourteen hours a day in the summer and sixteen hours a day in the winter. He was sometimes paid a small fee for his work and often laboured alongside the free Black community in Richmond.

A number of factors created a situation whereby the institution of slavery existed alongside the free Black community who, before the Civil War, numbered a quarter of a million in the American South: a flurry of manumissions during the Revolutionary War, immigration from the West Indies and Cuba, self-purchase, fugitivity, population growth and the addition of 'free people of colour' following the Louisiana Purchase. 'Free', of

RESURRECTION OF HENRY BOX BROWN.

'The Resurrection of Henry "Box" Brown', 1872

course, was a relative term in this context, and one that included segregation, lynching and huge societal barriers.[7]

In the Antebellum South, the 'free' Black community was predominantly located in urban areas like Richmond, where enslaved people had a greater level of autonomy compared to life among the enslaved people working on rural, agricultural fields. Brown, however, was still the legal property of another person, and he recalled the everyday brutality that was meted out to him and other enslaved people. In *The Narrative of Henry Box Brown*, he recalled how John F. Allen, an overseer and allegedly 'a very pious man', was particularly cruel and, 'for no other crime than sickness, inflicted two-hundred lashes' upon the bare back of an old, enslaved man.[8]

In the mid-1830s, Brown sought and secured permission to marry another enslaved person called Nancy (the union was not legally binding), and together they had three children. But

Brown recalled in harrowing detail how he and his family were blackmailed and ultimately separated by Nancy's legal owner – who sold his 'property', Nancy, and the children in 1848:

> My agony was now complete, she with whom I had travelled the journey of life in chains, for the space of twelve years, and the dear little pledges God had given us I could see plainly must now be separated from me for ever.[9]

It was in this tormented state of complete separation that Brown took direct action, journeying for freedom in a box bound for Philadelphia.

* * *

Between 1790 and 1860, the number of enslaved peoples in the United States grew. In the 1840s there were around 3 million enslaved people in America; by 1861 there were around 4 million concentrated around Chesapeake Bay, eastern Virginia, the coasts of South Carolina and Georgia and the Mississippi River Valley alone.[10]

At the same time, however, abolitionists fought back: they formed anti-slavery societies, held conferences, boycotted products and assisted so-called 'fugitive slaves', via the 'Underground Railroad', for instance, which helped enslaved people to reach Mexico, Canada and the free states of America. Brown's escape was daring and inventive and capitalised on the miracle of the modern postal service, which became a crucial channel for abolitionist communication – petitions, letters, literature – and, in Brown's case, a conduit to liberation, despite Southern attempts at controlling the system.[11]

Abolitionists also deployed lecturers, who spoke on the evils of slavery, and orators, who were themselves formerly enslaved, were seen as particularly valuable. They could speak from authentic and powerful first-hand experience; they were proof that Black people had humanity and were fellow Christians; and their stories of suffering struck a chord.

Henry Brown was soon to join their ranks. Indeed, he'd become an important symbol and standard-bearer of the abolitionist cause described by William Still, a free African American and 'conductor' for the railroad, as a 'man of invention as well as a hero'.[12]

Once safely in Philadelphia, Brown was introduced to the white American Quaker, Lucretia Mott, an abolitionist and women's rights activist whose husband James Mott helped establish the American Anti-Slavery Society in 1833. By 1840, the organisation had around 2,000 auxiliary societies and a total membership of approximately 150,000–200,000 people. They deployed abolitionist agents and lecturers across America, and they quickly saw Henry Brown as an appealing candidate. He had a strong singing voice, an incredible story of escape, and he was a powerful speaker who appealed to the emotions. He might have been uneducated, relatively illiterate and lacking in political nous, but he was quick-witted and a fast learner. Furthermore, he had a knack for theatricality which would stand him in good stead.[13]

Brown's life story was speedily written up by the lifelong anti-slavery campaigner Charles Stearns, who claimed that *The Narrative of Henry Box Brown* (this first account being published in 1849) derived from Brown's own testimony.[14] Brown joined Stearns on a book tour across Massachusetts. They appeared in numerous towns, with Stearns doing most of the talking.

But Brown was soon beginning to hold his own. He would mount the stage to describe the horrors of slavery, concluding with a song sung by the enslaved. In April 1850, he unveiled a pictorial illustration of plantation life, described by one paper as a 'novel mode of advancing the anti-slavery cause'.[15] The 'Mirror of Slavery Panorama' was Brown's idea and supplemented his developing routine of lecture and song.

During Brown's tours across the North, he met prominent Black abolitionists, including Frederick Douglass and William Wells Brown, who were both revered on the anti-slavery circuit. Douglass, who had escaped slavery in Maryland, became an agent for the Massachusetts Anti-Slavery Society in the early 1840s and in the face of racist interrogations over whether it was possible for a formerly enslaved person to possess such oratorical and intellectual gifts, he published the *Narrative of the Life of Frederick Douglass, an American Slave* (1845), in part to quell the racist doubters.

William Wells Brown, formerly enslaved in Kentucky, escaped to Ohio in 1834 and began working for the abolitionist cause. 'In the year 1842, I conveyed, from the first of May to the first of December, sixty-nine fugitives over Lake Erie to Canada', he wrote.[16] In 1843, he was engaged as a lecturer by the Western New York Anti-Slavery Society and in 1847 became a lecture agent for the Massachusetts Anti-Slavery Society. In lecturing against slavery, Wells Brown 'went forth to battle against slavery at the South, and its offspring, prejudice against colored people, at the North', wrote his daughter.[17]

In 1847 he published *Narrative of William W. Brown, A Fugitive Slave*, the first of many publications. A few years later, on 18 September 1850, the United States Congress passed the Fugitive Slave Act, which charged the Federal Government with finding, returning and trying 'fugitive slaves'. The act forced hundreds of formerly enslaved African Americans to embark on another journey towards freedom. Henry Brown was among them.

Armed with his experience of enslavement, his oratorical skills, his printed narrative and illustrated panorama, and accompanied by his friend, a free African American, James C. A. Smith, who had financially helped Brown when he was enslaved, Brown journeyed to Britain. On 1 November 1850, Brown and Smith arrived in Liverpool and within two weeks the pair began their abolitionist exhibitions. On 15 November, the *Liverpool Mercury* reported:

> All the horrors of the slave trade, with its demoralising effects on the slave and slaveholder, are graphically delineated, and with a simple, earnest, and unadorned eloquence, described by Mr. Brown, himself a fugitive slave.[18]

Brown and Smith concluded the exhibition with a 'slave song', and all who attended left 'in another frame of mind', wrote the press.[19]

The duo appeared in Liverpool, Manchester, Lancaster, Bolton and Leeds. In Burnley, where the pair were met by large crowds, they received endorsements from two white clergymen, which gave their shows even greater credence. They boosted their popularity by performing minstrel songs, sometimes at the expense of their abolitionist message, and in another publicity-generating move, Brown was transported in a box from Bradford to Leeds as a 're-enactment' of his escape.[20] On arrival, the box was placed on a coach and paraded through the city, accompanied by a band of musicians.

'The procession was attended by an immense concourse of spectators', wrote the *Leeds Mercury*, 'Mr. C. A. Smith, a coloured friend of Mr Brown's, rode in the coach with the box, and afterwards opened it at the Music Hall.'[21] After emerging from inside, Brown proceeded to deliver his lecture with a focus on his escape and, 'after a short but interesting account of his adventures', the newspaper report continued, 'he proceeded to exhibit his panorama'. This was a large canvas displaying over 100 scenes, which were carefully coordinated to reveal American hypocrisies: a 'slave auction' depicted in front of Congress; another auction alongside celebrations of American Independence Day. The *Leeds Mercury* was clear that the panorama offered 'representations strikingly illustrative of American institutions and inconsistencies'.[22]

The disparagement of America and the extolling of Britain was accentuated by Brown's 'slave narrative'. The first account written by Charles Stearns was supposedly composed from Brown's 'statement of facts', but the second version, printed in England and sold at his shows was, it was emphasised in the title and on the front cover, 'written by himself'. Although the narrative was probably dictated to a journalist, the writing focused much more on Brown's personal experiences and reflected his voice better than Stearns' version.[23]

The text formed part of the popular 'slave narrative' literary genre, better described as 'liberation or emancipation narratives', which typically focused on childhood experiences, the ordeals of enslavement and, crucially, the protagonist's desire to escape to freedom, the dangers of that escape and the joys of liberation post-escape. Emancipation narratives engaged with hope and the possibilities of freedom, titillating and inspiring an increasingly literate public, who devoured the tales of abuse and the daring flights to freedom. The genre quenched a thirst for sensationalism, but the publications were packaged as morality tales that echoed the Christian tradition, in which the morally determined eventually succeed, despite the obstacles.[24] They were a powerful weapon in the abolitionist arsenal, and Henry Brown used his to expose American hypocrisy: 'While America is boasting of her freedom and making the world ring with her professions *of equality*, she holds millions of her inhabitants in bondage.'[25]

* * *

According to the press, by March 1852, over 365,000 Britons had seen Henry Brown's exhibitions, an extraordinary number in little over a year since his arrival in Liverpool.[26] He was now performing solo, however, having parted ways with James C. A. Smith.

The exact reasons for the separation are unclear, but Brown's cherishment of the fruits of British freedom played a part. He enjoyed smoking, gambling, drinking, swearing and eating (by modern standards he was obese), which ran contrary to the weighty expectations placed on Black abolitionists, who were supposed to be morally unimpeachable, respectable and pious. James C. A. Smith revealed Brown's 'moral failings' in letters to their abolitionist sponsors, which exacerbated tensions between the two friends.[27]

Although their parting by June of 1851 was a disappointing conclusion to their friendship, it did mark a new stage in Brown's journey. He'd been tethered to the abolitionists but now he would pursue his own path. So, he proceeded to establish his own networks beyond religious and abolitionist circles. He joined friendly societies and the Freemasons – and he confronted challenges alone.

In March 1852, Brown had to contend with an aggressive review of his performance at the Wolverhampton Corn Exchange. It was penned by the editor of the *Wolverhampton and Staffordshire Herald*, Thomas Brindley, who opined that Brown's show was 'a mass of contradictions and absurdities', which, 'instead of benefitting the cause of abolition', merely generated 'disgust at the foppery, conceit, vanity and egotistical stupidity of the Box Brown school'.[28] Brindley turned his scorn on the audience, many of whom were working class, 'full of fulsome compliment to the bejewelled "darkey" whose portly figure and overdressed appearance bespeak the gullibility of our most credulous age and nation'.[29] This racist rant plumbed new depths when Brindley reported the moment a member of the audience asked Brown whether the Dismal Swamp was in Virginia or Carolina. In mocking tones, Brindley gave Brown's response as:

'Well, he daint sacly know; taint somewhere in de middle of de state.'

'But,' continued the interrogator, 'is it not on the boarders of North and South Carolina?'

'Well, he daint know you might put it in Carolina but he taut it was in Virginny.'[30]

The popular wave of minstrelsy that was sweeping the country had a negative effect on Brown's credentials as a performer. The racism taking hold in Britain also had an impression on James Watkins, another formerly enslaved man who had fled America following the Fugitive Slave Act and was lecturing some twenty-seven miles away. On arriving in Britain, Watkins 'applied to some large Liverpool merchants who, after asking me a great many questions, declared that they could not think of employing a "n****r who would steal"', he wrote. Watkins reported hearing English mothers threatening naughty children with being handed over to 'Black Sam' or 'The Black Man', and he observed with dismay:

> We have public exhibitions in pot-houses and low singing rooms of men who black their faces, and perform such outlandish antics as were never seen amongst the negroes, and who profess to imitate, but who in reality only caricature men of my race.[31]

Frederick Douglass called minstrels a 'pestiferous nuisance', while the Black abolitionist Sarah Parker Remond referred to them as 'vulgar men'.[32] Ira Aldridge's memoir noted that the minstrel-inspired laughter only stopped when whites were confronted with images of 'Blacks torn from their homes and dying by dozens in the foetid hold of a ship, or suffering the cruelest [*sic*] tortures of slavery', but these images merely reinforced another long-held notion of Black victimhood – and the minstrel quickly turned any pity into mirth.[33]

Henry Brown, however, was ready to take a stand. He did this alone, without his old partner James C. A. Smith and without the support of other abolitionists. In July 1852, he sued the racist editor Thomas Brindley for libel – and won. 'Henry "Box" Brown, the escaped Negro slave,' reported the *Blackburn Standard*, 'has obtained a verdict for £100 [...] the editor having described his exhibition in contemptuous terms, and thereby materially curtailed the receipts.'[34]

Libel laws being what they are, Brown won on the basis of lost earnings and not on what we would now call hate speech on the part of the racist editor. Yet, the *Morning Post* commented, 'The black man, the fugitive slave, who had been hunted from the shores of America, recovered damages' in a 'British court of justice'.[35] This became the crucial point in the British press: in telling this story, commentators could ignore homegrown racism and instead focus on benign British justice. Brown's victory was fashioned into a self-congratulatory national discourse and yet... Brown had triumphed in the courts; his pride was intact and he walked away with £100 in his pocket.

* * *

Henry Brown continued to deliver abolitionist entertainment to the British public. To remain competitive in the varied world of Victorian entertainment, he offered little gimmicks to entice the crowds: 'PRESENTS GIVEN AWAY EVERY EVENING!'[36] He lowered the admission fee, advertised 'Mr Box Brown's brass band' and he did what many great showmen did – he diversified his acts and made his performances topical.[37]

At the height of the mania for *Uncle Tom's Cabin*, when eleven different stage versions were running in December 1852 alone, Brown jumped at the chance of acting in a stage version at the Adelphi Theatre in Sheffield. He subsequently commissioned pictorial illustrations of *Uncle Tom's Cabin*, which he displayed in Staffordshire, Birmingham and Derby, among other places.[38] He commissioned a panorama of the Indian Rebellion, with scenes including 'The fearful Massacre at Cawnpore', 'The Severe Battle at Lucknow' and 'The Relief of Lucknow'.[39] Brown delivered a speech which described the scenes but also played into the audiences' fears about non-white Others (which, incidentally, included himself but which, as a corollary, increased his receipts).[40]

And alongside his 'most gorgeous and artistically painted PANORAMA OF THE INDIAN WAR!!' as the press praised it, there was Brown's panorama of American slavery.[41] Then, in 1861 when the American Civil War started to rage, Brown commissioned yet another panorama covering that tumultuous event. He also acted in a number of dramas, including a play loosely based on his life. 'Mr Brown's powerful acting [...] is really worthy of the highest commendation', noted the press.[42]

From the early 1860s, Brown also began to perform mesmerism and magic onstage. He was not the first Black mesmerist – G. W. Stone and Henry Edward Lewis had been hypnotising British audiences since the 1850s – and Brown was not the only Black magician either – the formerly enslaved John Brown was also doing the rounds – yet Henry 'Box' Brown upped the ante.[43] He appeared in African robes, introduced mind-reading and conjuring tricks and proclaimed himself 'King of all Mesmerists', giving entertainments on 'Magic, Animal Magnetism, Mesmerism, Electro-Biology, and Phrenology', as one verbose advertisement boasted.[44]

Offstage, his life had developed in new directions too. In the press, Brown claimed that he tried to purchase the freedom of his still-enslaved wife and children in America but, unable to secure their freedom, he felt justified in marrying twenty-one-year-old teacher Jane Floyd, a tin miner's daughter from Cornwall, on 28 November 1855. Interracial marriages were not uncommon and there had been Black people in Cornwall since the eighteenth century, so it was perhaps unsurprising that Jane's father and one of her brothers witnessed the marriage in a sign of approval.[45]

Jane accompanied her husband on his numerous tours, appearing onstage and picking up admiring reviews. On Wednesday, 7 April 1858, for example, hundreds of people crammed inside Cornwall's Circus for an exhibition of the Panorama of the Indian Rebellion. 'The descriptive part was ably conducted by Mrs Box Brown', stated the *Jersey Independent and Daily Telegraph*.[46]

The Browns' first child, Agnes Jane Floyd Brown, was born on 25 August 1860 and their second child Edward Henry on 28 October 1864. Around six years later, Jane gave birth to twins, Annie Amelia Helena and Mary Emma Martha, but tragically – and all too commonly – Mary died five months later. John Floyd Brown, born on 26 October 1871, died seven months later of bronchitis and convulsions, and in October 1874 the Browns had to bury their eldest child, Agnes, who died from inflammation of the kidneys.[47] There are no records or recollections of how these losses impacted the Browns, but they must have been heartbreaking, and perhaps they reignited Henry Brown's trauma of familial loss back in America.

A few months after burying their fourteen-year-old daughter, the Browns left England for America, which had by now abolished slavery following the Unionist victory in the American Civil War. Perhaps Henry Brown hoped to be reunited with Nancy and their children?

He certainly lived to see the marriages of his British-born children, Edward and Annie, and the births of his grandchildren too. Brown continued retelling the story of his escape in the box into the late 1880s, but we do not know what happened to his first, American family. There is no indication that they were reunited with their father, who died in Toronto on 15 June 1897. Jane Brown lived on until 1924.[48]

* * *

Henry Brown was unashamedly an entertainer. He appealed to the working classes in particular and he never allowed himself to be defined by the expectations of abolitionists. He maintained 'a trickster-like presence and an ever-changing, innovative performance art', writes historian Martha J. Cutter, 'that melded theatre, street shows, magic, painting, singing, print culture, visual imagery, acting, mesmerism, and even medical treatments'.[49] Cutter contends that Brown's turn to mesmerism and magic was a means of taking back control after enduring the traumas of slavery and racism. Operating under numerous sobriquets – The King of All Mesmerists, The African Chief, Dr Henry Brown, Professor of Electro-Biology – these acts certainly made his presence onstage political.[50] A Black man psychologically controlling white audiences through hypnotism was a potent reversal of racial control.[51]

But from this distance, it is impossible to tell whether these acts were conceived with a self-consciously political motivation. In her brilliant biography of Brown, Kathleen Chater is right to warn against imputing contemporary notions of identity and trauma back onto the past; rather, as she suggests, we would do better to assume that Brown created personae that fitted with the entertainment scene in which he operated. He was a professional entertainer with familial responsibilities, and he never displayed the overtly political stance of other abolitionists.[52]

Yet he still operated within the context and lineage of Black abolitionists in Britain. From the 1830s, many Black abolitionists travelled to Britain to erect a 'moral cordon', isolating America from the global community by igniting popular opinion against slavery.[53] There were James McCune Smith (1831); Moses Roper (1835); Charles Lenox Remond (1840); Frederick Douglass (1845) and William Wells Brown (1849). In the 1850s and 1860s there were Henry Highland Garnet, Sarah Parker Remond, Reverend Samuel Ward, Ellen Craft,

William Craft and Julia Jackson. In 1876, Josiah Henson came and in the early 1890s, Ida B. Wells. Individual tactics differed, personal circumstances and motivations varied but, on the whole, these Black abolitionists had the primary aim of propagating abolitionism and anti-racism, and in doing so, they helped mould Britain. They did not seek to overthrow the American government or request British military intervention; instead, they sought to inflame public opinion by revealing American abuses and hypocrisies of the kind described by Nathaniel Paul in July 1833:

> Perhaps it is not generally known that in the United States of America – that land of freedom and equality – the laws are so exceedingly liberal that they give to man the liberty of purchasing as many negroes as he can find means to pay for, and also the liberty to sell them again.[54]

A nation that enslaved millions of people but boasted of its free institutions, Christianity and democracy amounted to 'an asp in a basket of flowers', stated Black abolitionist Charles Lenox Remond.[55] America was a threat to the moral and international order, and Britain needed to know about it. And while many Black abolitionists vehemently denounced America (and indeed Britain for its role in slavery too), they did not only preach lamentations. They dreamed of a brighter tomorrow; a more egalitarian America; a country free from slavery and segregation.

For many of these campaigners, life was affirmed in Britain. A number of African Americans seemingly perceived Britain as an egalitarian haven which was largely free from racist sentiment. So, on the one hand, William Wells Brown expressed his sense of awe coming into the port of Liverpool, where everything 'seems to be built for the future as well as the present', and on stepping ashore 'no sooner was I on British soil, than I was recognized as a man, and an equal'.[56] For Frederick Douglass, the experience of being in Britain seems positively dizzying:

> I breathe, and lo! the chattel becomes a man. I gaze around in vain for one who will question my equal humanity, claim me as his slave, or offer me an insult. I employ a cab – I am seated beside white people – I reach the hotel – I enter the same door – I am shown into the same parlor – I dine at the same table – and no one is offended. No delicate nose grows deformed in my presence. I find no difficulty here in obtaining admission into any place of worship, instruction, or amusement, on equal terms with people as white as any I ever saw in the United States. I meet nothing to remind me of my complexion. I find myself regarded and treated at every turn with the kindness and deference paid to white people.[57]

The Black academic William G. Allen wrote that Englishmen demonstrated an 'entire absence of prejudice against color', and categorically stated that in England 'Color claims no precedence over character'.[58] And certainly, some Black abolitionists found themselves judged not completely on the colour of their skin but on the content of their character – that 'Moral order embodied in the individual', wrote Samuel Smiles in *Self-Help* (1859).[59]

With the components of self-restraint, perseverance, effort and courage in the face of adversity, the notion of character was imperative in Victorian Britain, and formerly enslaved orators were recognised for these qualities.[60] To many Victorians, it was morals which made the man, not class or hereditary status – a sentiment particularly important to the burgeoning middle classes who hoped to join the ranks of fashionable society. And this emphasis on character, over class or colour, left a space for Black abolitionists to find a receptive audience.

On the other hand, however, the idea that Britain was some egalitarian haven was more of a construct than a reality. On one level, it constituted clever political messaging – Black abolitionists massaged the national ego by proclaiming the tolerance in Britain in order to endear audiences to their abolitionist cause. It was also true that, compared to America where slavery, segregation and lynching were rampant, Britain appeared to be an accepting place. But, as we saw in the introduction, Black abolitionists, and Black people more generally, did experience racism in Britain. Henry Brown was racially mocked; James Watkins was denied employment; William G. Allen faced racism and discrimination when he became the director of a school for the poor. Frederick Douglass praised the tolerance he received in England, but he also saw that 'the higher the colored man rises in the scale of society, the less prejudice does he meet'.[61]

Colour prejudice and racism existed, but socially elevated individuals like Douglass received an element of protection. And while Black abolitionists might have been lionised, they also had to 'break through the limits of their expected roles as beggars, servants, comic performers, or uncultured abolitionist speakers', as historian Laura Korobkin notes.[62] And as we will see in the following chapter, some Black abolitionists had yet another barrier to overcome, too: their gender.

16

Daring to be Heard: Sarah Parker Remond
(1826–94)

American despotism would yet have to meet a bitter day of reckoning. It would yet be quoted in solemn warning to other states and nations. It carried within itself the seeds of its own decay, and it would involve in its own destruction that of the slave system which has so long and so viciously upheld it. The 'glorious Union' would be severed, and the sooner the better; liberty and slavery are ever incompatible, and only when the American people can be got to comprehend and appreciate genuine liberty, would the last fetter on the limbs of the slave be broken.[1]

Sarah Parker Remond, Dublin, 1859

'I was born at Salem, Massachusetts,' Sarah Remond stated in a short mid-century interview, 'the youngest but one of ten children of John and Nancy Remond.'[2] Her parents were relatively wealthy entrepreneurs and abolitionists who lived among the free Black population in the coastal city of Salem, located about fourteen miles from Boston. John Remond was an active member of the Massachusetts Anti-Slavery Society and Nancy was a founding member of the Salem Female Anti-Slavery Society (1834). Both were auxiliaries to the American Anti-Slavery Society, formed by Arthur Tappan and William Lloyd Garrison, that 'young and noble *apostle of liberty*', as Sarah Remond described the latter.[3]

Although Black women were typically excluded from the ideals of white Victorian womanhood, Nancy Remond trained her offspring in the skills demanded of all respectable women – proficiency in cooking, knitting and general domestic duties – and instilled in her children an inner strength 'to enable them to meet the terrible pressure which prejudice against colour would force upon them', Sarah Remond recalled.[4] The Remonds were defined and burdened by the white perception of their inferiority. They were treated with 'contempt', 'worse than criminals'; the colour of their skin the 'gigantic shadow', the 'huge sphinx' that defined their life.[5]

When Sarah Remond was eventually allowed to attend a racially mixed public school, she could already detect the corruption of childhood – 'We were frequently made to feel that prejudice had taken root' – and it wasn't long before the white parents decided that the Black children should be educated away from their broods.[6] Although African Americans in Massachusetts had been emancipated since the late eighteenth century, segregation in schools, the military and public accommodation divided Black and white children. And in 1849, the Supreme Court of Massachusetts declared that separate but equal schools did not violate the right of equality enshrined in the Massachusetts Constitution.

Even before that declaration, however, the gifted Remond was told by her teacher, in front of her class one morning, that she could no longer attend the school because she was Black. Some of her classmates were enraged, a few expressed sympathies, but all Remond could do was to weep 'bitter tears'.

Yet therein lay the moment that would define her life: 'I thought of the great injustice practised upon me, and longed for some power to help me to crush those who thus robbed me of my personal rights'.[7] This was a cry from her soul, that inner sanctum her mother encouraged her to cultivate, and for the remainder of her life she was determined to crush the white aggressors and their system of cruel injustice.

* * *

Denied the opportunity of effectively educating their children in Salem, John and Nancy relocated the family to Newport, Rhode Island, in 1835. They hoped to find relative freedom and better prospects, but the town was built on the backs of the enslaved and awash with the spirit of slavery. White families had amassed wealth from the blood of human bondage, and amid the bitter spirit of prejudice were rumours that slave chains 'could still be seen in the cellars of some of the houses of the elder citizens', recalled Sarah Remond.[8]

Newport was a microcosm of the Northern states and no better than Salem. Black people were barred from hotels, omnibuses, places of amusement and other public sites. Certain schools were for whites only. God was to be worshipped separately.

Remond's life testified to the fact that segregation was 'an immense disadvantage to the descendants of the African race', she stated, 'and a great drawback to their elevation'.[9] 'Slavery is indeed gone,' wrote Douglass after the Emancipation Proclamation, 'but its shadow still lingers over the country and poisons more or less the moral atmosphere of all sections of the republic.'[10]

Yet, despite the oppressive atmosphere, there was an influential free Black community in Newport. In the North, free African Americans had greater levels of freedom compared to those in the South: they owned land, homes and businesses, they were active in Black churches and schools and they sustained abolitionism through anti-slavery societies, print media and the Underground Railroad.

In Newport, the free Black community were of 'an elevated character, and for industry, morality, and native intellect, would compare favourably with any class in the community', recalled Remond.[11] She spent her days attending a private school for Black children, exploring the natural beauty of Newport and devouring the daily and weekly newspapers that flooded her home. She immersed herself in the libraries of friends and she relished English and American literature, 'which *even* prejudice could not deprive me' of.[12] Libraries, literary societies, churches, schools and the press were important institutions providing education, support and training to members of the free Black community, and Sarah Remond took advantage of them all.

In the summer of 1840, her older brother, Charles Lenox Remond, travelled with William Lloyd Garrison to London, where the World's Anti-Slavery Convention first met, with the aim of strengthening and internationalising the fight against slavery. The convention brought together different abolitionist societies, which broadly fell into two camps: those who favoured immediate abolition, and those who tended towards gradualism. The divisions were evident and became more entrenched, yet Charles Lenox Remond brought a steely determination and unwavering moral conviction to the convention. When female delegates were barred from attending, Lenox walked out in protest. He lectured across the British Isles railing against slavery and colonialism while establishing contacts between American and British abolitionists that would benefit the cause.

As he lectured in Britain, his sister in America lamented the Fugitive Slave Law and decried the Dred Scott decision of 6 March 1857. Scott was an enslaved Black man who sued his owners after they took him into a free state. The case went all the way to the Supreme Court, which declared, in *Dred Scott v. Sandford*, that an enslaved person who resided in a free state was not entitled to freedom, African Americans could not be citizens and the Missouri Compromise (1820), which ruled the

Wisconsin Territory free, was unconstitutional. These decrees pushed the union closer to Civil War and were proof that if one studied the political history of America, it 'would neither elevate humanity, nor advance the moral progress of the world', Remond lamented.[13]

The one glimmer of hope was the abolitionist cause, which Sarah Remond wholeheartedly embraced. She and her sisters were members of the Salem Female Anti-Slavery Society, which organised events and sponsored abolitionist lecturers, providing a training ground for Sarah who, by 1856, was lecturing for the American Anti-Slavery Society. From 1856–58, she toured America denouncing slavery and segregation. She moved in the highest political echelons and confronted the violence of racist Americans who were dismayed at a Black female abolitionist lecturer. She also honed her speaking skills, bracing herself for an imminent international tour.

* * *

Sarah Parker Remond, Manchester, 1859:

> [...] it remains for me to tell you what are the principles of those abolitionists who have originated that glorious movement with which I am identified. Their principles are in accordance with the precepts of Christianity, and their means of action are those of moral suasion; they are working earnestly and devotedly to awaken the moral feelings of the nation, and to arouse public opinion on behalf of the slave. It was thus that the abolition of slavery in your own colonies was brought about through much opposition. Far greater opposition is encountered in America, where the evil is on the spot, and is interwoven with all the institutions of the country; and far greater efforts are needed to bring the moral power of the nation to bear upon the question.[14]

* * *

On 29 December 1858, Sarah Parker Remond set sail for Europe. She was driven by a desire to find freedom, receive a proper education and serve the anti-slavery cause. She was thirty-two years old and travelled alone. 'To ride upon the waves of the ocean three thousand miles is really an event,' she wrote, 'but I know that, no matter how I go, the spirit of prejudice will meet me.'[15]

Back across the waters which carried African men, women and children into slavery, Remond now travelled towards the major port of the British Empire. Paradoxically, the Liverpool docks where slave ships were built became Remond's gateway to a new freedom and a new identity. Her imminent arrival was hailed in the pages of London's monthly newspaper, the *Anti-Slavery Advocate*: 'Miss Sarah P. Remond, a colored lady, a zealous and able anti-slavery lecturer [...] is entitled to our confidence, kindness and respect.'[16] She arrived on 12 January 1859 and was met by leading anti-slavery campaigners. They opened the doors to Britain's social elite and Sarah Parker Remond stepped right through.[17]

Remond delivered her first lecture at the Tuckerman Institute, Liverpool, on the evening of 21 January. She was introduced by Reverend William Henry Channing, a Unitarian minister, who began by praising Remond's family for their 'most active part in the abolition movement', before reassuring the crowd that it was possible for a woman to speak in public without sacrificing her womanhood.[18]

Remond stared out at the crowded assembly. The house was full. She began her lecture without notes. According to the *Liverpool Mercury*, as she entered her exhortation, 'she had a clear, musical voice, a distinct utterance, and – if it be not a needless remark of a lady – we may add she has at her command a great flow of language'.[19] She spoke for an hour and a half on themes that she would reemphasise in years to come: the cruelty of slavery; the suffering of female slaves; the apathy of American Christians. And she appealed to the 'moral and religious sympathy and influence of free England in the abolition movement'.[20] At the conclusion of her talk she was loudly applauded. One observer stated that Remond had an ability to stir 'one's innermost soul'.[21]

According to the press, she was the ideal Victorian lady: demure, deferential, gentle and graceful, and she comported herself with a 'calmness of manner' and the 'utmost readiness and clearness, with an admirable choice of words, and with a womanly dignity'.[22] Remond effectively toed the line. She conformed to notions of the virtuous woman, despite operating within the male public realm, and the day after her Tuckerman lecture, a prominent abolitionist confirmed in a letter to the press:

> She is not seeking either pecuniary gain or personal popularity, but, moved by a deep feeling of the wrongs of her coloured brethren, she is visiting this country with the object of arousing sympathy of the religious and philanthropic people of England towards her race.[23]

This helped quieten jittery patriarchal nerves. Remond was moved by womanly compassion. Her sphere was religious and philanthropic, not political. These were respectable callings for women in Victorian Britain.

Beneath the veneer of her respectable comportment and words was a Black abolitionist-feminist clarion call. An attendee at the National Women's Rights Convention in 1858, Remond saw the abolitionist cause through the prism of Black female suffering and solidarity. 'Women are the worst victims of slave power', she emphasised.[24]

Remond has rightly been described as a 'Black proto-feminist', who actively resisted the negative stereotypes of Black women – the asexual mammies, the hypersexual Jezebels, the grimacing Aunt Jemimas – and in so doing, played her part in an evolving Black feminist tradition which reached back to the 1830s.[25]

This multifaceted tradition assumed a multi-dimensional approach to liberation born out of the twin experiences of being both Black and a woman. There were different forms of Black feminism, but a foundational principle was that issues of 'race', class and sex were inextricable, and that Black women's

Sarah Parker Remond, n.d.

experiences of those intersections engendered distinct needs and perspectives. Sojourner Truth and Harriet Tubman asserted these truisms in America; Zilpha Elaw, Ellen Craft and Harriet Jacobs brought them to Britain in the 1840s; and Sarah

Parker Remond trod in their footsteps.[26] So by speaking out in Britain, Remond internationalised not only the abolitionist cause but Black feminism too.[27]

From Liverpool, Remond headed to the nearby town of Warrington, which had previously hosted Moses Roper and Frederick Douglass and boasted its own Warrington Anti-Slavery Society. As the doors opened on the evening of 24 January, an eager audience spilled into the hall. Within ten minutes, 'not a foot of standing room could be obtained', claimed the *Warrington Times*, as Remond launched into her emotive lecture.[28]

She railed at the moral decay that putrefied the American Government. She condemned the American churches that supported and legitimised slavery. She lamented the segregation and discrimination in the North. And she felt the full force of her own inadequacy. 'Almost overpowered and overwhelmed, for what tongue could describe the horrors of American slavery? Who could give the faintest idea of what the slave mother suffered?' she cried.[29]

But the case of Margaret Garner came close. She had escaped the bonds of slavery, having suffered 'the degradation that a woman could not mention', and fled with her children as far as Cincinnati. 'There she stood amidst magnificent temples dedicated to God,' railed Remond, 'but no sympathy or help was afforded her.'[30] When her slaveholder found her in hiding, Garner grabbed a knife and stabbed her two-year old daughter to death. Freedom came through a butcher's knife, wielded by a mother.

In sharing this story, Remond humanised the individuals trapped in a system thousands of miles away. She tapped into the audience's hunger for sensationalism.[31] And she horrified an audience steeped in a culture that elevated motherhood and family unity. Remond then brought the horror closer to home:

> Yes I can tell you English men and women, that women are sold into slavery with cheeks like the lily and the rose, as well as those that might compare to the wing of the raven. They are exposed for sale, and subjected to the most shameful indignities. The more Anglo-Saxon blood that mingles with the blood of the slave, the more gold is poured out when the auctioneer has a woman for sale, because they are sold to be concubines for white Americans. They are not sold for plantation slaves.[32]

Audiences recognised the figure of the 'mulatta' or 'white slave', who appeared in theatre and fiction, often in service of a conventional plotline: a beautiful, seemingly white, young woman who is ignorant of her enslaved status falls in love but discovers, or remembers, that she is, in fact, Black and formerly enslaved (her father often being the slaveowner) – a revelation which usually forces her back into slavery.

In the 1840s, the 'mulatta' trope was propelled into public consciousness by the white American abolitionist Lydia Maria Child, and was reinforced in the 1850s by Stowe's *Uncle Tom's Cabin*. In Remond's speeches, this familiar literary character was used to evoke empathy, concealing in its belly the anti-slavery message, and to challenge the audience's racialised imagery of slavery.[33]

Remond's talk in Warrington was met with thunderous applause, and at the end of that month she was invited back. This time a small fee was charged for admittance, but this did not diminish the crowds.[34] The Mayor of Warrington chaired the meeting and felt compelled to state that a female lecturer was novel but, then again, a woman was on the throne, and Remond had letters of recommendation. What was more, she was speaking on an important topic. Remond thanked the audience 'from the depths of an overflowing soul' and promised to speak on behalf of the victims of slavery whose voices were silenced in a country where 'sixteen hundred million dollars were invested in the bone, blood and sinews of men and women', and where slaveholders were entrenched in every department of government.

Remond's presence was radical, but her rhetoric was at times conservative: she presented slavery as an affront to Christianity and the Victorian cult of domesticity, discussing 'slave mothers torn from their children, fathers separated from their loved ones'. And she reminded her audience that white children were not always safe either. They too could be kidnapped and sold into slavery. Appealing to the nationalist, religious and moral sentiments of the audience, she declared:

[…] as English men and women in the land of Clarkson and Wilberforce – as the people who still kept before the world the high standard which those great men raised – with a determination of soul, to send their Christian and moral sympathy across the Atlantic, and say to those tyrants – 'Give up those men and women, and restore to them those God-given rights, and as far as you can, atone to them for the great injury you have inflicted on them.'[35]

But there was a righteous anger to her rhetoric: she told her audiences that she supported moral suasion but she never shirked from raising taboo subjects like rape, and she was clear that enslaved people had the right 'to fight for the freedom of their race'.[36] Indeed, she prophesied that 'the spirit of revenge was forming – it was coming upwards in the breast of a slave' and 'that the great American republic was destined to be sundered'.[37] Two years hence, the American Civil War would leave 620,000 bodies in its wake.

A couple of days later, still in Warrington, Remond addressed a predominantly female audience. In her lectures, she drew on notions of 'sisterhood' to try and appeal to white women, creating a bond that transcended racial divisions and prejudice and instead focused on female solidarity.[38] At this meeting, she especially emphasised the suffering of enslaved women and hinted at the rape and abuse they received. 'The fearful amount of licentiousness,' noted the *Warrington Times*, 'was realised by the fact that there were 800,000 mulattoes in the Southern States of America – the fruits of licentiousness – bringing nothing but desolation in the hearts of the mother who bore them.'[39]

At the conclusion of the talk, cut short due to her own exhaustion, Remond was presented with a watch inscribed, 'Presented to S. P. Remond by Englishwomen, her sisters, in Warrington, 2 February, 1859'. Remond responded in a manner that made her audience purr with delight:

> I have been received here as a sister by white women for the first time in my life. I have been removed from the degradation which overhangs all persons of my complexion; and I have felt most deeply that since I have been in Warrington and in England, I have received a sympathy I never was offered before. I had therefore no need of this testimonial of sympathy, but I receive it as the representative of my race with pleasure.[40]

Sarah Parker Remond was a success in Warrington. In addition to raising $100 for the American Anti-Slavery Society, her lectures galvanised abolitionist sentiment and led to an unprecedented 3,522 locals signing a petition against slavery. This was only the start. Between 1859 and 1861, she gave more than forty-five lectures across England, Ireland and Scotland on the themes of the injustices of segregation, the horrors of slavery, the plight of women and the corruption of the American Church and State.

Although her very presence as a Black woman onstage was transgressive, her message struck a chord with conservative Victorian Britons because much else about her – her relatively wealthy background, her lighter complexion, her manners and eloquence – seemed respectable and safe.

Daring to be Heard: Sarah Parker Remond

* * *

In October 1859, Sarah Remond realised her dream of receiving a proper education, enrolling at Bedford College in London, where she studied a range of subjects including Latin and French. While studying, she continued to give lectures and organise for the abolitionist cause. She was active in the Freedman's Aid Association, which gathered funds for the formerly enslaved, and in 1863 she helped form the Ladies' London Emancipation Society, an activist abolitionist group which sought to inform the British about the American Civil War. She embraced the women's suffrage cause too, being one of 1,500 signatories on an 1866 petition.

In 1865, she was granted citizenship of the United Kingdom. A year later, having graduated as a nurse, Remond left England to further her medical training at the prestigious Santa Maria Nuova Hospital in cosmopolitan Florence, which had a notable history of training women doctors. After graduating, she went on to practise medicine for more than twenty years, and in 1877, aged fifty, she married a white Italian named Lazzaro Pintor and moved into the upper echelons of white Florentine society.

Little is known of her later life. She passed away on 13 December 1894 and was buried in the Protestant Cemetery in Rome.

She left behind an enormous contribution: she helped to build and develop the transatlantic antislavery movement, joining the ranks of her brother Charles Lenox Remond, Frederick Douglass, William Wells Brown and Henry 'Box' Brown. Like Sojourner Truth in America, she advocated for abolitionism and women's rights in public spaces that were often sceptical or downright hostile to Black women. She developed networks with white abolitionists and feminists, and she internationalised pluralistic Black feminism too. The journey to Britain was a political act of female empowerment, an assertion of female agency, and Remond was clear that she would depend upon herself alone.

In her lectures, she advocated for women's involvement in the abolitionist cause, using Florence Nightingale as a role model and appealing for 'especial help from the women of England'.[41] She used the language and emotions of sentimental fiction, espousing themes of domesticity, womanhood and marriage, which were shockingly undermined – for white British audiences of the time – in Margaret Garner's story, with the aim of eliciting an emotional response based on pity and empathy.[42] Remond also sought to elicit empathy by alluding to oppressions closer to home, drawing attention to the plight of English seamstresses but arguing that enslaved women were far more degraded, supporting white female suffrage but also urging her white sisters to 'demand for the black woman the protection and rights enjoyed by the white'.[43] In this sense, she recognised and articulated the experience of many Black women in Britain: freedom did not entail equal consideration or equal 'privileges'; there were other barriers for Black women to overcome.[44]

As such, while Remond stroked the national ego to curry favour with her audiences, she never flinched from revealing British hypocrisies and flaws. She could tell her audience that 'as a rule, the heart of Old England beats truly to the anti-slavery cause', but in Manchester and Liverpool 'she found something that approximated more to the pro-slavery spirit of America'.[45]

And at one lecture in September 1859, she left her audience in no doubt that British prosperity was dependent on the plight of the enslaved:

When I walk through the streets of Manchester, and meet load after load of cotton, I think of those eighty thousand cotton plantations on which was grown the one hundred and twenty-five millions of dollars' worth of cotton which supply your market, and I remember that not one cent of that money has ever reached the hands of the labourers.[46]

Britain was not as morally impeccable as it liked to believe, and Sarah Parker Remond was not the only Black abolitionist – or Black feminist – to call Britain out.

17

Crossing Borders: Ellen Craft and William Craft
(EC: 1826–91) (WC: 1824–1900)

In late December 1848, Ellen Craft cut her hair, placed her right arm in a sling and wrapped bandages around her face. She donned a pair of men's trousers and green-tinted spectacles. This enslaved woman, the product of her slave-owning white father raping her enslaved mother, was preparing to pass as a white, rich, disabled, free gentleman. Her husband William Craft, who was also born enslaved, would act as her Black servant. This huge gamble was a desperate attempt to escape the shackles of slavery so that the couple could start a family in freedom.

Thus disguised, the Crafts headed to the station in Macon, Georgia, and boarded a train to another city in the state, Savannah, some 200 miles away. Ellen took her seat in the first-class carriage while William took his place in the 'negro car'. Just before the train was about to leave, William caught sight of a cabinetmaker for whom he had previously worked. The man was directing questions to the ticket seller and began searching the carriages, clearly driven by an intuitive fear that the Crafts were making an escape. He saw but did not recognise Ellen in her disguise, and then the train moved off just before he got to the 'negro car' where he would have discovered William.

As the train shuffled along the tracks, it was soon apparent that Ellen had taken a seat next to a close friend of her slave-owner. Ellen was convinced the escape attempt had come to a premature conclusion until the gentleman said to her, 'It is a very fine morning, sir.'[1] Ellen feigned deafness to avoid being drawn into conversation.

Reaching Savannah, the fugitive freedom-seekers boarded a steamer bound for Charleston, South Carolina. Ellen swiftly went to bed, no doubt traumatised and exhausted by the day's events and eager to avoid conversation with the other passengers. William slept on the deck as there were no places provided for Black travellers. In the morning, Ellen ate breakfast with the other passengers and found herself next to the captain, who was impressed by her 'servant':

> You have a very attentive boy, sir; but you had better watch him like a hawk when you get on to the North. He seems all very well here, but he may act quite differently there. I know several gentlemen who have lost their valuable n****rs among them d—d cut-throat abolitionists.[2]

A slave trader confirmed that taking an enslaved person to the North was incredibly risky and offered to purchase William and take him back to the South. Ellen declined the offer.

The steamer eventually arrived in Charleston and the couple headed to the city's best hotel, where Ellen, still disguised, was treated with the utmost care. The next day, she and William continued their journey by steamer and train to Baltimore, Maryland. They had to contend with suspicious authorities and racist passengers, one of whom was particularly irked by the fact that William wore 'a devilish fine hat'. 'It always makes me itch all over, from head to toe, to get hold of every d—d n****r I see dressed like a white man', he sneered behind tobacco-stained teeth.[3] Ellen and William promptly left the carriage.

When they eventually arrived in Baltimore, they had to confront the border patrols, which were particularly vigilant because many enslaved freedom-seekers attempted to enter the free state of Pennsylvania. At the train station, an officer declared that William and his 'master' needed to report to the authorities. Although paralysed with fear, William believed that 'the good God, who had been with us thus far, would not forsake us at the eleventh hour'.[4]

The eagle-eyed officer warned that it was against state rules to take an enslaved person into the free state of Philadelphia, unless the slaveowner could satisfy the authorities that he had a right to do so, and the officer was not satisfied with Ellen's excuses. He flatly refused to let the pair travel any further.

They had fallen into 'deep waters and were about to be overwhelmed', as their narrative puts it, but at that moment the train conductor entered the office and confirmed that the pair had travelled with him from Washington.[5] As the train's bell rang for its onward departure, the officer reluctantly let the pair proceed, owing in part to the invalid state of the disguised Ellen, and they swiftly boarded the train.

The Crafts arrived in Philadelphia the next morning – Christmas Day – and as they left the station, Ellen grasped William by the hand, 'Thank God, William, we're safe!'[6] She leant upon her husband and burst into tears.

In Philadelphia, the Crafts were assisted by the underground abolitionist network and, though Ellen was naturally fearful of white abolitionists, convinced that white people would draw them back into slavery, her fears were soon subdued by the kindness they received. On their first day in the city, the Crafts were given a reading lesson. Three weeks later, they could spell and write their names.

They went on to Boston, a key centre of the antislavery movement, and legally married in 1850. They subsequently partnered with William Wells Brown, joining the anti-slavery lecture circuit as the story of their escape spread through lectures, newspapers and visual media.

The camera was an instrument of resistance for many Black abolitionists, challenging white representations of 'the likeness of the negro, rather than of the man', as Frederick Douglass put it.[7] Ellen Craft posed for a daguerreotype in her masculine disguise: her direct gaze, cleft chin, pale skin tone and unapologetic masculine appearance undermined more commonplace visual representations of the meek, Black fugitive victim.[8]

As the image circulated, the Crafts undertook further lecture tours, and to make a living they established successful furniture-making and needlework businesses. But, as for many other formerly enslaved people, including those whom we have met earlier such as Henry 'Box' Brown, the Fugitive Slave Act placed the Crafts' hard-won new life under threat, and so they were forced to undertake another journey.

In November 1850, they boarded the SS *Cumbria* and sailed for England: 'May God ever smile upon England and upon England's good, much-beloved, and deservedly-honoured Queen, for the generous protection that is given to unfortunate refugees of every rank, and of every colour and clime.'[9] Stepping ashore, they finally felt 'free from every slavish fear'.[10]

The above narrative comes from *Running a Thousand Miles for Freedom* (1860), which was first published in London and included Ellen's daguerreotype on the title page. This text was unlike other emancipation narratives, which predominantly dealt with the singular enslaved man who overcame insurmountable obstacles, thus enshrining 'the Black American meta-narrative of heroic or noble victimization', writes scholar Gerald L. Early.[11] *Running a Thousand Miles*, on the other hand, demonstrates 'connection, collaboration, and partnership' between husband and wife, as academic Barbara McCaskill notes.[12]

Ellen Craft, 1853

The Crafts' story merges the drama of escape with the nineteenth-century literary tradition of victory through resolve and independence, all wrapped up in the romantic Christian dream of marriage and family.[13] As such, the memoir served the market for didactic books that contained a moral message: self-sufficiency and self-help were key ingredients in the realisation of freedom.[14]

Historian C. Riley Snorton observes how in the Crafts' narrative Black fugitivity intersects with gender fungibility, which turned cross-dressing and other forms of 'passing' into acts of empowerment that were also criminal.[15] Some enslaved people illegally disguised themselves as white or naturally appeared white – the enslaved man William Grimes, for instance, who wrote, 'They always took me to be a white man'.[16] Josephine Brown, daughter of William Wells Brown, recalled how her father found a painter who literally painted a fugitive white. She wrote:

> In an hour, by Mr. Brown's directions, the black man was as white, and with as rosy cheeks, as any of the Anglo-Saxon race, and disguised in the dress of a woman, with a thick veil over her face.[17]

This fugitive and the Crafts weren't the only enslaved people to use cross-dressing as a means of disguise. Harriet Jacobs walked to her free grandmother's house by donning a sailor's suit. 'I performed,' she wrote in 1861.[18]

Cross-dressing was not always associated with the enslaved, however. Readers in the Northern states might have remembered the infamous case of the Black sex worker, Peter Sewally, alias Mary Jones, who was charged with grand larceny in 1836. Sewally appeared in court, pleading not guilty, attired in a wig, white earrings and a dress. Challenging moral, racial and gender boundaries, Sewally was dubbed 'the Man-Monster' by the white press. He represented a leviathan of Black citizenship in contrast to virtuous white America.[19] In Britain, Elijah (or Eliza) Scott, described in the British press as 'a man of colour', was accused of assault with intent to commit sodomy, and like Sewally, he'd been 'in the habit of walking the streets at night, attired like a woman for the basest of purposes', wrote the press, and was imprisoned for twelve months.[20] Scott was one of many male sex workers plying their trade in London and one of many arrested for dressing as a woman.[21] At a time when scientific racism was establishing fixed, biological and hierarchical categories of difference, Sewally and Scott suggested another reality.

The Crafts' story had a similar effect, illuminating the mutability of gender and 'race', while merging Blackness with performativity. The story of Ellen's escape disrupted racial, gender, class and normative categories. And her whiteness was a central component of their overall celebrity, too.

While Remond evoked the 'mulatta' in her lectures, Craft was the literal embodiment.[22] In contemporaneous accounts, she was described as white rather than Black or 'mulatto' – she resisted these accounts by aligning herself with her Black ancestry – and her presence destabilised already confused definitions of whiteness in America (according to which, for instance, people of third- or fourth-generation African descent were considered white in many Southern slavery-promoting states). As a whole, therefore, despite its conformity in some respects with popular tropes of the liberation narrative, *Running a Thousand Miles* was unsettling to white readers. Ellen Craft's person disrupted popular perceptions of what a Black enslaved woman looked like and her means of asserting her agency in her fight for freedom was transgressive in both America and Britain.

* * *

Ellen and William Crafts' early months in Britain coincided with two key events in spring 1851. First, at the end of March, the census was conducted. The Crafts were registered in Leeds living with the Quaker, William Armistead. Under the column 'Rank, Profession, or Occupation', William Craft was described as a 'cabinet maker'. The words 'Fugitive Slave' were added and underlined. Beneath William's was the entry for Ellen: 'Wife of Wm Craft Fugitive Slave'. She was registered as twenty-four-years old; William as twenty-six.[23]

Then, a couple of months later, Ellen and William attended the Great Exhibition of the Works of Industry of All Nations in Hyde Park, which opened on 1 May. The international exhibition, which was organised and overseen by Prince Albert, sought to demonstrate Britain's greatness to the world and bore the motto, 'The Earth is the Lord's and all that therein is'.[24]

The Lord's world was brought together in the enormous Crystal Palace, which housed around 100,000 objects from over 14,000 contributors in a multistorey building over 500 metres long. The British displays occupied half of the space. The pitiful American section contained 500 exhibits sparsely arranged in a 40,000 square-foot area. There was a block of zinc from New Jersey, boat oars from Boston, bars of soap from Texas and a neoclassical sculpture by Hiram Powers, *The Greek Slave*, a statue of a Greek woman stripped and chained at a slave market. Towering above all the exhibits was a large pasteboard eagle, the symbol of American greatness.

Ellen and William Craft walked into the American section and, positioning themselves next to Powers' statue, produced a page from *Punch* magazine which depicted a Virginian woman enslaved in chains. The Crafts were joined by a handful of others, including William Wells Brown, who, according to a letter published in Still's *The Underground Railroad*, shouted, 'As an American fugitive slave, I place this Virginia Slave by the side of the Greek Slave, as its most fitting companion.'[25]

The stunt prompted a small crowd to gather around the protesters. *Punch*'s Virginian Slave was promptly removed by a tight-lipped white American as the protestors continued to rile the American delegation by promenading through the Great Exhibition for six or seven hours, William Craft walking arm in arm with a white abolitionist named Amelia Thompson. William Still wrote:

> To see the arm of a beautiful English young lady passed through that of a "n****r," taking ices and other refreshments with him, upon terms of the most perfect equality, certainly was enough to "rile" the slave-holders who beheld it; but there was no help for it.[26]

* * *

Under the sponsorship of abolitionists, the Crafts proceeded to receive an education at the Ockham School in Surrey and were subsequently offered jobs. William taught carpentry to boys and Ellen domestic crafts to girls. In October 1852, they welcomed their first son into the world and three years later, their second. The Crafts had five children in total, all born and raised in England.

They remained prominent anti-slavery activists. They sat on the Executive Committee of the London Emancipation Committee, established in May 1859 with the aim of influencing British public opinion against slavery. Ellen Craft attended meetings and developed networks among white and Black abolitionists, opening her home to Sarah Parker Remond and the Black pastor and abolitionist John Sella Martin; offering assistance to formerly enslaved individuals and becoming involved with a range of organisations, such as the

London Emancipation Committee and the Women's Suffrage Organisation. In the mid-1860s, she raised enough money to bring her enslaved mother from America to England.[27] And she and William continued to undertake anti-slavery speaking tours in England and Scotland.

Constrained by gender norms, Ellen nonetheless mounted the stage, using silence as a performative tool. She would sit or stand in the background while William Craft recounted their story of escape. But at the end of his speech, Ellen would step towards the audience, emerging as corporeal proof of the sexual violence experienced by enslaved women like her mother, and the embodiment of the fact that Black people could 'take care of themselves', as she quipped to one white gentleman.[28]

Ellen would sometimes answer questions, make jokes onstage, or write to the press in gestures of agency and protest. She emphasised her Black identity and would continue resistance and remembrance in private by singing abolitionist songs such as 'I Shall Not Be a Slave Anymore'.[29] She also drew on the realities of domestic labour and motherhood as a vehicle for her activism. She challenged the prevalent racist notion that 'mulatta' women were sterile by appearing onstage with her eldest son, literally performing motherhood.[30]

She was unafraid to challenge white, male authority. At a dinner party in 1867, Ellen was seated next to the former Governor of Jamaica, Edward John Eyre, who, just two years earlier, had violently suppressed the Morant Bay Rebellion of 1865. Among other acts of violence, he ordered the arrest of Jamaican businessman and politician George William Gordon who, without due process, was tried for high treason and executed. Ellen turned to Eyre and asked him, 'Do you not yourself, sir, feel now that poor Gordon was unjustly executed?'[31] Eyre did not know how to respond and swiftly headed to the other side of the room.

* * *

William Craft likewise continued to engage in activism and protest. He was elected to the John Anderson Committee, formed in 1861 to welcome and support the fugitive John Anderson, and two years later, he directly challenged scientific racism at a meeting of the British Association for the Advancement of Science, which was being held in Newcastle.

The weather that August day was gloomy and dark as incessant rain and thunder pounded down from the skies. But snug inside Section E of the British Association, in the area devoted to geography and ethnology, Dr James Hunt, a founding member of the Anthropological Society, was presenting his conference paper to a packed crowd. It was entitled 'Physical and Mental Character of the Negro':

> The capacity of the negro is limited to imitation. The prevailing impulse is for sensuality and rest. No sooner are the physical wants satisfied all psychical effort ceases, and the body abandons itself to sexual gratification and rest. […] Life has for the negro no longer any value when he cannot supply the physical wants; he never resists by increased activity, but prefers to die in a state of apathy, or he commits suicide. The negro has no love for war; he is only driven to it by hunger. War from passion or destructiveness is unknown to him.[32]

Dr Hunt, who did much to popularise scientific racism, dwelt at length on the supposed inability of Africans to better themselves, that Victorian evangelical obsession. He stressed the weakness of their family lives and their propensity to 'drunkenness, gambling, and ornamentation of the body'. As he spoke, members of the audience either cheered or jeered. Hunt then closed his talk with some firm conclusions:

1. That there is as good reason for classifying the negro as a distinct species from the European as there is for making the ass a distinct species from the zebra.
2. That the negro is inferior intellectually to the European.
3. That the analogies are far more numerous between the negro and apes than between the European and apes.[33]

Craft now rose to address the room. He asserted that 'though he was not of pure African descent, he was black enough to attempt to say a few words'. He described how his grandparents had 'pure negro blood', his grandfather was a proud 'chief of the West Coast' and 'through the treachery of some white men, who doubtless thought themselves greatly his superiors, he was kidnapped and taken to America'. He reminded the crowd about prominent Black Victorians such as Sarah Forbes Bonetta, and to supportive laughter, he jibed:

> When Julius Caesar came to this country, he said of the natives that they were such stupid people that they were not fit to make slaves of in Rome. It had taken a long time to make Englishmen what they are now.[34]

Craft then dismantled Hunt's thesis. In response to Hunt's claim that 'the thick skull and woolly head of the negro' was 'a mark of inferiority', Craft retorted, 'If the Almighty had not provided him with these in the hot climate he [the negro] would be as muddy-headed as certain persons who called themselves philosophers.' In response to the idea that people of African descent lacked mental development and could never be civilised, Craft retorted, 'Under his treatment the mind of the negro child was capable of a very high degree of culture'.[35] He concluded:

> Looking at the coloured people in America, and the long generations of oppression that had been exhibited towards them by all classes of white men, the wonder in his mind was not that so many of that race now occupied so respectable position, intellectually and morally, but that the soul had not been crushed out of them altogether.[36]

William Craft regained his seat to rapturous applause.

* * *

On the final day of the annual meeting, 2 September 1863, attendees headed out for excursions. The inventor Sir William Armstrong took a delegation to nearby Whitney, where they witnessed his Armstrong guns in action (a few years later, those same guns would be aimed at samurai fighters in the Boshin War, 1868–69).[37] The spectators had an agreeable time, though the poor weather brought the outing to an earlier than planned conclusion. Later that evening, however, spirits were lifted as an unusually large crowd gathered to hear William Craft give another talk.

He began by reminding the audience that he had once been enslaved and that 'he now considered himself an Englishman of African parentage, unfortunately born in America'. The subject of his talk would be his recent visit to Dahomey, where he had sought to 'change the bad habits of the people', which included human sacrifice and the trade in human slaves.[38] Supported by the British Government, but not representing it, Craft had been given a royal welcome by the King of Dahomey. Craft recalled the executed bodies displayed in the marketplace, and the thousands of Dahomean female warriors, 'Amazons, attired in the gayest garments', plus the hundreds of young women who 'danced very prettily', who took part in the official celebrations. During his talk, Craft offered an ethnographic exposé: human sacrifices did occur in Dahomey (though never of women or children); the King 'was quite black enough, but not quite so black as he had been painted' and different tribes were marked by different tattoos. Craft displayed several artifacts to his audience, including the backbone of a boa constrictor, before concluding that Dahomey could be encouraged to forgo slavery if their cotton industry became more profitable.[39] He was warmly applauded for his words.

No doubt, Craft was promoting British interests in West Africa. He espoused ideas shared by the likes of the African Aid Society, founded in July 1860 with the aim of abolishing slavery and promoting Christianity in Africa. They subscribed to the idea that if cotton production flourished in Africa, Britain would no longer require cotton from the slave-owning states of the American south. This would consequentially dampen the slaveowners' profits and ultimately lead to emancipation.[40] In actively supporting these ideas – notably the necessity of British involvement in West Africa and the need for Africa to embrace elements of Western culture – Craft has subsequently been accused of embracing and promoting Britain's colonial and imperial ambitions.[41]

In the end, though, the Crafts resist simple categorisation. Historians have to contend with and accept the paradoxes and contradictions of their story.[42] They have been portrayed as glorious heroes and lovers who triumphantly emerged from slavery to liberation, but the passing of the Fugitive Slave Act revealed that freedom in the North was precarious. Britain wasn't an island free from racism either. According to one acquaintance, Ellen detected and resented the 'amount of pro-slavery feeling among the English, the bigotry of the majority of people and anti-slavery people, [and] the small number of actual working abolitionists'.[43]

She remained constrained by gender norms, yet she also spoke out. And some forty years later, towards the close of the century, another African American woman would do the same.

Building on the work of Sarah Parker Remond, Ellen Craft and other Black abolitionists, Ida B. Wells developed networks, contacts and organisations to spread her message of anti-racism, becoming part of a cohort of Black campaigners and activists who sought profound and lasting reform.

18

Anti-Racism: Ida B. Wells
(1862–1931)

The voice of the people is the voice of God, and I long with all the intensity of my soul for the Garrison, Douglas[s], Sumner, W[h]ittier and Phillips who shall rouse this nation to a demand that from Greenland's icy mountains to the coral reefs of the Southern seas, mob rule shall be put down and equal and exact justice be accorded to every citizen of whatever race, who finds a home within the borders of the land of the free and the home of the brave.[1]

Ida B. Wells, February 1893

Ida B. Wells – educator, editor, feminist, activist – delivered these lines in a speech at the Tremont Temple, Boston, on 13 February 1893. As she praised prominent abolitionists who came before her, she herself was taking up the baton. A few months after this oration – which, seventy years later, echoed through Dr Martin Luther King's geographically expansive 'I have a dream', 'From every mountainside, let freedom ring' – Ida B. Wells came to England on the first of two tours in 1893 and 1894. She lectured across the country, from Portsmouth to Huntley near Aberdeen, often delivering a single talk to hundreds of people.[2]

She was invited by writer Isabelle Mayo and the Quaker, Catherine Impey, the founder of the anti-racist journal *Anti-Caste: Devoted to the Interests of Coloured Races*, whom we briefly met in Chapter 2. Mayo and Impey hoped Wells would emulate Frederick Douglass' triumphant 1845 tour of Britain, and certainly, by May 1893, the British press could proclaim that she 'has been lecturing with great success on a subject somewhat new to British audiences', lynch law in the United States.[3]

In the 1830s, and therefore in the context of the campaign for abolition, British commentators generally saw lynching as a form of anarchy, but over the intervening decades minds had been changed, primarily thanks to the efforts of American commentators who argued that lynching was a form of 'justice' necessary in frontier communities. They also argued that lynching expressed popular sovereignty, which checked the supposed dangers posed to white women by Black men.

British commentators largely bought into the lie, believing that perhaps lynching constituted a forgivable form of extra-legal violence, which maintained law and order and corrected wrongs (mainly sexual) allegedly perpetrated by Black men.[4] But Ida B. Wells maintained that all lynching was immoral and debased USA society as a whole. Lynching was an expression of white supremacy, the myth of Black rapists was exactly that – a myth – and lynching was not an expression of popular sovereignty but rather one of despotism and depravity. She injected a counternarrative into Britain with remarkable success, emulating the Black abolitionists who had come before.

Born enslaved in 1862 and freed under the terms of the Emancipation Proclamation of 1 January the following year, Wells went on to work as a teacher, journalist and editor of a Memphis paper, the *Evening Star*. In 1889, she was elected as secretary to the National Colored Press Association, and that year she became the editor of another Memphis paper, *Free Speech and Headlight*, having purchased a third interest, which made her an equal partner.

Following the lynching of a close friend in Memphis (one of a 1,000 cases reported between 1883 and 1884; we can assume the real number was much higher), Wells used the power of her pen and voice to attack lynching. She gave lectures in Wilmington, Delaware, Pennsylvania and Washington, and in 1892 published *Southern Horrors*, which contained many of the arguments she would mount in Britain.[5]

Wells challenged the unreliable reports of lynching in the Southern press. She showed that Black men were brutalised for having consensual sex with white women and she revealed that only about thirty per cent of Black victims had actually been *accused* of rape before they were lynched.[6] 'Even to the better class of Afro-Americans,' she wrote in *Southern Horrors*, 'the crime of rape is so revolting they have too often taken the white man's word and given lynch law neither the investigation nor condemnation it deserved.'[7] As the academic Angela Y. Davis argues, Wells defied 'the central role played by the fictional Black rapist in the shaping of post-slavery racism'.[8]

And there was more patent radicalism in her work. 'A Winchester rifle should have a place of honor in every black home,' Wells wrote, 'and it should be used for that protection which the law refuses to give.' This, plus a combination of 'boycott, emigration and the press', were needed to stamp out lynch law. She concluded, 'The gods help those who help themselves.'[9]

Through her actions, Wells stepped outside the confines of respectable, Black womanhood. She stood up in the Southern pit of sexual violence, white supremacy and racist mythology and she called it out. She was met with ambivalence or outright hostility in America, so, when presented with the opportunity of taking her message to Britain, she jumped at the chance.[10]

In the UK, her primary focus was on exposing lynching, but in interviews and lectures Wells denounced American segregation more broadly. This was a clever strategy, since British newspapers were largely conservative, hence shocking accounts of lynching could have met with editorial resistance. Furthermore, discussions of American racial segregation gave British audiences a context for understanding lynching and, by lamenting segregated churches in America, allowed Wells to connect with British Christians.[11] She also championed the term Afro-American over 'negro' because the latter overlooked nationality 'and we are all Americans', she stressed. In one interview, she added, 'Some of the "coloured" people are not distinguishable from the whites, so far has their negro blood been diluted, but they are all Afro-Americans – that is, Americans of African descent.'[12] This point, incidentally, was equally applicable to Britain: African blood coursed through Great Britain's veins.

But in America, unlike in Britain, there was formal, legal segregation. During the period of Reconstruction following the Civil War, and especially after the election of President Rutherford B. Hayes in 1876, the Southern states redrafted their constitutions, eradicating the rights of Black citizens. (The infamous 1896 case *Plessy v. Ferguson* subsequently upheld the Jim Crow laws.) And so, in 1884, seventy-one years before the Montgomery bus boycott triggered by fifteen-year-old Claudette Colvin and seamstress Rosa Parks, Ida B. Wells registered her own protest by refusing to move to the 'Jim Crow Car', as it was called.

As the conductor dragged her away, she bit his hand and subsequently hired a lawyer. She sued the company and won – only for that victory to be overturned by the Tennessee State Supreme Court. Wells was ordered to pay $200 in costs.

On tour in Britain, she regaled this injustice to audiences before turning her scorn on lynching. 'The mob are no longer content with shooting and banging, but burn negroes alive', she stressed.[13] On 6 July 1894, the *Leeds Mercury* reported on one of her lectures:

> [Lynching] happened not during the days of the Spanish Inquisition, not during the Dark Ages of the world, these crimes were not committed by the cannibals of the South Sea Islands – had they been so committed there would have been a terrible outcry – but were committed in the glare of the nineteenth century civilization, and by men who belonged to the Anglo-Saxon race, who boasted of their Christianity. The world was singularly silent, and the tone of condemnation and the voice that ought to cry shame on such deeds had been very hesitating and undecided. The world, she believed, had done so little regarding this matter because it knew so little it was her mission to give to the world the black people's side of the story.[14]

Wells should not be seen as a marginal figure or a lone militant in 1890s Britain; rather, she was at the centre of the British reform movement.[15] Building on earlier Black abolitionist campaigns, she effectively forged links with MPs, editors and aristocrats. She drew on the remnants of anti-slavery networks and developed new contacts too. She amplified the anti-racist sentiments expressed in *Anti-Caste*, providing a national platform for the journal.

On her second tour in 1894, she worked as a foreign correspondent for a Chicago newspaper, the *Daily Inter-Ocean*, ensuring that she had a voice in America too. In Britain, she shared a platform with the Black editor of the Christian paper *Lux*, Celestine Edwards, who used his networks to spread her message.

In working with Edwards, Wells engaged with the nascent Black British press, which would find further expression in the short-lived the *Pan-African*, launched by Henry Sylvester

Williams in 1901, and the *African Times and Orient Review*, founded by Dusé Mohamed Ali in 1912 (and running until 1920). Edwards and Wells both impressed audiences with their anti-racist rhetoric and in 1893 jointly edited the final edition of *Anti-Caste*, which was then reconfigured into the even larger journal *Fraternity*, edited by Edwards. This journal became the official organ of the Society for the Recognition of the Brotherhood of Man, established by Wells and Catherine Impey to oppose racism in all its ugly forms.[16]

* * *

Ida B. Wells, 1893

In the 1870s and 1880s, British periodicals and papers were proliferating, thanks to rising literacy rates, cheaper modes of production, innovative technologies in printing and paper production, new networks of distribution and the abolition of the duty on papers (1861). Furthermore, telegraph cables reached across to America (1858), the Black Sea (1868) and India (1869), bringing faster communications and international news. These developments enabled Wells to propagate her message and she took full advantage of them all.

But much like Sarah Parker Remond, Ellen Craft and Zilpha Elaw, Wells had to navigate 'double jeopardy': the fact of being both Black and a woman.[17] She talked publicly about murder, rape and consensual sex between Black men and white women, and in her person she represented the antithesis to patriarchal notions of passive, fragile and happily domestic womanhood.[18]

Furthermore, she lectured at a time when W. T. Stead's scandalous newspaper article, 'The Maiden Tribute of Modern Babylon' (1885), revealed the sex trafficking of young girls and ignited a moral panic over 'white slavery'. But Wells suggested that Black women were also threatened by male sexuality and, even more challengingly, that Black men were endangered both by white women's lust and by white men's desire to crush the fantasies of white women.[19]

Her presence and her words were transgressive and powerful, so she needed to establish her own personal legitimacy in America and Britain by conforming to gendered notions of propriety, engaging with religious networks and working closely with white allies. She was caught in what historian Nicole King describes as a paradox of the Victorian feminist: to tell the *truth* about lynching, Wells had to *perform* the role of a conventional, respectable lady.[20] So she presented herself as a humble, gentle woman forced into public life because of the horrors of lynching.[21]

But this requirement for performance did not limit her action or impact. She rallied the British into signing anti-lynching petitions. She helped form the Anti-lynching Committee, which included some twenty MPs and received an initial donation from a dozen Africans living in London. In the Committee's 1894–95 report, it was stated that they regularly met and lobbied governors in Arkansas, Tennessee, Mississippi, Kentucky, Louisiana, Texas, Florida, Alabama, Georgia, South Carolina and Ohio. Some 2,000 anti-lynching materials were sent to governors and editors.[22] Her work went on and on.

In America she established a civic club for Black women. 'As these ladies are able and fearless advocates of woman suffrage,' proclaimed the *Woman's Journal*, 'it may be expected that the Woman's Era Club will take the lead in educational work for the movement among colored women.'[23] She also helped set up the National Association of Colored Women's Clubs in 1896, which tackled civil rights and women's suffrage, and in 1913 she founded Chicago's Black women's suffrage group, the Alpha Suffrage Club. She was also part of the founding of the National Association for the Advancement of Colored People (NAACP), which went on to become the United States' most famous civil rights organisation.

In Britain, alongside the petitions, the Anti-lynching Committee and the Society for the Recognition of the Brotherhood of Man, she embedded a new narrative, using her experiences of Southern racism to expose the realities of racism to thousands of Britons. In the process, she challenged prevailing views and confused understandings on the subject of American lynching. In 1893, following the lynching of Henry Smith in Texas, the British *Daily Chronicle*'s reporting included mealy-mouthed language such as 'tragedy', 'not wonderful' and 'strong provocation', as if Smith had courted the mob.

But in 1894, after Wells had spoken out during her British tour, even the conservative *Economist* could admit that 'race hatred', not rape, caused the lynching of innocent people in America.[24] That change, that awakening to reality, was largely down to Ida B. Wells.

* * *

Wells was not alone. She was among a chorus of powerful Black female voices challenging white supremacy. A year before her *Southern Horrors* was published, the African American author Lucy Ann Delany published *From the Darkness Cometh the Light, or, Struggles for Freedom* (1891), which recounted her fight for freedom from slavery. A year later, Frances Ellen Watkins Harper's novel *Iola Leroy; or, Shadows Uplifted* (1892) explored a raft of social and political issues including abolition and reconstruction. Also in that year, Anna Julia Haywood Cooper published *A Voice from the South: By a Black Woman of the South* (1892), fomenting a growing Black feminist tradition that stretched from Sojourner Truth's 'Ain't I a Woman' speech (1851) to Harper's *We Are All Bound Up Together* (1866) to Fannie Barrier Williams' *Intellectual Progress of the Colored Women of the US since the Emancipation Proclamation* (1893).

Anna Julia Haywood Cooper, who also came to Britain in 1900, was, like Wells, born into slavery and freed following emancipation. Aged nineteen, she married a man of the ministry, but his death two years later enabled her to begin a career as a teacher (impossible while she was married).

As a self-supporting widow, Cooper obtained a BA, MA and ultimately a PhD. Her dissertation pre-empted the insights of Aimé Césaire and C. L. R. James by showing how early capitalism was dependent on slavery through a comparative study of the French and Haitian revolutions.[25] In 1887, she was recruited to teach at Washington Colored High School, followed by M Street High School and then the renowned Dunbar High School.

In her book *A Voice from the South* (1892), published in the same year as Wells' *Southern Horrors*, Cooper argued that the future of the entire African American community rested on the moral, intellectual and spiritual development of Black women. 'Womanhood: a vital element in the regeneration and progress of a race,' she wrote. She argued that women brought a unique grace and sensibility to education. 'Let us then, here and now, recognize this force and resolve to make the most of it—not the boys less, but the girls more.'[26] And she argued that educated Black women needed to support their peers, echoing the motto of the National Association of Colored Women, 'Lifting as We Climb'.[27]

She went further, too, criticising the depictions of Black women by authors such as Harriet Beecher Stowe and critiquing Black men for securing higher education for themselves but not for their sisters and mothers: '[...] while our men seem thoroughly abreast of the times on almost every other subject, when they strike the woman question they drop back into sixteenth century logic'.[28] Black men were the 'muffled chord', she argued. Black women were the 'mute and voiceless note' – they had 'no language – but a cry'.

She challenged the suffrage movement, highlighting the 'paralyzing grip of caste prejudice' and their failure to fight racism, and stressing that the greatest potential in the women's movement lay not with white women but with the women 'confronted by both a woman question and a race problem'.[29] In short, Cooper believed Black women should be at the forefront of social change and there were many individuals to cite and praise: Phillis Wheatley, Frances Watkins Harper, Sojourner Truth, Amanda Smith, Sarah Woodson Early, Martha Briggs, Charlotte Fortin Grimke, Fannie Jackson Coppin and Edmonia Lewis.

A Voice from the South was a powerful articulation of Black feminism.[30] Key tenets of Black feminist thought were informed and strengthened by her work, including the premise that gender and 'race' are intimately connected and that both are informed by class, sexuality and nationhood: an early expression of 'intersectionality'.[31] Furthermore, in following in Wells' footsteps and coming to Britain in 1900, Cooper internationalised her ideas and became yet another significant Black female activist in Britain at the close of the nineteenth century.

* * *

Two other such activists were Charlotte Manye and Alice Victoria Kinloch, both campaigning in 1890s Britain for political support and social change for their fellow Black South Africans. Manye was a member of the African Jubilee Singers and later the founder of the African Methodist Episcopal Church in South Africa. Speaking to W. T. Stead's *Review of Reviews* in 1891, she declared:

> Let us be in Africa as we are in England. Here we are treated as men and women. Yonder we are but as cattle. But in Africa, as in England, we are human. Can you not make your people at the Cape as kind and just as your people here?[32]

Kinloch, born in the Cape around 1863, came to Britain probably in mid-1895, a year after Ida B. Wells. Kinloch wrote a pamphlet and spoke to large crowds in Newcastle-upon-Tyne, York, Manchester and London. Her major theme was 'the ill treatment of the Natives throughout South Africa, but principally on the Compound System as obtains throughout the Mining Districts'.[33] The Compound System erected fences to create closely guarded barracks, which contained Black workers who were subject to degrading treatment.

Henry Sylvester Williams from Trinidad and Thomas J. Thompson from Sierra Leone, who were both studying at the Inns of Court, met and interviewed Kinloch. Together, they agreed in 1897 to form the African Association, which had the following aims:

> To encourage a feeling of unity: to facilitate friendly intercourse among Africans in general; to promote and protect the interest of all subjects claiming African descent, wholly or in part, in British Colonies and other places, especially in Africa, by circulating accurate information on all subjects affecting their rights and privileges as subjects of the British Empire and by direct appeals to the Imperial and local governments.[34]

As Sylvester Williams wrote in a private letter, 'The Association is the result of Mrs Kinloch's work in England and the feeling that as British Subjects we ought to be heard in our own affairs.'[35] Williams, who recognised his British status, also recognised the role of a Black woman in the anti-racist fight (a recognition that was not always forthcoming) and she, too, acknowledged the collective endeavour:

> [...] with some men of my race in this country, I have formed a society for the benefit of our people in Africa [...] I think the time has come for us to bear some of our responsibilities, and in so doing we will help the Aborigines' Protection Society.[36]

The following day, on 15 October 1897, the African Association was formally launched in the presence of 'twelve or fifteen negroes', wrote the press. And that evening, Kinloch delivered a speech which concluded, 'I am trying to educate people in this country in regard to the iniquitous laws made for blacks in South Africa.'[37]

Kinloch returned to South Africa in February 1898, leaving behind an organisation that had the support of Dadabhai Naoroji MP, Britain's first Indian Parliamentarian, and boasted Booker T. Washington as a patron. The African Association lobbied

Parliament, sought reforms and sought to educate on issues concerning injustices in Africa and the Caribbean colonies. And a couple of years later, the African Association, seeking to create a new platform from which Black women and men could speak out, inaugurated the first Pan-African Conference of 1900.

Pan-Africanism, as Professor Hakim Adi explains, can be 'viewed as one river with many streams and currents'.[38] It is a helpful metaphor which takes us to the source: the belief in the 'unity, common history and common purpose of the peoples of Africa and the African diaspora', Adi writes, 'and the notion that their destinies are interconnected'.[39] Alongside this stress on unity, there is the call for liberation from social, political, cultural and economic oppression – emancipation for Africa as a continent and for African peoples around the world – and a belief that the cornerstone of liberation is a united, independent Africa.

Although Pan-Africanism has ancient roots, it primarily emerged in response to the African diaspora, created by the enslavement and transportation of Africans, and Pan-Africanism entered a new phase in the context of anti-colonial struggles after 1945 as well. But it was at the First Pan-African Conference in 1900 that the terms 'Pan-African' and 'Pan-Africanism' were established; international Pan-African contacts and networks were cemented; the principle of self-governance was forcefully asserted; and a powerful and influential movement was formally initiated, which would reverberate well into the twentieth century and beyond.

19

Looking Forward: The Pan-African Movement

July 1900, and a heatwave was scorching London, causing city folk to sweat as they scanned newspaper articles about the Boer War in South Africa, the Asante insurrection on the Gold Coast and the first Pan-African Conference held at Westminster Town Hall. Delegates from around the world met to discuss slavery, colonialism, racism and ways to fight these global scourges.

Representatives hailed from across the British Empire, the United States, Ethiopia, Liberia, Haiti and the Caribbean, with a total of thirty-seven delegates and roughly ten other participants and observers. The Chairman, Bishop Alexander Walters, an African American clergyman and civil rights leader, formally opened the conference on 23 July with an address to the assembled guests and members of the press:

> It had been the misfortune of the negro in America, he said, to live among a people whose laws, traditions, and prejudices had been against them for centuries. It had been ever the policy of a certain class of Americans to keep the negro down. Even as far back as revolutionary times when America was fighting for her independence and help was needed from every class, the negro was ignored. But from the beginning the struggle

of the negro had been an upward one. The opposition to the emancipation of the coloured man was greater even than that to his enlistment in the army. That object was attained, however, to the great surprise of the negro's enemies, and his next achievement was his emancipation in 1868.[1]

At this point the conference erupted into applause. Everyone knew there was much work still to be done, but Walters was touching upon a clear trajectory of struggle and achievement: official African American enrolment into the army (1862); the 13th Amendment, which outlawed slavery (1865); the 14th Amendment, which granted citizenship to 'all persons born or naturalized in the United States', including the formerly enslaved (1868); and the 15th Amendment, which gave former slaves the right to vote (1870). Bishop Alexander continued:

In all those achievements the hand of God was plainly seen. The negro had been educated, and was standing before the world as a cultured man, and yet the world was told he belonged to a race of rapists. In order to obtain his full social and political rights the negro was determined to fight to the end – though it might be a long and severe struggle.[2]

More applause. The guests included the former Attorney General of Liberia Frederick Johnson, and the Haitian diplomat and aide-de-camp to the Ethiopian Emperor, Benito Sylvain, as well as Samuel Coleridge-Taylor, John Archer, Reverend Attoh-Ahjuma, Frederick J. Loudin and W. E. B. Du Bois.

C. W. French, of St Kitts, read a paper on the 'Conditions Favouring a High Standard of American Humanity', recounting that in the West Indies, 'the feeling of the planters, which had come down from the old cursed days of slavery, was such that land was denied the coloured man for the cottages which alone would give him security and independence'. He concluded with the statement that 'the only remedy would be a system of local government, giving the coloured people a voice in the control of their own affairs'.[3]

After French came Anna Jones from Kansas who, in a paper entitled 'The Preservation of Race Equality', discussed the growing presence of Black people in science, literature and the arts. She stressed the 'development of race consciousness, which led them to strive for a freer and happier life,' reported the *London Daily News*, and she declared that the 'oppression and repression to which her race has been subjected are serving a divine purpose in fitting it to hold its own in the world'.[4]

Originally from Canada, Jones had worked as a teacher in Indianapolis and St Louis and as an assistant principal at the Wilberforce Institute in Chatham, Ontario. Between 1885 and 1892 she was 'lady-principal' at Wilberforce University, which bestowed her a second honorary MA, in recognition of her contribution to teaching. From there, she moved to Kansas, where she became the principal of Douglass High School. In 1893, she was described as 'a scholar, profound teacher, a race lover, a Christian lady, struggling hard to make practical leaders of an oppressed people'.[5]

At the Pan-African Conference, Jones was one of a number of African American women delegates, including the educators and civil rights activists Ella D. Barrier and her sister, Fannie Barrier Williams. There was also Jane Rose Roberts, the widow of Liberia's first president, and Anna Julia Haywood Cooper.

On the evening of 23 July, Cooper addressed the conference with a paper entitled 'The Negro Problem in America': '[…] her people were now passing through the most severe ordeal that the race had known. They were passing through the fiery furnace of the white man's jealousy and selfishness.'[6] She stated that 'the negro problem of today is the white man's problem – and, it was humanity's problem' and she proclaimed that 'America was the land of destiny for the inheritance of the enslaved race'. Prophetically, she affirmed, 'America would never be at peace with herself until the negro problem was settled outright.'[7]

* * *

The African Association, which convened the first Pan-African Conference, existed within a broader nexus of student politics in Britain. The vice chairman, Thomas J. Thompson, and, the secretary, Henry Sylvester Williams, studied at the Inns of Court, while the assistant secretary, Moses Da Rocha, was a medical student at Edinburgh University.

From the eighteenth century onwards, West African students had studied in Britain. By the middle of the nineteenth, Queen's College in Taunton received a number of Black school-age students, while older Black students attended the universities of Oxford, Cambridge, Edinburgh, Durham and London. For Black female students, Portway College in Reading was a popular institution.[8]

Throughout this long history of study abroad, West African student politics sought to fight discrimination in the 'Mother Country' and promote unity among the peoples of Africa. The Pan-African Conference was a manifestation of this goal, with UK reporters noting the novelty of Africans from across the globe converging on London to unite for 'the attainment of equality and freedom'.[9]

But Pan-Africanism had roots beyond student politics. Hakim Adi has explored the multiple forerunners to the emergence of Pan-Africanism, which included the Haiti Revolution, the independence of Liberia and, as it was then known, Abyssinia (all seen as symbolic of African achievement), and the movement known as Ethiopianism, which challenged racism in African churches and was associated with the phrase 'Africa for the Africans'. Adi also highlights prominent individuals such as Martin Robin Delany, who celebrated the 'common cause' among the people of the African diaspora, and James Africanus Horton, 'the father of modern African political thought', who advocated for self-governance in Africa and challenged Victorian racism.[10]

In the late eighteenth century, the Black abolitionist organisation, the Sons of Africa, publicly campaigned against Britain's involvement in the slave trade, seeking to speak for their 'whole race' in recognition of their 'common calamity', as they expressed it.[11] They were perhaps the first Pan-African organisation whose members, which included the formerly enslaved men Ottobah Cugoano and Olaudah Equiano, attacked Western slavery and linked their suffering to the suffering of all the peoples of Africa, becoming pioneers of Pan-Africanism, whose cause was reasserted at the First Pan-African Conference some 100 years later.

* * *

During the First Pan-African Conference – with full days on 23, 24 and 25 July – there were papers and discussions on numerous pressing issues. William Meyer, a West Indian medical student at Edinburgh University, challenged scientific racism. 'Some people were trying to prove that negroes were worthless and depraved persons who had no right to live', he exclaimed. 'Some German scientists had pronounced the negro to be not a man, but an entity stage above the ape.' But such racist reasoning was being 'contradicted by the progress being made by young Negroes in colleges and at universities' and he called on 'England as a Christian nation to act up to its principles and to do justice to the black race'.[12]

Practical issues were addressed too. The African Association merged into a new Pan-African Association with Bishop Walters serving as president, Reverend Henry B. Brown as vice president and Henry Sylvester Williams as general secretary. Members of the elected executive committee included the composer Samuel Coleridge-Taylor and Jane Cobden Unwin, who strove for the rights of minorities and oppressed peoples in South Africa. The aims of the association were:

1. To secure to Africans throughout the world true civil and political rights.
2. To meliorate the conditions of our brothers on the continent of Africa, America and other parts of the world.
3. To promote efforts to secure effective legislation and encourage our people in educational, industrial and commercial enterprise.
4. To foster the production of writing and statistics relating to our people everywhere.
5. To raise funds for forwarding these purposes.[13]

The conference also universally approved the *Address to the Nations of the World*, which contained that famous phrase repeated in Du Bois' *The Souls of Black Folk* (1903), 'The problem of the twentieth century is the problem of the colour line'. The *Address* concluded:

Let the nations of the world respect the integrity and independence of the free Negro states of Abyssinia, Liberia, Haiti, and the rest, and let the inhabitants of these states, the independent tribes of Africa, the Negroes of the West Indies and America, and the black subjects of all nations take courage, strive ceaselessly, and fight bravely, that they may prove to the world their incontestable right to be counted among the great brotherhood of mankind. Thus we appeal with boldness and confidence to the Great Powers of the civilized world, trusting in the wide spirit of humanity, and the deep sense of justice and of our age, for a generous recognition of the righteousness of our cause.[14]

The day after the conference formally concluded, the *Westminster Gazette* ran with the story, 'The Pan-African Movement', which was featured below a headline that read, 'Race Riots at New Orleans. Threat to Wipe Out All Negroes.' A reporter for the *Westminster Gazette* spoke to Henry Sylvester Williams, who explained the nature of the movement:

> I felt that it was time some effort was made to have us recognised as a people, and so enable us to take our position in the world. We were being legislated for without our sanction – without a voice in the laws that were made to govern us. My idea of bringing about some alteration in this respect was confined in the first place to the British Colonies, but the scheme developed into a Pan-African one. Our object now is to secure throughout the world the same facilities and privileges for the black as the white man enjoys.[15]

In this interview, Williams proceeded to outline the discrimination and economic barriers in the West Indies. He echoed a theme of the conference – 'that there is an attempt in the world to-day to re-enslave the negro race' – and, when asked by the reporter, 'What political power have you in the West Indies?', he responded, 'To-day we have none'. But he promised that a Pan-African Conference would be held triennially, with an office established in London and branches throughout the world.

'This first Conference has been a great success', he rightly proclaimed, but white authority was seemingly indifferent.[16] Indeed, a petition was sent to Queen Victoria, denouncing the 'acute ill-treatment of the natives of South Africa', but there was no response.[17] In January 1901, nearly half a year after the conference, Williams finally received a letter from Secretary of State for the Colonies, Joseph Chamberlain's office, which read:

Sir: I am directed by Mr Secretary Chamberlain to state that he has received the Queen's commands to inform you that the Memorial of the Pan-African Conference respecting the situation of the native races in South Africa has been laid before Her Majesty, and that she was graciously pleased to command him to return an answer to it on behalf of her Government.

Mr Chamberlain accordingly desires to assure the members of the Pan-African Conference that, in settling the lines on which the administration of the conquered territories is to be conducted, Her Majesty's Government will not overlook the interests and welfare of the native races.[18]

Meanwhile, the Boer War continued to rage and, within separate concentration camps, Boers and Black Africans were contained and starved.

* * *

After the conference, Henry Sylvester Williams travelled to Jamaica, Trinidad and America, establishing branches of the Pan-African Association, before returning to London, where he then founded the *Pan-African* journal, which aimed to be 'the mouthpiece of the millions of Africans and their descendants'.[19] He also finished his legal studies and was called to the Bar in June 1902. In 1984, historian Peter Fryer correctly claimed that Williams was 'probably the first barrister of African descent to practise in Britain'.[20] He was right to be cautious because Frederick Cole from rural Sierra Leone had become a member of the Honourable Society of the Inner Temple in September 1879 and was called to the Bar four years later. Cole was, it should be noted, an alumnus at the University of Oxford and a committed Pan-Africanist, who was referred to as 'the n****r' while at Oxford.[21]

In 1906, Williams joined the Fabian Society and was elected to Marylebone Borough Council as a Progressive candidate in the same year. That year also saw the election of John Archer, a Black British activist and attendee at the 1900 Pan-African Conference (Archer also served as a Progressive on Battersea Borough Council, later becoming mayor in 1913).

By this point, Queen Victoria had died, on 22 January 1901, and her son, Edward, had assumed the throne, marking a new era.[22]

The Pan-African movement continued to make waves in British and international life throughout the long Edwardian era (1901–14) and beyond. Bandele Omoniyi, a student from present-day Nigeria, published *A Defence of the Ethiopian Movement* (1908), which openly criticised colonial rule.[23] The author, actor and publisher Dusé Mohamed Ali advanced the cause of Pan-Africanism through his publishing of the *African Times and Orient Review* from 1913–20. The Pan-Africanist Joseph Ephraim Casely-Hayford, who was called to the Bar in 1896, offered financial assistance to Dusé Mohamed Ali's journal and participated in Booker T. Washington's International Conference on the Negro in 1912.

Two years later, the Jamaican journalist Marcus Garvey and his first wife, the activist Amy Ashwood Garvey, established the Universal Negro Improvement Association and African Communities League, which aimed to establish 'a universal confederacy among the race', backed with 'racial pride and love', and called for self-determination for people of African descent.[24] This anti-colonial, Pan-African organisation was the largest and most influential of its time.

The First Pan-African Conference paved the way for the First, Second, Third and Fourth Pan-African Congress in 1919, 1921, 1923 and 1927 respectively. In the 1930s, Pan-Africanism began manifesting in the Rastafarian movement, the 'Negritude' movement and the nationalist struggles in Africa – different streams of the 'Pan-African River', to borrow Adi's metaphor once again.[25]

At the Fifth Pan-African Congress, held in Manchester in 1945, there were nearly 100 delegates, representing some fifty organisations, with around 200 audience members. The chair was held by the seventy-seven-year-old W. E. B. Du Bois. Future leaders of independent African states were present, including Kwame Nkrumah, Nnamdi Azikiwe and Jomo Kenyatta, who developed networks and strategies for independence struggles in the shadow of the Second World War.

Pan-Africanism informed the twentieth-century civil rights movement, which, like Pan-Africanism, originated in the resistance against slavery and its monstrous offspring, segregation, both aiming to champion the rights and common struggles of peoples in Africa and throughout the diaspora. Furthermore, the independence movements in Africa strengthened the civil rights movement in the West. Malcolm X, for example, was inspired by the anti-colonial struggles in Africa: his Organization of Afro-American Unity, stated clearly in its founding document, 'We have one destiny and we've had one past.'[26]

In Britain, the Universal Coloured People's Association, founded in the late 1960s, brought Black Power to Britain, opposing all forms of racism while propagating politics from Garveyism to Maoism to Pan-Africanism.[27] And at the turn of the twenty-first century, the African Union was formed as the continental union of African states, replacing the Organisation of African Unity, first established in 1963. At their twentieth summit, held in May 2013, the African Union published an account of Pan-Africanism which stated that, fundamentally, Pan-Africanism is 'a belief that African peoples both on the continent and in the diaspora, share not merely a common history, but a common destiny'.[28]

These words, chosen by a group working towards common goals, underline the belief, shared by us and stated in the opening pages of this book, that the past is inextricably linked to the present – and to our future. And key to envisioning and shaping the future is an understanding – and a recognition – of our past.

Conclusion:
Not the First, Not the Last

Over a decade into the twenty-first century, Norwell Roberts was proclaimed 'Britain's First Black Police Officer'.[1] He had joined the Metropolitan Police in 1967, risen to the rank of detective sergeant and in 1996 received the Queen's Police Medal. Norwell Roberts was rightly honoured after a distinguished career fighting crime on the streets and racism in the force, but he wasn't 'Britain's First'.

Robert Branford joined the Metropolitan Police on 24 September 1838. He progressed through the ranks to become sergeant, inspector and finally superintendent of M-Division (Southwark) in 1856. According to one Victorian chief inspector who knew Branford personally, he 'possessed a thorough knowledge of police matters in general. I should say he was about the only half-caste superintendent officer the Met ever had'. When Branford wasn't in the room, officers called him 'the n****r'.[2] Norwell Roberts wasn't 'the first', then, but neither was Robert Branford – at least outside of the Met.

John Kent was a British-born Black constable appointed to his post in 1835.[3] Two years later, he became a supernumerary officer in Carlisle City Police. He was a big, muscular, no-nonsense cop, known as 'Black Kent' among the residents of

Carlisle, 'an active and intelligent policeman'.[4] His son, William, emigrated to Australia; his daughter, Jane, ended her days in a mental asylum; and his other daughter, Mary, married and mothered three surviving children. Their descendants still reside in Carlisle.[5]

So, we should recognise Norwell Roberts, but not as 'the first'. We should recognise Robert Branford, but not as 'the first'. And we should recognise John Kent but not, necessarily, as 'the first'. In the Old Bailey records for the year 1746, Thomas Latham was described as a 'Negro, Constable'.[6]

* * *

There is something seemingly irresistibly tempting with that label, 'the first'. It crops up again and again, sometimes in rather convoluted ways: 'one of the first Black Scottish footballers' (Robert Walker from the late 1870s); 'the world's first Black person to play association football at international level' (Andrew Watson from 1881); 'the world's first Black professional footballer' (Arthur Wharton from 1886); 'the first known Black women's footballer in Britain' (Emma Clarke from 1897); 'the world's first Black professional footballer to score in the English football league' (William Gibb Clarke in 1901).[7]

There is nothing inherently wrong with these statements (though they are forever qualified and corrected), but to proclaim someone as 'the first' opens up potential pitfalls. It can promote the flawed and misleading narrative of Black exceptionalism.[8] In certain cases, the 'first' can perpetuate the idea that the Black British presence began when HMT *Empire Windrush* docked in Tilbury in 1948, which, as we have seen, is demonstrably false. And the label obscures another truism, too: so much of history, and Black history in particular, lies buried in the archives. There is a vast terrain of the unknown which is slowly being revealed.

Conclusion: Not the First, Not the Last

The Victorian archives have made colour hard to see. Ethnicity was overlooked by Victorian recordkeepers, Black assimilation led to archival obfuscation, and we as a society have, until recently, turned a blind eye as well. But despite the blind spots and haziness, a moment's readjustment brings the Black presence into focus.

Black Victorians were evident from the picket lines to the police force to the criminal courts, as defendants and prosecutors, officers, lawyers and barristers. From workhouses and asylums to the corridors of Buckingham Palace. They were found on country estates as landowners or as servants of the well-to-do. They were found begging on the streets, performing on the streets, sweeping the streets. They were found modelling for artists, gazing out from the canvas, the photograph, the engraving, the sculpture, the magazine, the newspaper. They appeared as sexualised 'Others'; they appeared as paragons of virtue, freedom and self-determination. They appeared in theatres, music halls, freak shows, circuses, fairs, ethnographic exhibitions and concert halls.

Black Victorians delivered Shakespeare, abolitionist dramas, spirituals, minstrel songs and classical music. They gave speeches and lectures; they wrote letters, novels, poems, articles and autobiographies. They spearheaded powerful polemics and political movements concerning abolitionism, Black feminism and Pan-Africanism.

Black Victorians were found in the pulpit, chapels, churches and in the missionary drive. They could be defenders of the faith or defenders of the nation, battling on land and sea for Britain's global ambitions. They were celebrities, and they were anonymous; they were writers, they were composers; they were fugitives, they were rooted. They were working, middle and upper class and they operated both inside and outside the social structures of their time.

Black Victorians did not exist in isolation and, crucially, they were not occasional landmarks in the Victorian landscape – they helped create the landscape. They were not simply present but pivotal. They were not simply bystanders but builders. They were not mere onlookers but active participants. Faced with challenges, burdened by external perceptions, they were often confined to the margins, yet at the same time central and integral to a world which, ultimately, birthed our own.

* * *

Recently, thanks to the work of scholars from different fields whose labours have informed our book, the picture of the age is being restored in a broad project of historical remembrance. But this remapping of Black history onto British history has unsurprisingly generated debate and controversy The act of remembering and the stone edifice of memorialisation are often confused: removing the statue of a slaveholder does not, for example, constitute forgetting – it corrects contemptuous commemoration. Recognising the historical reality of slavery need not generate furious attacks from seemingly patriotic defenders of Great Britain. A confident nation can look at its past honestly and sincerely, praising the good, acknowledging the bad and seeking to build a better tomorrow.

New work which recentres the decentred need not be denounced as political correctness; rather, it's historical diligence. And highlighting the hidden aspects of our past can lead to necessary, positive change: the Black nurse, Mary Seacole, added to the national curriculum; a statue of Arthur Wharton erected; Black plaques to honour people of African descent put in place; local history societies and projects and initiatives engaging, recalling and remembering our history.

But as Olivette Otele makes clear in her book, *African Europeans*, 'simply remembering is not the ultimate goal' – resistance is required; 'a collective degree of consciousness' is required; an engagement with Black radicalism is required – 'movements that have shifted perceptions around definitions of whiteness, white supremacy and notions of white fragility'.[9] This was (and is) epitomised in Black Lives Matter; it was (and is) epitomised in the #MeToo movement – initiated by the African American activist, Tarana Burke – and it was, is and will be incumbent on us all to continue remembering and resisting until the work is done.

For our part, this book is a tiny contribution to the cause. We have attempted to heed Carter G. Woodson's exhortation to engage in historical recollection and celebration, while making room for the larger context. Woodson, a key figure of the Harlem Renaissance, established 'Negro History Week' in 1926, choosing the second week of February as it marked the birthdays of Frederick Douglass and Abraham Lincoln. The week was officially expanded into a month in the mid-1970s and, thanks in large part to the leadership of the Pan-African activist, Akyaaba Addai-Sebo, Black History Month came to the UK in October 1987, as part of the African Jubilee Year.

Back in the late 1920s, Woodson highlighted a paradox that this book has sought to embrace – the act of highlighting and therefore isolating Black Victorians in order to emphasise their indivisible place in the wider Victorian world, and it seems fitting to end with his words:

> It is not so much a Negro History Week as it is a History Week. We should emphasize not Negro History, but the Negro in history. What we need is not a history of selected races or nations, but the history of the world void of national bias, race hate, and religious prejudice. There should be no indulgence in undue eulogy of the Negro. The case of the Negro is well taken care of when it is shown how he influenced the development of Civilization.[10]

We hope that we have demonstrated how Victorian society was shaped and informed by Black agency, ambition and achievement, and we also hope that in some ways you – like we – have been touched by the personal and sometimes elusive stories of these Black Victorians.

Acknowledgements

Our first acknowledgement is to Dr Michael Woolf, who brought us both together. He is the father to one of us, the thought partner to another, and he has guided us both professionally and personally, including with support and insights in the writing of this book. We both love him dearly and want to express our thanks.

Black Victorians would not exist without the work of others. They include – but are not limited to – Hakim Adi, Caroline Bressey, Kathleen Chater, Peter Fryer, Paul Gilroy, Jeffrey Green, Gretchen Holbrook Gerzina, Bernth Lindfors, David Olusoga, Edward Scobie, Folarin Shyllon and Ron Ramdin. We are also indebted to the many archivists, librarians and others who have assisted with the research. They include – but are not limited to – Mark Aston, Elli Clarke, Sean Creighton, Hannah Dale, Ivana Frlan, Melissa Harrison, Roger Hull, Jenny Hunt, David Luck, Ruth Macdonald, Abby Matthews, Anthony Morton, Louise Neilson, Kathryn Newman, Jo Parker, Rachel Roberts, Louise Smith, Susan Smith and Annette Wickham.

We would like to extend special thanks to Onyeka Nubia and Michael I. Ohajuru for their vital feedback and time. We would also like to thank Rose Paine and Vivienne Richmond for their reflections on Fanny Eaton and Part One respectively; Guy Woolf and Professor Vernon Trafford for their insightful comments on the manuscript; and Mark Stevens at the Berkshire Record Office for his invaluable assistance.

A special thanks to all those who helped in bringing the project to fruition, including the renowned agent and author Andrew Lownie; the incredible designer Leah Jacobs-Gordon; and, at Duckworth Books, the equally impressive Matt Casbourne, Pete Duncan and Rob Wilding. Also, Maria Nae and Hodan Ibrahim for their sensitivity notes; Sarah Wright, Christian Müller and Danny Lyle for their copyediting, proofreading and typesetting skills; Angela Martin for taking the book out into the world, and the editor extraordinaire Rowan Cope, who has been instrumental.

Further Reading

If you enjoyed this book, we encourage you to learn more. Some of the works suggested below have been marginalised for non-academic reasons, but please note that this list is not exhaustive and all these authors have a body of work that you can explore. This list should therefore be understood as offering preliminary suggestions from a rich and ever-growing historiography.

Adi, Hakim, *Pan-Africanism: A History* (2018)
Ali, Dusé Mohamed, 'Leaves from an Active Life', *The Comet* (1937–1938)
Bourne, Stephen, *Black Poppies: Britain's Black Community and the Great War* (2019)
Bressey, Caroline, *Empire, Race and the Politics of Anti-Caste* (2015)
Chater, Kathleen, *Untold Histories: Black people in England and Wales during the period of the British slave trade, c.1660–1807* (2009)
Costello, Ray, *Black Salt: Seafarers of African Descent on British Ships* (2012)
Dabydeen, David, et. al. (eds.), *The Oxford Companion to Black British History* (2007)
Fryer, Peter, *Staying Power: The History of Black People in Britain* (1984, 2018), which includes John Archer's 'J. R. Archer's Presidential Address to the Inaugural Meeting of the African Progress Union, 1918' (See appendix)
Gerzina, Gretchen H., (ed.), *Black Victorians/Black Victoriana* (2003)
Gilroy, Paul, *The Black Atlantic: Modernity and Double Consciousness* (1999)
Green, Jeffrey, *Black Edwardians: Black People in Britain 1901–1914* (1998)
Hall, Stuart, *Selected Writings on Race and Difference*, ed. by Paul Gilroy and Ruth Wilson Gilmore (2021)
Hoyles, Martin, *William Cuffay: The Life & Times of a Chartist Leader* (2013)
James, C. L. R., *The Black Jacobins* (1938)
Kaufmann, Miranda, *Black Tudors: The Untold Story* (2017)
Marsh, Jan, (ed.), *Black Victorians: Black People in British Art 1800–1900* (2015)
Nubia, Onyeka, *England's Other Countrymen: Black Tudor Society* (2019)
Olusoga, David, *Black and British: A Forgotten History* (2017)
Otele, Olivette, *African Europeans: An Untold History* (2020)
Qureshi, Sadiah, *Peoples on Parade: Exhibitions, Empire, and Anthropology in Nineteenth-Century Britain* (2011)
Ramdin, Ron, *The Making of the Black Working Class in Britain* (1987, 2017)
Rashidi, Runoko, *The Global African Community: The African presence in Asia, Australia, and the South Pacific* (1995)
Robinson, Cedric J., *Black Marxism: The Making of the Black Radical Tradition* (1983)
Rogers, J. A., *World's Great Men of Colour*, Vols. 1 and 2 (1995)
Scobie, Edward, *Black Britannia: A History of Blacks in Britain* (1972)

Sherwood, Marika, *Origins of Pan-Africanism: Henry Sylvester Williams, Africa, and the African Diaspora* (2011)
Shyllon, Folarin, *Black People in Britain 1555–1833* (1977)
Van Sertima, Ivan, *Black Women in Antiquity* (1984)
Vasil, Phil, *The First Black Footballer: Arthur Wharton 1865–1930* (1999)
Williams, Eric, *Capitalism & Slavery* (1944)

Bibliography

ARCHIVAL MATERIAL
Newspaper articles are cited in the notes but are not included in the list of references.
Berkshire Record Office, Reading (BRO)
  D/H14/D2/1/1/1-7 (kindly transcribed by Mark Stevens)
  D/H14/D2/2/1/19, Case file number 19: John Flinn
  D/H14/D2/2/1/914, Case file number 914: Joseph Peters
  D/H14/D2/2/1/1146, Case file number 1146: Joseph Fennell
  D/H14/D2/2/1/1147, Case file number 1147: William Brown
Bethlem Museum of the Mind, Beckenham (BMOTM)
  Admission Registers 1683–1902
  Criminal Patient Admission Registers 1816–64
  Incurable & Criminal Patient Casebooks 1778–1864
Black Cultural Archives, London (BCA)
  BCA/5/1/85
  COLETAY/1-4
  Ephemera/163
  GLADSTONE/1-14
  SEACOLE/1-10
Haringey Archive and Local History, London (HALHL)
  Photograph, Sister Freda
  Photograph, Walter Tull
  Photograph, Asarto Ward
Cadbury Research Library, University of Birmingham (CRL, UB)
  CA1/079, West African Mission, Original Papers of Rev. Samuel Adjai Crowther
  CA3/04/1-150, Nigeria-Niger Mission, Original Papers of Rev. Samuel Adjai Crowther
  CMS Periodicals
Cheltenham College Archives (CCA)
  College Register (1872)
  Nomination of Pupil: Alamayu
Cheltenham Ladies' College Archive (CLCA)
  Cheltenham Ladies' College Magazine (1891, 1895)
  Grace Wood's Diary (1881)
Cumbria Archive Service, Carlisle (CAS)
  Black History Files
  Kent Family File
Lambeth Palace Library, London (LPLL)
  Benson 113, E. W. Benson Papers, Official Letters, 1892
  Benson 166, E. W. Benson Papers, Official Letters, 1890–94

LC 11, Lambeth Conference Papers, 1878
LC 17, Lambeth Conference Papers, 1888
LC 25, Lambeth Conference Papers, 1888
LC 34, Lambeth Conference Papers, 1888
Tait 139, Official Letters London, 1864, July–Nov
Tait 140, Official Letters London, 1864, Nov–1865 Jan
Tait 159, Official Letters London, Natal 1866–69
Tait 234, Official Letters Canterbury, 1877
Tait 287, Official Letters Canterbury, 1882

Lancashire Archives (LA)
QJC/8, Calendar of Prisoners Kirkdale Session

Liverpool Record Office (LRO)
614 RAI 5/1, Rainhill Asylum Admissions Register
614 RAI 11/1, Rainhill Asylum Casebook File

London Metropolitan Archives (LMA)
SC/GL/BFS/001, Bartholomew Fair Folder
SC/GL/ENT/50–184, Grainger Entertainment Folder
SC/GL/NOB/C/O26/5-026/51, Noble Collection

Lothian Health Services Archive (LHSA)
LHB1/16/23, George Rice
LHB1/116/2, George Rice

Museum of Croydon (MC)
AR1149/1, Samuel Coleridge-Taylor: Material relating to Concerts
AR1149/2, Samuel Coleridge-Taylor: Published Works and Press
AR1149/4, Samuel Coleridge-Taylor: Samuel Coleridge-Taylor Network

National Fairground Archives, Sheffield (NFA)
178T1.1–178T1.186, John Bramwell Taylor, Box One
178T1.187–178T1.295, John Bramwell Taylor, Box Two
178T1.296–178T1.342, John Bramwell Taylor, Box Three
Turner Database (Online resource accessed onsite)

Medway Archives Centre, Strood (MAC)
E/MED 942.23 JOY, Celebrating the Black Presence in the Medway Towns
MED 920/BON, Sarah Forbes Bonetta
VF MED 920/COLE/2, Samuel Coleridge-Taylor
VF MED 920/CUF, William Cuffay

The Salvation Army International Heritage Centre, William Booth College (SAIHC, WBC)
CAR/7/1, Jamaica, 1888–99
C/BUR/1, Photograph of Joe Norton
SS/2/1/1, Women's Social Work 'Girls' Statement Books, 1890
War Cry, 1879–90

The Sandhurst Collection, Surrey (SCS)
RMC_WO_151_Vol_2_1864–81, Cadet Register

Sutton Archives, London (SAL)
39/1–25, Papers of Dr George Rice

Trinity College Library, Cambridge, Papers of A. J. Munby (TCLC, MUNB)
MUNB, 1–65, Diaries of A. J. Munby
MUNB, 97, Arthur Munby's Notebooks

Bibliography

Waltham Forest Archives and Local Studies Library, London (WFA, LSLL)
W 31.5, Fuegians
W 31.5, 22906, Pamphlet
W85.211, Pamphlet
Electronic Archives
Ancestry: https://www.ancestry.co.uk/
Archives of Women's Political Communication (AWPC): https://awpc.cattcenter.iastate.edu/
Black Abolitionist Archive (BAA): https://libraries.udmercy.edu/find/special_collections/digital/baa/
British Library (BL): https://www.bl.uk/onlinegallery/features/blackeuro/homepage.html
British Newspaper Archive: https://www.britishnewspaperarchive.co.uk/
Dictionary of African Christian Biography (*DACB*): https://dacb.org/
Durham Country Record Office: *The Story of Jimmy Durham* (DCRO, SJD), http://www.durhamrecordoffice.org.uk/article/10689/The-Story-of-Jimmy-Durham
Hansard, UK Parliament: https://hansard.parliament.uk/
Queen Victoria's Journals (QVJ): http://www.queenvictoriasjournals.org
The National Archives, Black Presence: Asian and Black History in Britain, 1500–1850 (TNA, BP): https://www.nationalarchives.gov.uk/pathways/blackhistory/
The Old Bailey Proceedings Online, 1674–1913: www.oldbaileyonline.org
The Transatlantic Slave Trade Database: http://www.slavevoyages.org/assessment/estimates
V&A Museum: https://www.vam.ac.uk/

ONLINE DATABASES, EXHIBITIONS & REFERENCES
Black History Month: https://www.blackhistorymonth.org.uk/
Black Past: https://www.blackpast.org/
British Library: 'Black Britain and Asian Britain': https://www.bl.uk/subjects/black-britain-and-asian-britain
Black Alumni of Dartmouth: https://badahistory.net/view.php?ID=124
English Heritage, 'Black History': https://www.english-heritage.org.uk/learn/histories/black-history/
Frederick Douglass in Britain and Ireland: http://frederickdouglassinbritain.com/
Jeffrey Green: https://jeffreygreen.co.uk/
Oxford English Dictionary (*OED*): http://www.oed.com
Oxford Dictionary of National Biography (*ODNB*): http://www.oxforddnb.com/index.jsp
Peter Higginbotham, 'The Workhouse': http://www.workhouses.org.uk/
Royal Collection Trust, 'Black and Asian History and Victorian Britain' (RCT, BAVB): https://www.rct.uk/collection/themes/trails/black-and-asian-history-and-victorian-britain
Royal College of Music (RCM), 'Samuel Coleridge-Taylor and the Musical Fight for Civil Rights': https://www.rcm.ac.uk/museum/exhibitions/
Runaway Slaves in Eighteenth-Century Britain: https://www.runaways.gla.ac.uk/
Slave Trade Act 1843: https://www.legislation.gov.uk/ukpga/Vict/6-7/98/enacted

The Dictionary of Victorian London: http://www.victorianlondon.org/
The U.S. National Archives and Records Administration: https://www.archives.gov/exhibits/featured-documents/emancipation-proclamation
The Samuel Coleridge-Taylor Society: https://sctf.org.uk/
University College London, 'Black Londoners': https://www.ucl.ac.uk/equiano-centre/projects/black-londoners-1800–1900
University College London, Centre for the Study of the Legacies of British Slavery, Legacies of British Slavery Database: http://wwwdepts-live.ucl.ac.uk/lbs/

PRIMARY SOURCES (INCLUDING MODERN REPRINTS)

Albert, Edward, *Brief Sketch of the Life of Edward Albert* (London: R. Atkinson, n.d.).
Aldridge, Ira, *The Black Doctor* (Online: Alexander Street Press, 1847).
Ali, Dusé Mohamed, 'Leaves from an Active Life', *The Comet* (Lagos: 1937–1938).
Anon., *Memoir and Theatrical Career of Ira Aldridge, the African Roscius* (London: Onwhyn, 1848 or 1849).
Anon., 'Mr Coleridge-Taylor', *Musical Times*, 50:793 (1909), pp. 153–58.
Anon., 'Samuel Coleridge-Taylor. Born August 15, 1875. Died September 1, 1912', *Musical Times*, 53:836 (1912), pp. 637–39.
Archer, Thomas, *The Pauper, the Thief and the Convict: Sketches of some of their Homes, Haunts and Habits* (London: Groombridge and Sons, 1865).
Brown, Henry 'Box', *Narrative of the Life of Henry Box Brown, Written by Himself* (Manchester: Lee and Glynn, 1851).
Brown, Josephine, *Biography of an American Bondman, by His Daughter* (Boston: R. F. Wallcut, 1856).
Brown, William Wells, *Narrative of William W. Brown, A Fugitive Slave. Written by Himself* (Boston: Anti-Slavery Office, 1847).
Brown, William Wells, *Three Years in Europe; or, Places I Have Seen and People I Have Met* (London: Charles Gilpin, 1852).
Brown, William Wells, *The Black Man, His Antecedents, His Genius, and His Achievements* (New York: Thomas Hamilton, 1863).
Cavanagh, Timothy, *Scotland Yard Past and Present: Experiences of Thirty-Seven Years* (London: Chatto and Windus, 1893).
C. C., *Anecdotes of Alamayu: The Late King Theodore's Son* (London: William Hunt, 1870).
Chapin, Walter, *The Missionary Gazetteer* (Woodstock: David Watson, 1825).
Childe, A. F., *Good out of Evil, or, The History of Adjai, The African Slave-Boy* (London: Wertheim and Macintosh, 1853).
Coleridge-Taylor, Jessie S. Fleetwood, *Genius and Musician: A Memory Sketch or Personal Reminiscences of My Husband, Genius and Musician S. Coleridge-Taylor 1875–1912* (London: John Crowther, 1943).
Cooper, Anna Julia, *A Voice from the South*, with intro. by Mary Helen Washington (Oxford: Oxford University Press, 1988 [1892]).
Craft, William [& Ellen], *Running a Thousand Miles for Freedom; or, the Escape of William and Ellen Craft from Slavery* (London: William Tweedie, 1860).
Cugoano, Ottobah, *Thoughts and Sentiments on the Evil and Wicked Traffic of the Slavery and Commerce of the Human Species, Humbly Submitted to the Inhabitants of Great Britain, by Ottobah Cugoano, a Native of Africa* (London, 1787).

Bibliography

Darwin, Charles, *The Descent of Man, and Selection in Relation to Sex* (London: John Murray, 1871).

De Lisle, Beauvoir, *Reminiscences of Sport and War* (London: Eyre & Spottiswoode, 1939).

Dickens, Charles, 'A Walk in a Workhouse', *Household Words*, 1:9 (1850), pp. 204–07.

Dickens, Charles, *The Personal History of David Copperfield* (London: Bradbury and Evans, 1850).

Dickens, Charles, *Great Expectations* (New York: P. F. Collier, 1861).

Disraeli, Benjamin, *Sybil; or, The Two Nations* (London: Henry Colburn, 1845).

Douglass, Frederick, *Narrative of the Life of Frederick Douglass, an American Slave. Written by Himself* (Boston: Anti-Slavery Office, 1845).

Douglass, Frederick, 'Farewell to the British People: An Address Delivered in London, England, March 30, 1847', https://glc.yale.edu/farewell-british-people (accessed 27 November 2021).

Douglass, Frederick, *My Bondage and My Freedom* (New York & Auburn: Miller, Orton & Mulligan, 1855).

Douglass, Frederick, 'The Color Line', *North American Review*, 132:295 (1881), pp. 567–77.

Du Bois, W. E. B., 'To the Nations of the World', BlackPast.org – https://www.blackpast.org/african-american-history/1900-w-e-b-du-bois-nations-world/ ([1900] accessed 14 August 2021).

Du Bois, W. E. B., *The Souls of Black Folk*, ed. and intro. by Brent Hayes Edwards (Oxford: Oxford University Press, 2007 [1903]).

Easton, Rev. H., *A Treatise on the Intellectual Character, and Civil and Political Condition of the Colored People of the United States; and the Prejudice Exercised Towards Them* (Boston: Isaac Knapp, 1837).

Eden, F. M., *The State of the Poor or an History of the Labouring Classes in England* (London: J. Davies, 1797).

Elaw, Zilpha, *Memoirs of the Life, Religious Experience, Ministerial Travels and Labours of Mrs. Zilpha Elaw, An American Female of Colour* (London: By the Authoress, 1846).

Engels, Friedrich, *The Condition of the Working-Class in England in 1844*, trans. by Florence Kelley Wischnewetzky (London: George Allen & Unwin, 1943 [1892]).

Equiano, Olaudah, *The Interesting Narrative of the Life of Olaudah Equiano, Or Gustavus Vassa, The African, Written By Himself* (London: Printed for and sold by the Author, 1789).

Evans-Gordon, William Eden, *The Alien Immigrant* (London: William Heinemann, 1903).

Forbes, Frederick E., *Dahomey and The Dahomans: Being the Journals of Two Missions to The King of Dahomey, and Residence at his Capital, in the years 1849 and 1850* (London: Longman, Brown, Green, and Longmans, 1851).

Frost, Thomas *Circus Life and Circus Celebrities* (London: Tinsley Brothers, 1873).

Galton, Francis, *Inquiries into Human Faculty and its Development* (London: Macmillan, 1883).

Greenwood, James, *The Wilds of London* (London: Chatto and Windus, 1874).

Grimes, William, *Life of William Grimes, the Runaway Slave, Brought Down to the Present Time. Written by Himself* (New Haven: W. Grimes, 1825).

Hastings, Adrian, *The Church in Africa 1450–1950* (Oxford: Clarendon Press, 1994).

Higgens, Annie C., 'Queen Victoria's African Protégée', *Missionary Quarterly Token*, 101 (1881), p. 6.

Hill, Matthew Davenport, *Our Exemplars, Poor and Rich* (London: Cassell, Pete, and Galpin, 1861).

Hunt, James, *The Negro's Place in Nature: A Paper Read Before the London Anthropological Society* (New York: Van Evrie, Horton, 1864).

Jacobs, Harriet Ann, *Incidents in the Life of a Slave Girl. Written by Herself*, ed. by L. Maria Child (Boston: Published for the Author, 1861).

Knox, Robert, *The Races of Men: A Fragment* (London: Henry Renshaw, 1850).

Lombroso, Cesare, *Criminal Man: According to the Classification of Cesare Lombroso Briefly Summarised by his Daughter Gina Lombroso-Ferrero* (London: G. P. Putnam's Sons, 1911 [1876]).

Mathews, Mrs [Anne Jackson], *The Life and Correspondence of Charles Mathews the Elder, Comedian* (London: Warne and Routledge, 1860).

Mayhew, Henry, *London Labour and the London Poor*, 4 Vols., (Project Gutenberg, 2017–20 [1851, 1861–65]).

Mayhew, Henry, and John Binny, *The Criminal Prisons of London and Scenes of Prison Life* (London: Griffin, Bohn, 1862).

Merriman-Labor, A. B. C., *Britons Through Negro Spectacles; or, A Negro on Britons* (London: Imperial and Foreign Company, 1909).

O'Donoghue, Edward Geoffrey, *The Story of Bethlehem Hospital from its Foundation in 1247* (New York: E. P. Dutton, 1915).

Page, Jesse, *Samuel Crowther: The Slave Boy who Became Bishop of the Niger* (New York: Fleming H. Revell, 1889).

Pratt, Ann, and Public Hospital and Lunatic Asylum (Kingston, Jamaica), *Official documents on the case of Ann Pratt, the reputed authoress of a certain pamphlet, entitled 'Seven months in the Kingston Lunatic Asylum, and what I saw there'* (Jamaica, Kingston & Spanish Town: Jordon & Osborn, 1860).

Prichard, James Cowles, *The Natural History of Man; Comprising Inquiries into the Modifying Influence of Physical and Moral Agencies of the Different Tribes of the Human Family* (London: H. Bailliere, 1843).

Prince, Mary, *The History of Mary Prince, a West Indian Slave. Related by Herself. With a Supplement by the Editor. To Which Is Added, the Narrative of Asa-Asa, a Captured African* (London: Whestley and Davis, 1831).

Sala, George Augustus, *Gaslight and Daylight with Some London Scenes They Shine Upon* (London: Chapman & Hall, 1859).

Sanger, 'Lord' George, *Seventy Years a Showman*, with an intro. by Kenneth Grahame (New York: Dutton and Company, 1926 [1910]).

Schön, James Frederick and Samuel Crowther, *Journals of the Rev. James Frederick Schön and Mr. Samuel Crowther: who, with the sanction of Her Majesty's government, accompanied the expedition up the Niger, in 1841, in behalf of the Church Missionary Society* (London: Hatchard and Son, 1842).

Smiles, Samuel, *Self Help: With Illustrations Of Conduct And Perseverance, Popular Edition* (London: John Murray, 1897 [1859]).

Spencer, Herbert, *The Principles of Biology*, Vol. I, (Oxford: Williams and Norgate, 1898).

Spinner, Jr., Thomas J., *A Political and Social History of Guyana, 1945–1983* (London: Westview Press, 1984).

Bibliography

Still, William, *The Underground Railroad: Authentic Narratives and First-Hand Accounts*, ed. by Ian Frederick Finseth (Mineola: Dover Publications, 2007).

Stock, Eugene, *The History of the Church Missionary Society. Its Environment, Its Men and Its Work*, Vol. II (London: Church Missionary Society, 1899).

Thicknesse, Philip, *A Year's Journey through France and Part of Spain*, Vol. II (London: W. Brown, 1778).

Walker, David, *Walker's Appeal, in Four Articles; Together with a Preamble, to the Coloured Citizens of the World, but in Particular, and Very Expressly, to Those of the United States of America* (Boston: David Walker, 1830).

Walker, Whimsical, *From Sawdust to Windsor Castle* (London: Stanley Paul, 1922).

Wallett, W. F., *The Public Life of W. F. Wallett, The Queen's Jester: An Autobiography*, ed. by J. Luntley (London: Bemrose and Sons, 1870).

Walter, *My Secret Life*: http://www.freeinfosociety.com/media/pdf/2674.pdf (accessed 2 August 2021).

Watkins, James, *Struggles for Freedom; or The Life of James Watkins, Formerly a Slave in Maryland, U.S.* (Manchester: Printed for James Watkins, 1860).

Wedderburn, Robert, *The Horrors of Slavery; Exemplified in The Life and History of the Rev. Robert Wedderburn, V.D.M* (London: R. Wedderburn, 1824).

Wells, Ida B., *Southern Horrors and Other Writings: The Anti-Lynching Campaign of Ida B. Wells*, ed. by Jacqueline Jones Royster (New York: Bedford Books, 1997 [1892]).

Wild, Sam, *The Original, Complete and only Authentic Story of 'Old Wild's'* (London: Vickers, 1888).

SECONDARY SOURCES

Adas, Michael, *Machines as the Measure of Men: Science, Technology, and Ideologies of Western Dominance* (Ithaca: Cornell University Press, 1989).

Adeloye, Adelola, 'Some Early Nigerian Doctors and Their Contribution to Modern Medicine in West Africa', *Medical History*, 18:3 (1974), pp. 275–93.

Adi, Hakim, 'Bandele Omoniyi: A Neglected Nigerian Nationalist', *African Affairs*, 90:361 (1991), pp. 581–605.

Adi, Hakim, *West Africans in Britain 1900-1960: Nationalism, Pan-Africanism and Communism* (London: Lawrence & Wishart, 1998).

Adi, Hakim, *Pan-Africanism: A History* (London: Bloomsbury, 2018).

Anand, Anita, *Sophia: Princess, Suffragette, Revolutionary* (London: Bloomsbury, 2015).

Andrews, Jonathan, Asa Briggs, Roy Porter, Penny Tucker and Keir Waddington, *The History of Bethlem* (London: Routledge, 1997).

Andrews, William L. (ed.), *Three Black Women's Autobiographies of the Nineteenth Century* (Bloomington: Indiana University Press, 1986).

Anim-Addo, Joan, 'Queen Victoria's Black "Daughter"', in *Black Victorians/Black Victoriana*, ed. by Gretchen H. Gerzina (New Brunswick: Rutgers University Press, 2003), pp. 11–19.

Appiah, Kwame Anthony, 'The Case for Capitalizing the *B* in Black', *Atlantic*, 18 June 2020 – https://www.theatlantic.com/ideas/archive/2020/06/time-to-capitalize-blackand-white/613159/ (accessed 27 November 2021).

Arnold, Catharine, *Bedlam: London and Its Mad* (London: Simon & Schuster, 2008).

Aschkenasy, Nehama, *Woman at the Window: Biblical Tales of Oppression and Escape* (Detroit: Wayne State University Press, 1998).

Ashby, LeRoy, *With Amusement For All: A History of American Popular Culture since 1830* (Lexington: University Press of Kentucky, 2006).

Atwal, Priya, *Royals and Rebels: The Rise and Fall of the Sikh Empire* (London: Hurst & Company, 2020).

Basu, Shrabani, *Victoria & Abdul: The True Story of the Queen's Closest Confidant* (Cheltenham: History Press, 2011)

Beasley, Edward, *The Victorian Reinvention of Race: New Racisms and the Problem of Grouping Human Sciences* (Oxford: Routledge, 2010).

Beckert, Sven, *Empire of Cotton: A New History of Global Capitalism* (London: Penguin, 2014).

Behrman, Cynthia F., 'The After-Life of General Gordon', *Albion: A Quarterly Journal Concerned with British Studies*, 3:2 (1971), pp. 47–61.

Berlin, Ira, *Slaves Without Masters: The Free Negro in the Antebellum South* (Oxford: Oxford University Press, 1974).

Bhavnani, Reena, Heidi Safia Mirza and Veena Meetoo, *Tackling the Roots of Racism: Lessons for Success* (Bristol: The Policy Press, 2005).

Blackett, R. J. M., 'Fugitive Slaves in Britain: The Odyssey of William and Ellen Craft', *Journal of American Studies*, 12:1 (1978), pp. 41–62.

Blackett, R. J. M., *Building an Antislavery Wall: Black Americans in the Atlantic Abolitionist Movement 1830–1860* (Baton Rouge: Louisiana State University Press, 1983).

Blanchard, Pascal, Gilles Boëtsch and Nanette Jacomijn Snoep, 'Human Zoos: The Invention of the Savage', in *Human Zoos: The Invention of the Savage*, ed. by Pascal Blanchard, Gilles Boëtsch and Nanette Jacomijn Snoep (Paris: Musée du Quai Branly, 2011), pp. 20–54.

Blockett, Kimberly, 'Disrupting Print: Emigration, the Press, and Narrative Subjectivity in the British Preaching and Writing of Zilpha Elaw, 1840–1860s', *MELUS*, 40:3 (2015), pp. 94–109.

Bolt, Christine, 'Race and the Victorians', in *British Imperialism in the Nineteenth Century*, ed. by C. C. Eldridge (London: Palgrave, 1984), pp. 126–47.

Bolt, Christine, *Victorian Attitudes to Race* (London: Routledge, 2007).

Bourne, Stephen, *Black Poppies: Britain's Black Community and the Great War* (Cheltenham: History Press, 2019)

Bourne, Stephen, *Under Fire: Black Britain in Wartime 1939–45* (Cheltenham: History Press, 2020).

Brantlinger, Patrick, *Taming Cannibals: Race and the Victorians* (Ithaca: Cornell University Press, 2011).

Bressey, Caroline, 'Forgotten histories: three stories of black girls from Barnardo's Victorian archive', *Women's History Review*, 11:3 (2002), pp. 351–74.

Bressey, Caroline, '"Of Africa's Brightest Ornaments": A Short Biography of Sarah Forbes Bonetta', *Social & Cultural Geography*, 6:2 (2005), pp. 253–66.

Bressey, Caroline, *Empire, Race and the Politics of Anti-Caste* (London: Bloomsbury, 2015).

Bressey, Caroline, 'Victorian Photography and the Mapping of the Black Prescence in Britain', in *Black Victorians: Black People in British Art 1800–1900*, ed. by Jan Marsh (Hampshire: Manchester Art Gallery and Birmingham Art Gallery, 2015), pp. 68–77.

Bibliography

Bressey, Caroline, 'The Next Chapter: The Black Presence in the Nineteenth Century', in *Britain's Black Past*, ed. by Gretchen H. Gerzina (Liverpool: Liverpool University Press, 2020), pp. 315–30.

Brown, Vincent, *Tacky's Revolt: The Story of an Atlantic Slave War* (Cambridge, Mass.: Harvard University Press, 2020).

Busby, Margaret (ed.), *Daughters of Africa: An International Anthology of Writing of Women of African Descent* (London: Jonathan Cape, 1992).

Byerman, Keith, 'Creating the Black Hero: Ira Aldridge's The Black Doctor', in *Ira Aldridge: The African Roscius*, ed. by Bernth Lindfors (Rochester: University of Rochester Press, 2007), pp. 180–90.

Cain, Joe, 'John Edmonstone: References from Charles Darwin' – https://profjoecain.net/charles-darwin-referencing-john-edmonstone-taxidermy (accessed 13 June 2021).

Charmantier, Isabelle, 'Linnaeus and Race', *The Linnean Society* – https://www.linnean.org/learning/who-was-linnaeus/linnaeus-and-race (accessed 12 June 2021).

Chater, Kathleen, *Untold Histories: Black people in England and Wales during the period of the British slave trade, c. 1660–1807* (Manchester: Manchester University Press, 2009).

Chater, Kathleen, 'Job Mobility amongst Black People in England and Wales during the Long Eighteenth Century', in *Belonging in Europe – The African Diaspora and Work*, ed. by Caroline Bressey and Hakim Adi (London: Routledge, 2011).

Chater, Kathleen, *Henry Box Brown: From Slavery to Show Business* (Jefferson: McFarland, 2020).

Chatterjee, Ronjaunee, Alicia Mireles Christoff and Amy R. Wong, 'Undisciplining Victorian Studies', *Victorian Studies*, 62:3 (2020), pp. 369–91.

Cima, Gay Gibson, *Performing Anti-Slavery: Activist Women on Antebellum Stages* (Cambridge: Cambridge University Press, 2014).

Cohen, Ashley L., 'Julius Soubise in India', in *Black Britain's Past*, ed. by Gretchen H. Gerzina (Liverpool: Liverpool University Press, 2020), pp. 215–34.

Colley, Linda, *Britons: Forging the Nation 1707–1837* (New Haven: Yale University Press, 2005).

Collini, Stefan, *Public Moralists: Political Thought and Intellectual Life in Britain, 1850–1930* (Oxford: Clarendon Press, 1991)

Costello, Ray, *Black Salt: Seafarers of African Descent on British Ships* (Liverpool: Liverpool University Press, 2012).

Costello, Ray, *Black Tommies: British Soldiers of African Descent in the First World War* (Liverpool: Liverpool University Press, 2015).

Cowhig, Ruth M., 'Ira Aldridge in Manchester', in *Ira Aldridge: The African Roscius*, ed. by Bernth Lindfors (Rochester: University of Rochester Press, 2007), pp. 126–34.

Cox, Jeffrey, 'Worlds of Victorian Religion', in *The Victorian World*, ed. by Martin Hewitt (London: Routledge, 2014), pp. 433–48.

Crais, Clifton and Pamela Scully, *Sara Baartman and the Hottentot Venus: A Ghost Story and a Biography* (Princeton: Princeton University Press, 2009).

Curtis, L. Perry, Jr., *Apes and Angels: The Irishman in Victorian Caricature* (Washington: Smithsonian Institution Press, 1997).

Cutter, Martha J., 'Will the Real Henry "Box" Brown Please Stand Up?', *Commonplace: The Journal of Early American Life*, http://commonplace.online/article/will-the-real-henry-box-brown-please-stand-up/ (accessed 7 September 2021).

Dabydeen, David, John Gilmore and Cecily Jones (eds.), *The Oxford Companion to Black British History* (Oxford: Oxford University Press, 2007).

Davies, Gareth H. H., *Pablo Fanque and the Victorian Circus: A Romance of Real Life* (Cromer: Poppyland Publishing, 2017).

Davis, Angela Y., *Women, Race and Class* (London: Penguin, 1981).

Deacon, Harriet, 'Racism and Medical Science in South Africa's Cape Colony in the Mid- to Late Nineteenth Century', *Osiris*, 15 (2000), pp. 190–206.

Delap, Lucy, *Knowing Their Place: Domestic Service in twentieth-century Britain* (Oxford: Oxford University Press, 2011).

Dennis, Rutledge M., 'Social Darwinism, Scientific Racism, and the Metaphysics of Race', *Journal of Negro Education*, 64:3 (1995), pp. 243–52.

Desmond, Adrian and James Moore, *Darwin's Sacred Cause: Race, Slavery and the Quest for Human Origins* (London: Penguin Books, 2010).

Diangelo, Robin, *White Fragility: Why It's So Hard for White People to Talk About Racism* (London: Penguin Books, 2019).

Douglas, Bronwen, 'Climate to Crania: science and the racialization of human difference', in *Foreign Bodies: Oceania and the Science of Race 1750–1940*, ed. by Bronwen Douglas and Chris Ballard (Canberra: ANU Press, 2008), pp. 33–96.

Drescher, Seymour, 'Antislavery Debates: Tides of Historiography in Slavery and Antislavery', *European Review*, 19:1 (2011), pp. 131–48.

Elebute, Adeyemo, *The Life of James Pinson Labulo Davies: A Colossus of Victorian Lagos* (Lagos: Prestige, 2017).

Ellis, Samantha, 'Paul Robeson in *Othello*', *Guardian*, 2 September 2003.

Emsley, Clive, *The Great British Bobby: A History of British Policing from the 18th Century to the Present* (London: Quercus, 2009).

Evans, Nicholas M., 'Ira Aldridge: Shakespeare and Minstrelsy' in *Ira Aldridge: The African Roscius*, ed. by Bernth Lindfors (Rochester: University of Rochester Press, 2007), pp. 157–79.

Eze, Emmanuel C., 'On Double Consciousness', *Callaloo*, 34:3 (2011), pp. 877–98.

Fanon, Frantz, *Black Skin, White Marks*, trans. by Richard Philcox (London: Penguin Books, 2008).

Ferrari, Roberto C., 'Fanny Eaton: The "Other" Pre-Raphaelite Model', *PRS Review*, 22:2 (2014), pp. 3–19.

Field, Corinne T., 'Old-Age Justice and Black Feminist History: Sojourner Truth's and Harriet Tubman's Intersectional Legacies', *Radical History Review*, 2021:139 (2021), pp. 37–51.

Figes, Lydia, 'Fanny Eaton: Jamaican Pre-Raphaelite Muse' – https://artuk.org/discover/stories/fanny-eaton-jamaican-pre-raphaelite-muse (accessed 2 August 2021).

Fisch, Audrey, *American Slaves in Victorian England: Abolitionist Politics in Popular Literature and Culture* (Cambridge: Cambridge University Press, 2000).

Foucault, Michel, *Madness and Civilization: A History of Insanity in the Age of Reason*, trans. by Richard Howard (London: Routledge, 2009).

Bibliography

Fryar, Christienna D., 'Imperfect Models: The Kingston Lunatic Asylum Scandal and the Problem of Postemancipation Imperialism', *Journal of British Studies*, 55 (2016), pp. 709–27.

Fryar, Christienna D., 'The Narrative of Ann Pratt: Life-Writing, Genre and Bureaucracy in a Postemancipation Scandal', *History Workshop Journal*, 85 (2018), pp. 265–79.

Fryer, Peter, *Staying Power: The History of Black People in Britain* (London: Pluto Press, 2018).

Gendre, Kevin Le, *Don't Stop the Carnival: Black Music in Britain*, Vol. I (Leeds: Peepal Tree Press, 2008).

Gerzina, Gretchen H., *Black England: Life Before Emancipation* (London: Allison & Busby, 1999).

Gilman, Sander L., *Difference and Pathology: Stereotypes of Sexuality, Race, and Madness* (Ithaca: Cornell University Press, 1985).

Gilroy, Paul, *The Black Atlantic: Modernity and Double Consciousness* (London: Verso, 1999).

Gilroy, Paul, *There Ain't No Black in the Union Jack* (London: Routledge, 2002).

Gossman, Norbert J., 'William Cuffay: London's Black Chartist', *Phylon*, 44:1 (1983), pp. 56–65.

Gould, Stephen Jay, *The Mismeasure of Man* (New York: W. W. Norton, 1981).

Green, Jeffrey and Paul McGilchrist, 'Samuel Coleridge-Taylor: A Postscript', *Black Perspective in Music*, 14:3 (1986), pp. 259–66.

Green, Jeffrey, '"The Foremost Musician of His Race": Samuel Coleridge-Taylor of England, 1875-1912', *Black Music Research Journal*, 10:2 (1990), pp. 233–52.

Green, Jeffrey, *Black Edwardians: Black People in Britain 1901–14* (London: Frank Cass, 1998).

Green, Jeffrey, *Samuel Coleridge-Taylor, A Musical Life* (London: Routledge, 2011).

Greenhow, Ray, *Britain's First Black Policeman: The Life of John Kent A Police Officer in Cumberland 1835–1846* (Carlisle: Bookcase, 2018).

Hall, Catherine, Keith McClelland and Jane Rendall, 'Introduction', in *Defining the Victorian Nation: Class, Race, Gender and the British Reform Act of 1867*, ed. by Catherine Hall, Keith McClelland and Jane Rendall (Cambridge: Cambridge University Press, 2000), pp. 1–70.

Hall, Kermit L., James W. Ely, Jr. and Joel B. Grossman (eds.), *The Oxford Companion to the Supreme Court of the United States* (Oxford: Oxford University Press, 2005).

Hanley, Ryan, 'Slavery and the Birth of Working-Class Racism in England, 1814–1833', *Transactions of the Royal Historical Society*, 26 (2016), pp. 103–23.

Hartman, Saidiya, *Wayward Lives, Beautiful Experiments: Intimate Histories of Social Upheaval* (London: Serpent's Tail, 2019).

Heaton, Matthew M., *Black Skins, White Coats: Nigeria Psychiatrists, Decolonization, and the Globalization of Psychiatry* (Athens, Ohio: Ohio University Press, 2013).

Heng, Geraldine, *The Invention of Race in the European Middle Ages* (Austin: University of Texas, 2018).

Hibbert, Christopher, *Queen Victoria in Her Letters and Journals* (Stroud: Sutton Publishing, 2000).

Hoermann, Raphael, '"Fermentation will be Universal": Intersections of Race and Class in Robert Wedderburn's Black Atlantic Discourse of Transatlantic Revolution', in *Britain's Black Past*, ed. by Gretchen H. Gerzina (Liverpool: Liverpool University Press, 2020), pp. 295–314.

Hollis, Patricia, 'Anti-Slavery and British Working-Class Radicalism in the Years of Reform', in *Anti-Slavery, Religion, and Reform: Essays in Memory of Roger Anstey*, ed. by Christine Bolt and Seymour Drescher (Folkestone: Wm Dawson & Sons, 1980), pp. 294–315.

Hooker, J. R., 'The Pan-African Conference 1900', *Transition*, 46 (1974), pp. 20–24.

Horsman, Reginald, 'Origins of Racial Anglo-Saxonism in Great Britain before 1850', *Journal of the History of Ideas*, 37:3 (1976), pp. 387–410.

Hoyles, Martin, *William Cuffay: The Life & Times of a Chartist Leader* (Hertford: Hansib Publications, 2013).

Isaac, Benjamin, *The Invention of Racism in Classical Antiquity* (Princeton: Princeton University Press, 2004).

Isaac, Benjamin, Joseph Ziegler, Miriam Eliav-Feldon, 'Introduction', in *The Origins of Racism in the West*, ed. by Benjamin Isaac, Joseph Ziegler, Miriam Eliav-Feldon (Cambridge: Cambridge University Press, 2009), pp. 1–31.

James, Leslie, and Daniel Whittall, 'Ambiguity and Imprint: British racial logics, colonial commissions of enquiry, and the creolization of Britain in the 1930s and 1940s', *Callaloo*, 39:1 (2016), pp. 166–84.

Jando, Dominique, *Philip Astley & The Horsemen who Invented the Circus (1768–1814)* (San Francisco: Circopedia, 2018).

Jones, Victoria, 'Mislike me not for my complexion' – https://www.shakespeare.org.uk/explore-shakespeare/blogs/mislike-me-not-my-complexion/ (accessed 26 August 2021)

Kaufmann, Miranda, *Black Tudors: The Untold Story* (London: Oneworld, 2017).

Kay, Charles, 'The Marriage of Samuel Coleridge-Taylor and Jessie Walmisley', *Black Music Research Journal*, 21:2 (2001), pp. 159–78.

Killingray, David, 'The Black Atlantic Missionary Movement and Africa, 1780s–1920s', *Journal of Religion in Africa*, 33:1 (2003), pp. 3–31.

Killingray, David, 'Rights, Land, and Labour: Black British Critics of South African Policies before 1948', *Journal of Southern African Studies*, 35:2 (2009), pp. 375–98.

Killingray, David, 'Significant Black South Africans in Britain before 1912: Pan-African Organisations and the Emergence of South Africa's First Black Lawyers', *South African Historical Journal*, 64:3 (2012), pp. 393–417.

King, Colin, '"They diagnosed me a schizophrenic when I was just a Gemini". The other side of madness', in *Reconceiving Schizophrenia*, ed. by Man Cheung Chung, K. W. M. Fulford and George Graham (Oxford: Oxford University Press, 2007), pp. 11–28.

King, Nicole, 'A Colored Woman in Another Country Pleading for Justice in Her Own', in *Black Victorians/Black Victoriana*, ed. by Gretchen H. Gerzina (New Brunswick: Rutgers University Press, 2003), pp. 88–109.

Kiste, John Van Der, *Sarah Forbes Bonetta: Queen Victoria's African Princess* (South Brent: A&F, 2018).

Bibliography

Korobkin, Laura, 'Avoiding "Aunt Tomasina": Charles Dickens Responds to Harriet Beecher Stowe's Black American Reader, Mary Webb', *English Literary History*, 82:1 (2015), pp. 115–40.

Koven, Seth, *Slumming: Sexual and Social Politics in Victorian London* (Princeton: Princeton University Press, 2004).

Lambert, David and Elizabeth Cooper, 'The Changing Image of the West India Regiments' – https://www.bl.uk/west-india-regiment/articles/the-changing-image-of-the-west-india-regiments# (accessed 19 August 2021).

Langford, Paul, *Englishness Identified: Manners and Characters, 1650–1850* (Oxford: Oxford University Press, 2000).

Langton, Winifred and Fay Jacobsen, *Courage: An Account of the Lives of Eliza Adelaide Knight and Donald Adolphus Brown* (Sabon: Geoff Gamble, 2007).

Laud, Derek, *The Problem with Immigrants* (London: Biteback Publishing, 2015).

Law, Robin, 'Dahomey and the Slave Trade: Reflections on the Historiography of the Rise of Dahomey', *Journal of African History*, 27:2 (1986), pp. 237–67.

Leach, S., et al. 'A Lady of York: Migration, Ethnicity and Identity in Roman Britain', *Antiquity*, 84:323 (2010), pp. 131–45.

Lindfors, Bernth, 'Charles Dickens and the Zulus', in *Africans On Stage: Studies in Ethnological Show Business*, ed. by Bernth Lindfors (Bloomington: Indiana University Press, 1999), pp. 62–80.

Lindfors, Bernth, *Ira Aldridge: The Early Years 1807–1833* (Rochester: University of Rochester Press, 2007).

Lindfors, Bernth, '"Mislike me not for my complexion...": Ira Aldridge in Whiteface', in *Ira Aldridge: The African Roscius*, ed. by Bernth Lindfors (Rochester: University of Rochester Press, 2007), pp. 180–90.

Lindfors, Bernth, '"Nothing Extenuate, nor set down aught in malice": New Biographical Information on Ira Aldridge', in *Ira Aldridge: The African Roscius*, ed. by Bernth Lindfors (Rochester: University of Rochester Press, 2007), pp. 50–67.

Lindfors, Bernth, *Ira Aldridge: Vagabond Years, 1833–1852* (Rochester: University of Rochester Press, 2011).

Lindfors, Bernth, *Ira Aldridge: Performing Shakespeare in Europe, 1852–1855* (Rochester: University of Rochester Press, 2013).

Lindfors, Bernth, *The Theatrical Career of Samuel Morgan Smith* (Trenton: African World Press, 2018).

Little, Kenneth, *Negroes in Britain: A Study of Racial Relations in English Society* (London: Routledge, 1948).

Llewellyn, Briony, 'Observations and Interpretation: Travelling Artists in Egypt', in *Black Victorians: Black People in British Art 1800–1900*, ed. by Jan Marsh (Hampshire: Manchester Art Gallery and Birmingham Art Gallery, 2015), pp. 34–45.

Lorimer, Douglas A., *Science, Race Relations and Resistance: Britain, 1870–1914* (Manchester: Manchester University Press, 2013).

Lott, Eric, *Love and Theft: Blackface Minstrelsy and the American Working Class* (Oxford: Oxford University Press, 1993).

Lowther, Bob, *Watching Over Carlisle: 140 years of the Carlisle City Police Force 1827–1967* (Carlisle: P3 Publications, 2010).

Martin, Tony, *The Pan-African Connection: From Slavery to Garvey and Beyond* (Dover, Mass: The Majority Press, 1983).

McCalman, Iain, *Radical Underworld: Prophets, Revolutionaries and Pornographers in London, 1795–1840* (Cambridge: Cambridge University Press, 1988).

McCaskill, Barbara, 'Ellen Craft: The Fugitive Who Fled as a Planter', in *Georgia Women: Their Lives and Times*, ed. by Ann Short Chirhart and Betty Wood (Athens: University of Georgia Press, 2009).

McCaskill, Barbara, *Love, Liberation, and Escaping Slavery: William and Ellen Craft in Cultural Memory* (Athens: University of Georgia Press, 2015).

McClintock, Anne, *Imperial Leather: Race, Gender and Sexuality in the Colonial Contest* (London: Routledge, 1995).

McKenna, Neil, *Fanny and Stella: The Young Men Who Shocked Victorian England* (London: Faber and Faber, 2013).

MacKenzie, John M., 'Introduction', in *Imperialism and Popular Culture*, ed. by John M. MacKenzie (Manchester: Manchester University Press, 1986), pp. 1–16.

McNish, James, 'John Edmonstone: the man who taught Darwin taxidermy' – https://www.nhm.ac.uk/discover/john-edmonstone-the-man-who-taught-darwin-taxidermy.html (accessed 13 June 2021).

Marche, Montaz, 'Uncovering Black Women in Eighteenth- and Nineteenth-Century Britain' – https://www.ucl.ac.uk/history/news/2019f/oct/uncovering-black-women-eighteenth-and-nineteenth-century-britain (accessed 13 June 2021).

Marsh, Jan, 'The Black Presence in British Art 1800–1900: Introduction and Overview', in *Black Victorians: Black People in British Art 1800–1900*, ed. by Jan Marsh (Hampshire: Manchester Art Gallery and Birmingham Art Gallery, 2015), pp. 12–22.

Maxwell, David, 'Christianity', in *The Oxford Handbook of Modern African History*, ed. by John Parker and Richard Reid (Oxford: Oxford University Press, 2013), pp. 263–80.

May, Vivian M., *Anna Julia Cooper, Visionary Black Feminist: A Critical Introduction* (London: Routledge, 2007).

Midgley, Clare, 'Anti-Slavery and Feminism in Nineteenth-Century Britain', *Gender & History*, 5:3 (1993), pp. 343–62.

Mullen, Lincoln, 'These Maps Reveal How Slavery Expanded Across the United States' – https://www.smithsonianmag.com/history/maps-reveal-slavery-expanded-across-united-states-180951452/ (accessed 7 September 2021).

Morrison, Michael A., 'Paul Robeson's Othello at the Savoy Theatre, 1930', *New Theatre Quarterly*, 27:2 (2011), pp. 114–40.

Murray, Hannah-Rose, *Advocates of Freedom: African American Transatlantic Abolitionism in the British Isles* (Cambridge: Cambridge University Press, 2020).

Murrell, Denise, *Posing Modernity: The Black Model from Manet and Matisse to Today* (New Haven: Yale University Press, 2018).

Myers, Norma, *Reconstructing the Black Past: Blacks in Britain, c. 1780–1830* (London: Frank Cass, 1996).

Myers, Walter Dean, *At Her Majesty's Request: An African Princess in Victorian England* (New York: Scholastic Inc., 1998).

Nelson, Charmaine, 'Vénus Africaine: Race, Beauty and African-Ness', in *Black Victorians: Black People in British Art 1800–1900*, ed. by Jan Marsh (Hampshire: Manchester Art Gallery and Birmingham Art Gallery, 2015), pp. 46–56.

Bibliography

Ney, Stephen, 'Samuel Ajayi Crowther and the Age of Literature', *Research in African Literatures*, 46:1 (2015), pp. 37–52.

Nubia, Onyeka, *Blackamoores: Africans in Tudor England, Their Presence, Status and Origins* (London: Narrative Eye, 2013/2014).

Nubia, Onyeka, *England's Other Countrymen: Black Tudor Society* (London: Zed Books, 2019).

Nunn, Pamela Gerrish, 'Rebecca Solomon's A Young Teacher', *Burlington Magazine*, 130 (1988), pp. 769–70.

Nyong'o, Tavia, *The Amalgamation Waltz: Race, Performance, and the Ruses of Memory* (Minneapolis: University of Minnesota Press, 2009).

Olson, Lester C., 'The Personal, the Political, and Others: Audre Lorde Denouncing "The Second Sex Conference"', *Philosophy & Rhetoric*, 33:3 (2000), pp. 259–85.

O'Grady, Lorraine, 'Olympia's Maid: Reclaiming Black Female Subjectivity', in *Art, Activism, and Oppositionality: Essays from Afterimage*, ed. by Grant H. Kester (Durham, NC: Duke University Press, 1998).

Olusoga, David, *Black and British: A Forgotten History* (London: Pan Books, 2017).

O'Quinn, Daniel, 'Theatre and empire' in *The Cambridge Companion to British Theatre, 1730–1830*, ed. by Daniel O'Quinn and Jane Moody (Cambridge: Cambridge University Press, 2009), pp. 233–46.

Otele, Olivette, *African Europeans: An Untold History* (London: Hurst & Company, 2020).

Palmer, William, 'How Ideology Works: Historians and the Case of British Abolitionism', *Historical Journal*, 52:4 (2009), pp. 1039–51.

Parsons, Neil, *King Khama, Emperor Joe, and the Great White Queen* (Chicago: University of Chicago Press, 1998).

Parssinen, T. M. and I. J. Prothero, 'The London Tailors' Strike of 1834 and the Collapse of the Grand National Consolidated Trades' Union: A Police Spy's Report', *International Review of Social History*, 22:1 (1977), pp. 65–107.

Perlman, Merrill, 'Black and White: Why Capitalization Matters', *Columbia Journalism Review* (2015) – https://www.cjr.org/analysis/language_corner_1.php (accessed 27 November 2021).

Phillips, Mike, 'Samuel Coleridge-Taylor: Black Europeans' – https://www.bl.uk/onlinegallery/features/blackeuro/homepage.html (accessed 2 January 2021).

Porter, Roy, 'The Patient's View: Doing Medical History from below', *Theory and Society*, 14:2 (1985), pp. 175–98.

Porter, Roy, *Madness: A Brief History* (Oxford: Oxford University Press, 2002), pp. 118–22.

Pratt, Richard H., '*The Advantages of Mingling Indians with Whites*', *Americanizing the American Indians: Writings by the 'Friends of the Indian' 1880–1900* (Cambridge, Mass: Harvard University Press, 1973), pp. 260–71.

Press, Jon, 'The Collapse of a Contributory Pension Scheme: The Merchant Seamen's Fund, 1747–1851', *Journal of Transport History*, 5:2 (1979), pp. 91–104.

Prizel, Natalie, '"The Dead Man Come to Life Again": Edward Albert and the Strategies of Black Endurance', *Victorian Literature and Culture*, 45:2 (2017), pp. 293–32.

Qureshi, Sadiah, *Peoples on Parade: Exhibitions, Empire, and Anthropology in Nineteenth-Century Britain* (Chicago: University of Chicago Press, 2011).

Qureshi, Sadiah, 'Meeting the Zulus: Displayed Peoples and the Shows of London', in *Popular Exhibitions, Science and Showmanship, 1840–1910*, ed. by Joe Kember, John Plunkett and Jill A. Sullivan (London: Pickering & Chatto, 2012), pp. 185–98.

Rainsbury, Anne, 'Nathaniel Wells: The Making of a Black Country Gentleman', in *Britain's Black Past*, ed. by Gretchen H. Gerzina (Liverpool: Liverpool University Press, 2020), pp. 253–74.

Ramdin, Ron, *The Making of the Black Working Class in Britain* (London: Verso, 2017).

Reay, Barry, *Watching Hannah: Sexuality, Horror and Bodily De-formation in Victorian England* (London: Reaktion Books, 2002).

Reinhardt, Mark, 'Who Speaks for Margaret Garner? Slavery, Silence, and the Politics of Ventriloquism', *Critical Inquiry*, 29:1 (2002), pp. 81–119.

Rice, Alan, *Radical Narratives of the Black Atlantic* (London: Continuum, 2003).

Richards, Paul, 'Africa in the Music of Samuel Coleridge-Taylor', *Africa: Journal of the International African Institute*, 57:4 (1987), pp. 566–71.

Richards, Paul, 'A Pan-African Composer? Coleridge-Taylor and Africa', *Black Music Research Journal*, 21:2 (2001), pp. 235–60.

Rinehart, Nicholas T., 'Black Beethoven and the Racial Politics of Music History', *Transition*, 112 (2013), pp. 117–30.

Ritchie, Joy and Kate Ronald (eds.), *Available Means: An Anthology of Women's Rhetoric(s)* (Pittsburgh: University of Pittsburgh Press, 2001).

Robbins, Hollis, 'Fugitive Mail: The Deliverance of Henry "Box" Brown and Antebellum Postal Politics', *American Studies*, 50:1/2 (2009), pp. 5–25.

Roberts, Pamela, *Black Oxford: The Untold Stories of Oxford University's Black Scholars* (Oxford: Signal Books, 2013).

Robinson, Jane, *Mary Seacole: The Charismatic Black Nurse Who Became a Heroine of the Crimea* (London: Robinson, 2005).

Ruggles, Jeffrey, *The Unboxing of Henry Brown* (Richmond: Library of Virginia, 2003).

St Leon, Mark Valentine, 'Celebrated at first, then implied and finally denied: the erosion of Aboriginal identity in circus, 1851–1960', *Aboriginal History*, 32 (2008), pp. 63–81.

Salenius, Sirpa, *An Abolitionist Abroad: Sarah Parker Remond in Cosmopolitan Europe* (Boston: University of Massachusetts Press, 2016).

Salenius, Sirpa, 'Transatlantic Interracial Sisterhoods: Sarah Remond, Ellen Craft, and Harriet Jacobs in England', *Frontiers: A Journal of Women Studies*, 38:1 (2017), pp. 166–96.

Salenius, Sirpa, 'Sarah Parker Remond's Black American Grand Tour', in *Women and Migration: Responses in Art and History*, ed. by Deborah Willis, Ellyn Toscano and Kalia Brooks Nelson (Cambridge: Open Book Publishers, 2019), pp. 265–71.

Salesa, Damon Ieremia, *Racial Crossings: Race, Intermarriage, and the Victorian British Empire* (Oxford: Oxford University Press, 2011).

Saxon A. H., *The Life and Art of Andrew Ducrow & The Romantic Age of the English Circus* (Hamden: Archon Books, 1978).

Bibliography

Scanlan, Padraic X., *Freedom's Debtors: British Antislavery in Sierra Leone in the Age of Revolution* (New Haven: Yale University Press, 2017).

Scanlan, Padraic X., *Slave Empire: How Slavery Built Modern Britain* (London: Robinson, 2020).

Scobie, Edward, *Black Britannia: A History of Blacks in Britain* (Chicago: Johnson Publishing Company, 1972).

Scull, Andrew, *Madness in Civilization: A Cultural History of Insanity from the Bible to Freud, from the Madhouse to Modern Medicine* (London: Thames & Hudson, 2016).

Shapin, Steven, 'The Invisible Technician', *American Scientist*, 77:6 (1989), pp. 554–63.

Sharpe, Christina, *In the Wake: On Blackness and Being* (Durham, NC: Duke University Press, 2016).

Shepherd, Jade, '"I am very glad and cheered when I hear the flute": The Treatment of Criminal Lunatics in Late Victorian Broadmoor', *Medical History* 60:4 (2016), pp. 473–91.

Sherwood, Marika, *Origins of Pan-Africanism: Henry Sylvester Williams, Africa, and the African Diaspora* (Oxford: Routledge, 2011).

Shillington, Kevin, *History of Africa*, 4th edition (London: Red Globe Press, 2019).

Showalter, Elaine, *The Female Malady: Women, Madness and English Culture 1830–1980* (London: Virago, 1987), pp. 23–50.

Shyllon, Folarin, *Black People in Britain 1555–1833* (Oxford: Oxford University Press, 1977).

Silkey, Sarah L., *Black Woman Reformer: Ida B. Wells, Lynching, and Transatlantic Activism* (Athens: University of Georgia Press, 2015).

Snorton, C. Riley, *Black on Both Sides: A Racial History of Trans Identity* (Minneapolis: University of Minnesota Press, 2017).

Stansell, Christine, *The Feminist Promise: 1792 to the Present* (New York: The Modern Library, 2010).

Steinbach, Susie L., *Understanding the Victorians: Politics, Culture and Society in Nineteenth-Century Britain* (Oxford: Routledge, 2017).

Stevens, Mark, *Broadmoor Revealed: Victorian Crime and the Lunatic Asylum* (Barnsley: Pen and Sword History, 2013).

Stringer, Chris, *Homo Britannicus: The Incredible Story of Human Life in Britain* (London: Penguin Books, 2006).

Summerfield, Penny, 'Patriotism and Empire: Music-Hall Entertainment, 1870–1914', in *Imperialism and Popular Culture,* ed. by John M. Mackenzie (Manchester: Manchester University Press, 1986), pp. 17–48.

Summers, Martin, '"Suitable Care of the African When Afflicted With Insanity": Race, Madness, and Social Order in Comparative Perspective', *Bulletin of the History of Medicine*, 84:1 (2010), pp. 58–91.

Swartz, Sally, 'The Black Insane in the Cape, 1891–1920', *Journal of Southern African Studies*, 21:3 (1995), pp. 399–415.

Sweet, Matthew, *Inventing the Victorians* (London: Faber and Faber, 2001).

Thompson, E. P., *The Making of the English Working Class* (London: Victor Gollancz, 1965).

Turner, John M., 'Pablo Fanque, Black Circus Proprietor', in *Black Victorians/ Black Victoriana*, ed. by Gretchen H. Gerzina (New Brunswick: Rutgers University Press, 2003), pp. 20–38.

Turner, Michael J., '"Setting the Captive Free": Thomas Perronet Thompson, British Radicalism and the West Indies, 1820s–1860s', *Slavery and Abolition*, 26:1 (2005), pp. 115–32.

Vasili, Phil, *The First Black Footballer: Arthur Wharton 1865–1930* (London: Frank Cass, 1999).

Virdee, Satnam, *Racism, Class and the Racialized Outsider* (Basingstoke: Palgrave Macmillan, 2014).

Walls, Andrew F., 'The Legacy of Samuel Ajayi Crowther', *International Bulletin of Missionary Research*, 16:1 (1992), pp. 15–21.

Walls, Andrew F., 'Buxton, Thomas Fowell', in *Biographical Dictionary of Christian Missions*, ed. by Gerald H. Anderson (New York: Macmillan Reference USA, 1998), p. 105.

Ward, Steve, *Beneath the Big Top: A Social History of the Circus in Britain* (Barnsley: Pen and Sword History, 2014).

Waters, Hazel, 'Ira Aldridge's Fight for Equality', in *Ira Aldridge: The African Roscius*, ed. by Bernth Lindfors (Rochester: University of Rochester Press, 2007).

Waters, Hazel, *Racism on the Victorian Stage: Representation of Slavery and the Black Character* (Cambridge: Cambridge University Press, 2007).

Weintraub, Stanley, *Albert: Uncrowned King* (London: John Murray, 1997).

Williams, C. Peter, *The Ideal of the Self-Governing Church: A Study in Victorian Missionary Strategy* (New York: E. J. Brill, 1990).

Wills, Shomari, *Black Fortunes: The Story of the First Six African Americans Who Survived Slavery and Became Millionaires* (New York: HarperCollins, 2018).

Wilson, A. N., *The Victorians* (London: Arrow Books, 2003).

Wilson, Carter A., *Racism: From Slavery to Advanced Capitalism* (London: Sage Publications, 1996).

Winder, Robert, *Bloody Foreigners: The Story of Immigration to Britain* (London: Abacus, 2013).

Wood, Marcus, 'William Cobbett, John Thelwall, Radicalism, Racism and Slavery: A Study in Burkean Parodics', *Romanticism on the Net*, 15 (1999) – https://doi.org/10.7202/005873ar

Wood, Marcus, *Blind Memory: Visual Representations of Slavery in England and America, 1780–1865* (Manchester: Manchester University Press, 2000).

Woodson, Carter G., 'The Celebration of Negro History Week, 1927', in *Journal of Negro History*, 12:2 (1927), pp. 103–09.

Woolf, John, *The Wonders: Lifting the Curtain on the Freak Show, Circus and Victorian Age* (London: Michael O'Mara Books, 2019).

Zackodnik, Teresa C., '"I Don't Know How You Will Feel When I Get through": Racial Difference, Woman's Rights, and Sojourner Truth', *Feminist Studies*, 30:1 (2004), pp. 49–73.

Zackodnik, Teresa C., *The Mulatta and the Politics of Race* (Jackson: University Press of Mississippi, 2004).

Zackodnik, Teresa C., 'Ida B. Wells and "American Atrocities" in Britain', *Women's Studies International Forum* 28 (2005), pp. 259–73.

Zackodnik, Teresa C., *Press, Platform, Pulpit: Black Feminist Publics in the Era of Reform* (Knoxville: University of Tennessee Press, 2011).

List of Illustrations

1. Dr Rice with Hospital Staff, *c.* 1910–20. Images from the George Rice Collections. Reproduced courtesy of London Borough of Sutton Local Studies and Archives.
2. Sketch of Broadmoor, 1880s. ILN sketches. Reproduced courtesy of Berkshire Record Office.
3. John Flinn's entry into Bethlem archives, 1861. By permission of Bethlem Museum of the Mind.
4. Edward Albert, *Brief Sketch of the Life of Edward Albert* (n.d.). Reproduced courtesy of University of Washington Libraries, Special Collections, Call # HV4545.A4 / b B74.
5. William Cuffay, *Reynold's Political Instructor*, Saturday, 13 April 1850. Reproduced courtesy of Medway Archives Centre.
6. Sarah Forbes Davies by Camille Silvy, albumen print, 15 September 1862. Reproduced courtesy of National Portrait Gallery, London, NPG Ax61384.
7. Victoria Davies while at Cheltenham Ladies College, *c.* 1881. Reproduced courtesy of Cheltenham Ladies' College Archive.
8. Samuel Ajayi Crowther, (LC 37, f.95), 1888. Reproduced courtesy of Lambeth Palace Library.
9. Samuel Ajayi Crowther, James Johnson, Henry Johnson and friends at the Wilberforce Oak in 1873, (Tait 219 f. 119). Reproduced courtesy of Lambeth Palace Library.
10. James Francis Durham with Sergeant Stuart, *c.* 1887–89. De Lisle, *Reminiscences*, photograph opposite page 29. Reproduced by permission of Durham County Record Office.
11. James Durham with sheep (1900–10), D/DLI 7/194/8. Reproduced by permission of Durham County Record Office.
12. Samuel Coleridge Taylor, *c.* 1900, PH-97-14251. Image courtesy of Croydon Archives.
13. Ira Aldridge as Othello, 1887. Schomburg Center for Research in Black Culture, Jean Blackwell Hutson Research and Reference Division, The New York Public Library Digital Collections.
14. Pablo Fanque, *c.* 1860. Reproduced courtesy of V&A Images, The Victoria and Albert Museum.
15. Fanny Eaton in Simeon Solomon's *The Mother of Moses*, 1860 (first exhibited 1860; undated), Simeon Solomon (1840–1905), Oil on canvas, 24 × 19 7/8 in. (61 × 50.5 cm), frame: 36 5/8 × 32 × 2 1/4 in. (93 × 81.3 × 5.7 cm), Delaware Art Museum, Bequest of Robert Louis Isaacson, 1999.
16. Edgar Degas, *Miss LaLa at the Cirque Fernando*, 1879, pastel sketch on faded blue paper, 46.4 × 29.8 cm (18 1/4 × 11 3/4 in.), 2004.93. The J. Paul Getty Museum, Los Angeles.
17. Portrait of Mrs Fanny Eaton by Simeon Solomon. Graphite on paper, 7 November 1859. PD.55-1959. © The Fitzwilliam Museum, Cambridge.

18. Fanny Eaton in Dante Gabriel Rossetti's *The Beloved ('The Bride')*, 1865–66. Purchased with assistance from Sir Arthur Du Cros Bt and Sir Otto Beit KCMG through the Art Fund 1916. Photo: Tate.
19. 'The Resurrection of Henry "Box" Brown', 1872. Schomburg Center for Research in Black Culture, Manuscripts, Archives and Rare Books Division, The New York Public Library Digital Collections.
20. Sarah Parker Remond, n.d., Box 4 Photo. 81.448, Collection of the Massachusetts Historical Society.
21. Ellen Craft, 1853. Schomburg Center for Research in Black Culture, Manuscripts, Archives and Rare Books Division, The New York Public Library Digital Collections.
22. Ida B. Wells, 1893. Schomburg Center for Research in Black Culture, Manuscripts, Archives and Rare Books Division, The New York Public Library Digital Collections.

Notes

INTRODUCTION

1. Mrs Mathews (Anne Jackson), *The Life and Correspondence of Charles Mathews the Elder, Comedian* (London: Warne and Routledge, 1860), p. 385.
2. Clifton Crais and Pamela Scully, *Sara Baartman and the Hottentot Venus: A Ghost Story and a Biography* (Princeton: Princeton University Press, 2009).
3. Pascal Blanchard, Gilles Boëtsch and Nanette Jacomijn Snoep, 'Human Zoos: The Invention of the Savage', in *Human Zoos: The Invention of the Savage*, ed. by Pascal Blanchard, Gilles Boëtsch and Nanette Jacomijn Snoep (Paris: Musée du Quai Branly, 2011), pp. 20–54.
4. Crais and Scully, *Sara Baartman and the Hottentot Venus*, pp. 75–81.
5. I am grateful to colleagues at Islington Council for the honest conversations and reflections.
6. Peter Fryer, *Staying Power: The History of Black People in Britain* (London: Pluto Press, 2018), p. xvii.
7. Kenneth Little, *Negroes in Britain: A Study of Racial Relations in English Society* (London: Routledge, 1948); James and Daniel Whittall, 'Ambiguity and Imprint: British racial logics, colonial commissions of enquiry, and the creolization of Britain in the 1930s and 1940s', *Callaloo*, 39:1 (2016), pp. 166–84 (p. 180).
8. Fryer, *Staying Power*, p. xvii.
9. Frantz Fanon, *Black Skin, White Marks*, trans. by Richard Philcox (London: Penguin Books, 2008), pp. ix–x.
10. John Woolf, *The Wonders: Lifting the Curtain on the Freak Show, Circus and Victorian Age* (London: Michael O'Mara Books, 2019).
11. Ronjaunee Chatterjee, Alicia Mireles Christoff and Amy R. Wong, 'Undisciplining Victorian Studies', *Victorian Studies*, 62:3 (2020), pp. 369–91 (p. 370).
12. Cited in Natalie Prizel, '"The Dead Man Come to Life Again": Edward Albert and the Strategies of Black Endurance', *Victorian Literature and Culture*, 45:2 (2017), pp. 293–320 (p. 296, 306).
13. See, for example, Jane Robinson, *Mary Seacole: The Charismatic Black Nurse Who Became a Heroine of the Crimea* (London: Robinson, 2005) and Phil Vasili, *The First Black Footballer: Arthur Wharton 1865–1930* (London: Frank Cass, 1999).
14. Olivette Otele, *African Europeans: An Untold History* (London: Hurst & Company, 2020), p. 8.
15. Kwame Anthony Appiah, 'The Case for Capitalizing the *B* in Black', *The Atlantic*, 18 June 2020 – https://www.theatlantic.com/ideas/archive/2020/06/time-to-capitalize-blackand-white/613159/ (accessed 27 November 2021); Merrill Perlman, 'Black and White: Why Capitalization Matters', *Columbia Journalism Review* (2015) – https://www.cjr.org/analysis/language_corner_1.php (accessed 27 November 2021).

16 Catherine Hall, Keith McClelland and Jane Rendall, 'Introduction', in *Defining the Victorian Nation: Class, Race, Gender and the British Reform Act of 1867*, ed. by Catherine Hall, Keith McClelland and Jane Rendall, (Cambridge: Cambridge University Press, 2000), pp. 1–70 (pp. 45–46).

17 Paul Gilroy, *There Ain't No Black in the Union Jack* (London: Routledge, 2002), pp. 35–38.

18 *Ibid.*, pp. 35, xxii.

19 Cited in Reena Bhavnani, Heidi Safia Mirza and Veena Meetoo, *Tackling the Roots of Racism: Lessons for Success* (Bristol: The Policy Press, 2005), p. 16.

20 *Oxford English Dictionary* (*OED*), 'racism, n.' – http://www.oed.com (accessed 27 November 2021). First uttered in 1902 by the American Richard Henry Pratt, who also declared, 'Kill the Indian in him, and save the man', reflecting his aim to 'civilise' Native Americans. Richard H. Pratt, *"The Advantages of Mingling Indians with Whites," Americanizing the American Indians: Writings by the "Friends of the Indian" 1880–1900* (Cambridge, Mass: Harvard University Press, 1973), pp. 260–71.

21 Benjamin Isaac, Joseph Ziegler, Miriam Eliav-Feldon (eds.), 'Introduction', in *The Origins of Racism in the West*, (Cambridge: Cambridge University Press, 2009), pp. 1–31 (p. 11).

22 Bhavnani, Mirza and Meetoo, *Tackling the Roots of Racism*, p. 15.

23 Ryan Hanley, 'Slavery and the Birth of Working-Class Racism in England, 1814–1833', *Transactions of the Royal Historical Society*, 26 (2016), pp. 103–23 (p. 104). Race prejudice could equally be called 'anti-Black racism' (racial stereotyping, prejudice or discrimination); see: *The Oxford Companion to Black British History*, ed. by David Dabydeen, John Gilmore and Cecily Jones (Oxford: Oxford University Press, 2007), p. 389.

24 Chatterjee, Christoff and Wong, 'Undisciplining Victorian Studies', p. 373.

25 Cited in Lester C. Olson, 'The Personal, the Political, and Others: Audre Lorde Denouncing "The Second Sex Conference"', *Philosophy & Rhetoric*, 33:3 (2000), pp. 259–85 (p. 259).

26 Cited in Otele, *African Europeans*, p. 5.

27 Christina Sharpe, *In the Wake: On Blackness and Being* (Durham, NC: Duke University Press, 2016), p. 13.

28 Robin Diangelo, *White Fragility: Why It's So Hard for White People to Talk About Racism* (London: Penguin Books, 2019), p. 26.

PART ONE: CONTEXT AND CONCEALMENT

CHAPTER 1

1 *Oxford Dictionary of National Biography* (*ODNB*), W. B. Squire and David J. Golby. 'Bridgetower, George Augustus Polgreen (1780–1860), violinist' – http://www.oxforddnb.com/index.jsp (accessed 2 January 2021). See also Mike Phillips, 'Black Europeans' – https://www.bl.uk/onlinegallery/features/blackeuro/homepage.html (accessed 2 January 2021).

2 Cited in Adrian Desmond and James Moore, *Darwin's Sacred Cause: Race, Slavery and the Quest for Human Origins* (London: Penguin Books, 2010), pp. 22–24.

Notes

3   Cited in *ibid.*, p. 19.
4   Cited in *ibid.*, pp. 35–37.
5   Cited in *ibid.*, p. 21.
6   James McNish, 'John Edmonstone: the man who taught Darwin taxidermy' – https://www.nhm.ac.uk/discover/john-edmonstone-the-man-who-taught-darwin-taxidermy.html (accessed 13 June 2021).
7   Charles Darwin, *The Descent of Man, and Selection in Relation to Sex* (London: John Murray, 1871), pp. 231–32.
8   Steven Shapin, 'The Invisible Technician', *American Scientist*, 77:6 (1989), pp. 554–63.
9   Lothian Health Services Archive (LHSA), George Rice, LHB1/116/2. See also: LHSA, George Rice, LHB1/16/23.
10 *Black Alumni of Dartmouth*, 'George Rice' – https://badahistory.net/view.php?ID=124 (accessed 21 November 2021).
11 Sutton Archives, London (SAL), Papers of Dr George Rice, 39/10.
12 SAL, Papers of Dr George Rice, 39/1–25.
13 SAL, Papers of Dr George Rice, 39/23/1–3.
14 Chris Stringer, *Homo Britannicus: The Incredible Story of Human Life in Britain* (London: Penguin Books, 2006), pp. 134–59.
15 S. Leach et al., 'A Lady of York: Migration, Ethnicity and Identity in Roman Britain', *Antiquity*, 84:323 (2010), pp. 131–45; David Olusoga, *Black and British: A Forgotten History* (London: Pan Books, 2017), pp. 29–56.
16 Miranda Kaufmann, *Black Tudors: The Untold Story* (London: Oneworld, 2017); Onyeka Nubia, *England's Other Countrymen: Black Tudor Society* (London: Zed Books, 2019).
17 The National Archives, 'Black Presence: Asian and Black History in Britain, 1500–1850' (TNA, BP) – https://www.nationalarchives.gov.uk/pathways/blackhistory/ (accessed 13 July 2021), CO 268/1, ff. 8, 10 (24 Sept 1672).
18 'Estimates', *The Trans-Atlantic Slave Trade Database* – http://www.slavevoyages.org/assessment/estimates (accessed June 2021).
19 Cited in Kathleen Chater, *Untold Histories: Black people in England and Wales during the period of the British slave trade, c. 1660–1807* (Manchester: Manchester University Press, 2009), p. 89.
20 Slavery did not technically exist as an institution in Britain, although many individuals regarded their servants as enslaved; Chater, *Untold Histories*, p. 95.
21 *Ibid.*, pp. 25–32.
22 Norma Myers, *Reconstructing the Black Past: Blacks in Britain, c. 1780–1830* (London: Frank Cass, 1996), p. 77.
23 Ashley L. Cohen, 'Julius Soubise in India', in *Black Britain's Past*, ed. by Gretchen H. Gerzina (Liverpool: Liverpool University Press, 2020), pp. 215–34.
24 Gretchen H. Gerzina, *Black England: Life Before Emancipation* (London: Allison & Busby, 1999), p. 183.
25 Caroline Bressey, 'The Next Chapter: The Black Presence in the Nineteenth Century', in *Britain's Black Past*, ed. by Gretchen H. Gerzina (Liverpool: Liverpool University Press, 2020), pp. 315–30 (p. 326).
26 Montaz Marche, 'Uncovering Black Women in Eighteenth- and Nineteenth-Century Britain' – https://www.ucl.ac.uk/history/news/2019/oct/uncovering-black-women-eighteenth-and-nineteenth-century-britain (accessed 13 June 2021).

27　Bressey, 'The Next Chapter', in *Britain's Black Past*, ed. by Gerzina, pp. 315–30 (p. 334).
28　*Ibid.*
29　Ancestry – https://www.ancestry.co.uk/, Metropolitan Police Pension Registers, 1852–1932 (accessed 27 November 2021). My thanks to Cheryl Lovelace, the living relative of the 'dark' William Lovelace, who I learnt, thanks to Lovelace's DNA analysis, had no African ancestry.
30　See, for example, Haringey Archive and Local History, London (HALHL), Photographs, Sister Freda, Walter Till, Asarto Ward; Waltham Forest Archives and Local Studies Library, London (WFA, LSLL), Fuegians W 31.5, Pamphlet W 31.5, 22906, Pamphlet W85.211.
31　Jan Marsh, 'The Black Presence in British Art 1800–1900: Introduction and Overview', in *Black Victorians: Black People in British Art 1800–1900*, ed. by Jan Marsh (Hampshire: Manchester Art Gallery and Birmingham Art Gallery, 2015), pp. 12–22 (p. 14).
32　Paul Gilroy, *The Black Atlantic: Modernity and Double Consciousness* (London: Verso, 1999), p. 13.
33　Ray Costello, *Black Salt: Seafarers of African Descent on British Ships* (Liverpool: Liverpool University Press, 2012), pp. 123–24.
34　Cited in *ibid.*, p. 92.
35　This was based on looking at each year over a period of fourteen years in the early to mid-nineteenth century, Henry Mayhew, *London Labour and the London Poor*, 4 vols (Project Gutenberg, 2017–20 [1851, 1861–65]), vol. 3, p. 418.
36　'Sigismund Stiebel', University College London, Centre for the Study of the Legacies of British Slavery, Legacies of British Slavery Database – http://wwwdepts-live.ucl.ac.uk/lbs/ (accessed 27 November 2021).
37　Susie L. Steinbach, *Understanding the Victorians: Politics, Culture and Society in Nineteenth-Century Britain* (Oxford: Routledge, 2017), pp. 65–71.

CHAPTER 2

1　Christopher Hibbert, *Queen Victoria in Her Letters and Journals* (Stroud: Sutton Publishing, 2000), pp. 1, 23.
2　Robert Winder, *Bloody Foreigners: The Story of Immigration to Britain* (London: Abacus, 2013), pp. 146–55.
3　Linda Colley, *Britons: Forging the Nation 1707–1837* (New Haven: Yale University Press, 2005), pp. 147–94; Paul Langford, *Englishness Identified: Manners and Characters, 1650–1850* (Oxford: Oxford University Press, 2000), pp. 267–75.
4　Ottobah Cugoano, *Thoughts and Sentiments on the Evil and Wicked Traffic of the Slavery and Commerce of the Human Species, Humbly Submitted to the Inhabitants of Great Britain, by Ottobah Cugoano, a Native of Africa* (London, 1787), pp. 11, 110.
5　Olaudah Equiano, *The Interesting Narrative of the Life of Olaudah Equiano, Or Gustavus Vassa, The African, Written By Himself* (London: Printed for and sold by the Author, 1789), p. iii.
6　Mary Prince, *The History of Mary Prince, a West Indian Slave. Related by Herself. With a Supplement by the Editor. To Which Is Added, the Narrative of Asa-Asa, a Captured African* (London: Whestley and Davis, 1831), p. 23.

Notes

7   Vincent Brown, *Tacky's Revolt: The Story of an Atlantic Slave War* (Cambridge, Mass: Harvard University Press, 2020), pp. 1–15, 237–49.
8   The factors behind the abolition of slavery are complex and the subject of a rich historiography. See Seymour Drescher, 'Antislavery Debates: Tides of Historiography in Slavery and Antislavery', *European Review*, 19:1 (2011), pp. 131–148.
9   William Palmer, 'How Ideology Works: Historians and the Case of British Abolitionism', *The Historical Journal*, 52:4 (2009), pp. 1039–51.
10 Michael Adas, *Machines as the Measure of Men: Science, Technology, and Ideologies of Western Dominance* (Ithaca: Cornell University Press, 1989), p. 268.
11 Frederick Douglass, 'Farewell to the British People: An Address Delivered in London, England, March 30, 1847' – https://glc.yale.edu/farewell-british-people (accessed 27 November 2021).
12 R. J. M. Blackett, *Building an Antislavery Wall: Black Americans in the Atlantic Abolitionist Movement 1830–1860* (Baton Rouge: Louisiana State University Press, 1983), p. 196.
13 Olusoga, *Black and British*, pp. 246–48.
14 Cited in Audrey Fisch, *American Slaves in Victorian England: Abolitionist Politics in Popular Literature and Culture* (Cambridge: Cambridge University Press, 2000), p. 69.
15 Cited in Alan Rice, *Radical Narratives of the Black Atlantic* (London: Continuum, 2003), p. 177.
16 David Walker, *Walker's Appeal, in Four Articles; Together with a Preamble, to the Coloured Citizens of the World, but in Particular, and Very Expressly, to Those of the United States of America* (Boston: David Walker, 1830), p. 47.
17 Harriet Ann Jacobs, *Incidents in the Life of a Slave Girl. Written by Herself*, ed. by L. Maria Child (Boston: Published for the Author, 1861), p. 275.
18 Frederick Douglass, 'The Color Line', *The North American Review*, 132:295 (1881), pp. 567–77 (p. 572).
19 Cited in Matthew Sweet, *Inventing the Victorians* (London: Faber and Faber, 2001), p. xiv.
20 Cited in Padraic X. Scanlan, *Slave Empire: How Slavery Built Modern Britain* (London: Robinson, 2020), pp. 299–330.
21 Slave Trade Act 1843 – https://www.legislation.gov.uk/ukpga/Vict/6-7/98/enacted (accessed 27 November 2021).
22 Scanlan, *Slave Empire*, pp. 257–98.
23 Cited in *ibid.*, p. 352.
24 Sven Beckert, *Empire of Cotton: A New History of Global Capitalism* (London: Penguin, 2014), p. 244.
25 *Ibid.*, pp. 243–46.
26 W. E. B Du Bois, *The Souls of Black Folk*, ed. and intro. by Brent Hayes Edwards (Oxford: Oxford University Press, 2007 [1903]), p. 8.
27 Gilroy, *The Black Atlantic*, p. 1.
28 Edward Scobie, *Black Britannia: A History of Blacks in Britain* (Chicago: Johnson Publishing Company, 1972), p. vii; Jacobs, *Incidents in the Life of a Slave Girl*, p. 119.
29 Cited in Gilroy, *The Black Atlantic*, p. 162.
30 Cited in *ibid.*, p. 221.

31 Cited in Emmanuel C. Eze, 'On Double Consciousness', *Callaloo*, 34:3 (2011), pp. 877–98 (p. 881).
32 Carter A. Wilson, *Racism: From Slavery to Advanced Capitalism* (London: Sage Publications, 1996), pp. 48–55.
33 Olusoga, *Black and British*, pp. 69–71.
34 Chater, *Untold Histories*, p. 79.
35 Cited in Fryer, *Staying Power*, p. 154.
36 Cited in *ibid.*, p. 161.
37 Isabelle Charmantier, 'Linnaeus and Race', *The Linnaeus Society* – https://www.linnean.org/learning/who-was-linnaeus/linnaeus-and-race (accessed 12 June 2021).
38 Cited in Bronwen Douglas, 'Climate to Crania: Science and the Racialization of Human Difference', in *Foreign Bodies: Oceania and the Science of Race 1750–1940*, ed. by Bronwen Douglas and Chris Ballard (Canberra: ANU Press, 2008), pp. 33–96 (p. 33).
39 *Ibid.*
40 James Cowles Prichard, *The Natural History of Man: Comprising Inquiries into the Modifying Influence of Physical and Moral Agencies of the Different Tribes of the Human Family* (London: H. Bailliere, 1843), p. 26.
41 Damon Ieremia Salesa, *Racial Crossings: Race, Intermarriage, and the Victorian British Empire* (Oxford: Oxford University Press, 2011), pp. 141–47.
42 James Hunt, *The Negro's Place in Nature: A Paper Read Before the London Anthropological Society* (New York: Van Evrie, Horton, 1864), p. 23.
43 Cited in Salesa, *Racial Crossings*, p. 150.
44 *Ibid.*, pp. 148–49.
45 Stephen Jay Gould, *The Mismeasure of Man* (New York: W.W. Norton, 1981), p. 73.
46 Edward Beasley, *The Victorian Reinvention of Race: New Racisms and the Problem of Grouping Human Sciences* (Oxford: Routledge, 2010), p. 17.
47 Olusoga, *Black and British*, pp. 280–22.
48 Cited in Bernth Lindfors, 'Charles Dickens and the Zulus', in *Africans On Stage: Studies in Ethnological Show Business*, ed. by Bernth Lindfors (Bloomington: Indiana University Press, 1999), pp. 62–80 (p. 72).
49 Cited in *ibid.*, p. 76.
50 Cited in Sadiah Qureshi, 'Meeting the Zulus: Displayed Peoples and the Shows of London', in *Popular Exhibitions, Science and Showmanship, 1840–1910*, ed. by Joe Kember, John Plunkett and Jill A. Sullivan (London: Pickering & Chatto, 2012), pp. 185–98 (p. 195).
51 Rev. H. Easton, *A Treatise on the Intellectual Character, and Civil and Political Condition of the Colored People of the United States; and the Prejudice Exercised Towards Them* (Boston: Isaac Knapp, 1837), p. 40.
52 Cited in Olusoga, *Black and British*, pp. 369–72.
53 Cited in Seth Koven, *Slumming: Sexual and Social Politics in Victorian London* (Princeton: Princeton University Press, 2004), p. 62.
54 Marcus Wood, 'William Cobbett, John Thelwall, Radicalism, Racism and Slavery: A Study in Burkean Parodics', *Romanticism on the Net*, 15 (1999) – https://doi.org/10.7202/005873ar.
55 Satnam Virdee, *Racism, Class and the Racialized Outsider* (Basingstoke: Palgrave Macmillan, 2014), pp. 9–73.

Notes

56 Reginald Horsman, 'Origins of Racial Anglo-Saxonism in Great Britain before 1850', *Journal of the History of Ideas*, 37:3 (1976), pp. 387–410.
57 Cited in Beasley, *The Victorian Reinvention of Race*, pp. 16–17.
58 Mayhew, *London Labour and the London Poor*, Vol. 4, p. 425.
59 *Ibid.*
60 *Ibid.*, p. 426.
61 *Ibid.*
62 Costello, *Black Salt*, pp. 212–13.
63 *Ibid.*, pp. 123–24.
64 Mayhew, *London Labour and the London Poor*, Vol. 4, pp. 425–26.
65 *Ibid.*, p. 481.
66 *Ibid.*, Vol. 1, p. 419; Henry Mayhew and John Binny, *The Criminal Prisons of London and Scenes of Prison Life* (London: Griffin, Bohn, 1862), p. 44.
67 Cited in A. N. Wilson, *The Victorians* (London: Arrow Books, 2003), p. 217.
68 Cited in Salesa, *Racial Crossings*, p. 171.
69 Cited in *ibid.*, p. 173.
70 Douglas A. Lorimer, *Science, Race Relations and Resistance: Britain, 1870–1914* (Manchester: Manchester University Press, 2013), p. 21.
71 Herbert Spencer, *The Principles of Biology*, Vol. I (Oxford: Williams and Norgate, 1898), pp. 263–64.
72 Rutledge M. Dennis, 'Social Darwinism, Scientific Racism, and the Metaphysics of Race', *The Journal of Negro Education*, 64:3 (1995), pp. 243–52 (p. 244).
73 Francis Galton, *Inquiries into Human Faculty and its Development* (London: Macmillan, 1883), pp. 24–25. Galton was in no doubt that 'Negroes' were vastly inferior and that the 'Arab is little more than an eater up of other men's produce; he is a destroyer' (Francis Galton, *Letter to the Editor of The Times*, 5 June 1873).
74 Dennis, 'Social Darwinism, Scientific Racism, and the Metaphysics of Race', pp. 243–52.
75 Beasley, *The Victorian Reinvention of Race*, p. 20.
76 Cited in Neil Parsons, *King Khama, Emperor Joe, and the Great White Queen* (Chicago: University of Chicago Press, 1998), p. 27.
77 John M. MacKenzie, 'Introduction', in *Imperialism and Popular Culture*, ed. by John M. Mackenzie (Manchester: Manchester University Press, 1986), pp. 1–16.
78 Gilroy, *The Black Atlantic*, pp. 88–90.
79 Cited in Caroline Bressey, *Empire, Race and the Politics of Anti-Caste* (London: Bloomsbury, 2015), p. 17.
80 Lorimer, *Science, Race Relations and Resistance*, p. 13.
81 Desmond and Moore, *Darwin's Sacred Cause*, p. 365.
82 Woolf, *The Wonders*, p. 239.
83 Cited in Lorimer, *Science, Race Relations and Resistance*, p. 44.
84 *Ibid.*
85 Jeffrey Green, '186: Americans Experience London Racism, 1903?' – https://jeffreygreen.co.uk/186-americans-experience-london-racism-1903/ (accessed 26 June 2021).
86 A. B. C. Merriman-Labor, *Britons Through Negro Spectacles; or, A Negro on Britons* (London: Imperial and Foreign Company, 1909), p. 176.
87 L. Perry Curtis Jr., *Apes and Angels: The Irishman in Victorian Caricature* (Washington: Smithsonian Institution Press, 1997), pp. 94–108.

88 Robert Knox, *The Races of Men: A Fragment* (London: Henry Renshaw, 1850), p. 245.
89 Cited in Rice, *Radical Narratives of the Black Atlantic*, p. 179.
90 Benjamin Isaac, *The Invention of Racism in Classical Antiquity* (Princeton: Princeton University Press, 2004); Geraldine Heng, *The Invention of Race in the European Middle Ages* (Austin: The University of Texas, 2018).
91 Christine Bolt, 'Race and the Victorians', in *British Imperialism in the Nineteenth Century*, ed. by C. C. Eldridge (London: Palgrave, 1984), pp. 126–47 (p. 126).
92 Sweet, *Inventing the Victorians*, pp. ix–xxiii.
93 William Eden Evans-Gordon, *The Alien Immigrant* (London: William Heinemann, 1903), p. 7.
94 Du Bois, *The Souls of Black Folk*, p. 15.
95 Du Bois, 'To the Nations of the World', BlackPast.org – https://www.blackpast.org/african-american-history/1900-w-e-b-du-bois-nations-world/ (accessed 14 August 2021).
96 Cited in Christine Bolt, *Victorian Attitudes to Race* (London: Routledge, 2007), p. 209.

PART TWO: STRUGGLE AND SURVIVAL

CHAPTER 3

1 *Weekly Dispatch* (London), 21 January 1883.
2 *Ibid.*
3 Saidiya Hartman, *Wayward Lives, Beautiful Experiments: Intimate Histories of Social Upheaval* (London: Serpent's Tail, 2019), p. 10.
4 *Ibid.*, pp. 31–32.
5 *Weekly Dispatch* (London), 21 January 1883.
6 *St James's Gazette*, 19 April 1883.
7 Winifred Langton and Fay Jacobsen, *Courage: An Account of the Lives of Eliza Adelaide Knight and Donald Adolphus Brown* (Sabon: Geoff Gamble, 2007), p. 34.
8 Thomas J. Spinner, Jr., *A Political and Social History of Guyana, 1945–1983* (London: Westview Press, 1984), pp. 6–7.
9 Langton and Jacobsen, *Courage*, p. 43.
10 Ancestry.com, Elizabeth Ann Burrus (Burrows), Family Tree.
11 Langton and Jacobsen, *Courage*, p. 43.
12 *Weekly Dispatch* (London), 21 January 1883.
13 *Ibid.*
14 Sally Swartz, 'The Black Insane in the Cape, 1891-1920', *Journal of Southern African Studies*, 21:3 (1995), pp. 399–415.
15 Jade Shepherd, '"I am very glad and cheered when I hear the flute": The Treatment of Criminal Lunatics in Late Victorian Broadmoor', *Medical History* 60:4 (2016), pp. 473–91.
16 Cited in Mark Stevens, *Broadmoor Revealed: Victorian Crime and the Lunatic Asylum* (Barnsley: Pen and Sword History, 2013), p. 5.
17 Elaine Showalter, *The Female Malady: Women, Madness and English Culture 1830–1980* (London: Virago, 1987), pp. 23–50.
18 Cited in Shepherd, '"I am very glad and cheered when I hear the flute"', p. 474.

Notes

19 Berkshire Record Office, Reading (BRO), D/H14/D2/1/1/4, William Brown (kindly transcribed by Mark Stevens).
20 *Ibid.*
21 BRO, 1147: William Brown, D/H14/D2/2/1/1147, 12 July 1885.
22 *Ibid.*, 13 July 1885.
23 BRO, D/H14/D2/1/1/4, William Brown, Letters, 28 January 1885 and 25 March 1885.
24 BRO, D/H14/D2/1/1/4, William Brown, 25 March 1885.
25 The National Archives, 'The Dockyard Worker' – http://www.nationalarchives.gov.uk/pathways/census/pandp/people/dock.htm (accessed 27 November 2021).
26 Langton and Jacobsen, *Courage*.
27 Gilroy, *The Black Atlantic*, pp. 1–40.

CHAPTER 4

1 BRO, 19: John Flinn, D/H14/D2/2/1/19/2.
2 Lancashire Archives (LA), Calendar of Prisoners Kirkdale Session, 17 April 1855, QJC/8.
3 Liverpool Record Office (LRO), Rainhill Asylum Admissions Register, 614 RAI 5/1 and Rainhill Asylum Casebook File, 614 RAI 11/1.
4 LRO, Rainhill Asylum Casebook File, 614 RAI 11/1.
5 *Ibid.*
6 *Ibid.*
7 Catharine Arnold, *Bedlam: London and Its Mad* (London: Simon & Schuster, 2008), pp. 205–10; Jonathan Andrews, Asa Briggs, Roy Porter, Penny Tucker and Keir Waddington, *The History of Bethlem* (London: Routledge, 1997), pp. 436–63.
8 Edward Geoffrey O'Donoghue, *The Story of Bethlehem Hospital from its Foundation in 1247* (New York: E. P. Dutton, 1915), p. 353.
9 Bethlem Museum of the Mind (BMOTM), John Flinn (1861), Admission Registers 1683–1902; John Flinn (1861), Criminal Patient Admission Registers 1816–1864; John Flinn (1861), Incurable & Criminal Patient Casebooks 1778–1864. See also BRO, 19: John Flinn, D/H14/D2/2/1/19/1.
10 BMOTM, John Flinn (1861), Incurable & Criminal Patient Casebooks 1778–1864.
11 Roy Porter, *Madness: A Brief History* (Oxford: Oxford University Press, 2002), pp. 118–22.
12 Shepherd, "'I am very glad and cheered when I hear the flute'", pp. 485–90.
13 Cesare Lombroso, *Criminal Man: According to the Classification of Cesare Lombroso Briefly Summarised by his Daughter Gina Lombroso-Ferrero* (London: G.P. Putnam's Sons, 1911 [1876]), pp. 7, 15, 16, 21.
14 Martin Summers, '"Suitable Care of the African When Afflicted With Insanity": Race, Madness, and Social Order in Comparative Perspective', *Bulletin of the History of Medicine*, 84:1 (2010), pp. 58–91.
15 Colin King, 'They diagnosed me a schizophrenic when I was just a Gemini. "The other side of madness"', in *Reconceiving Schizophrenia*, ed. by Man Cheung Chung, K. W. M. Fulford and George Graham (Oxford: Oxford University Press, 2007), pp. 11–28.

16 Summers, '"Suitable Care of the African When Afflicted With Insanity"', pp. 58–91.
17 Sander L. Gilman, *Difference and Pathology: Stereotypes of Sexuality, Race, and Madness* (Ithaca: Cornell University Press, 1985), pp. 131–49.
18 Bolt, 'Race and the Victorians', in *British Imperialism in the Nineteenth Century*, p. 126.
19 BRO, D/H14/D2/1/1/1, John Flinn (kindly transcribed by Mark Stevens).
20 BRO, Notes from William Ross Tuchet (kindly transcribed by Mark Stevens).
21 BRO, D/H14/D2/1/1/1, John Flinn (kindly transcribed by Mark Stevens).
22 LRO, Rainhill Asylum Casebook File, 614 RAI 11/1.
23 Michel Foucault, *Madness and Civilization: A History of Insanity in the Age of Reason*, trans. by Richard Howard (London: Routledge, 2009), pp. 35–60. See also: Andrew Scull, *Madness in Civilization: A Cultural History of Insanity from the Bible to Freud, from the Madhouse to Modern Medicine* (London: Thames & Hudson, 2016), pp. 188–223.

CHAPTER 5

1 Remarkably, we can follow historian Roy Porter's plea for a medical history which captures patients' voices: Roy Porter, 'The Patient's View: Doing Medical History from below', *Theory and Society*, 14:2 (1985), pp. 175–98.
2 BRO, D/H14/D2/1/1/4, Joseph Peters (kindly transcribed by Mark Stevens).
3 Kevin Shillington, *History of Africa*, 4th edition (London: Red Globe Press, 2019), pp. 266–67.
4 BRO, D/H14/D2/1/1/4, Joseph Peters.
5 *Ibid.*
6 *Ibid.*
7 *Shipping and Mercantile Gazette*, 12 October 1876.
8 BRO, D/H14/D2/1/1/4, Joseph Peters (kindly transcribed by Mark Stevens).
9 Foucault, *Madness and Civilization*, pp. 35–60; Summers, '"Suitable Care of the African When Afflicted With Insanity"', pp. 58–91.
10 Harriet Deacon, 'Racism and Medical Science in South Africa's Cape Colony in the Mid-to Late Nineteenth Century', *Osiris*, 15 (2000), pp. 190–206; Matthew M. Heaton, *Black Skins, White Coats: Nigeria Psychiatrists, Decolonization, and the Globalization of Psychiatry* (Athens, Ohio: Ohio University Press, 2013), pp. 1–28.
11 Christienna D. Fryar, 'The Narrative of Ann Pratt: Life-Writing, Genre and Bureaucracy in a Postemancipation Scandal', *History Workshop Journal*, 85 (2018), pp. 265–79.
12 Christienna D. Fryar, 'Imperfect Models: The Kingston Lunatic Asylum Scandal and the Problem of Postemancipation Imperialism', *Journal of British Studies*, 55 (2016), pp. 709–27.
13 Ann Pratt and Public Hospital and Lunatic Asylum (Kingston, Jamaica), 'Official documents on the case of Ann Pratt, the reputed authoress of a certain pamphlet, entitled "Seven months in the Kingston Lunatic Asylum, and what I saw there"' (Jamaica, Kingston & Spanish Town: Jordon & Osborn, 1860), pp. 11–12.
14 Cited in Fryar, 'The Narrative of Ann Pratt', p. 265.

Notes

15 Fryar, 'Imperfect Models', pp. 709–27, and Fryar, 'The Narrative of Ann Pratt', pp. 265–79.
16 Gilroy, *The Black Atlantic*, p. 16.
17 Lemelle, and Kelley, 'Imagining Home', in *Imagining Home*, p. 9.
18 Mayhew, *London Labour and the London Poor*, Vol. 1, p. 182; Vol. 2, p. 481; Vol. 3, pp. 191, 302.
19 *Ibid.*, Vol. 4, p. 421.
20 *Ibid.*
21 George Augustus Sala, *Gaslight and Daylight with Some London Scenes They Shine Upon* (London: Chapman & Hall, 1859), pp. 145–56.
22 Mayhew, *London Labour and the London Poor*, Vol. 4, p. 421.
23 Charles Dickens, 'A Walk in a Workhouse', *Household Words*, 1:9 (1850), pp. 204–7 (p. 206).
24 Louis James Grant, 17 August 1840, 'The Old Bailey Proceedings Online, 1674–1913' – https://www.oldbaileyonline.org (accessed 25 June 2021).
25 See: Caroline Bressey, 'Victorian Photography and the Mapping of the Black Prescence in Britain', in *Black Victorians: Black People in British Art 1800–1900*, ed. by Jan Marsh (Hampshire: Manchester Art Gallery and Birmingham Art Gallery, 2015), pp. 68–77.
26 Gilroy, *The Black Atlantic*, p. 16.

CHAPTER 6

1 Mayhew, *London Labour and the London Poor*, Vol. 4, p. 491.
2 Benjamin Disraeli, *Sybil; or, The Two Nations* (London: Henry Colburn, 1845), p. 149.
3 Friedrich Engels, *The Condition of the Working-Class in England in 1844*, trans. by Florence Kelley Wischnewetzky (London: George Allen & Unwin, 1943 [1892]), pp. 23–24.
4 Mayhew, *London Labour and the London Poor*, Vol. 2, p. 493.
5 *Ibid.*, p. 491.
6 Prizel, '"*The Dead Man Come to Life Again*"', p. 295.
7 Mayhew, *London Labour and the London Poor*, Vol. 2, p. 491.
8 Ray Costello, *Black Salt*, pp. 79–84.
9 Jon Press, 'The Collapse of a Contributory Pension Scheme: The Merchant Seamen's Fund, 1747–1851', *The Journal of Transport History*, 5:2 (1979), pp. 91–104.
10 Prizel, '"*The Dead Man Come to Life Again*"', pp. 305–6.
11 Mayhew, *London Labour and the London Poor*, Vol. 2, p. 493.
12 *Ibid.*, p. 490.
13 *Ibid.*
14 *Ibid.*, pp. 465–67.
15 *Ibid.*, Vol. 1, p. 1.
16 Sadiah Qureshi, *Peoples on Parade: Exhibitions, Empire, and Anthropology in Nineteenth-Century Britain* (Chicago: University of Chicago Press, 2011), pp. 17–25; Seth Koven, *Slumming*, pp. 60–62.
17 Edward Albert, *Brief Sketch of the Life of Edward Albert* (London: R. Atkinson, n.d.), pp. 7–8. Gratefully reproduced in Prizel, '"*The Dead Man Come to Life Again*"', courtesy of the University of Washington Libraries.
18 Prizel, '"*The Dead Man Come to Life Again*"', p. 296.
19 Otele, *African Europeans*, p. 220.

PART THREE: CHURCH AND STATE

CHAPTER 7

1. TNA, BP, Reports of State Trials (New Series), Vol. 7, cols 467–68, 478, 480–82.
2. Cited in Norbert J. Gossman, 'William Cuffay: London's Black Chartist', *Phylon*, 44:1 (1983), pp. 56–65 (p. 63).
3. Charles Dickens, *Great Expectations* (New York: P. F. Collier, 1861), p. 57.
4. Medway Archives Centre, Strood (MAC), William Cuffay VF MED 920/CUF.
5. Charles Dickens, *The Personal History of David Copperfield* (London: Bradbury and Evans, 1850), p. 292.
6. T. M. Parssinen and I. J. Prothero, 'The London Tailors' Strike of 1834 and the Collapse of the Grand National Consolidated Trades' Union: A Police Spy's Report', *International Review of Social History*, 22:1 (1977), pp. 65–107.
7. E. P. Thompson, *The Making of the English Working Class* (London: Victor Gollancz, 1965), pp. 807–32.
8. *ODNB*, Peter Fryer, 'Cuffay, William (bap. 1788, d. 1870), Chartist'.
9. Cited in Martin Hoyles, *William Cuffay: The Life & Times of a Chartist Leader* (Hertford: Hansib Publications, 2013), p. 130.
10. MAC, William Cuffay, VF MED 920/CUF, *Northern Star and Leeds General Advertiser*, 24 September 1842.
11. *The Times*, 27 October 1848.
12. TNA, BP, The Chartists' Trial, CRIM 10/28, pp. 792, 822 & 852. Nonetheless, he resisted arrest and attempted to pass a loaded handgun to his wife.
13. *Ibid.*
14. *The Times*, 2 October 1848; MAC, William Cuffay, VF MED 920/CUF, *The Rochester, Chatham and Stroud Gazette, and Weekly Advertiser*, October 1848.
15. TNA, BP, Reports of State Trials (New Series), Vol. 7, cols 467–68, 478, 480–82.
16. *Ibid.*
17. *Punch*, 15:385 (1848), p. 230. Also see: *Punch*, 15:378 (1848), p. 154 and *Punch*, 15:368 (1848), p. 51.
18. Cited in Gossman, 'William Cuffay', pp. 56–65 (p. 63).
19. *The Times*, 2 October 1848.
20. Hoyles, *William Cuffay*, p. 202.
21. TNA, BP, Howell's State Trials, Vol. 33, cols.1549–51 (1826).
22. TNA, BP, 'The Cato Street Conspiracy'.
23. Robert Wedderburn, *The Horrors of Slavery; Exemplified in The Life and History of the Rev. Robert Wedderburn, V.D.M* (London: R. Wedderburn, 1824), p. 5.
24. Iain McCalman, *Radical Underworld: Prophets, Revolutionaries and Pornographers in London, 1795–1840* (Cambridge: Cambridge University Press, 1988), pp. 51–55.
25. Raphael Hoermann, '"Fermentation will be Universal": Intersections of Race and Class in Robert Wedderburn's Black Atlantic Discourse of Transatlantic Revolution', in *Britain's Black Past*, ed. by Gretchen H. Gerzina (Liverpool: Liverpool University Press, 2020), pp. 295–314 (p. 297)
26. Cited in *Ibid.*, p. 297.

Notes

27 Wedderburn, *The Horrors of Slavery*, p. 9.
28 Cited in Hoermann, "'Fermentation will be Universal'", p. 307.
29 TNA, BP, Reports of State Trials.
30 MAC, William Cuffay, VF MED 920/CUF.
31 Cited in Hoyles, *William Cuffay*, pp. 211–12.
32 Cited in *ODNB*, Fryer, 'Cuffay, William'.
33 TNA, BP, Reports of State Trials (New Series), Vol. 7, cols 467–68, 478, 480–82.
34 Brantlinger, *Taming Cannibals*, p. 111.
35 Gilroy, *The Black Atlantic*, p. 85.
36 Cited in Hoyles, *William Cuffay*, pp. 131–32.
37 MAC, William Cuffay, VF MED 920/CUF, *Reynold's Political Instructor*, 13 April 1850.
38 Michael J. Turner, "'Setting the Captive Free": Thomas Perronet Thompson, British Radicalism and the West Indies, 1820s–1860s', *Slavery and Abolition*, 26:1 (2005), pp. 115–32.
39 Ron Ramdin, *The Making of the Black Working Class in Britain* (London: Verso, 2017), pp. 19–20.
40 Virdee, *Racism, Class and the Racialized Outsider*, pp. 9–73.
41 Cited in Hanley, 'Slavery and the Birth of Working-Class Racism in England, 1814–1833', p. 122.
42 Cited in Wood, 'William Cobbett, John Thelwall, Radicalism, Racism and Slavery'.
43 Hanley, 'Slavery and the Birth of Working-Class Racism in England, 1814–1833', pp. 103–23.
44 Patricia Hollis, 'Anti-Slavery and British Working-Class Radicalism in the Years of Reform', in *Anti-Slavery, Religion, and Reform: Essays in Memory of Roger Anstey*, ed. by Christine Bolt and Seymour Drescher (Folkestone: Wm Dawson & Sons, 1980), pp. 294–315.

CHAPTER 8

1 Hibbert, *Queen Victoria in Her Letters and Journals*, p. 268.
2 Queen Victoria's Journals (QVJ), 9 November 1850 – http://www.queenvictoriasjournals.org (accessed 27 November 2021).
3 *Ibid.*
4 Cited in Kiste, *Sarah Forbes Bonetta*, p. 77–78.
5 Frederick E. Forbes, *Dahomey and the Dahomans: Being the Journals of Two Missions to the King of Dahomey, and Residence at his Capital, in the years 1849 and 1850* (London: Longman, Brown, Green, and Longmans, 1851), p. 10.
6 *Ibid.*, p. 208.
7 *Ibid.*, p. 10.
8 *Ibid.*, p. 207.
9 *Ibid.*, pp. 91–92.
10 Robin Law, 'Dahomey and the Slave Trade: Reflections on the Historiography of the Rise of Dahomey', *The Journal of African History*, 27:2 (1986), pp. 237–67.
11 Cited in Adeyemo Elebute, *The Life of James Pinson Labulo Davies: A Colossus of Victorian Lagos* (Lagos: Prestige, 2017), pp. 17–18.

12 Olusoga, *Black and British*, pp. 314–30.
13 Cited in Caroline Bressey, 'Of Africa's Brightest Ornaments: A Short Biography of Sarah Forbes Bonetta', *Social & Cultural Geography*, 6:2 (2005), pp. 253–66 (p. 254).
14 Forbes, *Dahomey and the Dahomans*, p. 208.
15 *Ibid.*
16 *Ibid.*, p. 207.
17 Cited in Elebute, *The Life of James Pinson Labulo Davies*, p. 37.
18 Walter Chapin, *The Missionary Gazetteer* (Woodstock: David Watson, 1825), p. 132.
19 Olusoga, *Black and British*, p. 334; Padraic X. Scanlan, *Freedom's Debtors: British Antislavery in Sierra Leone in the Age of Revolution* (New Haven: Yale University Press, 2017), p. 179.
20 Shillington, *History of Africa*, p. 264.
21 Andrew F. Walls, 'Buxton, Thomas Fowell', in *Biographical Dictionary of Christian Missions*, ed. by Gerald H. Anderson (New York: Macmillan Reference USA, 1998), p. 105.
22 Cited in Elebute, *The Life of James Pinson Labulo Davies*, p. 4.
23 Walter Dean Myers, *At Her Majesty's Request: An African Princess in Victorian England* (New York: Scholastic Inc., 1998), pp. 47–63.
24 John Van Der Kiste, *Sarah Forbes Bonetta: Queen Victoria's African Princess* (Devon: A&F, 2018), pp. 50–58.
25 Elebute, *The Life of James Pinson Labulo Davies*, p. 41.
26 Myers, *At Her Majesty's Request*, p. 63.
27 Annie C. Higgens, 'Queen Victoria's African Protégée', *Missionary Quarterly Token*, 101 (1881), p. 6.
28 *Ibid.*
29 *Ibid.*
30 Bressey, 'Of Africa's Brightest Ornaments', p. 258; Elebute, *The Life of James Pinson Labulo Davies*, pp. 51–52; Kiste, *Sarah Forbes Bonetta*, pp. 74–76; Myers, *At Her Majesty's Request*, pp. 101–02.
31 Bressey, 'Of Africa's Brightest Ornaments', p. 258.
32 *Brighton Gazette*, 14 August 1862.
33 Cited in Kiste, *Sarah Forbes Bonetta*, p. 77–78.
34 *Islington Gazette*, 23 August 1862.
35 *Ibid.*
36 Bressey, 'Of Africa's Brightest Ornaments', p. 258.
37 *Islington Gazette*, 23 August 1862.
38 See, for example, *Belfast Morning News*, 19 August 1862; *Dundee Courier*, 16 August 1862; *Cork Examiner*, 19 August 1862; *Windsor and Eton Express*, 16 August 1862.
39 *South East Gazette*, 14 August 1862.
40 MAC, Sarah Forbes Bonetta, MED 920/BON.
41 Cited in Bressey, 'Of Africa's Brightest Ornaments', p. 259.
42 *Brighton Gazette*, 14 August 1862.
43 *Brighton Guardian*, 20 August 1862.
44 Montaz Marche, 'Uncovering Black Women in Eighteenth- and Nineteenth-Century Britain' – https://www.ucl.ac.uk/history/news/2019/oct/uncov-

Notes

ering-black-women-eighteenth-and-nineteenth-century-britain (accessed 13 June 2021).
45 Shomari Wills, *Black Fortunes: The Story of the First Six African Americans Who Survived Slavery and Became Millionaires* (New York: HarperCollins, 2018).
46 Hakim Adi, *West Africans in Britain 1900-1960: Nationalism, Pan-Africanism and Communism* (London: Lawrence & Wishart, 1998), p. 8.
47 *ODNB*, John Evans, 'Wells, Nathaniel (1779–1852)'; Anne Rainsbury, 'Nathaniel Wells: The Making of a Black Country Gentleman', in *Britain's Black Past*, ed. by Gretchen H. Gerzina (Liverpool: Liverpool University Press, 2020), pp. 253–74.
48 One became an author, another was educated at the University of Oxford and another was educated at the University of Cambridge before entering the ministry.
49 *Hereford Journal*, 22 July 1835; *Hereford Times*, 26 November 1836; *Cardiff and Merthyr Guardian*, 13 March 1841; *Saint James's Chronicle*, 13 May 1845; *Saunders's News-Letter*, 21 March 1856.
50 *Hereford Journal*, 19 September 1827.
51 *Monmouthshire Merlin*, 2 March 1850.
52 *Hereford Times*, 21 June 1845; *Hereford Journal*, 11 June 1845; *Morning Post*, 12 December 1839; *Cardiff and Merthyr Guardian, Glamorgan, Monmouth, and Brecon Gazette*, 24 July 1847; *Hereford Journal*, 10 February 1841.
53 *Monmouthshire Beacon*, 27 June 1840.
54 Olusoga, *Black and British*, p. 332.
55 Joan Anim-Addo, 'Queen Victoria's Black "Daughter"', in *Black Victorians/Black Victoriana*, ed. by Gretchen H. Gerzina (New Brunswick: Rutgers University Press, 2003), pp. 11–19 (pp. 16–7).
56 Elebute, *The Life of James Pinson Labulo Davie*, p. 48.
57 Cited in Parsons, *Kling Khama, Emperor Joe and the Great White Queen*, p. 224.
58 QVJ, 16 July 1868.
59 C. C., *Anecdotes of Alamayu: The Late King Theodore's Son* (London: William Hunt, 1870), pp. 29, 72.
60 Cheltenham College Archives (CCA), Nomination of Pupil: Alamayu, 28 September 1872.
61 CCA, Cheltenham College Register, October 1872.
62 The Sandhurst Collection, Surrey (SCS), 'Alamayu, Prince (1880), Cadet Register, RMC_WO_151_Vol_2_1864–1881.
63 'Brief Biographies', in *Black Victorians*, ed. by Marsh, p. 187.
64 Cited in Shrabani Basu, *Victoria & Abdul: The True Story of the Queen's Closest Confidant* (Stroud: History Press, 2011), p. 84.
65 Priya Atwal, *Royals and Rebels: The Rise and Fall of the Sikh Empire* (London: Hurst & Company, 2020), pp. 211–13; Anita Anand, *Sophia: Princess, Suffragette, Revolutionary* (London: Bloomsbury, 2015).
66 Basu, *Victoria & Abdul*, pp. 241–62.
67 Kiste, *Sarah Forbes Bonetta*, p. 93.
68 QVJ, 9 December 1867.
69 QVJ, 29 March 1873.
70 QVJ, 24 August 1880.
71 CLCA, 'Chronicle', *Cheltenham Ladies' College Magazine* (Autumn 1895).

Black Victorians

72 CLCA, 'Marriages, Births and Deaths', *Cheltenham Ladies' College Magazine* (Spring 1891); Adelola Adeloye, 'Some Early Nigerian Doctors and Their Contribution to Modern Medicine in West Africa', *Medical History*, 18:3 (1974), pp. 275–93.
73 Derek Laud, *The Problem with Immigrants* (London: Biteback Publishing, 2015), p. 118.
74 Elebute, *The Life of James Pinson Labulo Davies*, pp. 76–79.

CHAPTER 9

1 *Kentish Chronicle*, 2 July 1864.
2 *Ibid.*
3 *East Kent Times*, 2 July 1864.
4 *East Kent Times*, 28 May 1864.
5 *East Kent Times*, 28 May 1864; *Kentish Gazette*, 10 May 1864.
6 *Kentish Gazette*, 8 November 1864.
7 Steinbach, *Understanding the Victorians*, pp. 260–78.
8 Adrian Hastings, *The Church in Africa 1450–1950* (Oxford: Clarendon Press, 1994), pp. 173–82, 242–48.
9 Jeffrey Cox, 'Worlds of Victorian religion', in *The Victorian World*, ed. by Martin Hewitt (London: Routledge, 2014), pp. 433–48.
10 *Dictionary of African Christian Biography* (*DACB*), Andrew F. Walls, 'Crowther, Samiel Ajayi (A)'.
11 Lambeth Palace Library, London (LPLL), LC 25, ff. 160–61, Lambeth Conference Papers, 1888.
12 Jesse Page, *Samuel Crowther: The Slave Boy Who Became Bishop of the Niger* (New York: Fleming H. Revell, 1889), p. 36; Cadbury Research Library, University of Birmingham (CRL, UB), CA1/079/1, West African Mission, Original Papers of Rev. Samuel Adjai Crowther.
13 CRL, UB, CA1/079/1, West African Mission, Original Papers of Rev. Samuel Adjai Crowther, 11 February 1837.
14 James Frederick Schön and Samuel Crowther, *Journals of the Rev. James Frederick Schön and Mr. Samuel Crowther: who, with the sanction of Her Majesty's government, accompanied the expedition up the Niger, in 1841, in behalf of the Church Missionary Society* (London: Hatchard and Son, 1842), pp. 259–60.
15 Page, *Samuel Crowther*, p. 64.
16 CRL, UB, CA1/079/4a, West African Mission, Original Papers of Rev. Samuel Adjai Crowther.
17 *Ibid.*
18 Schön and Crowther, *Journals of the Rev. James Frederick Schön and Mr. Samuel Crowther*, p. 265.
19 Hastings, *The Church in Africa*, p. 178.
20 CRL, UB, CMS Periodicals, *Church Missionary Record*, 21:4 (1830).
21 Eugene Stock, *The History of the Church Missionary Society. Its Environment, Its Men and Its Work*, Vol. II (London: Church Missionary Society, 1899), p. 113.
22 QVJ, 18 November 1851.
23 A. F. Childe, *Good out of Evil, or, The History of Adjai, The African Slave-Boy* (London: Wertheim and Macintosh, 1853), p. 107.
24 Page, *Samuel Crowther*, p. 112.
25 *Ibid.*, p. 118.

Notes

26 *Kentish Chronicle*, 24 September 1864.
27 *East Kent Times*, 28 May 1864.
28 *Ibid.*
29 *Ibid.*
30 Page, Samuel Crowther, p. 16.
31 *Ibid.*, p. 65.
32 *Ibid.*, p. 159.
33 *DACB*, Walls, 'Crowther'.
34 LPLL, Tait 234, f. 352, Official Letters Canterbury, 1877; Tait 287, ff.64–65, Official Letters Canterbury, 1882.
35 LPLL, LC 11, ff. 234–35, Lambeth Conference Papers, 1878.
36 LPLL, LC 17, ff. 157–63, Lambeth Conference Papers, 1888.
37 LPLL, LC 34, ff. 55–64, Lambeth Conference Papers, 1888.
38 David Maxwell, 'Christianity', in *The Oxford Handbook of Modern African History*, ed. by John Parker and Richard Reid (Oxford: Oxford University Press, 2013), pp. 263–80.
39 LPLL, Tait 140, f. 349, Official Letters London, 1864 Nov–1865 Jan; LPLL, Tait 139, ff. 389–90, Official Letters London, 1864 July–Nov.
40 C. Peter Williams, The Ideal of the Self-Governing Church: A Study in Victorian Missionary Strategy (New York: E. J. Brill, 1990), pp. 102–227.
41 *DACB*, Walls, 'Crowther'.
42 *DACB*, Owadayo, 'Crowther'.
43 LPLL, Benson 113, ff.125–32 E. W. Benson Papers, Official Letters, 1892.
44 LPLL, Benson 166, ff. 82–194, E. W. Benson Papers, Official Letters, 1890–94.
45 *DACB*, Owadayo, 'Crowther'.
46 Hastings, *The Church in Africa*, pp. 242–58.
47 David Killingray, 'The Black Atlantic Missionary Movement and Africa, 1780s–1920s', *Journal of Religion in Africa*, 33:1 (2003), pp. 3–31.
48 The Salvation Army International Heritage Centre, William Booth College (SAIHC, WBC), CAR/7/1, Jamaica 1888–99.
49 SAIHC, WBC, *War Cry*, 2 January 1888; C/BUR/1, Photograph of Joe Norton; *War Cry*, 2 January 1888; *War Cry*, 3 March 1888; *War Cry*, 8 February 1890.
50 Zilpha Elaw, *Memoirs of the Life, Religious Experience, Ministerial Travels and Labours of Mrs. Zilpha Elaw, An American Female of Colour* (London: By the Authoress, 1846), p. 141; Jeffrey Green, '149: Zilpha Elaw (C 1790–1873), American Preacher' – https://jeffreygreen.co.uk/149-zilpha-elaw-c-1790-1873-american-preacher/ (accessed 11 August 2021).
51 Elaw, *Memoirs Of The Life*, p. 140.
52 Kimberly Blockett, 'Disrupting Print: Emigration, the Press, and Narrative Subjectivity in the British Preaching and Writing of Zilpha Elaw, 1840–1860s', *MELUS*, 40:3 (2015), pp. 94–109 (p. 95).
53 *Ibid.*, p. 140.
54 William L. Andrews (ed.), *Three Black Women's Autobiographies of the Nineteenth Century* (Bloomington: Indiana University Press, 1986), pp. 1–22.
55 Elaw, *Memoirs Of The Life*, p. 7.

56 Stephen Ney, 'Samuel Ajayi Crowther and the Age of Literature', *Research in African Literatures*, 46:1 (2015), pp. 37–52; Andrew F. Walls, 'The Legacy of Samuel Ajayi Crowther', *International Bulletin of Missionary Research*, 16:1 (1992), pp. 15–21.

57 *DACB*, Mahoney, 'Nicol, George'.

CHAPTER 10

1 Cited in Cynthia F. Behrman, 'The After-Life of General Gordon', *Albion: A Quarterly Journal Concerned with British Studies*, 3:2 (1971), pp. 47–61 (p. 50, 49).
2 Shillington, *History of Africa*, pp. 311–19.
3 Durham Country Record Office, The Story of Jimmy Durham (DCRO, SJD) – http://www.durhamrecordoffice.org.uk/article/10689/The-Story-of-Jimmy-Durham (accessed 27 November 2021); *The Bugle*, 14 June 1894, p. 49.
4 DCRO, SJD, *The Bugle*, 14 June 1894, p. 49.
5 *Ibid.*
6 DCRO, SJD, Record of Services for 1885–86, D/DLI 2/2/135, p. 27.
7 Hansard, House of Commons, 'Egypt – The Military Expedition – The Battle Of Ginnis', Volume 305: debated on Tuesday, 11 May 1886 – https://hansard.parliament.uk/Commons/1886-05-11/debates/e33f486a-cb4c-4baf-99a284a5b2b01813/Egypt%E2%80%94TheMilitaryExpedition%E2%80%94The-BattleOfGinnis (accessed 19 August 2021).
8 DCRO, SJD, *The Bugle*, 14 June 1894, p. 49.
9 DCRO, SJD, *The Bugle*, 19 November 1896, pp. 1394-5.
10 *Dundee Evening Telegraph*, 2 February 1934.
11 Beauvoir De Lisle, *Reminiscences of Sport and War* (London: Eyre & Spottiswoode, 1939), pp. 27–28.
12 DCRO, SJD, *The Bugle*, 14 June 1894, p. 50.
13 *Ibid.*
14 *Ibid.*
15 *Ibid.*
16 DCRO, SJD, *The Bugle*, 27 October 1899, p. 3045.
17 DCRO, SJD, Photograph as baby, 1886, D/DLI 7/194/1.
18 DCRO, SJD, *The Bugle*, 27 October 1899, p. 3045.
19 DCRO, SJD, *The Bugle*, 14 June 1894, p. 50.
20 *Ibid.*
21 *Civil & Military Gazette* (Lahore), 18 May 1887.
22 DCRO, SJD, *The Bugle*, 28 July 1899, p. 2898.
23 *Ibid.* Also see DCRO, Photograph of band [1900–1910], D/DLI 7/194/10.
24 DCRO, Durham to Stella: Letter 17 April 1908, Courtesy of the DLI Museum.
25 *Evening Telegraph*, 2 February 1934.
26 DCRO, Details from the Marriage Certificate of James Francis Durham and Jane Green.
27 *Reynold's Newspaper*, 14 August 1910.
28 DCRO, Transcript of Digest of Services, June–August 1910, D/DLI 2/2/15.
29 David Lambert and Elizabeth Cooper, 'The Changing Image of the West India Regiments' – https://www.bl.uk/west-india-regiment/articles/the-changing-image-of-the-west-india-regiments (accessed 19 August 2021).

30 *Ibid.*
31 Ray Costello, *Black Tommies: British Soldiers of African Descent in the First World War* (Liverpool: Liverpool University Press, 2015), pp. 1–16, 91–112; Stephen Bourne, *Black Poppies: Britain's Black Community and the Great War* (Cheltenham: History Press, 2019); Stephen Bourne, *Under Fire: Black Britain in Wartime 1939–45* (Cheltenham: History Press, 2020).
32 *The Graphic*, 12 May 1906; *Tenbury Wells Advertiser*, 8 May 1906; *Bicester Herald*, 4 May 1906; *Longford Journal*, 5 May 1906.
33 Kaufmann, *Black Tudors*, pp. 7–31.
34 Kevin Le Gendre, *Don't Stop the Carnival: Black Music in Britain*, Vol. I (Leeds: Peepal Tree Press, 2008), pp. 56–69.

PART FOUR: THE ARTS

CHAPTER 11

1 Mike Phillips, 'Samuel Coleridge-Taylor: Black Europeans' – https://www.bl.uk/onlinegallery/features/blackeuro/homepage.html (accessed 2 January 2021).
2 *Ibid.*
3 Anon., 'Mr Coleridge-Taylor', *The Musical Times*, 50:793 (1909), pp. 153–58 (p. 153).
4 *Ibid.*
5 *Reynold's Newspaper*, 2 August 1908.
6 Anon., 'Mr Coleridge-Taylor', *The Musical Times*, 50:793 (1909), pp. 153–58 (p. 153).
7 Cited in Jeffrey Green and Paul McGilchrist, 'Samuel Coleridge-Taylor: A Postscript', *The Black Perspective in Music*, 14:3 (1986), pp. 259–66 (p. 260).
8 Anon., 'Mr Coleridge-Taylor', p. 154.
9 *Ibid.*, p. 156.
10 Anon., 'Samuel Coleridge-Taylor. Born August 15, 1875. Died September 1, 1912', *The Musical Times*, 53:836 (1912), pp. 637–39 (p. 638).
11 Royal College of Music (RCM), 'Samuel Coleridge-Taylor and the Musical Fight for Civil Rights' – https://www.rcm.ac.uk/museum/exhibitions/ (accessed 27 November 2021), Report (December 1892).
12 Anon., 'Mr Coleridge-Taylor', p. 154.
13 *The Times*, 15 September 1898.
14 Anon., 'Mr Coleridge-Taylor', p. 156.
15 Anon., 'Samuel Coleridge-Taylor', p. 638.
16 Cited in Green and McGilchrist, 'Samuel Coleridge-Taylor', p. 262.
17 Paul Richards, 'A Pan-African Composer? Coleridge-Taylor and Africa', *Black Music Research Journal*, 21:2 (2001), pp. 235–60.
18 Penny Summerfield, 'Patriotism and Empire: Music-Hall entertainment, 1870–1914', in *Imperialism and Popular Culture*, ed. by John M. Mackenzie (Manchester: Manchester University Press, 1986), pp. 17–48.
19 Paul Richards, 'Africa in the Music of Samuel Coleridge-Taylor', *Africa: Journal of the International African Institute*, 57:4 (1987), pp. 566–71.
20 RCM, Wedding Telegram.

21 Jessie S. Fleetwood Coleridge-Taylor, *Genius and Musician: A Memory Sketch or Personal Reminiscences of My Husband, Genius and Musician S. Coleridge-Taylor 1875-1912* (London: John Crowther, 1943), p. 20.
22 *Ibid.*, p. 14.
23 Charles Kay, 'The Marriage of Samuel Coleridge-Taylor and Jessie Walmisley', *Black Music Research Journal*, 21:2 (2001), pp. 159–78.
24 Coleridge-Taylor, *Genius and Musician*, p. 37.
25 *Ibid.*, p. 47.
26 Cited in Jeffrey Green, *Samuel Coleridge-Taylor, A Musical Life* (London: Routledge, 2011), p. 89.
27 BCA, COLETAY/1/19, *Twenty-four Negro Melodies* (1905).
28 *Ibid.*
29 *Ibid.*
30 Phillips, 'Samuel Coleridge-Taylor'.
31 Museum of Croydon (MC), Samuel Coleridge Taylor: Material relating to Concerts, AR1149/1/2.
32 *Reynold's Newspaper*, 2 August 1908.
33 *Ibid.*
34 Cited in Green, *Samuel Coleridge-Taylor*, p. 133.
35 MC, Samuel Coleridge Taylor: Published Works and Press, AR1149/2, *Penge & Anerley News*, 7 September 1912.
36 *Ibid.*; *ODNB*, Jeffrey Green, 'Taylor, Samuel Coleridge (1875–1912)'. For more on Coleridge-Taylor, see Jeffrey Green, '"The Foremost Musician of His Race": Samuel Coleridge-Taylor of England, 1875–1912', *Black Music Research Journal*, 10:2 (1990), pp. 233–52; Jeffrey Green, *Samuel Coleridge-Taylor, A Musical Life* (London: Routledge, 2011).
37 Gendre, *Don't Stop the Carnival*, pp. 60–68.
38 MC, AR1149/2, *Penge & Anerley News*, 7 September 1912.
39 BCA, COLETAY/2.
40 MC, AR1149/2, *Penge & Anerley News*, 7 September 1912.
41 RCM, Production of *Hiawatha* at the Royal Albert Hall, 1936.
42 Samantha Ellis, 'Paul Robeson in *Othello*', *Guardian*, 2 September 2003.
43 Michael A. Morrison, 'Paul Robeson's Othello at the Savoy Theatre, 1930', *New Theatre Quarterly*, 27:2 (2011), pp. 114–40.

CHAPTER 12

1 *Morning Advertiser*, 22 July 1858.
2 William Wells Brown, *The Black Man, His Antecedents, His Genius, and His Achievements* (Boston: R. F. Wallcut, 1863), pp. 119–20.
3 *Morning Chronicle*, 28 July 1858.
4 Anon., Memoir and Theatrical career of Ira Aldridge, the African Roscius (London: Onwhyn, 1848 or 1849), pp. 15–16.
5 Hazel Waters, 'Ira Aldridge's Fight for Equality', in *Ira Aldridge: The African Roscius*, ed. by Bernth Lindfors (Rochester: University of Rochester Press, 2007), pp. 97–125.
6 Bernth Lindfors, *Ira Aldridge: The Early Years 1807–1833* (Rochester: University of Rochester Press, 2007), pp. 17–20.

· Notes

7   Kathleen Chater, *Henry Box Brown: From Slavery to Show Business* (Jefferson, NC: McFarland, 2020), p. 86.
8   Daniel O'Quinn, 'Theatre and empire' in *The Cambridge Companion to British Theatre, 1730–1830*, ed. by Daniel O'Quinn and Jane Moody (Cambridge: Cambridge University Press, 2009), pp. 233–46.
9   Cited in TNA, BP, 'The Theatre'; Waters, 'Ira Aldridge's Fight for Equality', in *Ira Aldridge*, ed. by Lindfors, pp. 97–125 (p. 120).
10 Cited in Waters, 'Ira Aldridge's Fight for Equality', pp. 97–125 (p. 99).
11 Bernth Lindfors, '"Nothing Extenuate, nor set down aught in malice": New Biographical Information on Ira Aldridge', in *Ira Aldridge: The African Roscius*, ed. by Bernth Lindfors (Rochester: University of Rochester Press, 2007), pp. 50–67.
12 Scobie, *Black Britannia*, p. 131.
13 Anon., *Memoir and Theatrical Career of Ira Aldridge*, p. 16.
14 *Figaro in London*, 6 April 1833.
15 *Ibid*.
16 *Manchester Gazette*, 24 February 1827.
17 Anon., *Memoir and Theatrical Career of Ira Aldridge*, pp. 8–9.
18 Ira Aldridge, *The Black Doctor* (Online: Alexander Street Press, 1847), pp. 4–5.
19 Keith Byerman, 'Creating the Black Hero: Ira Aldridge's The Black Doctor', in *Ira Aldridge: The African Roscius*, ed. by Bernth Lindfors (Rochester: University of Rochester Press, 2007), pp. 180–90.
20 Byerman, 'Creating the Black Hero', in *Ira Aldridge*, ed. by Lindfors, pp. 207–08.
21 *Era*, 26 April 1857.
22 Cited in Victoria Jones, 'Mislike me not for my complexion' – https://www.shakespeare.org.uk/explore-shakespeare/blogs/mislike-me-not-my-complexion/ – (accessed 26 August 2021).
23 *Era*, 25 August 1867.
24 V&A, Iluminated Tribute Presented to Ira Aldridge – http://collections.vam.ac.uk/item/O1476384/illuminated-tribute-presented-to-ira-illuminated-manuscript-unknown/ (accessed 26 August 2021).
25 Waters, 'Ira Aldridge's Fight for Equality', in *Ira Aldridge*, ed. by Lindfors, p. 101.
26 *Morning Chronicle*, 28 July 1858.
27 *Ibid*.
28 Cited in Waters, *Racism on the Victorian Stage: Representation of Slavery and the Black Character* (Cambridge: Cambridge University Press, 2007), p. 93.
29 Eric Lott, *Love and Theft: Blackface Minstrelsy and the American Working Class* (Oxford: Oxford University Press, 1993), pp. 45–46.
30 Cited in *ibid*., p. 94.
31 Cited in Ruth M. Cowhig, 'Ira Aldridge in Manchester', in *Ira Aldridge: The African Roscius*, ed. by Bernth Lindfors (Rochester: University of Rochester Press, 2007), pp. 126–34 (p. 126).
32 Waters, *Racism on the Victorian Stage*, pp. 94–98.
33 Lindfors, *Ira Aldridge: Vagabond Years*, pp. 59–80; Waters, *Racism on the Victorian Stage*, pp. 114–29.
34 Cited Lindfors, *Ira Aldridge: Vagabond Years*, p. 74.
35 LeRoy Ashby, *With Amusement For All: A History of American Popular Culture Since 1830* (Lexington: University Press of Kentucky, 2006), pp. 85–91.

36 Waters, *Racism on the Victorian Stage*, pp. 89–113; Beasley, *The Victorian Reinvention of Race*, p. 16.
37 Cited in Bernth Lindfors, '"Mislike me not for my complexion…" Ira Aldridge in Whiteface', in *Ira Aldridge: The African Roscius*, ed. by Bernth Lindfors (Rochester: University of Rochester Press, 2007), pp. 180–90 (p. 182).
38 Cited in Lindfors, *Ira Aldridge: Vagabond Years*, p. 61.
39 Eric Lott, *Love and Theft: Blackface Minstrelsy and the American Working Class* (Oxford: Oxford University Press, 1993), pp. 45–46.
40 Waters, *Racism on the Victorian Stage*, pp. 63–65; Nicholas M. Evans, 'Ira Aldridge: Shakespeare and Minstrelsy' in *Ira Aldridge: The African Roscius*, ed. by Bernth Lindfors (Rochester: University of Rochester Press, 2007), pp. 157–79.
41 Lott, *Love and Theft*, pp. 46–47.
42 Victoria Jones, 'Mislike me not for my complexion' – https://www.shakespeare.org.uk/explore-shakespeare/blogs/mislike-me-not-my-complexion/ (accessed 26 August 2021).
43 *Era*, 25 August 1867.
44 Anon., *Memoir and Theatrical Career of Ira Aldridge*, p. 25.
45 Dabydeen, Gilmore and Jones (eds.), *The Oxford Companion to Black British History*, pp. 23–25.
46 Waters, 'Ira Aldridge's Fight for Equality', in *Ira Aldridge*, ed. by Lindfors, pp. 97–125 (pp. 105–08).
47 Chater, *Henry Box Brown*, p. 119.
48 See Bernth Lindfors, *The Theatrical Career of Samuel Morgan Smith* (New Jersey: African World Press, 2018); Chater, *Henry Box Brown*, pp. 118–20.
49 Bressey, 'The Next Chapter', in *Britain's Black Past*, ed. by Gerzina, pp. 315–30.

CHAPTER 13

1 F. M. Eden, *The State of the Poor or an History of the Labouring Classes in England* (London: J. Davies, 1797), p. 479.
2 Philip Thicknesse, *A Year's Journey Through France and Part of Spain*, Vol. II (London: W. Brown, 1778), p. 108.
3 Gareth H. H. Davies, *Pablo Fanque and the Victorian Circus: A Romance of Real Life* (Cromer: Poppyland Publishing, 2017), pp. 13–29.
4 Thomas Frost, *Circus Life and Circus Celebrities* (London: Tinsley Brothers, 1873), pp. 142, 192.
5 Dominique Jando, *Philip Astley & The Horsemen who Invented the Circus (1768–1814)* (San Francisco: Circopedia, 2018), p. 73.
6 Mayhew, *London Labour and the London Poor*, Vol. 3, p. 90.
7 *Hampshire Advertiser*, 15 February 1834.
8 *Ibid.*
9 Frost, *Circus Life and Circus Celebrities*, p. 97.
10 *The Era*, 21 July 1839.
11 W. F. Wallett, *The Public Life of W. F. Wallett, The Queen's Jester: An Autobiography*, ed. by J. Luntley (London: Bemrose and Sons, 1870), p. 74.
12 Frost, *Circus Life and Circus Celebrities*, p. 196.
13 *Preston Chronicle*, 28 May 1842.
14 *Leeds Times*, 13 May 1871.

Notes

15 Cited in John M. Turner, 'Pablo Fanque, Black Circus Proprietor', in *Black Victorians/Black Victoriana*, ed. by Gretchen H. Gerzina (New Brunswick: Rutgers University Press, 2003), pp. 20–38 (p. 23).
16 *Liverpool Mercury*, 8 October 1841.
17 Whimsical Walker, *From Sawdust to Windsor Castle* (London: Stanley Paul, 1922), pp. 8–9.
18 *Ibid.*, p. 9.
19 *Ibid.*
20 'Lord' George Sanger, *Seventy Years a Showman*, with an intro. by Kenneth Grahame (New York: Dutton and Company, 1926 [1910]), p. 1.
21 Cited in Steve Ward, *Beneath the Big Top: A Social History of the Circus in Britain* (Barnsley: Pen and Sword History, 2014), p. 86.
22 National Fairground Archives (NFA), Turner Database, Pablo Fanque.
23 *Freeman's Journal*, 1 April 1850.
24 *The Era*, 26 August 1905.
25 Mark Valentine St Leon, 'Celebrated at first, then implied and finally denied: the erosion of Aboriginal identity in circus, 1851–1960', *Aboriginal History*, 32 (2008), pp. 63–81 (p. 64).
26 Woolf, *The Wonders*, p. 249.
27 Sam Wild, *The Original, Complete and only Authentic Story of 'Old Wild's'* (London: Vickers, 1888), p. 225.
28 Cited in A. H. Saxon, *The Life and Art of Andrew Ducrow & The Romantic Age of the English Circus* (Hamden: Archon Books, 1978), p. 332.
29 NFA, Turner Database. Arthur Williams died from rheumatic fever on 11 January 1871.
30 NFA, John Bramwell Taylor, Box One, 178T1.1–178T1.186; John Bramwell Taylor, Box Two, 178T1.187–178T1.295; John Bramwell Taylor, Box Three, 178T1.296–178T.342; London Metropolitan Archives (LMA), Bartholomew Fair Folder, SC/GL/BFS/001; Noble Collection, SC/GL/NOB/C/O26/5-026/51; Grainger Entertainment Folder, SC/GL/ENT/50–184; Bartholomew Fair Folder, SC/GL/BFS/051.

CHAPTER 14

1 *Aberdeen Press and Journal*, 16 May 1860.
2 *Ibid.*
3 See Roberto C. Ferrari, 'Fanny Eaton: The "Other" Pre-Raphaelite Model', *PRS Review*, 22:2 (2014), pp. 3–19.
4 Marsh, 'The Black Presence in British Art 1800-1900', in *Black Victorians*, ed. by Marsh, pp. 12–22.
5 *Ibid.*
6 Qureshi, *Peoples on Parade*, pp. 47–100.
7 Denise Murrell, *Posing Modernity: The Black Model from Manet and Matisse to Today* (New Haven: Yale University Press, 2018), pp. 70–83.
8 See, for example, RCT, BAVB collection, including photographs and paintings of Prince Alamayu and Cetshwayo, King of the Zulus.
9 Marsh, 'The Black Presence in British Art 1800–1900', in *Black Victorians*, ed. by Marsh, pp. 12–22.

10   *Isle of Wight Observer*, 14 July 1860.
11   Marsh, 'The Black Presence in British Art 1800–1900', in *Black Victorians*, ed. by Marsh, pp. 12–22.
12   *ODNB*, Roberto C. Ferrari, 'Eaton [*née* Antwistle/Entwistle], Fanny (1835–1924)'.
13   His ethnicity is unknown and, because no wedding certificate has been found, Fanny Eaton's great-grandson claimed they never married.
14   Thomas Archer, *The Pauper, the Thief and the Convict: Sketches of some of their Homes, Haunts and Habits* (London: Groombridge and Sons, 1865), p. 128.
15   James Greenwood, *The Wilds of London* (London: Chatto and Windus, 1874), p. 1.
16   Lydia Figes, 'Fanny Eaton: Jamaican Pre-Raphaelite Muse' – https://artuk.org/discover/stories/fanny-eaton-jamaican-pre-raphaelite-muse (accessed 2 August 2021).
17   '*Punch*, Jan.–Jun. 1850', *The Dictionary of Victorian London* – http://www.victorianlondon.org/ (accessed 7 March 2022).
18   Pamela Gerrish Nunn, 'Rebecca Solomon's A Young Teacher', *The Burlington Magazine*, 13 (1988), pp. 769–70.
19   Nehama Aschkenasy, *Woman at the Window: Biblical Tales of Oppression and Escape* (Detroit: Wayne State University Press, 1998), pp. 16, 23.
20   Ferrari, 'Fanny Eaton', p. 4.
21   Trinity College Library, Cambridge, Diaries of A. J. Munby (TCLC, MUNB), 19, 1 May–10 July 1863, p. 111.
22   TCLC, MUNB, 4, 1 January–18 March, 1860, n.p.
23   Cited in Anne McClintock, *Imperial Leather: Race, Gender and Sexuality in the Colonial Contest* (London: Routledge, 1995), p. 108.
24   *Ibid.*, pp. 106–07.
25   Cited in Barry Reay, *Watching Hannah: Sexuality, Horror and Bodily De-formation in Victorian England* (London: Reaktion Books, 2002), pp. 84, 155.
26   *Ibid.*, pp. 81–90.
27   Cited in *ibid.*, p. 148.
28   Gilman, *Difference and Pathology*, pp. 76–108.
29   Lucy Delap, *Knowing Their Place: Domestic Service in Twentieth-century Britain* (Oxford: Oxford University Press, 2011), p. 174.
30   Ritter von Leopold Sacher-Masoch, *Venus in Furs*, trans. by Fernanda Savage, Project Gutenberg – https://www.gutenberg.org/cache/epub/6852/pg6852.html (accessed 2 August 2021).
31   See Kathleen Chater, 'Job Mobility amongst Black People in England and Wales during the Long Eighteenth Century', in *Belonging in Europe – The African Diaspora and Work*, ed. by Caroline Bressey and Hakim Adi (London: Routledge, 2011), pp. 9–26.
32   McClintock, *Imperial Leather*, p. 113.
33   See, for example, Walter, *My Secret Life* – http://www.freeinfosociety.com/media/pdf/2674.pdf (accessed 2 August 2021), Vol. 8 and Vol. 9., n.p.
34   Lorraine O'Grady, 'Olympia's Maid: Reclaiming Black Female Subjectivity', in *Art, Activism, and Oppositionality: Essays from Afterimage*, ed. by Grant H. Kester (Durham, NC: Duke University Press, 1998), pp. 268–87.
35   Charmaine Nelson, 'Venus Africaine: Race, Beauty and African-Ness', in *Black Victorians: Black People in British Art 1800–1900*, ed. by Jan Marsh (Hampshire: Manchester Art Gallery and Birmingham Art Gallery, 2015), pp. 46–56.
36   Murrell, *Posing Modernity*, p. 56.

Notes

37 *Ibid.*, pp. 7–83.
38 *Ibid.*, p. 83.
39 Cited in Briony Llewellyn, 'Observations and Interpretation: Travelling Artists in Egypt', in *Black Victorians: Black People in British Art 1800–1900*, ed. by Jan Marsh (Hampshire: Manchester Art Gallery and Birmingham Art Gallery, 2015), pp. 34–45 (p. 39).
40 Nelson, 'Venus Africaine: Race, Beauty and African-Ness', in *Black Victorians*, ed. by Marsh, p. 50.
41 Cited in Ferrari, 'Fanny Eaton', p. 7.
42 Cited in *Black Victorians*, Catalogue No. 72, ed. by Marsh, p. 149.
43 Figes, 'Fanny Eaton'.
44 Cited in Otele, *African Europeans*, p. 29.
45 Marcus Wood, *Blind Memory: Visual Representations of Slavery in England and America, 1780–1865* (Manchester: Manchester University Press, 2000), p. 23.

PART FIVE: FIGHTING FOR FREEDOM

CHAPTER 15

1 Cited in Hannah-Rose Murray, *Advocates of Freedom: African American Transatlantic Abolitionism in the British Isles* (Cambridge: Cambridge University Press, 2020), p. 48.
2 Henry 'Box' Brown, *Narrative of the Life of Henry Box Brown, Written by Himself* (Manchester: Lee and Glynn, 1851), p. 57.
3 *Ibid.*
4 *Ibid.*, p. 1.
5 Kermit L. Hall, James W. Ely, Jr., Joel B. Grossman (eds.), *The Oxford Companion to the Supreme Court of the United States* (Oxford: Oxford University Press, 2005), p. 295.
6 Brown, *Narrative of the Life of Henry Box Brown*, p. 16.
7 Ira Berlin, *Slaves Without Masters: The Free Negro in the Antebellum South* (Oxford: Oxford University Press, 1974), pp. 15–181.
8 Brown, *Narrative of the Life of Henry Box Brown*, pp. 24–26.
9 *Ibid.*, p. 44.
10 Lincoln Mullen, 'These Maps Reveal How Slavery Expanded Across the United States' – https://www.smithsonianmag.com/history/maps-reveal-slavery-expanded-across-united-states-180951452/ (accessed 7 September 2021).
11 Hollis Robbins, 'Fugitive Mail: The Deliverance of Henry "Box" Brown and Antebellum Postal Politics', *American Studies*, 50:1/2 (2009), pp. 5–25.
12 William Still, *The Underground Railroad: Authentic Narratives and First-Hand Accounts*, ed. by Ian Frederick Finseth (Mineola, New York: Dover Publications, 2007), p. 103.
13 Chater, *Henry Box Brown*, pp. 14–16.
14 *Ibid.*, pp. 19–22, 43–46.
15 Cited in *ibid.*, p. 27.
16 William Wells Brown, *Narrative of William W. Brown, A Fugitive Slave. Written by Himself* (Boston: Anti-Slavery Office, 1847), pp. 109–10.

17. Josephine Brown, *Biography of an American Bondman, by His Daughter* (Boston: R.F. Wallcut, 1856), p. 54.
18. *Liverpool Mercury*, 15 November 1850.
19. *Ibid.*
20. Chater, *Henry Box Brown*, pp. 37–41.
21. Cited in Fisch, *American Slaves*, pp. 73–4.
22. *Leeds Mercury*, 24 May 1851.
23. Chater, *Henry Box Brown*, pp. 19–22, 43–46.
24. The autobiographies also reflected urban exposé, religious conversion narratives and the rags-to-riches literary archetype, popularised in works such as Dickens' *Oliver Twist*. See Fisch, *American Slaves*, pp. 53–55; Chater, *Henry Box Brown*, pp. 19–20.
25. Brown, *Narrative of the Life of Henry Box Brown*, p. i.
26. *Wolverhampton Chronicle and Staffordshire Advertiser*, 24 March 1852.
27. Chater, *Henry Box Brown*, pp. 48–58.
28. *Wolverhampton Chronicle and Staffordshire Advertiser*, 17 March 1852.
29. *Ibid.*
30. *Ibid.*
31. James Watkins, *Struggles for Freedom; or The Life of James Watkins, Formerly a Slave in Maryland, U.S.* (Manchester: Printed for James Watkins, 1860), pp. 42–45.
32. Cited in Olusoga, *Black and British*, p. 281.
33. Anon., *Memoir and Theatrical Career of Ira Aldridge*, p. 7.
34. *Blackburn Standard*, 11 August 1852.
35. Cited in Fisch, *American Slaves*, p. 80.
36. *Bradford Review*, 5 January 1861.
37. *Kentish Independent*, 10 July 1858.
38. Chater, *Henry Box Brown*, pp. 86–88, 90–93.
39. *Jersey Independent and Daily Telegraph*, 10 March 1858.
40. Fisch, *American Slaves*, p. 82.
41. *Kentish Independent*, 10 July 1858.
42. Cited in Chater, *Henry Box Brown*, p. 115.
43. *Ibid.*, pp. 111–71.
44. *Thanet Advertiser*, 6 February 1869.
45. Chater, *Henry Box Brown*, pp. 83–84, 95–105.
46. *Jersey Independent and Daily Telegraph*, 7 April 1858.
47. Chater, *Henry Box Brown*, pp. 178–83.
48. *Ibid.*, pp. 185–200.
49. Martha J. Cutter, 'Will the Real Henry "Box" Brown Please Stand Up?', *Commonplace: The Journal of Early American Life* – http://commonplace.online/article/will-the-real-henry-box-brown-please-stand-up/ (accessed 7 September 2021).
50. *Ibid.*
51. Jeffrey Ruggles, *The Unboxing of Henry Brown* (Richmond: Library of Virginia, 2003), p. 174.
52. Chater, *Henry Box Brown*, p. 148–50.
53. Blackett, *Building An Antislavery Wall*, p. 196.
54. Black Abolitionist Archive (BAA) – https://libraries.udmercy.edu/find/special_collections/digital/baa/ (accessed 27 November 2021), Doc. No. 00611.

Notes

55 Cited in Blackett, *Building An Antislavery Wall*, p. 46.
56 William Wells Brown, *Three Years in Europe; or, Places I Have Seen and People I Have Met* (London: Charles Gilpin, 1852), pp. 7–8.
57 Frederick Douglass, *My Bondage and My Freedom* (New York & Auburn: Miller, Orton & Mulligan, 1855), p. 371.
58 *The Liberator*, 22 July 1853.
59 Samuel Smiles, *Self Help With Illustrations Of Conduct And Perseverance, Popular Edition* (London: John Murray, 1897 [1859]), p. 382.
60 Stefan Collini, *Public Moralists: Political Thought and Intellectual Life in Britain, 1850–1930* (Oxford: Clarendon Press, 1991), pp. 91–118.
61 Douglass, 'The Color Line', p. 576.
62 Laura Korobkin, 'Avoiding "Aunt Tomasina": Charles Dickens Responds to Harriet Beecher Stowe's Black American Reader, Mary Webb', *English Literary History*, 82:1 (2015), pp. 115–40 (p. 116).

CHAPTER 16

1 BAA, Doc. No. 20397.
2 Matthew Davenport Hill, *Our Exemplars, Poor and Rich* (London: Cassell, Pete, and Galpin, 1861), p. 276.
3 *Ibid.*, p. 284.
4 *Ibid.*, p. 276–77.
5 *Ibid.*, p. 277.
6 *Ibid.*
7 *Ibid.*, p. 279.
8 *Ibid.*, p. 280.
9 *Ibid.*, p. 281.
10 Douglass, 'The Color Line', p. 573.
11 Hill, *Our Exemplars*, p. 282.
12 *Ibid.*
13 *Ibid.*, p. 283.
14 BAA, Doc. No. 21295.
15 The *Anti-Slavery Advocate*, 1 November 1858.
16 *Ibid.*
17 Sirpa Salenius, *An Abolitionist Abroad: Sarah Parker Remond in Cosmopolitan Europe* (Boston: University of Massachusetts Press, 2016), p. 77.
18 *Liverpool Mercury*, 22 January 1859.
19 *Ibid.*
20 *Ibid.*
21 *Birmingham Daily Post*, 25 January 1861.
22 BAA, Doc. No. 21102.
23 *Warrington Standard and Lancashire and Cheshire Advertiser*, 22 January 1859.
24 The *Anti-Slavery Advocate*, 1 October 1859.
25 Sirpa Salenius, 'Sarah Parker Remond's Black American Grand Tour', in *Women and Migration: Responses in Art and History*, ed. by Deborah Willis, Ellyn Toscano and Kalia Brooks Nelson (Cambridge: Open Book Publishers, 2019), pp. 265–71.
26 Corinne T. Field, 'Old-Age Justice and Black Feminist History: Sojourner Truth's and Harriet Tubman's Intersectional Legacies', *Radical History Review*,

2021:139 (2021), pp. 37–51; Sirpa Salenius, 'Transatlantic Interracial Sisterhoods: Sarah Remond, Ellen Craft, and Harriet Jacobs in England', *Frontiers: A Journal of Women Studies*, 38:1 (2017), pp. 166–96.
27 Teresa Zackodnik, *Press, Platform, Pulpit: Black Feminist Publics in the Era of Reform* (Knoxville: University of Tennessee Press, 2011), p. 58.
28 *The Liberator*, 11 March 1859.
29 BAA, Doc. No. 20202.
30 *Ibid.*
31 Mark Reinhardt, 'Who Speaks for Margaret Garner? Slavery, Silence, and the Politics of Ventriloquism', *Critical Inquiry*, 29:1 (2002), pp. 81–119.
32 *Ibid.*
33 Teresa C. Zackodnik, *The Mulatta and the Politics of Race* (Jackson: University Press of Mississippi, 2004), pp. 42–74.
34 *The Liberator*, 11 March 1859.
35 *Ibid.*
36 *Birmingham Daily Post*, 25 January 1861.
37 BAA, Doc. No. 20202.
38 Teresa C. Zackodnik, '"I Don't Know How You Will Feel When I Get Through": Racial Difference, Woman's Rights, and Sojourner Truth', *Feminist Studies*, 30:1 (2004), pp. 49–73.
39 BAA, Doc. No. 20242.
40 *Ibid.*
41 The *Anti-Slavery Advocate*, 1 October 1859.
42 Salenius, 'Transatlantic Interracial Sisterhoods', pp. 166–96.
43 Cited in Clare Midgley, 'Anti-Slavery and Feminism in Nineteenth-Century Britain', *Gender & History*, 5:3 (1993), pp. 343–62 (p. 353).
44 *Ibid.*
45 BAA, Doc. No. 21295.
46 The *Anti-Slavery Advocate*, 1 October 1859.

CHAPTER 17

1 William (& Ellen) Craft, *Running a Thousand Miles for Freedom; or, the Escape of William and Ellen Craft from Slavery* (London: William Tweedie, 1860), p. 44.
2 *Ibid.*, pp. 46–47.
3 *Ibid.*, p. 67.
4 *Ibid.*, pp. 69–70.
5 *Ibid.*, pp. 72–73.
6 *Ibid.*, p. 79.
7 Cited in Barbara McCaskill, 'Ellen Craft: The Fugitive Who Fled as a Planter', in *Georgia Women: Their Lives and Times*, ed. by Ann Short Chirhart and Betty Wood (Athens: University of Georgia Press, 2009), pp. 82–105 (p. 92).
8 *Ibid.*, pp. 92–94.
9 Craft, *Running a Thousand Miles for Freedom*, p. 94.
10 *Ibid.*, p. 108.
11 Cited in Barbara McCaskill, *Love, Liberation, and Escaping Slavery: William and Ellen Craft in Cultural Memory* (Athens: University of Georgia Press, 2015), p. 57.
12 Cited in *ibid.*, p. 58.

Notes

13 R. J. M. Blackett, 'Fugitive Slaves in Britain: The Odyssey of William and Ellen Craft', *Journal of American Studies*, 12:1 (1978), pp. 41–62.
14 McCaskill, *Love, Liberation, and Escaping Slavery*, pp. 60–61.
15 C. Riley Snorton, *Black on Both Sides: A Racial History of Trans Identity* (Minneapolis: University of Minnesota Press, 2017), pp. 55–97.
16 William Grimes, *Life of William Grimes, the Runaway Slave, Brought Down to the Present Time, Written by Himself* (New Haven: W. Grimes, 1825), pp. 3, 49.
17 Brown, *Biography of an American Bondman*, p. 51.
18 Jacobs, *Incidents in the Life of a Slave Girl*, pp. 169–70.
19 Tavia Nyong'o, *The Amalgamation Waltz: Race, Performance, and the Ruses of Memory* (Minneapolis: University of Minnesota Press, 2009), pp. 96–102.
20 Cited in Chater, *Henry Box Brown*, p. 34.
21 Neil McKenna, *Fanny and Stella: The Young Men Who Shocked Victorian England* (London: Faber and Faber, 2013), pp. 105–06.
22 Zackodnik, *The Mulatta and the Politics of Race*, pp. 50–58.
23 Ancestry.com, 1851 England Census.
24 Cited in Stanley Weintraub, *Albert: Uncrowned King* (London: John Murray, 1997), p. 250.
25 Still, *The Underground Railroad*, pp. 346–47.
26 *Ibid.*
27 Barbara McCaskill, 'Ellen Craft', in *Georgia Women*, ed. by Chirhart and Wood, pp. 82–105.
28 Cited in Murray, *Advocates of Freedom*, p. 197.
29 Cited in Gay Gibson Cima, *Performing Anti-Slavery: Activist Women on Antebellum Stages* (Cambridge: Cambridge University Press, 2014), p. 211.
30 Cited in *ibid.*, pp. 223–24.
31 Cited in *ibid.*, p. 226.
32 *The Times*, 31 August 1863.
33 *Ibid.*
34 *Ibid.*
35 *Hereford Times*, 12 September 1863.
36 *Ibid.*
37 *The Times*, 4 September 1863.
38 *Ibid.*
39 *Ibid.*
40 Blackett, 'Fugitive Slaves in Britain', pp. 41–62.
41 Snorton, *Black on Both Sides*, p. 95.
42 McCaskill, *Love, Liberation, and Escaping Slavery*, pp. 14–17.
43 Cited in Murray, *Advocates of Freedom*, p. 209.

CHAPTER 18

1 Cited in Joy Ritchie and Kate Ronald (eds.), *Available Means: An Anthology of Women's Rhetoric(s)* (Pittsburgh: University of Pittsburgh Press, 2001), p. 203.
2 Frederick Douglas in Ireland and Britain – http://frederickdouglassinbritain.com/Map:Abolitionists/ (accessed 14 August 2021).
3 *East Anglian Daily Times*, 22 May 1893.

4 Sarah L. Silkey, *Black Woman Reformer: Ida B. Wells, Lynching, and Transatlantic Activism* (London: University of Georgia Press, 2015).
5 Bressey, *Empire, Race and the Politics of Anti-Caste*, p. 73.
6 Ida B. Wells, *Southern Horrors and Other Writings: The Anti-Lynching Campaign of Ida B. Wells*, ed. by Jacqueline Jones Royster (New York: Bedford Books, 1997 [1892]), p. 61.
7 *Ibid.*
8 Angela Y. Davis, *Women, Race and Class* (London: Penguin, 1981), p. 172.
9 Wells, *Southern Horrors and Other Writings*, pp. 68–72.
10 Christine Stansell, *The Feminist Promise: 1792 to the Present* (New York: The Modern Library, 2010), pp. 126–27.
11 Silkey, *Black Woman Reformer*, p. 66.
12 *East Anglian Daily Times*, 22 May 1893.
13 *Ibid.*
14 Ida B. Wells, 'Frederick Douglass in Britain and Ireland' – http://frederickdouglassinbritain.com/abolitionists/IdaBWells/ (accessed 27 November 2021).
15 Teresa Zackodnik, 'Ida B. Wells and 'American Atrocities' in Britain', *Women's Studies International Forum* 28 (2005), pp. 259–73.
16 Bressey, *Empire, Race and the Politics of Anti-Caste*, pp. 73–94.
17 Cited in Margaret Busby (ed.), *Daughters of Africa: An International Anthology of Writing of Women of African Descent* (London: Jonathan Cape, 1992), p. xxxx.
18 Murray, *Advocates of Freedom*, p. 300.
19 Zackodnik, 'Ida B. Wells and 'American Atrocities' in Britain', pp. 259–73.
20 Nicole King, 'A Colored Woman in Another Country Pleading for Justice in Her Own', in *Black Victorians/Black Victoriana*, ed. by Gretchen H. Gerzina (New Brunswick: Rutgers University Press, 2003), pp. 88–109 (p. 92).
21 Murray, *Advocates of Freedom*, p. 293
22 *Ibid.*, pp. 194–95.
23 *The Woman's Journal*, 17 March 1894.
24 Cited in Silkey, *Black Woman Reformer*, pp. 39, 113.
25 Vivian M. May, *Anna Julia Cooper, Visionary Black Feminist: A Critical Introduction* (London: Routledge, 2007), pp. 1–12.
26 Anna Julia Cooper, *A Voice from the South*, with intro. by Mary Helen Washington (Oxford: Oxford University Press, 1988 [1892]), p. 79.
27 *Ibid.*, p. xxx.
28 *Ibid.*, p. 75.
29 *Ibid.*, pp. 1, 116, 134.
30 *Ibid.*, p. li.
31 May, *Anna Julia Cooper*, pp. 169–88.
32 Cited in David Killingray, 'Rights, Land, and Labour: Black British Critics of South African Policies before 1948', *Journal of Southern African Studies*, 35:2 (2009), pp. 375–98 (p. 380).
33 Cited in David Killingray, 'Significant Black South Africans in Britain before 1912: Pan-African Organisations and the Emergence of South Africa's First Black Lawyers', *South African Historical Journal*, 64:3 (2012), pp. 393–417 (p. 402).
34 Cited in Adi, *West Africans in Britain 1900–1960*, pp. 9–10.
35 Cited in Killingray, 'Significant Black South Africans in Britain before 1912', p. 403.

36 *Ibid.*
37 *Ibid.*
38 Hakim Adi, *Pan-Africanism: A History* (London: Bloomsbury, 2018), p. 2.
39 *Ibid.*

CHAPTER 19

1 *Westminster Gazette*, 23 July 1900.
2 *Ibid.*
3 *London Daily News*, 24 July 1900.
4 *Ibid.*
5 Cited in Marika Sherwood, *Origins of Pan-Africanism: Henry Sylvester Williams, Africa, and the African Diaspora* (Oxford: Routledge, 2011), p. 250.
6 Cited in *ibid.*, p. 83.
7 Cited in *ibid.*
8 Adi, *West Africans in Britain 1900–1960*, p. 8.
9 Cited in Adi, *Pan-Africanism*, p. 21.
10 *Ibid.*, pp. 7–23.
11 Cited in Gerzina, *Black England*, p. 173.
12 Cited in Sherwood, *Origins of Pan-Africanism*, p. 86–88.
13 Cited in Fryer, *Staying Power*, p. 289.
14 Du Bois, 'To the Nations of the World'.
15 *Westminster Gazette*, 26 July 1900.
16 *Ibid.*
17 Cited in Ramdin, *The Making of the Black Working Class*, p. 54.
18 Cited in J. R. Hooker, 'The Pan-African Conference 1900', *Transition*, 46 (1974), pp. 20–4 (p. 26).
19 Cited in Fryer, *Staying Power*, p. 291.
20 *Ibid.*
21 Pamela Roberts, *Black Oxford: The Untold Stories of Oxford University's Black Scholars* (Oxford: Signal Books, 2013), pp. 2–3.
22 See Jeffrey Green, *Black Edwardians: Black People in Britain 1901–1914* (London: Frank Cass, 1998).
23 Hakim Adi, 'Bandele Omoniyi: A Neglected Nigerian Nationalist', *African Affairs* 90:361 (1991), pp. 581–605.
24 Cited in Adi, *Pan-Africanism*, p. 28.
25 Tony Martin, *The Pan-African Connection: From Slavery to Garvey and Beyond* (Dover, Mass: The Majority Press, 1983), pp. 3–29.
26 Cited in Adi, *Pan-Africanism*, p. 166.
27 See *ibid.*, pp. 178–81.
28 Cited in *ibid.*, *Pan-Africanism*, p. 1.

CONCLUSION

1 *The Voice*, 17 February 2021.
2 Timothy Cavanagh, *Scotland Yard Past and Present: Experiences of Thirty-Seven Years* (London: Chatto and Windus, 1893), p. 50. Special thanks to historian Stephen Bourne, who helped make the story of Robert Branford known.

3   Cumbria Archive Service, Carlisle (CAS), Kent Family Files.
4   Cited in Ray Greenhow, *Britain's First Black Policeman: The Life of John Kent A Police Officer in Cumberland 1835–1846* (Carlisle: Bookcase, 2018), p. 139. See also Bob Lowther, *Watching Over Carlisle: 140 years of the Carlisle City Police Force 1827–1967* (Carlisle: P3 Publications, 2010), pp. 44–48.
5   Greenhow, *Britain's First Black Policeman*, pp. 177–80.
6   As historian Kathleen Chater discovered: The Old Bailey Proceedings Online, 1674–113' – www.oldbaileyonline.org (accessed 14 June 2021), February 1746, trial of Catherine Burk (t17460226-13).
7   Statements proclaimed on Wikipedia.
8   To claim someone as 'the first' does not mean the biography or history is flawed. For a great example of this truism see Vasili, *The First Black Footballer*, esp. pp. 85–104.
9   Otele, *African Europeans*, pp. 220–21.
10 Carter G. Woodson, 'The Celebration of Negro History Week, 1927', in *The Journal of Negro History*, 12:2 (1927), pp. 103–09 (p. 105).

Index

A
abolition 17–18, 213, 230, 265
abolitionism 16, 90, 93, 96, 224, 239, 283
Aborigines' Protection Society 26, 123
activism 252
Adams Express Company 209
Addai-Sebo, A. 285
Address to the Nations of the World 275
Adewale, J. R. 117
Adi, H. 13, 269, 273, 279
Adventures of Huckleberry Finn (Twain) 58
Africa 8, 33, 51, 82, 102, 120, 125, 138, 203, 255, 269, 273–275, 279
   East 145
   North 7, 145, 180
   West 21, 100, 114, 117, 118, 122, 125, 145, 255
African Aid Society 255
African Americans 18–19, 22, 27–28, 33, 62, 132, 153, 164, 173, 177, 214–215, 224, 228–230, 255, 266, 271
African Association 33, 268–269, 273–274
African Communities League 278
African diaspora 51, 146, 160, 269, 274
African Europeans (Otele) 284
African Jubilee Singers 267
African Methodist Episcopal Church (South Africa) 267
African Times and Orient Review 262, 278
African Union 279
Afro-American 260
Ain't I a Woman (Truth) 265
Alabama (USA) 172, 264
Albert, E. 69, 70–78, 96
Aldridge, A. 150
Aldridge, I. 150, 157, 160, 161–178
Allen, J. F. 212
Allen, W. G. 225–226
Allenborough, G. 177
Ali, D. M. 262, 278
Alpha Suffrage Club 264
Am I Not a Man and a Brother? (Peckard) 206
American Civil War (1861–1865) 22, 31, 72, 164, 221–222, 231, 237–239, 260
American Colonization Society (ACS) 62
American intolerance 108
An Account of the Manners and Customs of the Modern Egyptians (Lane) 192
Anderson, J. 252
Anderson, R. 121, 132
Anecdotes of Alamayu 113
Anglo-Afghan War (1838–1842) 33
Anglo-Burmese Wars 142
Anglo-Saxons 3
Anglo-Zulu War (1879) 33
Anim-Addo, J. 112
Anthropological Society of London 26–27, 252
Anti-Caste: Devoted to the Interests of the Coloured Race 33, 258, 261–262
Anti-Lynching Committee 264
anti-racism 224, 256, 257–269
The *Anti-Slavery Advocate* 232
Anti-Slavery Society 210, 214–215, 227, 231, 238
Antigua 132
apprenticeships 20, 179
Archer, J. 271, 278
Arkansas (USA) 264

Armistead, W. 249
Armstrong, W. 254
Army Temperance Association 143
Astley, P. 180
Astley's Amphitheatre 180–181
Athenaeum 162
Australia 31, 64
   Tasmania 91
Austro-Hungarian Empire 162
autonomy 212
The Axe Laid to Root (Wedderburn) 90
Azikiwe, N. 279

B
Balkans 7
Barbados 24
Barbados Slave Code (1661) 24
Barret, J. 211
Barret, W. 211
Barrier, E. D. 272
Barrier Williams, F. 272
Battle of Ginnis (1885) 136–138
Batty, W. 179–181
Beckwith, J. 149
Beethoven, L. van 1–2, 5
   Violin Sonata No 9, Op. 47 in A major (Kreutzer Sonata) 1
Belle, D. E. 9
Belle Weekly Messenger 125
The Beloved (Rossetti) 198
Berlin Conference (1884–1885) 138
Bethlem Royal Hospital 46, 54–58
Birley, J. 139
Birmingham Land Conference 85
Black, L. 192
Black Atlantic 66, 69, 96
Black community 211–212, 229–230
The Black Doctor 168
Black feminism 234–235, 239, 266, 283
black fun 172
Black History Month 285
Black identity 155
black labour aristocracy 9
Black Lives Matter 285
The Black Man, His Antecedents, His Genius, and His Achievements (Wells Brown) 162
Black missionaries 130
Black models 191, 194
Black Sea 263
Black seafarers 12, 30, 72
Black servicemen 143
Blackburn Standard 220
blackface acts 172
blackface minstrelsy 174, 178
Blackness 248
Blake, W. 83
Boer War (1899–1902) 277
Bolt, C. 58
Bonetta, S. F. 13, 97–117, 120, 123, 134, 193, 253
born criminals 57
Boston (Massachusetts) 227, 244
Boyce, J. M. 197, 205
Branford, R. 281–282
Bressey, C. 10, 13, 107
Bridgetower, G. A. P. 1–2, 5, 13
Brief Sketch of the Life of Edward Albert or the Dead Man come to Life Again (Albert) 76
Briggs, M. 266
Brighton Gazette 105, 108
Brindley, T. 218–220
British Army 30, 143–146
British Association for the Advancement of Science 252
British Empire 31, 34, 114, 232, 270
British Guiana 44
British Navy 12
British tolerance 108
Britons Through Negro Spectacles (Merriman-Labor) 34
Broadmoor Criminal Lunatic Asylum 41–51, 52, 55–59, 61, 65
Bromby, C. H. 118
Brown, A. C. 45, 49–50, 61
Brown, A. J. F. 222
Brown, A. O. A. (Miss LaLa) 192
Brown, D. A. 45, 49–50
Brown, E. 41–45
Brown, H. ('Box') 157, 209–226, 239, 245

Index

Brown, Rev. H. B. 274
Brown, John 221
Brown, Josephine 247
Brown, J. F. 222
Brown, M. J. 45, 49–50
Brown, W. 41–51, 56, 61, 65–66, 69, 71, 77, 96
Buenos Aires 63
Bugle 137–142
Bulwer Lytton, E. 161–162
Burke, T. 285
Burrows, D. 43
Burton, R. 100
Buxton, T. F. 123

C

Campbell-Bannerman, H. 138
Canada 31, 131, 213, 272
Cannibal Club 26
Canterbury Cathedral 125–127
capitalism 81, 265
  industrial 82, 93
Capitein, J. 123
Caribbean 21, 33, 95, 131, 145, 269, 270
Carlisle (UK) 281–282
Carlyle, T. 28, 126
Carolinas, North and South (USA) 21, 172, 213, 218–219, 243, 264
Casely-Hayford, J. E. 278
Cato Street Conspirators (1820) 89
Caucasians 25
Césaire, A. 265
Chamberlain, J. 276
Channing, W. H. 232
Charleston (South Carolina) 243
Chartism 81, 85, 92–93
Chater, K. 223
Cheddar Man 7
Child, L. M. 236
China 21
Christianity 30, 102–103, 120–122, 128, 224, 231, 237, 255, 261
Christy Minstrels 173
Church of England 119, 134
Church Missionary Record 124
Church Missionary Society (CMS) 102–105, 120–123, 127, 130

circus 179, 182, 186
City Arabs 75
Civil and Military Gazette 141
civilisation 57–58, 120–122
  white 108
class 91–92, 267
  middle 19, 88, 95, 154, 187
  social 182
  working 12, 19, 29, 35, 46, 82, 85–86, 90–96, 149, 191, 206
Cobbett, W. 29, 95
Cole, F. 277
Coleridge-Taylor, S. 11, 146, 149–160, 271, 275
colonialism 16, 65, 230, 270
  cultural 128
colonisation 100
colour-blindness 10
colour-prejudice 154, 226
Colvin, C. 260
Combe, G. 3–4
Compound System 267
Confederates 22
Congress (USA) 215
consensual sex 259, 263
Cook, F. M. 6
Cooper, A. J. H. 265–267, 272
Coppin, F. J. 266
Corker, E. 185–186
County Asylums Act (1845) 53
Craft, E. 83, 223, 234, 242–256, 263
Craft, W. 224, 242–256
Crimean War (1853–1856) 145
Criminal Lunatics Act (1800) 46
Criminal Lunatics Act (1860) 46
Criminal Man (Lombroso) 57
criminaloids 57
criminals of passion 57
criminology 57
cross-dressing 247
Crowther, D. C. 128, 134
Crowther, S. A. 11, 117, 118–134
Cuba 211
Cuffay, M. A. 91
Cuffay, W. 81–96, 104
Cugoano, O. 10, 16, 274
Cullwick, H. 200
cultural bias 165

345

cultural colonialism 128
Cutter, M. J. 223
Cuvier, G. 25

D
Da Rocha, M. 273
Dahomey 99–100
Dahomey and the Dahomans (Forbes) 99
Daily Chronicle 264
Daily Inter-Ocean 261
Darby, J. 179
Darby, M. 179
Darby, W. 179–180
  see also Fanque, P.
Darmouth Alumni Magazine (1935) 6
Darwin, C. 4–5, 26, 32–34, 206
  theory of evolution 4, 32
Davidson, W. 88–89, 96
Davies, J. P. L. 105, 108, 120
Davies, V. 114–115
Davies, W. B. 143
Davis, A. Y. 259
De Lise, B. 137–141
The Death of Hiawatha (Coleridge-Taylor) 160
A Defence of the Ethiopian Movement (Omoniyi) 278
Degas, E. 192, 203
Delany, L. A. 265
Delany, M. R. 274
democracy 93, 224
Democratic Committee for Poland's Regeneration 86
The Descent of Man (Darwin) 34
diaspora 23, 279–280
  African 51
Dickens, C. 12, 27, 68, 82, 149
discrimination 72, 226, 235, 273, 276
Disraeli, B. 70
domestic servants 9
domestic sphere 197
domesticity 237, 240
double consciousness 23
Douglas, B. 25
Douglas, F. 18–20, 27, 35, 215, 219, 223–226, 229, 235, 239, 245, 258, 285

Dowling, R. H. 197
The Dream of Gerontius (Elgar) 153
Du Bois, W. E. B. 22, 36, 271, 275, 279
Dunbar, G. 177
Dunbar, P. L. 151
Duncan, A. 3
Durham, J. F. 134, 135–146, 153, 158
Durham Light Infantry (DLI) 136–145
Dyce, W. 189

E
Early, G. L. 245, 266
East Africa 145
East India Company 30
East Kent Times 119
Eastern Europe 180
Easton, H. 28
Eaton, F. 189–206
Eaton, J. 194
Economist 264
Edinburgh (Scotland) 3
Edmonstone, J. 2–5, 13
Edwards, C. 261–262
Egypt 135–136, 141, 153, 203
eighteenth century 9–12, 24–25, 46, 82–83, 100, 143–145, 206, 221, 228, 273274
Elaw, Z. 132–133, 234, 263
Elebute, A. 103, 112
Elgar, E. 152–153
Elijah (Mendelssohn) 160
emancipation 17, 44, 92, 194, 265, 269
emancipation narratives 133, 245
Emancipation Proclamation 229, 258
empire 16
empowerment 247
Encyclopaedia Britannica 37
Engels, F. 70
England 9, 27, 44, 52, 69, 74, 89–90, 96, 103–104, 110, 114, 123, 132–133, 164, 194, 217, 222, 225–226, 238–239, 245, 250–251, 257
English negrophilism 20

Index

Enlightenment 27
   Scottish 3
enslavement 4, 77, 217
Entwistle, J. 194
epilepsy 45, 48
equality 96, 164, 228
   racial 32
equestrianism 180
Equiano, O. 10, 17, 274
Era 169, 176
Este, H. 110
Ethiopia 270
Ethiopian Serenaders 173
Ethiopianism 273
ethnic diversity 12
ethnicity 10–11, 46, 283
Ethnological Society of London 25–27
eugenics 32
Europe 7, 33, 162, 170, 232
   Eastern 180
European missionaries 130–131
evangelism 193
Evans-Gordon, W. E. 36
Evening Star 258
evolutionary theory 57
exoticism 187
Eyre, E. J. 251

F

Fabian Society 278
Fanque, P. 178, 179–188
Fergusson, J. 139, 142
Ferrari, R. C. 198
First Matabele War (1893) 112
Fisher, F. 139
Fisk University Jubilee Singers 33, 156
Flinn, J. 50, 52–60, 65–66, 69, 71, 77, 96
Flood in the Highlands (Landseer) 189
Florida (USA) 264
Floyd, J. 221
Foote, J. 133
Forbes, F. E. 98–101, 105
Forman, R. 50
Foster, A. 132

Foster, M. 194
Fox, J. 82
France 84, 153
   Revolution (1789) 84
   Second Revolution (1830) 84
Fraser's Magazine 28
Fraternity 262
Free Speech and Headlight 259
Freedman's Aid Association 239
freedom seekers 244
Freeman, T. B. 13
Freemasons 218
Freetown (Sierra Leone) 102, 105, 121–122
French, C. W. 271
French Revolution (1789) 84
From the Darkness Cometh the Light, or, Struggles for Freedom (Delany) 265
Frost, T. 179–182
Fryar, C. 13, 65
Fryer, P. 277
Fugitive Slave Act (1850) 219, 230, 245, 255

G

Galapagos 4
Galton, F. 32
Garner, M. 235, 240
Garnet, H. H. 223
Garrick, D. 164
Garrison, W. L. 228–230
Garvey, A. A. 278
Garvey, M. 278
gender norms 251, 255
General Register Office 10
Georgia (USA) 213, 242, 264
Germany 84
Gerzina, G. H. 10, 13
Ghana 132
Ghezo 99–100
Gill, M. 165, 176
Gilroy, P. 66
Glasgow (Scotland) 3, 72
Glorious Revolution (1688) 16
Gordon, G. 135–136
Gordon, G. W. 251
Grand Lodge of Operative Tailors of London 84

Grand National Consolidated Trades Union 84
Grant, L. J. 68
Gray, K. 198
Great Britain 8–9, 15–22, 29–31, 37, 51, 81, 86, 99–101, 121, 136, 153–154, 159, 173, 176–177, 184, 206, 217–219, 223–226, 234–235, 239–241, 249, 255, 258–267, 273–274, 284
Great Exhibition 249–250
Great Public Meeting of the Tailors 85
Greater Britain Exhibition 34
The Greek Slave (Powers) 249
Green, J. 142
Green, T. 142
Greenwood, J. 75, 195
Grimes, W. 247
Grimke, C. F. 266
Gronniosaw, U. 10
Gross, G. 177

H
Haiti 17, 170, 270
Hall, W. E. 143
Harper, F. E. W. 265–266
Harris, W. J. 43
Hartman, S. 42
Hawkins, J. 8
Hayes, R. B. 260
Henderson, J. 184
Henson, J. 224
Hewlett, J. 164
Hiawatha's Wedding Feast (Coleridge-Taylor) 152–153, 157
Higgens, A. C. 104
Hillier, J. 187
History of Jamaica (Long) 24
The History of Mary Prince (Prince) 17
HMS *Beagle* (1831–1836) 4
HMS *Bonetta* 101
HMT *Empire Windrush* 282
Hodge, S. 145
Hogarth, W. 201
Holiday, H. 195
Holman, B. 149
Honourable Society of the Inner Temple 277
Hood, W. C. 55
The Horrors of Slavery (Wedderburn) 89–90
Horton, J. A. 143, 274
House of Commons 138
Hume, D. 3, 24
Hunt, J. 26, 35, 252
hypersexuality 202

I
immigration 211
imperialism 15, 18, 120, 146
Impey, C. 33, 258, 262
India 31–33, 113, 132, 141–142, 263
Indian Rebellion (1857–1859) 30–31, 145, 197, 220–222
industrial capitalism 82, 93
insane convict 56
insane criminals 57
insanity 52–53, 57, 66
Intellectual Progress of the Colored Women of the US since the Emancipation Proclamation (Williams) 265
interracial couples 13
interracial marriage 168, 221
Iola Leroy; or, Shadows Uplifted (Harper) 265
Ireland 143, 177, 186, 238
Islington Gazette 106
Israelites 193, 197
Italy 180

J
Jackson, J. 224
Jacobs, H. 20–22, 234, 247
Jamaica 31, 71, 82, 89, 131–132, 194
James, C. L. R. 265
Jephthah (Millais) 197
Jersey Independent and Daily Telegraph 222
Jeune, F. 118
John Anderson Committee 252
Johnson, F. 271
Johnson, H. 128–130
Johnson, J. 130
Jones, A. 272

Index

K
Karim, A. 113–114
Kauffman, A. 189
Kean, E. 171
Keckley, E. 83
Kent, J. 281–282
Kentish Chronicle 125
Kentish Gazette 119
Kentucky (USA) 215, 264
Kenyatta, J. 279
Kilham, H. 122
King, M. L. 257
King, N. 263
King of Dahomey 254–255
King Pepple 128
Kinloch, A. V. 267–268
Kirkdale Gaol 53, 58
Kitchener, H. 153
Kite, W. 184
Knight, E. A. 50
Knight, J. 9
Knox, R. 35
Korobkin, L. 226
Kreutzer, R. 1–2

L
Ladies' London Emancipation Society 239
Lambeth Palace Conference 128
Landseer, E. H. 189
Lane, E. W. 192
Langton, W. 50
Latham, T. 282
Lay Preaching (Stirling) 190
Le Grande, K. 146
Lee, J. 133
Leeds Mercury 216, 261
legitimacy 263
Lennon, J. 188
Lewis, E. 266
Lewis, H. E. 221
liberalism 16
Liberia 62, 131–132, 155, 270–273
Liberian Patriotic Hymn (Coleridge-Taylor) 155
Lincoln, A. 285
Linnaeus, C. 25
Lister, J. 6

Liverpool (UK) 12, 63, 67, 186, 215–217, 224, 232, 235, 240
Liverpool Mercury 184, 216, 232
Lombroso, C. 57–58
London (UK) 67, 72–73, 86, 124, 149–150, 166, 206, 230, 248, 264, 273, 276
London Daily News 272
London Dispatch 43
London Emancipation Committee 250–251
London Labour and the London Poor (Mayhew) 12, 67, 70
London Society of West India Merchants and Planters 167
Long, E. 24
Longfellow, H. W. 152–154
Loudin, F. J. 156, 271
Louisiana (USA) 264
    Purchase 211
Loyalist Claims Commission 72
Lux 261
lynching 226, 258–259, 263–265

M
Macaulay, H. 117
Macaulay, O. H. 134
Mace, J. 187
Macon (Georgia) 242
Madeira 71
Madox Brown, F. 197, 205
Mahdist army 136–137
The Maiden Tribute of Modern Babylon (Stead) 263
Manchester (UK) 240
Manet, E. 201–202
Mansel, H. 118
Mansfield, Lord 9
Manvell, M. A. 83
Marche, M. 10, 110
marginalisation 2
Marlow, S. 185–187
The Marriage of Victoria, Princess Royal, 25 January 1858 (Phillip) 190
Martin, A. H. 150
Martin, J. S. 250
martyrdom 136
Massachusetts (USA) 228

Boston 227, 244
Salem 227–229
Mathews, C. 171–175
Mayhew, H. 12, 29–30, 66–67, 70–75, 180
Mayne, C. 267
Mayo, I. 258
McCaskill, B. 245
McClintock, A. 200
McCune Smith, J. 223
melancholia 48
Memoir and Theatrical Career of Ira Aldridge, the African Roscius 168, 176
Memphis (Tennessee) 259
mental asylums 42
mental collapse 63
mental health 45
The Merchant of Venice (Shakespeare) 175–176
Merchant Seamen's Fund 72
Merriman-Labor, A. B. C. 34
Messiah (Handel) 160
Methodism 90
MeToo movement 285
Metropolitan Delegate Council 85
Metropolitan Police 281
Metropolitan Tailors' Charter Association 85
Mexico 213
Meyer, W. 274
Middle Ages 83, 202
middle class 19, 88, 95, 154, 187, 225
Middle East 145
migration 13
Millais, J. E. 197
Miss LaLa at the Cirque Fernando (Degas) 192, 203
missionaries 120, 128
Black 130
European 130–131
Mississippi (USA) 213, 264
Missouri Compromise (1820) 230
modernisation 6, 15
Molyneaux, P. 177
Mongolians 25
monogenism 4, 25–26
Moore, A. 195–197

moral therapy 46, 55–56, 66
Morant Bay Uprising (1865) 31, 251
Morning Chronicle 162, 170–171
The Morning Post 220
Morris, J. 198
Morrison, T. 23
Moser, M. 189
The Mother of Moses (Solomon) 190–194
The Mother of Sisera (Moore) 197
Mott, J. 214
Mott, L. 214
Mozart, W. A. 2
mulatta 236, 248, 251
Mulgrave, C. E. 132
Munby, A. 198–202
Murrell, D. 202–203
Musical Times 149–152
My Secret Life 202

N
Naoroji, D. 33, 268
The Narrative of Henry Box Brown, Written by Himself (Brown) 210–214
Narrative of the Life of Frederick Douglas, an American Slave (Douglas) 215
Narrative of William W. Brown, A Fugitive Slave (Wells Brown) 215
nation-states 131
National Anti-Militia Association 85
National Association for the Advancement of Colored People (NAACP) 264
National Association of Colored Women 266
National Association of Colored Women's Clubs 264
National Colored Press Association 258
National Gallery 189
National Land Company 85
National Women's Rights Convention (1858) 233
Native Agency Committee 103
Native Americans 153
negro car 242

Index

Negroes 25, 203, 274
Negroid 203
Nelson, C. 203
New World slavery 66
New York (USA) 67
New York Express 20
New Zealand 31
Newton, J. 23–24
Nichol, W. 107
Nichols, H. 132
Nicol, G. 134
Nicol, G. G. M. 134
Niger Expedition (1841) 122–123, 127–128
Nigeria 131
Nightingale, F. 240
nineteenth century 10–14, 21–22, 25–26, 30, 35–37, 55–57, 71, 75, 82, 91, 103, 111–112, 120, 131, 134, 146, 154, 164, 179, 187, 189, 202, 206, 247, 267, 273
Nkrumah, K. 279
North Africa 7, 145, 180
Norton, J. 132
Noyes, A. 159
Nubia, O. 13

O

O'Brien, W. C. 95
O'Donoghue, E. G. 55
O'Grady, L. 202
Ohio (USA) 215, 264
Okeadon War (1848) 99
Olusoga, D. 13, 102, 112
Olympia (Manet) 201–203
Omoniyi, B. 278
On the Origins of Species (Darwin) 26
Orange, W. 48, 61
Otele, O. 77, 284
Othello (Shakespeare) 160, 161
Other 22, 27, 168, 200–204, 221, 283
Otherness 202
Ottoman Empire 24
Owen, E. 110

P

The Padlock 167

Palestine 203
Pan-African Association 277
Pan-African Conference 33, 36, 269, 270–278
The Pan-African Journal 277
Pan-African Movement 270–280
Pan-Africanism 269, 273, 278–279, 283
Parks, R. 260
Parry, H. 151–152
Paul, N. 224
Peckard, P. 206
Pegwell Bay (Dyce) 189
Pennsylvania (USA) 244
People's Charter (1838) 85
Peterloo Massacre (1819) 89
Peters, J. 61–69, 71, 77, 96
Philadelphia (USA) 209–210, 213–214, 244
Phillip, J. 190
phrenology 3
Picton, C. 9
Pintor, L. 239
Poland 176
Polish uprising (1846) 86
polyamory 130
polygamy 128
polygenism 26
Poor Law Amendment Act (1834) 68, 84
Posing Modernity (Murrell) 202
poverty 12, 16, 22, 42, 68, 70, 84, 89–91, 96, 186
Powers, H. 249
Pratt, A. 65–66
Pre-Raphaelite Brotherhood 191, 194–197, 205–206
Preamble of the American Constitution 211
prejudice 107, 229
  colour 154, 226
Prichard, J. C. 25, 75
Prince, M. 10, 17
Prince Alamayu 113
Prince Albert 97, 106, 124, 249
Prince of Wales (future King George IV) 2
Princess Gouramma 113–114

private asylums 53
Prizel, N. 77
prostitute 202
public asylums 53
Punch 28, 88, 249–250

Q

Quaque, P. 123
Queen Victoria 15, 21, 86, 97, 101–106, 111–116, 124, 142, 184, 276–278
Qureshi, S. 14

R

Raban, J. 121–122
race 4, 14, 25–27, 31, 35, 46, 57, 91, 98, 101, 107, 111, 200–201, 248, 267
race riots 36
racial abuse 154–155
racial equality 32
racial identity 29
racial stereotypes 169
racism 24–27, 34–35, 58–59, 81, 95, 111, 133, 149, 160, 177, 219, 223, 226, 255, 262, 266, 270, 273–274
    anti 224, 256, 257–269
    scientific 248, 252, 274
    working class 95–96
Rainhill Asylum 53, 58–59
Rajah of Coorg 113
A Rake's Progress (Hogarth) 201
Ramdin, R. 13
Randle, A. 117
Randle, B.H. 117
Randle, J. 115
rape 237–238, 259, 263–265
realism 189
Reform Act (1832) 84
Reminiscences of Sport and War (De Lise) 139
Remond, C. L. 223–224, 230, 239
Remond, J. 227–229
Remond, N. 227–229
Remond, S. P. 219, 223, 227–241, 250, 256, 263
Review of Reviews (Stead) 267
The Revolt of Surinam (1825) 165

Reynold's Newspaper 143
Reynold's Political Instructor 93
Rhode Island (USA) 229
Rice, G. 5–6, 13
Rice, T. D. 173
Roberts, D. 203
Roberts, J. R. 272
Roberts, N. 281–282
Robeson, P. 160, 177
Robson, R. 142
Robson, S. 142
Roper, M. 209, 223, 235
Rossetti, D. G. 197–198, 205
Royal Academy of Arts (RA) 189, 193, 196–198
Royal African Company (RAC) 8
Royal Albert Hall 159
Royal Coburg 165
Royal College of Music (RCM) 150–154
Royal Navy 71
Royal Society of Musicians 2
Rump, A. 43–44
Rump, D. 44
Running a Thousand Miles for Freedom (Craft) 245, 248
Russia 162, 177

S

Saint-Domingue 17
Salem (Massachusetts) 227–229
Salem Female Anti-Slavery Society 231
Salvation Army 132
Sancho, I. 9, 164
Sandys, F. 197
Sanger, G. 185–186
Sass, J. E. 103
Savannah (Georgia) 242–243
Scandinavia 7
Schoen, E. 105
Schoen, J. F. 104, 117, 123, 130
scientific racism 248, 252, 274
Scobie, E. 13–14, 22
Scotland 2–3, 177, 192, 238, 251
    Edinburgh 3
    Glasgow 3, 72
Scott, D. 230

Index

Scott, E. 248
Scottish Enlightenment 3
Scramble for Africa 32, 130, 135
Seacole, M. 13, 284
Second French Revolution (1830) 84
segregation 18, 46, 224–226, 228–231, 235, 238, 260, 279
Self-Help (Smiles) 225
sensationalism 217
The Servant (von Bayro) 201
Seven Months in the Kingston Lunatic Asylum and What I Saw There (Pratt) 65
seventeenth century 8, 24–26, 55, 68
Sewally, P. 247–248
sex trafficking 263
sex workers 82, 247–248
sexual violence 251, 259
Sgt Pepper's Lonely Hearts Club Band (Beatles) 188
Shakespeare, W. 170, 175, 283
Sheppey Union Workhouse 48–49
Shipping and Mercantile Gazette 63
Shyllon, F. 13
Siddal, E. 196
Sierra Leone 62, 102–105, 114, 122, 125, 131, 150, 158, 267, 277
    Freetown 102, 105, 121–122
Sierra Leone Weekly 158
Singh, D. 114
sixteenth century 145, 211
Skertchly, J. A. 100
slave 24, 254
    white 236
slave chains 229
Slave Compensation Act (1837) 21
slave narratives 19, 217
slave trade 8–10, 16–18, 98–102, 120
slave trader 243
slavery 3, 8–9, 16–24, 32, 44, 57, 82–83, 92, 100, 132, 165–167, 177, 192, 200–201, 211–215, 221–226, 229–238, 242–244, 250, 255, 265, 270–271, 274, 279
    New World 66
    white 263
Slavery Abolition Act (1833) 16, 20–21, 167

slavery expeditions 8
slut 201
Smiles, S. 225
Smith, Adam 3
Smith, Amanda 132, 266
Smith, Andrew 75
Smith, H. 264
Smith, J. C. A. 215–219
Smith, S. 186
Smith, S. M. 177
Snorton, C. R. 247
social class 182
social hierarchy 110
Society for Effecting the Abolition of the Slave Trade (1787) 16
Society for the Propagation of the Gospel 119
Society for the Recognition of the Brotherhood of Man 262–264
Solomon, J. B. 9
Solomon, S. 190–195, 205
Somerset, J. 9
The Song of Hiawatha (Longfellow) 152
Sons of Africa 10, 16–17, 274
Soubise, J. 9, 164
The Souls of Black Folk (Du Bois) 36, 275
South East Gazette 107
South Africa 27, 267–268, 270, 275
    African Methodist Episcopal Church 267
South America 2–4
Southern Horrors 259, 265–266
sovereignty 258
Spencer, H. 31–32
SS *Cumbria* 245
St Andrew's Workhouse 179
Standard 166
Stead, W. T. 263, 267
Stearns, C. 214, 217
stereotypes 30, 174, 206, 233
    racial 169
Stevens, M. 61
Stiebel, G. 13
Stiebel, S. 13
Still, W. 214, 249–250
Stirling, J. 190
Stocks, W. F. 197, 205

Stone, G. W. 221
Stone, M. 195
Stowe, H. B. 28, 266
Strawberry Fields Forever (Beatles) 188
String-Players Club 157
Stuarts 8
Sub-Saharan Africans 7
Sudan 135–138, 153
Suffragette 50
Sunday Times 169
Supreme Court (USA) 230
Sweet, M. 35
Sylvain, B. 271
syphilis 66
Syria 7
Systema Naturae 25

T
Tappan, A. 228
Tasmania (Australia) 91
taxidermy 4
Taylor, D. P. H. 150
The Taylor's Complete Guide (1796) 83
Tewodros II 112
Tennessee (USA) 260, 264
Texas (USA) 249, 264
theory of evolution (Darwin) 4, 32
Thicknesse, P. 179
thirteenth century 55
Thompson, A. 250
Thompson, E. P. 84
Thompson, T. J. 267, 273
Tiger Bay 195
The Times 30, 34, 86–88, 135, 151, 165
Titus Andronicus (Shakespeare) 169, 177
Towerson, J. L. W. 8
Travis, T. 52
Triangular Trade 8
Trinidad 131, 267
A Trip to America 171–172
Trollope, A. 29
Truth, S. 234, 239, 265–266
tuberculosis 115
Tubman, H. 234
Tuchet, W. R. 59
Tuckerman Institute 232–232
Tudor period 8
Tuke, D. 57

Tull, W. 11
Twain, M. 58
twelfth century 145
twentieth century 36, 269, 279
twenty-first century 50, 279, 281
Twenty-four Negro Melodies (Coleridge-Taylor) 156

U
Uganda 153
Ukraine 170
Ulterior Committee 86, 89
Uncle Tom's Cabin (Stowe) 28, 77, 178, 220, 236
The Underground Railroad (Still) 249
United Kingdom (UK) 72, 132, 239, 260, 273, 285
   Carlisle 281–282
   Liverpool 12, 63, 67, 186, 215–217, 224, 232, 235, 240
   London 67, 72–73, 86, 124, 149–150, 166, 206, 230, 248, 264, 273, 276
   Manchester 240
   Warrington 235–238
United States of America (USA) 19–20, 33, 121, 133, 157–159, 172, 176, 184, 187, 213–214, 217, 221–226, 231, 234, 248, 251, 258–260, 263–265, 270
   ACS 62
   African Americans 18–19, 22, 27–28, 33, 62, 132, 153, 164, 173, 177, 214–215, 224, 228–230, 255, 266, 271
   Afro-American 260
   Alabama 172, 264
   Arkansas 264
   Carolinas, North and South 21, 172, 213, 218–219, 243, 264
   Civil War (1861–1865) 22, 31, 72, 164, 221–222, 231, 237–239, 260
   Congress 215
   Florida 264
   Georgia 213, 242, 264
   Kentucky 215, 264

Index

Louisiana 264
Louisiana Purchase 211
Massachusetts 228
Mississippi 213, 264
Native Americans 153
New York 67
Ohio 215, 264
Pennsylvania 244
Philadelphia 209–210, 213–214, 244
Rhode Island 229
Supreme Court 230
Tennessee 260, 264
Texas 249, 264
Virginia 209, 218
White House 158
Universal Coloured People's Association 279
Universal Negro Improvement Association 278
Unwin, J. C. 275
urban savage 75

V

Venn, H. 101–103, 107, 117, 120–121, 127, 130–132
Venus in Furs (von Sacher-Masoch) 201–202
Villiers, C. 151
Virginia (USA) 209, 218
Virginia Minstrels 173
A Voice from the South: By a Black Woman of the South (Cooper) 265–266
von Bayro, F. 201
von Bismarck, O. 138
von Brandt, A. P. 176
von Sacher-Masoch, L. 201

W

Walker, D. 20
Walker, T. D. 184
Wallett, W. F. 182–184, 188
Walmisley, T. A. 150, 154
Walters, A. 270–271, 274
Walters, H. A. 150
War Cry 132
Ward, S. 223
Warrington (UK) 235–238

Warrington Anti-Slavery Society 235
Warrington Times 235, 238
Washington, B. T. 157, 268, 278
Waters, W. 164
Waterton, C. 2–3
Watkins, J. 219, 226
Watts, P. 75
We Are All Bound Up Together (Harper) 265
Webb, R. 35
Wedderburn, J. 89
Wedderburn, R. 89–90, 96
Weekly Dispatch 42
Wells, I. B. 33, 224, 256, 257–269
Wells, N. 13, 110–111
Wells Brown, W. 161–162, 215, 223–224, 239, 245–249
Welsh, S. 105
West Africa 21, 100, 114, 117, 118, 122, 125, 145, 255
  Yorubaland 121, 124
West African Squadron 18
West End 164–166, 170
West Indian Regiments (WIRs) 145
West Indies 52, 211, 271, 276
Westminster Gazette 34, 276
Wharton, A. 284
Wheatley, P. 20, 266
white civilisation 108
white consciousness 23
White House (USA) 158
white privilege 127
white slave 236
white slavery 263
white supremacy 164, 258–259, 265
whiteness 193, 248
whitewashing 2, 13
Wilberforce, W. 95
The Wild's of London (Greenwood) 195
Williams, A. 187
Williams, F. 9
Williams, F. B. 265
Williams, H. S. 261–262, 267–268, 273–278
Winniett, W. 100
Wise, M. 118
Wolverhampton and Staffordshire Herald 218

Wolverhampton Corn Exchange 218
Woman's Journal 264
Women's Suffrage Organisation 251
Woods, W. D. 132
Woodson, C. G. 285
workhouse 68–69, 84, 188, 283
working class 12, 19, 29, 35, 46, 82, 85–86, 90–96, 149, 191, 206, 223
working class consciousness 84–87
working class racism 95–96
working class women 200

World Anti-Slavery Convention 21, 230
World War I (1914–1918) 36, 145
World War II (1939–1945) 279
Wright, R. 23

Y

Yorubaland (West Africa) 121, 124
A Young Teacher (Solomon) 197

Z

Zulus 27